★

GROWING UP
IN THE
Lone Star State

1 year 9 mos

★

GROWING UP IN THE

Lone Star State

NOTABLE TEXANS REMEMBER
THEIR CHILDHOODS

Gaylon Finklea Hecker & Marianne Odom

BRISCOE CENTER
FOR AMERICAN HISTORY
THE UNIVERSITY OF TEXAS AT AUSTIN

DISTRIBUTED BY TOWER BOOKS, AN IMPRINT
OF THE UNIVERSITY OF TEXAS PRESS

Requests for permission to reproduce material from this work
should be sent to:
Office of the Director
Dolph Briscoe Center for American History
University of Texas at Austin
2300 Red River Stop D1100
Austin, TX 78712-1426

⊗ The paper used in this book meets the minimum requirements
of ANSI/NISO Z39.48-1992 (R1997) (Permanence of Paper).

Library of Congress Control Number: 2020943696

ISBN (hardcover): 978-0-9997318-4-0

Endsheets: Detail from the back of the Le Moyne Stars Crib Quilt,
which features a rare Texas-themed fabric, c. 1845–1860. Ima
Hogg Quilt Collection, W2h30.76, Briscoe Center for American
History, University of Texas at Austin

Frontispiece: Samuel W. Lewis Jr., who grew up in Houston, as a
child. He later served as ambassador to Israel during the Jimmy
Carter administration. *Photo courtesy Samuel W. Lewis Jr.*

★

To Texans past, present, and future by birth or
spirit and everyone everywhere wise enough to cherish
childhood for its lasting impact on us all.

To Brent
my one in a million
Son-in-law
Much love
Momoban

Gaylon Finklea Hecker and Marianne Odom deserve Texas-size applause for weaving Texas tales that reveal the power of a Texas heritage. Texans have a devotion to their state like no other Americans. My father always said, "Texas is the place where people know when you're sick and care when you die." The stories of these Texans tell you why. I knew and loved 17 of the Texas luminaries in this book and have met many of the rest. All of their stories are worth sharing. All are inspirational to those who love our state and those who have yet to discover why.

—**LUCI BAINES JOHNSON, daughter of President Lyndon B. Johnson and Lady Bird Johnson**

Who knew that former Secretary of State Rex Tillerson was named for the singing cowboy Rex Allen? Or that Dan Rather used to ride on the backs of giant soft-shell turtles in Buffalo Bayou, or that Kathryn Crosby, the star of *The 7th Voyage of Sinbad* and the wife of Bing Crosby, once had a pet bobcat named Chester W. Nimitz Please. Those are only a few of the revelations found in this fascinating, eminently browsable collection of personal stories about Texas, and about the everlasting imprint a state with a uniquely powerful identity leaves upon its children.

—**STEPHEN HARRIGAN, author of** *Big Wonderful Thing: A History of Texas* **and** *The Gates of the Alamo*

The sky is definitely not the limit for Texas-born high achievers, such as NASA space shuttle pioneer Bob Crippen, whose childhood in the Big Thicket propelled him to reach far beyond those towering pines to the stars above them. These stories prove dreams really do come true with determination, hard work, and the courage to aim high.

—**CHARLIE DUKE, lunar module pilot of Apollo 16, retired U.S. Air Force brigadier general and motivational speaker**

Thank goodness Dr. Lauro Cavazos hasn't forgotten the poignant details of his rise from my grandfather's Big House on the King Ranch to the White House and all the boot-shining, rattlesnake-hunting, and cattle-breeding in between. The history of the ranch is so intertwined with the history of Texas, I think you ought to read his chapter first. But you can't go wrong anywhere you start. The true stories in this book are as wide-ranging and awe-inspiring as, well, the King Ranch.

—STEPHEN J. "TIO" KLEBERG, great-great-grandson of founder Captain Richard King and King Ranch Inc. board member

Our stories are the fabric of our lives. We are all storytellers at heart, and we all love to hear a good story from the earliest days of childhood to the fading days of old age. But those childhood stories are the best because they are conjured from indelible memories that are the DNA of who we are as adults. This book is full of surprises. I learned so much more about every Texan in the book and maybe a little more about myself in the process.

—TERRY LICKONA, executive producer of *Austin City Limits* and co-producer of the Grammy and Latin Grammy awards

"The Child is father of the Man," wrote Wordsworth. This idea is at the heart of what Gaylon Finklea Hecker and Marianne Odom set out to do in this book. And they have done it so well— shown how childhood influences shaped the lives of a panoply of accomplished Texas men and women.

—STRYKER MCGUIRE, editor at *Bloomberg* and former correspondent and editor at *Newsweek* who lived and reported in Texas during the 1970s and early 1980s

Growing Up in the Lone Star State is a little piece of Texas heaven. This book chronicles the poignant, tender, and often lean times of many of the state's most famous celebrities in the world of sports, politics, and Hollywood and should be a must-read for anyone who was smart enough to either be raised in Texas or got to the state as fast as they could. It's a brilliantly conceived idea. I can't think of an easier read than this highly entertaining, breezy book. In fact, it should be mandatory reading for all Texans.

—KIRK BOHLS, *Austin American-Statesman* sports columnist

"There's only one state and it's Texas." So sayeth none other than Debbie Reynolds, one of the many legendary Lone Star ladies captured in this utterly charming book. From Mary Kay Ash to Jaclyn Smith, these fabulous Yellow Roses amply illustrate the strength, grace, and compassion of Texas women.

—**SARAH BIRD**, screenwriter and novelist, author of *Daughter of a Daughter of a Queen*

I hate to admit it but reading this book was a humbling experience because I realized how much I didn't know about my home state. I mean, who knew the late Debbie Reynolds grew up on a diet of Texas jackrabbits and pinto beans or that Texas-raised Kathryn Crosby was Miss Fat Stock Show before she married Bing? Decades in the making, these childhood recollections of Texas writers, actors, athletes, politicians and a few who seem to fit no category are at once insightful, hilarious, informative and just a down right good read. I loved it.

—**BOB SCHIEFFER**, CBS News anchor, retired

Like no other Americans, Texans are born into a fraternal order of sorts. Weaned on a potion that makes defeat incomprehensible and surrender out of the question, they are a breed that cannot be vanquished. And no matter how far Texans roam from the Lone Star State, they forever remain a part of this loose herd. In their veracious, thought-provoking, sometimes deeply moving, often humorous oral histories, the authors document this never-say-uncle attitude with fascinating insights into the childhoods of nearly fifty tenacious Texans who represent the best in the worlds of arts, entertainment, sports, journalism, medicine, business, politics, science, and faith.

—**DAVID NELSON WREN**, Texas-born author of *Ardrossan: The Last Great Estate on the Philadelphia Main Line*

CONTENTS

FOREWORD

L ike many other residents of New England, I grew up hearing those Texas myths: everything was bigger in Texas, the oilmen richer, the steaks tastier, the women more beautiful, the cowboys tougher, etc., etc. Ad nauseam. That these myths seemed like tall tales to us didn't make them any less entertaining. We Yankees were happy to let Texans have their lies and exaggerations while remaining convinced that such a godforsaken, rattlesnake-infested, tornado-swept, heat-blasted no-man's-land couldn't possibly be as exceptional or as interesting as Texans claimed.

Well.

In 1994 I took a job in Texas as the local bureau chief for *Time* magazine. Though I came more or less voluntarily, the move was really a strategic escape from New York City. I figured I could stand anything for a couple of years, then I would be on my way to more glamorous jobs as a correspondent in Paris, Tokyo, or Rome. Twenty-five years later I am so deeply rooted in this state that, as I joke to my wife, I will probably leave here only one way: feet first. Texas, as I have been shocked and thrilled to discover, is every bit as crazy, original, exceptional, and downright unique as all them yarn-spinnin' Texans said it was. At *Texas Monthly* magazine, where I worked for the better part of a decade, we had meetings once a month where we would all bring our story ideas and discuss them. It never failed to amaze me that these meetings produced so many great ideas about people and places that we could have published *three* award-winning magazines a month. Iowa and Delaware are nice places, I am sure, but they don't generate great stories like that. They do not produce larger-than-life characters like that.

Which brings us to this remarkable book about the state and its exceptional residents. Its breadth and depth and astonishing lineup of superstars is proof that the authors are themselves exceptional Texans. It is hard to imagine the sort of gumption it took to persist in a forty-year-long project. Not to mention the energy and persistence in wrangling—I think wrangling is the proper word—their many and far-flung subjects.

I am pleased to report that *Growing Up in the Lone Star State* is as entertaining as our state gets. So many of these words just jump out at you. Here is Broadway and television star Sandy Duncan from Henderson, in East Texas, talking about learning to dance: "We'd hold on to poker tables as our ballet barre. . . . We'd do pliés to the rhythm of the pumps." I don't recall my sisters using similar techniques in Connecticut. Here's Jimmy Dean from Plainview, the dude who wrote the proto-rap song "Big Bad John" in ninety minutes and redefined breakfast sausage, talking about diet: "We ate beans for breakfast and drank water for lunch and swelled up for supper." And here's Henry Cisneros, one of my political heroes, with a take you might not expect on growing up in San Antonio's barrio: "It was a kind of Norman Rockwell existence, but all our faces were brown."

You get the idea. This is fantastic stuff. Enjoy.

S. C. "Sam" Gwynne is the author of the *New York Times* Best Sellers *Rebel Yell: The Violence, Passion, and Redemption of Stonewall Jackson* and *Empire of the Summer Moon: Quanah Parker and the Rise and Fall of the Comanches.*

PREFACE

rowing Up in the Lone Star State is not only a valuable compendium of historical information, but also a literary monument to persistence and the refusal to be daunted. Journalists Gaylon Finklea Hecker and Marianne Odom began the interviews for this book forty years ago. Their purpose was to record the memories of accomplished Texans to determine why and to what extent growing up in the Lone Star State influenced and shaped their future successes.

The resulting forty-seven oral history interviews preserve the recollections of a wide variety of successful Texans. The list includes educator and Prairie View A&M University president Ruth Simmons, Archbishop Patrick Flores, broadcast journalist Bob Schieffer, entertainer Sandy Duncan, former San Antonio mayor Henry Cisneros, and college football great Jerry LeVias. There are interviews with individuals whose papers are housed in the Briscoe Center, including journalists Liz Carpenter and Liz Smith, former US Senator Kay Bailey Hutchison, and former CBS News anchor Dan Rather. Other interviewees include former ExxonMobil CEO Rex Tillerson, who was largely responsible for ExxonMobil's donation of its massive historical collection to the Briscoe

Center, and San Antonio entrepreneur Red McCombs, whose memoir was published by the center in 2010.

These fascinating reminiscences span from the early 1900s through the race to the moon. Recalled are memories of childhoods spent in communities established by formerly enslaved men and women; on sprawling ranches, small farms, and land worked by sharecroppers and tenants; and in small towns and big-city neighborhoods, with stories as diverse as the Texas landscape. These interviews and the records that come with them to the Briscoe Center preserve historically valuable information that will be useful for teaching and research for many years to come.

For that reason, among others, I eagerly accepted Gaylon and Marianne's offer to preserve at the Briscoe Center their archive of the original interview recordings as well as the documents and photographs they accumulated as they carried out the project. In addition, it was obvious to me that the interviews deserve a wide audience that reaches beyond the reading room of the Briscoe Center. The Briscoe Center only publishes books that are based largely on our collections. The addition of Gaylon and Marianne's oral history archive to our holdings qualified it to be considered for publication as part of our book program.

Accordingly, Alison Beck, the Briscoe Center's director of special projects, and Holly Taylor, the center's editor and head of publications, worked with Gaylon and Marianne to shepherd this book into print. I want to acknowledge the outstanding job Alison and Holly did to prepare the authors' manuscript and to expand the number of historic photographs by including many from the Briscoe Center's collections. And, of course, I congratulate Gaylon and Marianne on the successful completion of a project long in creation. The result is well worth their effort and persistence.

Don Carleton
Executive Director
Briscoe Center for American History

INTRODUCTION
The Project of a Lifetime

T he copyright date on this book is 2021, but its birthdate was 1981. Its coauthors devoted a professional lifetime to never giving up on a good idea—collecting heartfelt memories of accomplished Texans to determine what, if anything, about growing up in the Lone Star State prepared them for success. In our relative youth, we considered this a quest to define a Texas mystique, an elusive trait acknowledged but difficult to define.

In the end, our efforts reveal a rich mosaic of "nowhere but" experiences that reflect an extraordinary state that cultivates bigger-than-life personalities. It was in the Lone Star State that some of the world's most successful Texans learned to play hard, work harder, never give up, and summon the courage to seek their dreams. Whether catapulted by the advantages of privilege or the courage born of adversity, all traced their drive to their early days on Texas soil. Interviewees with backgrounds as diverse as the state's weather acknowledged in detail the enduring impact of childhood influences—good, bad, or indifferent. Through their dear, relatable reminisces, we learn about ourselves.

At its inception, we were a lifestyle reporter and a fashion editor, both from East Texas, thrown together in a corner of the *San Antonio*

Express-News two blocks from the Alamo. We could not predict the decades it would take, the places we would go, the relationships we would forge, and the lessons in history, humanity, and life in general that would unfold.

What we did know was Texas had captured the imagination of American popular culture, seemingly branding a big T on entertainment, politics, publishing, and even network news. It was this wave of interest we wanted to ride. With the 1980 election of President Ronald Reagan and Vice President George H. W. Bush, Texas once again was big in the nation's capital more than a decade after LBJ had left town. Plenty of Texans showed up at black-tie-and-boots fetes at the 1981 inauguration, including the coauthors, dispatched by the *Express-News* to cover the social whirlwind. The assignment tested stamina, cemented a working relationship, and started this project on its journey.

Authors Gaylon Finklea Hecker and Marianne Odom took their Texas pride with them to New York City in 1982. *Photo courtesy Gaylon Finklea Hecker and Marianne Odom*

Whether or not Texas was at the epicenter of pop or political culture, the success of so many Texans was undeniable and enduring. When we compiled lists of well-known native Texans, there were respected sports legends, trendsetters, entertainers, icons in many fields, and other overachievers. It became a parlor game to think of diverse talents who claimed these roots. "I didn't know he—or she—was from Texas!" became a common refrain. The list convinced us we had the basis for a book.

Through the mid-1980s, twenty-eight notable Texans sat down for oral history interviews in which we probed deep into their hearts for what it was about growing up in Texas that shaped them into the adults they became. Recorded interviews were transcribed, divided into anecdotes, and hand edited by interviewees. Their reactions were overwhelmingly positive. They all wanted to talk about Texas.

After a valiant start, life got in the way for us, and the original manu-script languished in file drawers for twenty-seven years. Periodically, guilt-ridden, we'd shake our heads and commiserate, "We sure ought to dust off that book and make it into something. We said we would."

So after an unexpected life turn in 2013, the project was reborn, and we committed to seeing this project to fruition even if it took more than half our lives. It was our good fortune that childhood remembrances have no expiration date. With the passage of almost three decades, the recollections we'd assembled in the 1980s were every bit as valuable—if not more so, because some of the subjects had died—but the picture was incomplete. It didn't tell the whole story of growing up in Texas. The state had changed and so had we. The quest resumed for a more encom-passing picture.

As if providence guided us, two back-to-back interviews fell into place in December 2016. Hectic schedules cleared up. Some of the busiest, most elusive subjects suddenly wanted to sit down with us. We added nineteen interviews that lasted from thirty minutes backstage at a chilly rodeo arena to four and a half hours around a breakfast table in a cozy Houston home. The project again developed a life of its own.

The idea of a Texas mystique still made for a good conversation starter, but beneath that shiny veneer lay the real jewels. In addition to intimate recollections that impart the personal effects of race, class, and economic status, interviewees shared youthful perspectives of the triumphs and tragedies that impacted the state through the 1960s. Of course, they weren't strangers to challenges.

The oldest interviewees witnessed the struggle for women to earn the right to vote and weathered the Great Depression. Many remembered two world wars, while others recalled the Texas City explosion of 1947 and the tornado that devastated Waco in 1953. They experienced the advent of television and the nightly news, which helped many come to terms with the assassination of a president too close to home.

For the first interview in June 1981, folklorist and good-old-boy char-acter actor Guich Koock had responded promptly to an interview request and didn't disappoint. In full ten-gallon hat and well-worn boots, he sidled up to the bar in San Antonio's historic Menger Hotel, where Teddy Roo-sevelt had recruited Rough Riders in 1898, to share stories of an Austin childhood steeped in Texas lore and a loving, socially conscious family.

In contrast, the final interview in August 2018 expanded a side of the Texas tapestry that was underrepresented in early interviews. Representative Senfronia Thompson, the longest-serving African American and woman in the Texas Legislature, granted an interview in her office suite in the state capitol. She spoke frankly about the hardships and discrimination she faced while raised by her illiterate grandmother on a subsistence farm in the area of Houston that, fittingly, she has represented for almost fifty years.

The interviews revealed a snapshot in time from the early 1900s, when Texas was an agrarian state, through the growth of major cities and the country's race to the moon in the 1960s. From El Paso to Beaumont, Wichita Falls to Mission, interviewees recalled life in former slave colonies, gigantic ranches, tiny farms, sharecropper fields, one-horse towns, dangerous ghettos, and tony neighborhoods. Their stories were as diverse as the state's geography. They jumped the waves at Galveston, contemplated an empty horizon on the Llano Estacado, and marveled as torrents of oil bubbled from the rich East Texas fields, transforming wildcatters into millionaires overnight. In the Piney Woods, they looked up for stars veiled by the Big Thicket's loblollies. They sought fertile lands for farming or expansive ranches for raising livestock. They rode real bulls at real rodeos or admired the brave who did.

Many clung to the cultures their parents or ancestors brought with them from Mexico or Southern plantations. Regardless of their background, life was a struggle for families living off the land or following ever-ripening crops. People worshipped in their own churches, lived on their side of town, attended their own schools, watched movies in segregated theaters, and were laid to rest in separate cemeteries. Hardships added to their resolve to seek better lives.

Most recalled studying Texas history in school—the legislature mandated it be taught to all students—and singing "Texas, Our Texas" was sandwiched between the national anthem and a daily classroom prayer. They were taught, and most believed, they could do anything if they worked hard enough and set their minds to it. Their futures were as expansive as the abundant natural resources and the sheer size of the state. Name it—Texas had it. Great things were expected.

Like the rest of the country, Texas and Texans changed exponentially in the second half of the twentieth century. But the memories of the first half, especially those of cherished, simple childhoods, offer glimpses of an era that no longer exists or at best is getting hard to find.

Their reflections transcend the original premise of trying to define Texas exceptionalism through the lens of outstanding Texans. Their recollections rise above boots and cattle and cowboy hats—though there are plenty of those—to become universal stories of good, bad, hope, despair, poverty, wealth, depression, and inspiration.

Oral histories, like those captured here, document primary accounts as the subjects remember them. Recollections of childhood told from an adult perspective may conflict with subsequent interpretations of events. Some intimate memories are as vivid to storytellers as if they happened yesterday; others are hazy as if filtered through the gauze of time. Yet their importance remains clear and irrefutable. Despite the capriciousness of memory, these endearing and colorful stories reveal poignant experiences that inspired hopes and dreams and laid the foundation for a lifetime of accomplishments. Whether it is nature or nurture that shapes young lives, these outstanding Texans prove the Lone Star State is a good place to make a good start.

The authors interview Henry Cisneros at his grandparents' home in San Antonio, where he resides today, December 2016. *Photo by Marvin Hecker*

Richard Overton on the front porch of his home in Austin on a street later named for him.
Photo courtesy Volma Overton Jr.

BIRTH NAME	**RICHARD ARVINE OVERTON**
BORN	May 11, 1906, in St. Mary's Colony, Bastrop County, to Jim Gentry Overton and Elizabeth "Lizzie" Franklin Overton
DIED	December 27, 2018
INTERVIEW	His home, Austin, Texas, February 18, 2017

RICHARD OVERTON
A Marksman Way Back When

Richard Overton was the oldest living World War II veteran and the oldest man in the United States when he died in 2018 at 112. He was honored with a funeral in Austin worthy of his status as a national treasure and laid to rest in the Texas State Cemetery. At age thirty-six, he was drafted and entered the military in 1942. He served in the all-Black 1887th US Army Engineer Aviation Battalion and spent seventeen tumultuous months in 1944 and 1945 at Pearl Harbor, Iwo Jima, Okinawa, and other islands in the Asiatic-Pacific campaign. After the war, he built his home on the street the City of Austin renamed for him in 2017. He worked as a courier in the capitol under four governors and the state Treasury Department. President Barack Obama honored him on Veterans Day in 2013 at Arlington National Cemetery. Overton's celebrity led to a 2016 YouTube documentary distributed by National Geographic, guest appearances at events such as the 2016 US Army All-American Bowl in San Antonio, and regular visits from dignitaries and well-wishers.

I was a good boy. My daddy was just crazy about me. Of course, he was crazy about me, more so than he was any of the others, because we would sit down by the fireplace every morning and get us some Gordon's gin. He drank that Gordon's gin, and I helped him drink it. And he'd get out there every morning, when it was cold or anytime, and sit at the fireplace out there at Creedmoor.

And I'll never forget, I'd get up and put my elbow on his knee, and he'd tell me different words and learn me everything. And then I got up in size to walk around, and I didn't need everything. My daddy didn't whip me at all, but he whipped some of the others. They didn't do what he said do, and he always had a big belt. But he was crazy about me. My daddy just liked me. That was all.

My daddy would always buy me bicycles and horses. And I got big enough, and he'd buy me a car. He'd buy me anything I wanted. He bought me a horse and a buggy. Old Frank was kind of a racehorse, a brown, tan horse. I hooked him to a buggy. I used to ride him, and I used to ride my little cousins around on Old Frank.

We were ten kids. Six girls, four boys. Out of the children, I was close to the middle. I had four of them older than I was.

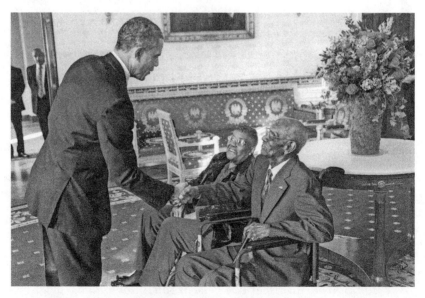

President Barack Obama greets Richard Overton, with Earlene Love-Karo, November 11, 2013. Overton, then 107 years old, attended the Veterans Day Breakfast at the White House.
White House photo by Lawrence Jackson

I had some pictures of me as a kid, but they all burned up. The house caught fire, and my oldest sister had it in the books. The fire burned up the Bibles and all the stuff.

My mother was nice, a nice lady. It was busy around our house. I done everything. I was a good helper around the house. You bet your life, I helped her cook and clean. She cooked on a potbelly stove. That cookstove had four little caps on the top. It was a small stove.

And they've got little washbowls and little old washstands. And you hang some clothes over that. That's a washstand.

We had a dirt floor packed real tight. That ground is just as hard like a floor.

At that time, you'd sleep anywhere. You could sleep on the porch or outside the wall, on top of the ceiling. You could sleep on the floor or you could sleep out on the driveway. You can sleep anywhere you wanted. And now you can't walk down your driveway—you better not try to sleep out there.

A lot of people had sleeping porches. We had porches, but they didn't have no screen wire on them. We'd get your fur and a pallet and sleep on them porches—nice and cool out there.

When we were kids, we didn't get toys for Christmas. Later on, they'd give you some toys, but when you first started out early on, your sock would be hanging by the fireplace. You'd get an onion and popcorn and an apple.

They weren't making much toys then. Daddy wasn't able to buy any.

Out in the country, we used to hunt opossums, rabbits, ducks. I could kill anything. People would come from town. I'd carry them out in the field where I knew the birds was. I used to kill birds, and they'd carry some birds back to town.

I was known as a great shooter. Went hunting with my cousins, and everybody else was trying to hit something. I was known as a marksman way back when.

We ate what we killed. That's the reason I killed them. Oh, I'm telling you, I eat ducks and rabbits. I eat opossums and squirrels. Squirrels, that's good meat. My mother cooked them.

I had some bird dogs and sold them bird dogs for one hundred dollars a dog. Every year I'd have puppies, and I'd sell them. I raised cats and dogs and calves and turkeys and chickens and doves.

At Pleasant Valley, I had everything I wanted to have. And people would have these cows they'd draw milk from. Well, they'd have calves. For every calf, they had to have ten or twelve cows. They'd take the milk and give me one of the calves. They couldn't keep the calf. I'd keep them and sell them. I knew how to make money. I never was broke.

We lived in St. Mary's here in Texas in Bastrop County. We moved to different houses. My daddy would move us.

I worked on a farm, lived on a farm—picked cotton, chopped cotton, drove teams and plowed, pulled corn, shocked hay, drove trucks, did all kind of fieldwork. I don't know what all I did do. For a lot of people, they never did nothing, but I did all that stuff.

You'd be out in the field working and twelve o'clock come. He didn't have no bell; he'd hit a dadgum cow horn. If you were picking cotton, you'd drop that sack right then and go and eat your dinner for an hour. And when he hit that bell again, you'd go back right to the same sack you was in and start from there.

I used to pick cotton in Big Spring. That's where I helped my older brother and his wife. They had to pick cotton.

I went to school in the country between Creedmoor and Pleasant Valley. I went to eleven grades. I was a good schoolboy. I could tell the teacher a lot of things. I liked all the subjects—all of them.

We had great big geographies. You could see all the states and cities, and they had all them roads. We went to those places. Somebody read about them and told about them, but they didn't go there. But we went and walked into those places.

Lot of these people say, "I heard about it."

But I went there. That's how I can tell them about it.

I was a baseball player. I started playing in school. I played all the way up until I got grown. I could play all the places, but my regular place was first base. I was a home run hitter. I didn't dream about being a professional baseball player. I was in school.

I was crazy about school, but I had to quit. My daddy died, so my mother had to take over. I was older than four or five of the kids, and I had to take care of them, so I had to quit.

I was driving a car bringing the teachers to town in the evening. There were two schools over here on Twelfth Street at night. That's how I made my living.

My family went to church. I had to go. It was Baptist. I was fourteen years old. We were in Pleasant Valley or maybe it was the little white church in St. Mary's.

I was baptized in the river. There was a little space beside the river. There was some singing, but I don't remember the minister.

The women in my family sang church songs. Oh, God, yeah. Some of them can sing them now. Boy, they used to could sing, especially the young ones. They had good voices.

I never sang in the choir, but I always sang in church. I sing now. I like singing to myself. I liked all the songs. I remember them all, but I can't name one.

Like I said, my daddy drank that Gordon's gin, and I helped him drink it. When I got up in size, I wanted to drink gin, gin, gin. But I never got drunk, never did go to jail, nothing.

I started smoking cigars when I was eighteen. I guess if I had put all them cigars together, I could have made a house out of them. I smoked four and five and six a day, sometimes ten a day. They don't hurt my health. I didn't inhale it. I had one a while ago, but I didn't light it up.

Richard Overton was thirty-six years old when he entered the army during World War II. *Photo courtesy Richard Overton*

A Speedy Draft in Texas

I was down here near Bastrop, and some boys said there were soldiers down there.

"Why you ain't in the army?"

I said, "I ain't old enough."

I was thirty-six.

That was Sunday.

Monday morning I got up and I had a letter: "Come in to San Antonio. Signed, Uncle Sam."

The youngest of nine children, Sarah McClendon poses with two older brothers and a sister.
Photo courtesy McClendon House, Tyler, Texas

BIRTH NAME	**SARAH NEWCOMB McCLENDON**
BORN	July 8, 1910, in Tyler to S. S. McClendon and Anne Bonner McClendon
DIED	January 8, 2003
INTERVIEW	White House Press Room, Washington, DC, November 30, 1984

SARAH McCLENDON

Feminist at an Early Age

Sarah McClendon became an institution in the Washington press corps by peppering officials, especially presidents, with tough questions at news conferences for six decades. After graduating from the University of Missouri School of Journalism in 1931, she worked as a reporter in Tyler and Beaumont. She joined the Women's Army Corps in 1942, where she served as a public relations officer for the surgeon general. As a lieutenant who insisted on her rights, she was the first officer to give birth at a military hospital. As a young widow, she began her own McClendon News Service in 1946, which covered Washington news for member newspapers and individual subscribers. She related her experiences in two books, My Eight Presidents *in 1978 and* Mr. President, Mr. President! My Fifty Years of Covering the White House *in 1996. Her family home in Tyler, the McClendon House, listed in the National Register of Historic Places, is open to visitors.*

At the time I was born, Tyler was a Victorian city that tried to be a center of culture. It was a very lovely place. My people had lived there since 1830, and some of them went to the Civil War from Tyler.

I'm the youngest of nine. My mother was forty-three when I was born. It's wonderful to have a big family and to be the youngest, because all of my brothers and sisters had to take care of me. They helped send me to school when money was short.

As a student, I played around. I didn't think studying was necessary, but I loved to read. I read like mad when I was eight, nine, and ten, and I've never read as much since. We had a good library in the house. I absolutely loved history and politics, but mainly I loved English and didn't care for math and science.

We had some grand educators and ministers around Tyler. I had some wonderful teachers in high school and at Tyler Junior College. I looked up to them very highly. Mattie Jones taught all nine children in our family.

I read newspapers because my father said everybody had to read them. To be educated, he thought you had to read the *Dallas News*. He read everything in it every day. In the summer, we had Chautauquas with lectures for about a week and programs for children in the libraries that I went to.

In my town, the families would go all out to entertain the young people in their homes in town and at the lake. For instance, if we were having a Valentine or Halloween party, the mother and maybe her friends would work for days to make decorations for the whole house and beautiful cakes. Everything would be done in an exquisite way to carry out a motif. It is amazing to think about all the pain and trouble our parents went to for us to be entertained.

I was a spoiled brat. At times, I'm afraid, I was a juvenile delinquent. For instance, we didn't do very much but ride around town. Sometimes I moved some of the red lamps from the road construction and put them on the doorstep of somebody who was real prissy.

As a child, I was ugly, towheaded, and always wearing hand-me-downs. I didn't mind that. I loved my brothers and sisters. They were wonderful to me and I was very happy. One of the nicest things that ever happened to me was on a birthday. My family always did so much for my birthdays. I looked out the window and they had put up some new swings for me. I loved to have swings in the yard.

I lived in the wonderful old house in Tyler that I was born in. My uncles and aunts built it around 1878, and it was restored as a center for history and community activity in Tyler. Our great big house had a great big yard where we could rake leaves in piles and jump in them. We had a lake behind us and woods. My sister took us through the woods and told us the names of leaves, trees, and little animals. We found snakes and turtles.

We decorated the whole house at Christmastime with evergreens from the trees around. We made wreaths for each window. On Christmas morning, we lined up to go into the parlor, and I could go in first because I was the youngest. Each of us had our presents on a chair, because there were so many of us we couldn't put all the gifts at the fireplace.

When I was eight or nine, the circus came to town, and the circus wagons bogged down in the mud right in front of my house. We had very heavy red clay in the roads and no pavement. They had to use the elephants and camels to pull the circus wagons out. I got to ride the elephants and the camels. And the acrobats came into our yard and practiced on our swings.

I credit my gutsiness to my parents. My family was never well-to-do, but I had uncles and aunts who were. My father, S. S. McClendon, said he would have had some money if he hadn't had so many children to provide for.

He was very interested in politics. As a big family sitting around the dinner table, we spent a lot of time talking. Then we would sit out on the big porch in the summertime at night with guests and relatives and eat watermelon and talk politics.

When I was six, my mother, Anne Bonner McClendon, was a leader in the women's movement. Her friend was Mrs. Cone Johnson of Tyler, a national leader in trying to get women the right to vote. They made speeches to organize people in East Texas to get women interested in voting. My mother had no day care center to leave me in, so she took me with her. I enjoyed hearing them make those speeches. Then when

I got home, my brothers would put me up on the table and let me mimic the speeches.

My father had had his own book and stationery business, and then he had the dealer agency for ballroom pianos. He became one of the first credit merchants in East Texas. For thirty years, he was the Smith County Democratic Party chairman, and he ran the Democratic elections.

My father came from Louisiana, and after the Civil War there was no place for him to go to school. His mother told him, "Go out in the woods on Sunday afternoons and read Shakespeare and the Bible."

He did, and he became quite a well-known speaker. When he and my mother married, they said they would always help people—the sick and the poor—and they would always take part in public events. My father became quite a champion of the underdogs, the Catholics and the Jews, the foreigners and the Blacks. My family's social consciousness may have come from struggling after the Civil War.

My grandfather was M. H. Bonner. He went to Marshall, Texas, and started a law practice with J. Pinckney Henderson, who was elected the first governor of Texas in 1845. Henderson, Texas, was named for him. He had been a foreign diplomat who represented the Texas Republic at the Court of St. James's and of France. My grandfather was the circuit-rider judge in East Texas, and his father had been a circuit-riding preacher in East Texas. My grandfather went on to become a member of the Texas Supreme Court, and his picture is in the capitol in Austin. My great-uncle, T. R. Bonner, had been a commander of troops in the Civil War and became speaker of the Texas House of Representatives.

The family was mainly lawyers then. I thought surely I'd be a lawyer, but I didn't know how I'd ever make any money being a woman.

My brother Sidney was one of the first to go to World War I from the University of Texas. He was in law school and in the first officer candidate school, which later became a powerful organization in Texas political and business life. Then my brother Charles also went to the war.

You can imagine the shock of a family in East Texas who had not traveled abroad. The idea of the sons going overseas was a terrible thing. As a child, I used to go with my older sisters and wait at the railroad tracks near our house as loads of troops went off to war. We'd stand under the trees and watch. Sometimes the soldiers wanted us to write them. They would put a penny in a note with their address on it and then throw it

Sarah McClendon asks questions at a briefing in the
White House Press Room, 1984. *Photo by Harry Young*

to us from the train. I have such a memory of this war. When they came
back, they never said a word about it. They were in shock still. It was
just so awful.

As children we were taught in our schools to be very patriotic. We
marched in all the parades on patriotic days. We learned to sing all those
songs about Texas and about the nation. That's why I was motivated to
volunteer for the army in World War II. My brothers went to the first
war, and I'd always said if there was another war, I was going.

A junior college teacher of mine, a very fine woman from Columbia,
Missouri, where the very strong University of Missouri Journalism School is, said I had the attributes of a reporter and that I should try
to be one. She said she knew I wrote a lot of themes, I did a lot of questioning, and I was always talking.

She said, "You, McClendon, will go to the university for journalism,
and you will learn how to be a reporter."

I'm so glad I did. But I had to scrimp and borrow money from my brothers and sisters. Otherwise, I could never have done it, because that was a very hard time for us. My family didn't have any money.

It was so wonderful to be a reporter in Tyler because the oil boom came in during that time, and it brought people from all over the world. It was absolutely fascinating. I'll never forget when I first started working for the *Tyler Courier-Times-Telegraph*, my very dignified sisters came home one day horrified.

They harped, "Sarah, we saw you sitting on a bench on the courthouse square today interviewing this old tramp."

Because I was a woman, I was told I couldn't cover a lot of stories. I was determined to prove that as a woman reporter, I could cover anything a man could. Women have to work twice as hard.

One night while I was dancing in one of those beautiful homes, I found out there had been a murder at the motor courts. So I got my date to go with me, and we left to cover the murder. That was a great shock to my family. I was never considered a lady. They never wanted me to touch anything like that or to go into any place that was bad.

They would have liked for me to go to Hollins College in Virginia, where most of my family had gone. But we couldn't afford it. They wanted me to be a quiet lady. But my mother encouraged me to have a career. She said too many people married so young and then had children and couldn't have a career. She wanted people to go forward and take part in public life.

I was timid. I was scared to go to Europe or anywhere by myself. My father kept pushing me and pushing me, and he said, "Go, go. Don't forget that Woodrow Wilson met three men at the Democratic Convention and those men later became members of his cabinet. Contacts are the main thing. Always make good contacts."

My mother had wanted to be a writer. She wrote something every day. She kept diaries, and I have a whole batch of beautiful letters she wrote to the members of her family. She wrote the history of the Episcopal church and the history of education in Tyler.

My sisters say Mother wasn't a feminist, but I tell them she certainly was. I went with her to make those speeches. They didn't know all that, and they never were suffragettes.

I've been a feminist ever since I was a child, and I certainly combine it with my journalism today.

———

Usually what makes a good reporter is having enough courage to try and try again to get the story that other people are not getting, to try to pull out the story that other people are trying to cover up. The reason Texas turned out so many fine journalists is because Texans are such individualists. It goes with the Texas personality.

All these things came out of my childhood and I'm amazed to see how they spin over to your later life.

Childhood portrait of Claudia Alta Taylor, in or near Karnack, Texas, c. 1915. *LBJ Presidential Library photo*

BIRTH NAME	**CLAUDIA ALTA TAYLOR**
BORN	December 22, 1912, in Karnack to Thomas Jefferson Taylor and Minnie Lee Pattillo Taylor
DIED	July 11, 2007
INTERVIEW	LBJ Ranch, Stonewall, Texas, August 10, 1981

LADY BIRD JOHNSON
A Southern Upbringing

Lady Bird Johnson took her reverence for natural beauty to the White House, where as first lady from 1963 to 1969 she created a Keep America Beautiful campaign and lobbied Congress to pass the Highway Beautification Act to plant wildflowers along the nation's thoroughfares. A businesswoman in her own right, owning radio and television stations in Austin, the wife of the thirty-sixth president of the United States, Lyndon B. Johnson, modernized the structure of the first lady's office by adding her own chief of staff, an outside liaison with Congress, and a press secretary. After the president died in 1973, she oversaw the Town Lake Beautification Project in Austin, renamed Lady Bird Lake after her death. She and actress Helen Hayes founded the National Wildflower Research Center in Austin in 1982. President Gerald Ford bestowed on her the Presidential Medal of Freedom in 1977. In 1988 she was the first president's wife to receive the Congressional Gold Medal.

Perhaps I have a drawl. I am a bit more Southern, because we in Texas are many regions. I happen to come from deep East Texas, which is much more a part of the Old South. It's about twelve miles from the Louisiana line, and I spent the first twenty-one years of my life there. That was home.

Actually, I was born and raised entirely out in the country. Karnack was the closest post office. Our house was an old, red brick Greek revival, perhaps Georgian, made by slaves down in the pasture. It had white columns in the front and long side porches.

We hadn't owned it all that time. My father just came to Texas at the turn of the century. My father was Thomas Jefferson Taylor, and my mother was Minnie Lee Pattillo Taylor. In 1899 or 1900, he came to Texas from Clark County, Alabama, stayed about a year, went back and got my mother to marry him, and they settled near Karnack.

As the years passed, he accumulated a good amount of land. He had two country stores and a gin. Cotton was the way of life, and Karnack was a very small agricultural community. My daddy's store was the main business. It was probably known to a lot of sporting fishermen because they would go through Karnack on their way to Caddo Lake, which is a beautiful, wild lake full of cypress trees hanging with Spanish moss, sloughs and bayous, and a few crocodiles and big catfish.

Among the servants in the house, there was a very nice, refined Black nurse named Alice Tittle. She was my nurse, and she is said to have given me the name Lady Bird when I was two months old. She said of me, "She's as pretty as a little lady bird."

However, that was a nickname and not uncommon in the South. People usually outgrow them, and if I had my life to live over, I would make sure that I outgrew it.

My two brothers—one was eight years older and one was twelve years older—were sent off to school before I was big enough to be companionable with them. And my mother died when I was five. I feel terribly sorry for my mother herself and my father about that. But I don't feel sorry for myself, because when you're five you don't know too much what you're missing.

I remember my mother was tall and slim and fast and swept around the house with such agility and grace that I couldn't keep up as I waddled around behind her. She usually dressed in white and had artistic tastes.

In her lifetime, the house had a good deal of company, and we had quite a lot of servants. I have a delightful old picture of everybody all lined up in the front yard—all the servants, the cook with the great big bushy white apron and big white cap, and the nurse with the big apron on and the washerwoman and everybody else and my two brothers looking like ragamuffins out in front.

After my mother died, her maiden sister, Effie Mason Pattillo, came to live with me to be the feminine influence in the house. She was a dear, gentle, wonderful woman but very innocent and completely unworldly. She had a great love of nature, and perhaps that is one of the things she gave me.

I was shy and I'm sure people thought of me as lonely. But I never thought of myself as lonely, because I had all the world to walk in. I walked in the woods in the spring, and I searched for the first violets, and I knew every branch, as we called them. If they were bigger, they were called creeks. I used to go around in little bateaux with a good friend or by myself, and it never occurred to any of us that it was dangerous or lonesome.

> I never thought of myself as lonely, because I had all the world to walk in.

My mother used to read to me. She was an omnivorous reader. She read me fairy stories, the Greek and Roman myths and legends, and German folk stories. Of course, for a five-year-old, these were pretty limited. But she had a good little library of children's books for me. Lamb's version of Shakespeare was one thing I remember. I particularly missed reading when she died.

Then I discovered, lo and behold, my daddy could read. I was amazed because I thought it was a wonderful gift that my mother possessed, and if anybody could read, surely they'd spend a lot of time doing it. I never thought of my daddy doing it. He would do a lot of figuring and book work and maybe read the newspaper, but he went to bed early and got up early. When he found out I was hooked on books, he began to read to me every night. The fare then turned to adventure stories and nature stories and Zane Grey.

My daddy influenced my childhood very much. He was very handsome and physically one of the strongest people I've ever known. I'd like to think I look like my father, but I'm afraid my nose didn't take after anybody.

He couldn't bear to say if he ever was sick. He was always so proud when he got back from his annual physical examination. From the time he was sixty, the doctor said he looked like a man of forty-five. And as the years progressed, it went on like that.

He was big, strong, handsome, and determined, but I knew him to be gentle and loving. I expect a lot of people thought he was stern and forbidding. His name in the countryside was Captain Taylor, and the name that some of the Black folks called him was Mr. Boss.

However, he certainly had an understanding side, because I have met countless Black people since who have said, "Your daddy lent me money to start off to college," or "I was trying to build myself a house and the bank wouldn't lend me money, and your dad lent me money to start my first house."

In the interval between my mother's death and when Aunt Effie arrived, my daddy used to take me with him to the store at night during ginning season. This began in late August and lasted until the last bale was ginned in October or early November. The gin would run very late

First Lady Hillary Clinton, Texas Governor Ann Richards, and Lady Bird Johnson
at an event related to the Liz Carpenter Lecture Series at the University of Texas, 1993.
*Photo by Larry Murphy, UT News and Information, Ann W. Richards Papers, Briscoe
Center for American History, University of Texas at Austin*

at night. It was a big and important season of the year, and he would stay down there until nine o'clock or later. So we'd sleep at the store.

It was a great big, cavernous, red brick building, the only big building in the little community. The second floor had things like furniture and coffins and plows and farm tools. The downstairs had lanterns and kerosene lamps, chewing tobacco, the candy counter with which I was very familiar, dry goods, shoes, and everything that it took to live on.

In those days, the economy was such that you had tenants. About 95 percent of them were Black, and they would rent a farm, and you would charge them a certain portion of the cotton they would raise sharecropping. He would sell them everything from the store, because it would take a mule and a wagon a very long time to drive into Marshall, the closest town.

When I spent the night in the store, I noticed these great big, long wooden boxes and I said, "What's that, Daddy?"

He paused just a moment and said, "Dry goods, honey."

He knew not to tell me that they were coffins because I had been listening, as all little children did, to countless ghost stories from my Black nurse. Our old house, having been built before the Civil War, naturally had its quota of ghost stories. They had an effect, and to this day, when I go back there, I have an eerie feeling.

Our house was so far in the country, I had few people to play with except an occasional imported child. Black children were my main playmates.

A lot of the family back in Alabama were Baptists. But all of my life, my father was a mainstay of the Methodist church in Karnack. I think my mother was, too. Some of us went to church every Sunday, but my father had the idea that as long as we were represented somehow, that was enough.

When I visited in Alabama in the summertime, my father's branch of the family was much stricter. My mother, had she lived on, I feel sure, would not have been strict. My Alabama kinfolks didn't believe in dancing or playing cards on Sunday. A funny thing, it was all right to play dominoes, but not cards. I never quite got the difference. Forty-two was the domino game they played.

I knew my grandmother, my father's mother. She had four husbands and thirteen children and lived to be eighty-some-odd years old. All of those children except one grew up to maturity, and that one died in an accident. So she was a strong survivor. I have often thought of that when I have been in demanding situations with a lot of trouble. I hope I take after my grandmother.

I went to a school called Fern, which was a one-room schoolhouse heated in the winter by a stovepipe right up to the ceiling, and a chalkboard, and a teacher's desk at one end, and by the door a small closet for your cloak. The big boys always lit the fire in the stove and kept it going in the wintertime. One teacher taught everybody from the primer, as it was called, through seventh grade, where it came to an end.

In some course, I got a B. I was about eight years old, and I was wretched and crushed. The high point of the day was when Daddy arrived home from work. I always ran to the gate to meet him. This particular day, he could see something was the matter. He asked me, and I told him.

He said, "Honey, it's just one day. It's just one lesson. You've got days and weeks and months ahead of you to learn that and to get better than anybody, and don't let one day affect you."

This was a very backward rural community, and thirteen students were the most we had. There was one itinerant white family with five children in the school, and they moved off in the middle of the year. That left about four months of school where I was the only child.

The effect was that if you applied yourself at all, you could make two grades a year if you wanted to, and it was all right with the teachers if you did. I made two grades a year quite frequently. So I graduated from high school when I was fifteen, which was a mixed blessing: I was not at all that adult. Other girls were adventuring with lipstick and dates. I was still wearing saddle shoes or the comparable thing in those days and feeling very shy around boys and most people. I imagined that they were all more sophisticated than I was.

I went off to St. Mary's School for Girls in Dallas, which in September 1928 had very high intellectual standards. But it was terribly old-fashioned and had rigid rules, like you had to have a chaperone if you went anywhere. If you went to downtown Dallas, you certainly had a

Lady Bird Johnson at the LBJ Ranch near Stonewall, Texas,
June 1, 1991. *LBJ Library photo by Frank Wolfe*

chaperone, and the chaperone was supposed to sit downstairs in the living room if anybody came to see you.

In many ways, it was a wonderful experience. It opened the doors of the theater to me, and I've loved it ever since. I made the acquaintance of several teachers, real teachers, who excited me about learning and also taught me that it wasn't wrong or crazy to doubt and question.

After two years at St. Mary's, I went to the University of Texas. I was seventeen years old and very, very eager to see the world. I did not have any clear notion of what I wanted to do with my life. It was obvious to me as I went along through the university that I wanted to emerge with some kind of a skill so I could get a job. So I took enough courses in education to get a second-class teacher's certificate, thinking that if I liked it, I could return and upgrade it to first class. But I didn't want to teach in the little rural town down the road. I was interested only in teaching some place like Hawaii or Alaska. I even had the names of congressmen from two regions to write and make inquiries about it, but I never got that far.

I also got a degree in journalism because I got a good many dates with newspaper people, met a bunch of them, and decided that it was a very interesting, exciting life, which puts you in the forefront of where things are happening. I wanted to be where things were happening and to see the world.

I remember one time my daddy said something that startled me. I was about to graduate from the university, and I was talking about whether I would try to get a job teaching or try to get my foot in the door as a secretary.

I said, "Maybe I'll just come back here and live at the brick house."

My daddy said with a sharpness that was totally untypical of him, "Oh, no you won't."

I didn't know what to think of it, because I knew he loved me, and I knew he was lonesome.

"There's more in life for you," he said.

He had spent his whole life there, but it was very clear he did not want me to limit my horizons to that little country town.

Washington in the Rearview Mirror

Lady Bird Johnson with her daughters, Lynda and Luci, 1947. *Christianson-Leberman photo, Sam Rayburn Papers, Briscoe Center for American History, University of Texas at Austin*

My children had a lasting bond with Texas. We would come home to Texas the day Congress adjourned and not go back to Washington until between Christmas and New Year's. It was always a wrenching, sad time and a hard household to manage after my first week or so in Washington because the girls hadn't wanted to go. They felt transplanted.

I remember leaving the ranch with Luci when she was about eight, and she was saying, "I don't want to go. You're not a real mother or you'd let me live in Texas."

Mary Martin, three and a half years old. *Photo courtesy Doss Heritage and Culture Center*

BIRTH NAME	**MARY VIRGINIA MARTIN**
BORN	December 1, 1913, in Weatherford to Preston Martin and Juanita Presley Martin
DIED	November 3, 1990
INTERVIEW	The Mansion, Dallas, Texas, June 11, 1983

MARY MARTIN
The Gift of Talent

Mary Martin, the theater and film actress and singer beloved as Peter Pan on stage and television in the 1950s, became an overnight sensation singing "My Heart Belongs to Daddy" in Cole Porter's Leave It to Me! in 1938. Martin won a Tony Award for Peter Pan in 1955 and as Nellie Forbush in South Pacific in 1950 and Maria von Trapp in The Sound of Music in 1960. She won an Emmy for the televised version of Peter Pan. Martin also appeared on radio and in movies in a career that spanned seven decades. She has a star for recording on the Hollywood Walk of Fame and one for radio on Hollywood Boulevard. Martin was inducted into the American Theater Hall of Fame in 1973 and was recognized for career achievements in 1989 at the Kennedy Center Honors. She was the mother of actor Larry Hagman, who personified Texans to viewers around the world as J. R. Ewing in the 1980s television series Dallas.

I get my musical abilities from my mother's side of the family. She met my daddy at Weatherford College, where he was studying to be a young lawyer. She married very young and gave up the violin then. But I heard her play when I was a little girl, and she was fabulous.

When I was five, she had me taking lessons on her violin down at Weatherford College. I could immediately play anything that I'd heard, but I couldn't read the notes. My mother and teacher didn't know that. I'd hear a song once, and I could play it. I can still pick out songs on the violin, but it sounds awful. I played violin in *I Do! I Do!*, the same old violin. I played "Time to Get Married."

I taught myself dancing. I was what you call one of those "natural" dancers. But I did take what they called elocution from Auntie Flo, Mrs. Flo Hutchison. I was her strongest pupil because I loved it so much; I loved performing. I gave an hour and a half recital when I was twelve. If I had an audience of one, I'd perform. I was just on all the time.

It never occurred to me to be anything but an entertainer. That's the way it was. I learned things very quickly. In chapel or school, I could hear a song and sing it immediately. I could learn the words in about ten minutes, no more.

My earliest remembrance of performing was at age five at our firehouse. I was like their mascot. The firemen let me go out in the truck to drive around. The biggest thrill of my entire childhood, and probably the biggest thrill of my life, was when the firemen let me slide down the brass pole.

So when I did *Peter Pan*, Richard [Halliday], my husband, knew how much I loved that fire pole, and he told the producer. When the scenery was made, they had a fireman's pole to slide down into Never Never Land underneath where the pirates couldn't get them. I knew exactly how to slide down it.

One of my favorite lines in the entire show was when Tiger Lily had to say, "Peter Pan, you are the sun, the moon, and the stars."

And Peter at the top would say, "Yes, I know," and slide down the pole.

I get my energy from both my parents. My mother had tremendous energy. So did my sister. I call it adrenaline. I get tired, but as long as I know something is coming up, my adrenaline goes to work.

My positive outlook and exuberance must come from the genes in my family. I've had many fabulous things happen in my life, and I've had bad things, too.

I have an inner voice, always there, that tells me what I should do and when I'm not doing the right thing. I don't know what it is, but I have always been tuned into it. I had it from the beginning; it did not develop. I think my mother had it, too.

You can take the girl out of Texas, but you can't take Texas out of the girl—ever. I originally entitled my book [*My Heart Belongs*] "The Square," for the square in Weatherford, my hometown. It has a courthouse in the middle. When my father was young, he was a judge in that courthouse. And then he became a famous lawyer and tried many cases there. So the book is partly about me at the age of five going around the square and going from one store to another, because I knew everybody in the entire place. This was a ritual. I went every day of my life around this square.

Everybody knew me, and I certainly knew everybody by their first name. They were all my closest friends: the man at the grocery store, the man who cut my hair. When I was made a Distinguished Citizen

Mary Martin won a Tony and Emmy for her performances as Peter Pan. *Photo courtesy Doss Heritage and Culture Center*

of Weatherford, I shook hands with seventy-five people. I remembered everybody's name and nickname that was in my age bracket.

My father was a fabulous actor in the field of law. He could make the jury cry or laugh. I used to slip into the courthouse and listen. His voice had tremendous power.

My daddy called me Baby all the time. I got so mad at him one time. When I was twelve, he had a baby bed moved into our room at the Rice Hotel.

I asked the man, "What's that for?"

And he said, "It's for Mr. Preston Martin and his wife and baby."

I couldn't even look. I knew what he was talking about.

My mother was very, very clever. She could make anything. All my clothes were beautifully handmade. My father bought me my first store-bought dress when I was about six or seven.

I frightened my mother every single day of her life. She would say, "What have you done now?"

I would ruin my clothes when I climbed trees and fences. I jumped off the roof of the garage and broke my collarbone. I always thought I could fly.

My mother was born in a place called Brenham, Texas. She was what they called a "change-of-life baby." Her brothers and sisters were all married. Her father apparently loved horses and carriages. He was killed in front of their house by frightened horses when she was a very little girl. Then her mother died soon after that.

Actress Mary Martin, right, with First Lady Nancy Reagan, April 1988. *Photo by Dirck Halstead, Dirck Halstead Photographic Archive, Briscoe Center for American History, University of Texas at Austin*

The sisters and brothers raised this little girl. One of the sisters was married to a German violinist, so she was raised as a violinist. Her sister also had a little girl my mother's age, and they practiced eight hours a day together on the violin.

I loved my daddy and loved my mother and I loved my sister. I favored both my parents. It was a very loving and close family. My sister was eleven or twelve years older, and we didn't see each other much. I was sort of an only child because my sister was so much older and away at school most of the time.

She was born with what they called then "leakage of the heart." They said she would never live past sixteen. When I was little, she was in bed all the time, and I didn't know what was the matter with her. Mother would send me up with trays of food, and I'd stop on the steps and eat most of it. She never told Mother.

I had heard the expression "leakage of the heart," and I would hide to see if her heart leaked. I never saw it. She got better after she was sixteen, and the valves started closing. That was because they suddenly said she had to have physical exercise. She learned to ride horses and jump hurdles. She learned ballet and was a toe dancer. She went to Columbia University in New York and majored in physical education.

We sounded exactly alike. I always thought she was prettier than I was. She had a very pretty nose; mine was always round. And she had huge, beautiful brown eyes.

I had a tremendous curiosity about religion. I went to Methodist Sunday school when I was about four because they had birthday cake on everybody's birthday. And then I went to the Presbyterian church on Wednesday nights because they had a choir that I liked to sing in when I was little. I went to the Baptist church on Fridays because they had what they called BYTU, Baptist Youth Training Union, and they had refreshments. I wanted to go to the Catholic church, but I didn't understand a word they said. So I made friends with the priest, and we played baseball on Saturdays.

There wasn't an Episcopal church until later, when I was about eleven. I went to see what that was like and thought it was a sensation because it was showmanship—all those robes. They sang those beautiful songs, and then they had to kneel and everybody had to say something. It was a show. I told Mother I wanted to join the Episcopal church.

She said, "Then you have to study the catechism, because you have to know what it is you're getting into."

So I went to the father and said, "Whatever catechism is, I'd like to have one."

I studied and memorized and learned a lot, and my mother said I could join. The minister was also the Sunday school teacher. The first Sunday after I joined, his subject to this class of little twelve-year-old girls was talent. It's in the Bible. It says talent is God given. It's taken away as easily as it is given if it's not cared for. That's why my life has been so strict.

From that moment until this moment and until the rest of my life, it's the truth. If you don't take care of what's been given to you, it's taken away. When I studied at a dancing teachers' school in California, everybody went to the beach, and I wouldn't go. I went to another class. Everybody thought I was nuts. I did go with them once, and I thought I'd been struck dead.

Mary Kathlyn Wagner, age seven. *Photo courtesy Mary Kay Ash*

BIRTH NAME	**MARY KATHLYN WAGNER**
BORN	May 12, 1918, in Hot Wells to Edward Alexander Wagner and Lula Vember Hastings Wagner
DIED	November 22, 2001
INTERVIEW	Mary Kay Cosmetics Inc., Dallas, Texas, September 14, 1981

MARY KAY ASH
A Can-Do Attitude

With a borrowed $5,000 investment in 1963, Mary Kay Ash opened Beauty by Mary Kay in a tiny Dallas storefront, where she sold five cosmetic items. More than fifty years later, Mary Kay Incorporated, headquartered in Addison, Texas, nets $4 billion annually in direct sales by 3.5 million independent consultants in nearly forty countries. After encountering inequalities in the workplace, Ash launched the company with a business plan to empower a predominantly female workforce through entrepreneurship. The strategy promoted values, self-determination, and rewards, such as iconic pink Cadillacs. She shared her business philosophy in best-selling books, including Mary Kay on People Management *in 1984 and* Mary Kay: You Can Have It All *in 1995. In 1999 she was recognized as the* Texas Woman of the Century, *and in 2000 Lifetime Television named her the most outstanding woman in business in the twentieth century. An academic study at Baylor University in 2003 declared her the greatest female entrepreneur in American history.*

Back in the days before it was fashionable for women to work, my mother had to because my father contracted tuberculosis when I was two years old. In those days, tuberculosis patients were sent off to a sanitarium. They stayed there for three years or so and came back, being told not to ever do anything again, just to stay around the house.

My father's name was Edward Alexander Wagner. He was called Alex. Mother's name was Lula Vember because she was born on the last day of November. I favored my mother in looks. I look more like her every day. There were four of us children, but the next one to me was eleven years older. So when I was four or five, my next sister was already gone and married. I was almost an only child.

My parents had owned a hotel in Hot Wells, Texas, which has since burned down. It was like Hot Springs, Arkansas, except in a smaller version. My mother was an excellent cook, so she became very famous in that area. That's where everybody went on Sunday for dinner. Then on weekends, they brought their children and took those hot spring baths.

I was born in that hotel in Hot Wells. I was a blue baby before they knew what blue babies were. The hotel served hundreds of chickens a day, and so there was nothing available but hot chicken water to dunk me in. They stuck me down in the hot chicken water—feathers and all—and it saved my life. I guess that made me gasp to get enough oxygen.

My parents sold the hotel when I was two. They moved to Houston because of my father's illness. Mother couldn't run the hotel alone.

Knowing the restaurant end of the business very well, she managed a restaurant in Houston. It opened at six o'clock in the morning, so she left every morning at five o'clock and returned at nine o'clock at night. Hers was a seven-day-a-week job. For many years, I was asleep when she left and asleep when she came home. She was so tired from standing on her feet fourteen hours a day.

The restaurant she worked for first was in downtown Houston. Then after a while, she bought a little café out on Washington Avenue. It was near this depot, and the men from the depot were her main customers. They ate very heartily.

For the noon meal, you had to get there early because all the seats and stools were filled. She had wonderful things like chicken and dumplings. Chicken and dressing and barbecued beef were other big specialties.

She had cornbread every day of the week; cornbread just fit into the Depression era. Somehow, it's very filling and you can eat a little of it and feel like you've had a lot. Cornbread and black-eyed peas were par for the course. If you didn't like those, you just weren't Texan.

Her café was Wagner's Café. In the beginning, she had waffles. Waffles were one of those fads that were kind of like tacos are now. We jokingly called it Wagner's Wonderful Waffle Works. And they were good. She had all kinds of syrups—blueberry, strawberry, maple, and whatnot. Customers would eat six or eight waffles. The waffles were like a quarter apiece.

I was the waitress in the restaurant when I got a little older. Mother had more than she could do. She had a cook in the kitchen, but things would not quite suit her. So she would go in there and stir up something herself.

I have no early recollection of Mother baking cookies at home and all those things your mother is supposed to do. Instead, my daddy came home from the sanitarium when I was about six or seven. He could only sit around the house. I remember returning home from school, and my job was to clean up the house and fix my daddy's dinner and take care of him. We had all kinds of precautionary measures for sanitation.

I didn't know everybody didn't do that, so I never felt put upon. I always thought it was normal. Besides that, I enjoyed doing it. I loved cleaning up the house, and I loved doing things for him. My father thought I hung the moon. He was the one who petted me. If Mother wanted to punish me for something, he would take up for me. It was really a good relationship, and, of course, I felt very protective of him.

As the years went on, he got to the point where he could go out and he worked for L. B. Price Mercantile Company, which sold blankets and sheets and all kinds of things for the home. He would pile them in his car and go more or less door-to-door selling that stuff. This was in the Depression, when things like that were prevalent. The vegetable man used to come around in a wagon, and you bought your vegetables from the vegetable man. The iceman came, and you bought your ice, the egg man came, the milkman came, and the bread man came. There were no supermarkets like we have today.

When I would go to school, I would say, "Now, Daddy, don't forget we need a loaf of bread and we need some milk, and when the vegetable man comes, get some of this, and this and this."

Now my mother certainly became my mentor early in my life. She couldn't be there to show me how to do things. So when I needed help, which was frequently during the day, I would call and say, "Mother, Daddy wants potato soup for supper. What do I do?"

She would say, "Now, honey, you take this big pot you used yesterday. Remember? And I think two potatoes will be enough for the two of you. You take a cup of cream off of the top of the milk, and you . . ."

She would tell me in detail how to do everything. She always finished with, "You can do it now, honey. You can do it."

She probably wasn't sure I could do it, but that was her way of bolstering my confidence. I had to take responsibility as a child. That was the only way I could get things done. When I had to have a new dress, a new sweater, or a new pair of shoes or whatever, I didn't have anybody to do it for me.

So at seven, I was going downtown on a streetcar in Houston buying my own clothes. The biggest problem I had was getting clerks to wait on me. When I would go up with my forty-nine-cent dress, which dresses were in those days, and try to buy it, the lady would say, "Where's your mother?"

And I would say, "Well, my mother's working, but it's OK. If you don't believe me, I will give you the phone number."

The clerk would call to be able to sell me whatever I was trying to buy. Mother would say, "If she wants it and she has the money, it's all right."

She would emphasize again my ability to take care of myself.

The big thing in my life was to go downtown on Saturday morning. When I finished my shopping, I would go to Kress and have a pimento cheese sandwich and a Coke. It was a big deal. To this day, I'm crazy about pimento cheese. Whenever I see pimento cheese on a menu, I order it because it has been special all my life.

My mother's "you can do it" syndrome made a running thread through my life. I grew up with the idea that "you can do it." And then I had some teachers who, knowing that I did not have a mother at home to do everything for me, felt a little sorry for me and took special interest in me.

One teacher decided that I had a gift for extemporaneous speaking. So she decided to train me for the state extemporaneous speaking contest in seventh grade. We went through months of preparation on every subject under the sun because you weren't allowed to just choose a subject.

You had to pull a subject out of a hat and talk extemporaneously on that subject. I won second place in the state contest.

I spoke on Stone Mountain, Georgia, but in my mind I was talking about Mount Rushmore with the presidents' faces chiseled into a mountain. When I actually came face to face with both places in later years, it occurred to me after all those years that I had a mental picture of the wrong thing. But nevertheless, I won the contest.

I got a taste of how it felt to be onstage and to win. From that point forward, there was no stopping me. I had to win at everything. I wanted to sell the most May fair tickets and be the best of whatever there was.

Then I won a typing contest. Typewriters were very expensive in those days. Somehow my mother scrimped and saved and bought me a Woodstock typewriter, one of those old, clunk-clunk keyboards. Having that Woodstock typewriter and being able to type things that I had to write out, like speeches, made a big difference.

My mother was always egging me on. She saw to it that I got to Sunday school every single Sunday morning even though she couldn't take me. She would see that I had my clothes out and she would discuss with me what I was going to wear. She would see that I looked as good as the other children. I became an avid part of the Sunday school and the church.

My father was Catholic; my mother was Baptist. There was a conflict right there. As a matter of fact, I think he was excommunicated from the church when he married my mother.

One person who played quite a role and started shaping my childhood and my life was a little friend around the corner named Dorothy Zapp. She was the protected, cherished child of her family. She had long golden curls, which her mother corkscrewed every morning. She wore a little starched pinafore and looked like a little angel off a magazine cover. I was little Mary Kathlyn with a sugar-bowl haircut, which my mother gave me, and if my dress got ironed, I ironed it.

I would go over every morning to get Dorothy, and we would walk to school together two or three blocks away. Dorothy was one of these little, skinny "I don't want to eat my breakfast" types. Her breakfast looked scrumptious to me. It was always a tall glass of milk with ice and strawberry preserves and big plates of toast. So when Dorothy's mother would try to coax her to eat her breakfast, Dorothy would slip it to me. I ate her breakfast every day of the week. I still say she's the reason for my being plump, because I used to eat my breakfast and go over and eat hers, too.

I grew up feeling food was a very important part of life because we had so little of it. Whenever I got around food, I ate everything I could see. I think what you do as a child carries on into your adulthood. I've always had a very difficult time losing weight. Being overly plump has been the bane of my existence all my life.

There were little side perks from being Dorothy's friend. I knew I had to be her role model to get all those extras, those lovely breakfasts, those vacations, and their Christmas celebrations. If Dorothy made an A, I had to make an A-plus to remain the one she looked up to. Her parents would say things like, "Now, Dorothy, why don't you behave like Mary Kathlyn?"

My family couldn't afford to go on what people today call vacations. But Dorothy's family could. So I would get to go to her grandmother's farm with them, spend two weeks there, ride in their beautiful car, and do all these extra things that were not otherwise available to me.

Dorothy's grandmother's farm was in Weimar, Texas. They had a big, old house with the usual quilts on the bed. Her grandmother was a very warm, friendly woman, and she served wonderful meals. The farm was a different environment. We played in the swings in the trees and we had picnics. We watched her grandmother milk cows and gather eggs and do things that city children don't ever see.

At Christmas, Dorothy's family had the most beautiful Christmas tree. In those days, you didn't have ornaments; you had apples and oranges and popcorn and cranberry strings. They would have a tree every year that would reach their high ceiling. It was filled with candy and popcorn and corn—all really beautiful.

In contrast, we would go to the little forest that surrounded our house and cut down a little, scraggly pine tree and bring it home. It was awful compared to Dorothy's. So being part of Dorothy's life was worth all the trouble.

But I never knew we were poor. You accept whatever you have. And there was no way for me to know that there was anything different except for Dorothy. I thought she was a fairy princess, and I was glad to be a part of their family.

Dorothy's mother was like a surrogate mother to me. And so was another lady across the street from me, Mrs. Lula Bates. She had a daughter named Tilly. Tilly was four or five years older than I, and she was pretty and slim and tall. Tilly's mother knew how to entertain, and she did a lot of things. She'd have her church ladies over, and they would have nice little lunches. She would spend days fixing up all the things to go on the table. So from watching and helping her, I learned how to cook. She was an excellent cook and taught me how to make biscuits and how to do all the little things nobody was at home to teach me. I became part of their family, too.

Those two friends who were closest to me in my childhood are still close today. They are both retired now, and I can do little things for them that make me feel good. That gives me a chance to sort of repay some of the kindnesses of my childhood when I had nothing.

Mary Kay Ash's business plan empowered a predominantly female workforce. *Photo courtesy Mary Kay Cosmetics Inc.*

Denton Cooley, left, with his father and brother on Armistice
Day, 1922. *Photo courtesy Dr. Denton Cooley*

BIRTH NAME	**DENTON ARTHUR COOLEY**
BORN	August 22, 1920, in Houston to Dr. Ralph Clarkson Cooley and Mary Augusta Fraley Cooley
DIED	November 18, 2016
INTERVIEW	Texas Heart Institute, Houston, Texas, July 25, 1981

DR. DENTON COOLEY

A Quiet Achiever

D r. Denton Cooley performed the first successful human heart transplant in the United States in 1968 and implanted the first artificial heart in a human the next year. More than 118,000 open-heart operations are credited to him and his associates in Houston, more than any other group in the world. Cooley pioneered multiple techniques used in cardiovascular surgery and helped develop at least two hundred surgical aids, including the heart/lung machine. After graduating with highest honors from the University of Texas at Austin in 1941, he earned an MD in 1944 and completed surgical training in 1950 at Johns Hopkins University School of Medicine. He founded the Texas Heart Institute in 1962. Among his prestigious awards are the Presidential Medal of Freedom, the nation's highest civilian award, by President Reagan in 1984; the National Medal of Technology by President Clinton in 1998; the René Leriche Prize, the highest honor of the International Surgical Society; and the Boukalev Premium, Russia's highest award for cardiovascular surgery, from the Russian Academy of Medical Sciences.

I am a third-generation Cooley living in Houston. My grandfather came here in 1880 from Nebraska and developed an area known as the Houston Heights, where he built the first home and raised three sons. My grandfather's old Victorian house with spires, pillars, and lookouts fascinated me. It had a fantastic attic and a basement where mushrooms were grown. A beautiful, old livery stable had been converted into a garage, and there was a hayloft. It was a wonderful place for boys to play.

The reason the Heights was built is interesting. In the 1850s and 1860s, yellow fever devastated Houston. Approximately 20 percent of the population was wiped out in one year. This was before Walter Reed discovered that the mosquito, prevalent in swampy areas, was the carrier. Houston is certainly swampy. They say that in the early days there was so much mud down Main Street that you could lose a team of mules in it. People began to notice that most of the deaths from the fever were in the downtown Houston area, which is how the idea for a residential area outside of Houston and my grandfather's interest in its development were born. Before the trolley was built, people commuted to downtown by horseback.

My brother, Ralph, and I were raised in the Montrose section of Houston. It was new when I was born in 1920. My father was a prominent dentist. I went to the public schools, attending Montrose Grade School, Sidney Lanier Junior High School, and San Jacinto High School.

When I was a little boy, I was involved mostly in boy things. I always had athletic interests and played basketball, baseball, and football. I played basketball in high school, in the scholastic leagues, and on the varsity team at the University of Texas. Even during medical school, I played semiprofessional basketball in Baltimore. I benefited tremendously from those experiences as an athlete.

I was not a precocious youngster who won every science fair, but a quiet achiever, a normal little boy playing games in the neighborhood with my chums. I was shy and studious. I always made good grades, and science subjects were my favorites.

We did a lot of hunting as kids, mainly a result of my brother's passion for it. Since I was younger, I followed along. I suppose we might have been considered poachers. After school, we roamed the neighborhood with our small air rifles and BB guns, shooting blue jays and birds we thought were bad for the ecology. We never shot a redbird or a mockingbird or any songbirds. We also shot a few cats. Occasionally, we took a little fruit off the neighbors' trees. It was all challenging and mischievous.

Although we did not have a ranch or belong to a country club, we rode horses on a friend's ranch, located where NASA is today. The ranch belonged to a Houston Ford dealer named Raymond Pearson, one of my dad's best friends and my godfather. He liked us to come down, ride the horses, and work the cattle—all of the kinds of things youngsters dream of doing. Those are very fond memories.

I might have been somewhat subdued in having an older brother. He was a dominating force. He had asthma, and, it seemed to me, most of the family's emphasis was on his welfare.

For most of our vacations, Mother would take us away from Houston to places with more agreeable climates—usually we went to areas around Kerrville or even Colorado. One glorious summer, we drove to El Paso to spend the months of July and August. You can imagine how desirable that was prior to the days of air-conditioning. But it was all for my brother's asthma.

Even though my brother's health was paramount, there wasn't a great deal of rivalry between us. We grew up as best friends. We had one or two fights, as boys will do, but only

Practicing basketball in Gregory Gymnasium at the University of Texas, 1939. *Photo courtesy Dr. Denton Cooley*

when we were older and I was in medicine did our lives go in such different directions that we grew apart.

Although my brother was a year and a half older than I was, we graduated from high school the same year. He had dropped out briefly because of illness. In our high school annual, he was voted the most popular boy in school, which was the nicest achievement, and I was voted the most outstanding. That was the difference between us. I played basketball and made straight As, and he was more gregarious.

Dr. Denton Cooley at the Texas Heart Institute. *Photo courtesy the Texas Heart Institute*

Mother was my greatest influence when I was growing up. She was born in Marshall, Texas. Her father moved to Houston as part of an oil company in the early days. My mother had lived in the same neighborhood as Roy Cullen, who became the legendary oilman. She remembers when the Cullens couldn't pay their grocery bill. Her father was a salaried man, not one of the giants of exploration. But still they felt somewhat superior when she was a little girl because at least they were more or less stable.

She also knew Glenn McCarthy. He was really a typical, flamboyant, wildcat oil-well driller who made many of his deals with his fists rather than his brain. Edna Ferber's book *Giant* was based on McCarthy's life, and James Dean portrayed him in the movie. He typified what a young man could do with guts and a little courage.

My mother was a bright woman. I am told she was a beautiful young woman, the prettiest bride in Houston. She was well disciplined. She was a good mother. My dad, for instance, started a small business producing and selling dental products to supplement his professional income. She was the one who assembled the products, and my brother and I helped her. She enjoyed business and was well organized. She certainly could have done more than be a good housewife.

Mother taught us dedication, self-discipline, and how to work. I adored her, of course, growing up. Mother influenced my life so much that whenever I disappointed her, I vowed not to do it again. For example, when I was twelve years old, I went to a little girl's house for a neighborhood party with about twenty other children. My brother and I rode our bicycles, returning home about midnight. Mother was hysterical, worried about where her boys were at such a late hour. She was consumed in tears when we finally arrived—angrier at my brother than me because he was the older.

She made a simple statement to my brother, "Well, you'll have Bubba smoking cigarettes before we know it—drinking and smoking cigarettes."

That one statement Mother made always rang in my ear, and I was one of the few young people in our group who never smoked cigarettes. Whenever I think of this incident, I am thankful because of the harmful effects that we now know are associated with cigarette smoking.

As a youngster, I was always an achiever. My studiousness came from trying to please my parents. I didn't want to cause additional trouble, since they were always worried about my brother's health.

One of my fondest memories was from my junior high school years. Each year the American Legion recognized one boy and one girl in the graduating class. The winners were kept a surprise and were named during an assembly the last week of school. There were three hundred or four hundred students in my class. When the announcement of the American Legion award came, my name was called. My mother and dad had been notified that the award was to be given at eleven o'clock. They had come to the auditorium and were sitting in the back, unbeknownst to me. My parents sharing that moment with me was one of the highlights of my youth. It pleased them greatly, and, therefore, it pleased me.

My father was a really jovial, nice man, whom one book described as a "raconteur, bon vivant, and friend to everyone who came his way." My dad instilled in me a sense of family pride. He emphasized the importance of being a member of our family and what my obligations were to my parents and brother. He said that regardless of the circumstances, I should stand by my brother, that blood counts.

My father also had great pride in Houston, and he instilled that in me. He acted as though Houston belonged to him. He loved development of any kind, even a new drainage ditch. Every time ground was broken for a new building, he took an intense interest in it. Houstonians are unified by this feeling of belonging and responsibility to their city.

My father was very anxious for me to take his dental practice. He had a very good practice, and like most men, wanted to turn it over to his son. Thus, I went to the University of Texas with the idea of taking a predental course. At the end of my freshman year, I was a straight-A student in predental, which was the same as the premedical course.

What made me decide to become a doctor may sound rather silly. I went with a friend to his home in San Antonio to dove hunt. While we were there, we went to Santa Rosa Hospital to visit a young friend, a medical student. He was working in the emergency room, and it became very busy that night.

Our medical student friend asked, "Would you like to sew up some of these lacerations?"

I said, "Yeah, what do you do?"

He said, "Just get a needle and thread and start sewing them up."

It was a big thrill. I got so involved and enthusiastic that I went back to Austin and changed my curriculum to premed. It was something I had always considered in the back of my mind.

The Denton A. Cooley Building (dedicated in 2002) at the Texas Heart Institute at St. Luke's Episcopal Hospital in the Texas Medical Center, Houston. *Photo courtesy the Texas Heart Institute*

Opportunities Abound Back Home

There's a charisma associated with being the "Texas surgeon" or "cowboy surgeon," as I've been described in many publications. I always believed that Houston was the place to spend my life.

I think it is intriguing to many people that the kind of excellent medicine most often associated with institutions in the East is being practiced by someone in Texas. Yet we do more heart surgery at the Texas Heart Institute than any other institution in the world—twice as much as other major centers.

I have been everywhere in the world, and I haven't seen anywhere yet that offered more opportunity than Texas.

Mary Elizabeth Sutherland, age eight or nine, with her brothers. *Photo courtesy Christy Carpenter*

BIRTH NAME	**MARY ELIZABETH SUTHERLAND**
BORN	September 1, 1920, in Salado to Thomas S. Sutherland and Mary Elizabeth Robertson Sutherland
DIED	March 20, 2010
INTERVIEW	LBJ Presidential Library, Austin, Texas, July 16, 1981

LIZ CARPENTER
A Love of Words

L iz Carpenter was a reporter, author, feminist, media adviser, speechwriter, speaker, political humorist, and public relations expert performing at a level former Texas governor Ann Richards described as a "tilt-a-whirl at the State Fair with all the lights on and the music." Immediately after graduating from the University of Texas in 1942, she headed to Washington, DC, where for nearly twenty years she covered Congress, the White House, and federal agencies for primarily Texas and southwestern newspapers. She and her husband, Leslie Carpenter, founded the Carpenter News Bureau in 1945. As executive assistant to Vice President Lyndon B. Johnson, she drafted the speech Johnson delivered to the nation on November 22, 1963, after the assassination of John F. Kennedy. Carpenter served as press secretary and staff director to longtime friend Lady Bird Johnson from 1963 to 1969. In 1971, she helped found the National Women's Political Caucus and campaigned for passage of the Equal Rights Amendment as national co-chair of ERA America. Governor Mark White named her to the Texas Women's Hall of Fame in 1985. In 1936 her grandparents' plantation home in Salado rated a state historical marker, and in 1967 a plaque was added indicating she once lived there.

I'm a fifth-generation Texan. My people came here about 1830. It has always been a source of pride to me that we were in Texas when the writing and the fighting were done. The Sutherlands seem to have done more fighting. One seventeen-year-old boy, William, ended up getting killed at the Alamo. His father, Major George Sutherland, was at San Jacinto and had his horse shot out from under him.

The Sutherlands had large families of fifteen and sixteen kids, all double first cousins. Three brothers married three sisters, and they all moved to the Nueces Canyon and the Uvalde area. The first man in my family to come to Texas was Major George Sutherland on my father's side. He came by boat from Alabama and landed at old Indianola.

The other side of my family started with Sterling C. Robertson, and he was an empresario. He brought six hundred colonists from Tennessee by wagon and horseback.

The Robertsons were signers and writers of the Declaration of Independence on March 2, 1836, in old Independence. George Childress, nephew of Sterling C. Robertson, drafted the Declaration of Independence and signed it. In all, three kinsmen of mine were signers, including these two and William Menefee.

The Robertsons settled in Salado in Central Texas sixty miles north of Austin. The old Robertson house, which I love and grew up in, is there. It has a plaque on it, which tells about the house, Colonel Robertson, and me. It was built in 1854 and is the oldest house in Texas still occupied by the same family. It has never changed hands. My mother and father were married in the parlor of that house at Salado. For a wedding present, her father gave her a .44 Colt pistol.

"Never hesitate to use it if you need it," he told her as she set out to the Nueces Canyon to live on a remote ranch. My mother and father stopped at the old Menger Hotel in San Antonio for their honeymoon. It advertised itself as the finest hotel in the Southwest.

My mother gave me a great love of words. She, like many rural Texas women, read from a library that was brought across the Red River from Tennessee. She loved to quote the English poets Wordsworth, Tennyson, and Kipling.

48

Lady Bird Johnson, left, and Liz Carpenter aboard an aircraft returning
to Texas, November 3, 1960. *LBJ Library photo by Frank Muto*

I can still quote, "Break, break, break on thy cold gray stones, O Sea!
And I would that my tongue could utter the thoughts that arise in me."

She gave me that love of words and the desire to achieve. "Make something of yourself" was the phrase that was very often used by her. She
was Mary Elizabeth Robertson Sutherland.

My mother looked a little bit like me. She was short, five feet one or
two, and plump. She had a very saintly face; that's where we differ. White
hair has been a trademark of the Robertson women. We have pictures
of great-aunts with great coifs of white hair in the old-fashioned hairdo.

My mother had very clear brown eyes that were unafraid. She could
shoot very well. In those days, a Sunday afternoon pastime was to put a
can on the back fence, and everybody in the family could vie for it. She

could beat her brothers in marksmanship. It served her well out in the Nueces Canyon. There were panthers and polecats when she moved out there, and you never knew whether they were friends or foes.

She was a mother first, a reader and word lover second, and a house-wife third.

When we moved to Austin in 1928 to get educated at the university,

Liz Carpenter holds a sign supporting the Equal Rights Amendment, 1980.
The photograph is inscribed to Ann Richards. *Photo by David Woo, Ann W. Richards Papers,
Briscoe Center for American History, University of Texas at Austin*

we rented a marvelous old house on West Avenue. It was a great, open, hospitable place. The doors were never locked. There was always room for cousins to stay with us and sleep on the sleeping porch during the time they went through school. They wouldn't have been able to go to college otherwise. We accommodated lots of people in and out of the house. That gave an elasticity, a quality that has served me well.

My mother never put any pressure on me to marry. She never, like lots of mothers in that day, talked about "when you get married" or "your hope chest." Rather, it was "be self-reliant." She didn't shove me in any way.

Mother had baked pies in the suffrage movement. I had aunts in Washington who were lobbying for women to get the vote. We talked with great pride about women in my family who had achieved things, such as my great-aunt Birdie Johnson, who was the first female regent at what now is Texas Woman's University, a philanthropist, and the first Democratic national committeewoman.

There was never any feeling that I couldn't go as far as I wanted to go, because my mother and father believed in me. I started out wanting to be a missionary. That was from going to the Methodist church. I also had read Richard Halliburton, and I thought the only route I had to get to bathe in the Taj Mahal at midnight and to swim the Nile was to be a missionary and save the heathens around the world. That was strong when I was about seven. Then as I grew older and went to the movies, of course, I wanted to be a movie star.

But there was never any doubt from the time I was in grammar school that I was going to write. I wrote the school song for Woodridge School, my grammar school. I wrote the class prophecy at University Junior School, and I worked on the *Daily Texan* and was a journalism major at the University of Texas. So I never sat around soul-searching about what my profession would be. I was always bent in that direction.

My family was always interested in politics. It was always a big discussion at our dinner table. In the Depression, I think, this was a common thing all over the state. The name Hoover couldn't help anyone running for office in Texas. We all had too many memories of poor land, a tight, unhelpful government. Whether he's rightly or wrongly blamed, Herbert Hoover got the blame for the Depression.

Liz Carpenter with President Bill Clinton at the University of Texas at Austin, October 16, 1995. *Photo by Wally McNamee, Wally McNamee Photographic Archive, Briscoe Center for American History, University of Texas at Austin*

We sat around the dining room table eating pork and beans and cussing Hoover. Pork and beans and rice were the steady fare and, sometimes on lucky days, meat loaf.

My fondest childhood memories are centered around the whole aura of Salado: that wonderful old house with pallets on the floor, and my mother sitting in the passageway in the front hall and reading to me a variety of books about the Old South, including the Little Colonel books and Uncle Remus.

My uncle Sterling would saddle up the tamest mare for me to ride down to Norwood's Grocery Store and pick up the mail. Cool watercress in the creek and cleaning out the spring, simple things, were great pleasures.

Aunts on the Sutherland side would sing around the piano "How Great Thou Art." There was a reverence for older people and reverence for certain values I still think are important.

There was a basic goodness. We knew idleness was a sin. We believed you are your brother's keeper. I believe that to this day. There was a Christian ethic there of helping people who are in trouble, of being a stepping stone for them.

I have never been a pet lover, like dogs or cats. The only pet I ever owned was a chicken. It followed me all around the yard. Amazingly, that chicken knew me. I bottle-fed baby goats that were born in the spring. I was never in the dog business much.

I am the middle of five children. We were stretched over twenty years. My little brother, George, was my favorite playmate.

My mother had time for everybody because she was not a fastidious housekeeper. She offered love and thought. We might find a misplaced butcher knife in the living room couch or cobwebs in the fireplace, but her sense of values gave me a sense of security. I felt loved all my life.

My father had a happy buoyancy and grit, a feeling of "get up and go." He was an early riser. He wanted to get things done.

"Don't put off till tomorrow what you can do today."

He was the man who made things happen, and I think I got my energy from him. I got my wit from the Depression and from being in a big family. My mother was witty. She had read a lot and had a sense of humor that saw her through a lot of hard times.

A Reverence for the Hometown

When I go to Salado, I feel I'm in church. There is a reverence for ancestors and for the values that are still there. I still get hungry for watercress, and I still like to sit in a place called the "bathtub," a part of the creek hollowed out by water. I still like to have a picnic at Table Rock. I always will.

There was an open spirit of helpfulness in the frontier that still lives in Texas. Within our memory are ancestors who helped carve out this state and brought civilizing schools, churches, and leaders.

As a young registered nurse during World War II, 2nd Lt. Lillian Dunlap served in New Guinea, the Philippines, and the Admiralty Islands. *Photo courtesy US Army Medical Department Center of History & Heritage, Fort Sam Houston, Texas*

BIRTH NAME	**LILLIAN DUNLAP**
BORN	January 20, 1922, in Mission to Ira Dunlap and Mary Schermerhorn Dunlap
DIED	April 3, 2003
INTERVIEW	Her home, San Antonio, Texas, January 25, 1984

BRIGADIER GENERAL LILLIAN DUNLAP

A Tendency to Take Care of People

L illian Dunlap was the fourteenth chief of the Army Nurse Corps and the first who was already a brigadier general when she was appointed in 1971. She had served overseas in New Guinea, the Admiralty Islands, and the Philippines from 1943 to 1945; in Germany from 1954 to 1957; and in Okinawa from 1965 to 1966. She introduced the nurse practitioner role in the US Army and established the baccalaureate degree in nursing as a requirement for service in the Army Nurse Corps. To promote even higher standards, she helped establish a master of science curriculum in nursing at the University of the Incarnate Word in San Antonio, where an endowed professional chair bears her name. For her military service, she earned the Distinguished Service Medal, the Meritorious Service Medal, and the Army Commendation Medal with oak leaf cluster. She has been inducted into the Texas Women's Hall of Fame for public service and was an honorary fellow of the American Academy of Nursing.

I'm the first of five girls. My father, Ira Dunlap, was born in Sabinal, and his father was one of the first Anglo settlers in Mission in the early 1890s. My mother was born in Ledbetter in 1895, and I was born in 1922 in Mission. We moved to San Antonio when I was six months old.

Mother received her teaching certificate from the University of Texas when she was nineteen years old. She first taught in Edinburg and then at Mission. I've heard them tell the story that "Miss Mary" was a tiny little thing barely five feet tall. She looked like a child.

My father went to high school in Mission, and they met while my mother was teaching. He also went to Peacock Military Academy. They married in 1919, and she didn't teach school after that. We lived on Daddy's salary payday to payday. We knew there were people who had less than we did and more than we did.

Mother and Daddy had disagreements only over my sisters and me because Mother wanted the children to have things he thought we didn't need. She would hold back on her grocery money to give us things that we really could not afford.

I must say Daddy worked. He left home early. When he'd come home from work, we sisters would be on the front porch watching for him. We'd go racing out to the car to see who could be the first one to kiss him. Years later he told us the men in his carpool used to really tease him about that.

Our life centered around the family, church, school, and neighborhood. On Sundays we went to Sunday school, church, home for lunch, back to church for the young folks' league, then church at night. Daddy was Baptist and sang in the choir, and Mother was Methodist. We went to the church, either Baptist or Methodist, nearest us. When Daddy would go to the hospital with a church group to sing for the patients, he'd take me along. And he took me to weddings and funerals.

We always celebrated birthdays and anniversaries, and any special occasion became a family affair. For our birthdays, Mother would bake angel food cakes. It was very special to afford an angel food cake because it took thirteen egg whites. When the cake was cooking, there was no way we would run through the house or slam the door because the cake would fall. The only exception to angel food birthday cakes was for my sister, Lucile, who always had devil's food cake, white icing, and little red Valentine hearts.

Mother had four angels and one devil.

In the neighborhood, we played hide-and-seek, red rover, punch the icebox, crack the whip, and let's pretend.

I was a little on the tomboy side. We used to dig a hole in the ground for a cave and a winding tunnel leading to it. The top would be boards or cardboard. We'd crawl into our cave with a candle and have secret meetings. We had slingshots and berry shooters using the berries off the *Ligustrum* bushes, which hurt if you got hit. But the best ones were the chinaberries because they were gooey.

When Daddy wanted to call us in, he would stand out on the front porch and whistle. We knew we'd better run. To discipline us, Mother would spank us on the seat with her hand. Mother sometimes also "put us in the doghouse." But when we were real bad, Daddy would send us to break a switch off the hedge, take the leaves off, and switch our legs.

Lucile got a real bad spanking one time and her mouth washed out with soap. She had been chasing me and she hit me. I fell down with a sucker in my mouth and the stick stuck in the fleshy part of my cheek. Lucile said some nasty word, probably "damn."

The worst punishment was not to be able to go out and play. If we didn't have our homework done, we couldn't play. We'd stand with our noses pressed against the window watching the kids outside playing.

We still say, "Yes, ma'am," and "No, ma'am," to people who are senior to us. We were taught to respect our elders. When our parents told us to do something, we did it because we were supposed to mind.

Since I was the oldest, I learned to keep the babies if Mama went to the store or somewhere. As more of them came along, naturally, I had more of them to keep and helped change a lot of diapers. They all probably hated me, like all big sisters are hated, because they thought I was bossy.

As we got older, we all had our chores, like doing dishes. One would clear the table, one would wash, one would dry. The last baby didn't do much. In fact, when I went into nurse's training in '39, she was still just a baby peeking over the windowsill.

We always had kinfolks coming. They didn't call and ask if they could come; they just came. It was nothing for one aunt to come up from the Valley and bring some of her four children. Maybe Grandpa and a couple of friends would come with her. The adults and the company children would get to sleep on the mattresses, and we slept on pallets on the floor.

I went to seven different schools in San Antonio and Mission, and we lived in thirteen houses. That may be one reason I found it very easy to adjust to changes of station in the military.

When Grandpa Dunlap came to live with us, we rented a really pretty house with an acre of land on Ware Boulevard south of San Antonio in the country. When we lived in the country, we had cows, pigs, and chickens. And I learned to churn. Mama would put some milk in a fruit jar, and we'd shake it to make our own butter.

We used to make clabber. We put milk in a sack and hung it out on the clothesline and let it clabber. We loved to eat clabber and sugar. Grandpa loved that. We always had to have cornbread with buttermilk, and we ate the juice off the beans, called pot liquor.

The cow had a calf, and we named it Armistice Lucinda because it was born on Armistice Day and Mama's middle name was Lucinda.

Our grandpa was so good to us. Grandpa would give my mother money at the beginning of the school year to buy our school clothes, but he wanted us to wear long stockings with supporters and teddy underwear. By that time, girls were beginning to wear knee socks and anklets, but he wouldn't give Mama money to buy those.

He would take all the children in the neighborhood to the circus. He liked to go to the circus, too, and taking us was an excuse. He'd also take all the youngsters to see Shirley Temple movies because he liked Shirley Temple, too.

In South San, we lived across the street from a bootlegger. Sometimes people would make a mistake and knock on our front door instead of the bootlegger's door. Daddy would chase them away.

Uncle Tom was our rich bachelor uncle who would come visit us in our home in South San. Uncle Tom liked to chase fires. Every time we'd hear the fire siren, we'd jump in the car and chase the fire truck.

We had snow one time, and a neighbor took an apple crate and made a little sled so he could pull me around in the snow.

Until I went into the army, I had only been as far as Austin and Corpus Christi. And that was to visit kinfolks.

The first car I remember having was when we lived in South San. It was a gray, two-door coupe. There was space in the back so two children could get back there.

In Brackenridge Park in San Antonio, there was a donkey trail with donkeys you could ride for free. It was a treat to ride the donkeys. Mama would let us ride as long as she could stand it.

We would go to San Pedro Park to swim. We also went to swim out at old Hot Wells. You had to pay to swim there, so we didn't go very often. It also stunk because of the sulfur water. We'd smell like rotten eggs when we came out.

Another treat was to get to take a ride on Saturday or Sunday, if we'd been good. In those days, Fort Sam Houston was out in the country. After we left the post, we'd go down New Braunfels Avenue through Rattle-snake Hill. Daddy would make us get down on the floorboard and put our heads down so we couldn't see the prostitutes and the bars and all the sin and corruption going on.

Another great treat was to ride down to Alamo Plaza. Just to park there and watch people walk by was entertainment.

Also for recreation, we'd get up early, drive to the lower end of Medina Lake below the dam and cook breakfast. Mother would take the old skillet and put in butter and a piece of bread and make what we called "Medina Lake toast." It is still known as "Medina Lake toast" in our family, and we never realized why other people didn't know about it.

My first association with the annual Fiesta in San Antonio was when I was in the first grade. The school had a float and there was a penny-a-vote contest to see who would ride on it. Someone must have had some pennies because I won and got to ride on the float.

I was a cute little red-haired girl, and some of our friends who lived on a ranch near Boerne wanted me to stay with them. They had an outhouse and used the slop jar. They had a woodstove, and Mrs. Morris always made the best mush. One day I wanted mush and she told me if I would take this pail to the woodpile and get some wood chips, she'd make me some mush. I didn't come back. She came looking for me and there I was sitting at the woodpile with my little bucket full of wood chips. I was try-ing to figure out how she was going to make mush out of those wood chips.

Our folks made what we did fun. The women in the neighborhood would gather up the children, pack a lunch, and take us to Poteet to pick strawberries. We thought we were playing games.

During the summer, the five of us girls would go down to Woodlawn Lake. Mother would pack a lunch. We'd spend the day there playing ten-nis. We had four tennis racquets. The fifth one chased the balls.

We used to go up in the Hill Country and chop cedar trees for our Christmas trees. We'd bring them in, and we'd make our own Christmas decorations.

This was our way of life.

I don't really know what interested me in nursing. No one in the family was a nurse or doctor. My family told a story on me when I was in the second grade. My girlfriends and I made dollhouses out of cardboard boxes or we made houses with rooms outlined with rocks. Two of the little girls got sick and their mothers called my mother to see if I was sick. Come to find out, I had been playing that I was the doctor and they were my patients. I had some little pink calomel pills and had given them some to make them well.

We got a doll each Christmas and one other toy that we shared, like a table with chairs. We played hard with our dolls and wore them out so that next Christmas we needed another doll. I once cut off the leg of my doll and sewed it back on.

From watching the movies, I got the idea to make parachutes for my dolls. I'd go up on the roof of the little shed and throw my dolls off and I would jump, too. The cowboys did it in the movies, so why couldn't we do it, too?

If you analyzed my play habits, you could probably see I had the tendencies to take care of people.

I went through a stage when I played West Point. Women didn't go to West Point then. I read the series of books about someone at West Point, and I'd get the neighborhood kids and march them all around. I marched my sisters and anybody else around with broomsticks.

It was at that point, too, that I became interested in the Girl Reserves, which the YWCA sponsored. I was a good student and made the National Honor Society at Jefferson High School. I had skipped early grades and graduated very young. Being younger has always been a problem for me.

We didn't have any counselors in high school. I had said I wanted to be a nurse or I was interested in X-ray technology. I liked science and took all the sciences I could in high school. Another uncle had said that I was artistic, and he thought I had a career opportunity in commercial art. He would have paid for me to go to commercial art school.

I didn't want that, and mother didn't make me do it. Instead, she borrowed the $150 that it took for three years of nursing training at Santa Rosa Hospital from still another uncle so I could go into nurse's training. The other uncle wouldn't pay for that because he thought nursing was not something a professional woman should go into. It was not appropriate.

They wouldn't let me into the Santa Rosa Hospital School of Nursing because you had to be eighteen, and I was only sixteen. So I went to the University of San Antonio by Woodlawn Lake.

When I was seventeen, I still wanted to go into nursing, and Santa Rosa finally agreed to take me because they thought I was more mature than most eighteen-year-olds. When I graduated in nursing, there was a state requirement that you couldn't take the state board examination until you were twenty-one years old. I applied for state boards anyway, and they let me take them, and I passed.

In my senior year in nursing, World War II started, and the American Red Cross was recruiting nurses. They helped you process papers for going into the service and you got to wear a little pin that said "student nurse reserve." I was twenty years old.

I graduated in 1942. I went into the service for the war. Sister Bernice, the operating room supervisor, made me promise to come back when I got out of the army. Thirty-three years later, I retired. Sister Bernice had gone to her reward, and I didn't go back to work at Santa Rosa.

Lillian Dunlap was the first brigadier general appointed chief of the US Army Nurse Corps. *Photo courtesy US Army Medical Department Center of History & Heritage, Fort Sam Houston, Texas*

Liz Smith as a student at Robert Lee Paschal High School, Fort Worth, Texas, 1940.
Liz Smith Papers, Briscoe Center for American History, University of Texas at Austin

BIRTH NAME	**MARY ELIZABETH SMITH**
BORN	February 2, 1923, in Fort Worth to Sloan Smith and Sarah Elizabeth McCall Smith
DIED	November 12, 2017
INTERVIEW	American Place Theatre, New York City, May 2, 1982

9

....

LIZ SMITH
The Thrill of Reading

O ften described as the Doyenne of Dish, Liz Smith chronicled
celebrity show business gossip for fifty-seven years through
syndicated newspaper columns, major magazines, television,
and websites. She began ghostwriting the Cholly Knickerbocker
gossip columns for Hearst newspapers in the 1950s. By 1976 she was
churning out her own for the New York Daily News, Newsday, and the
New York Post, the only writer to have a column in three major New
York City newspapers simultaneously. She was entertainment editor of
Cosmopolitan and Sports Illustrated at the same time. After reporting
on the glitterati on WNBC-TV's Live at Five for eleven years, she was
a regular on the Fox News Network. Her books included The Mother
Book in 1978 and an unsurprisingly frank memoir, Natural Blonde, in
2000. She led high-profile fund-raising efforts that netted millions for
charitable causes, including AIDS services, Literacy Partners, the New
York Restoration Project, and the New York Landmarks Conservancy.

———

I was just an ordinary little child. I am from Fort Worth, and I lived at 1919 Hemphill Street in a very ordinary house where I was born in the back room. I wasn't even born in a hospital; that's how old-fashioned my family was.

My older brother was born in Ennis, Texas, but Bobby, my younger brother, was born in the same room I was born in. None of us was born in a hospital; the doctor came to the house. People just didn't go to the hospital to have babies. That was a holdover from the old days when people lived out on the farm.

Fort Worth was a nice town to grow up in. It had a beautiful park and a wonderful zoo. When I lived there, it was a beautiful small town. I had one uncle who lived in Dallas, and once in a blue moon we'd go see him. But we just didn't go to Dallas otherwise, and I never knew anything much about Dallas. I took the rivalry with Dallas very seriously.

I remember one of my cousins took me away to San Antonio for the weekend when I was about eleven. I was so impressed with the Alamo, I wrote this giant-sized letter. My brothers made so much fun of me. They said that it was corny.

My mother was from Mississippi, and she was just glad she had gotten out of Mississippi. My father was born in Putnam, Texas, out near Cisco.

He had been very, very poor. He had had to quit school in the fourth grade. He was totally self-educated, but he was very bright. He was not patriotic. He was a true iconoclast.

My father's parents lived with us. And my grandmother, on my mother's side, also lived with us. So I was very much under the influence of grandmothers.

My grandfather was a metalsmith, and his name was Jerome Bonaparte Smith. We always claim that he was named for Napoleon's brother who settled in Louisiana. He was a wonderful old man. He made cast-iron skillets for my mother. He was a wit, and everybody loved Boney.

My father used to tell wonderful stories about how they grew up in this terrible place near Cisco, and they didn't have any toys. He had about four brothers and three sisters. They would collect corncobs. They would round them up and pretend they were their cattle. They would take hot wires and burn their brands on them and then make little fences out of stones and try to get more "cows" than the others. Those were their toys. Then at Christmas, they would get an orange.

Liz Smith as a journalism major at the University of Texas in the 1940s.
She wrote for the *Daily Texan* and *Ranger* magazine. *Liz Smith Papers, Briscoe Center for American History, University of Texas at Austin*

We thought that was horribly primitive. I mean, I was a little child in a city. There we were living in a nice town and a nice house with trees, and we had a maid. I had nice toys and all that stuff. I was definitely from the middle class.

I look a lot like my mother. In fact, we all look like my mother. I don't

---

look very much like my father. He was real small and wiry, only five foot seven. He didn't weigh enough to get in the army during World War I.

My mother was a wonderful person. I couldn't say I resemble her personality-wise. She wanted me to wear little white gloves and be a debutante. Given my brothers, I never had a chance to be the genteel little lady my mother wanted.

I wanted to be like Tom Mix; he was my real idol. I have a picture of myself in a cowboy outfit that one of my aunt's boyfriends bought me. It had leopard chaps, boots, a hat, and everything.

I had one girlfriend on the block, Louise Lewis, and she was the only little girl I'd ever played with until I went to school. I was so shocked at little girls; they didn't want to play rough. I'd always had a lot of dolls, but I always scalped them.

But I had a lot of friends of both sexes after I went to school. Making friends was easy for me. I was very outgoing and rambunctious. I wasn't very serious minded, I must say. I had the longest adolescence of anyone.

My fondest childhood memory is of learning to read. I wanted so badly to read before I ever learned, I would just put books down and look at them for hours. I kept thinking, "I will figure out what this means eventually."

I think I learned to read before I ever went to school. I must have been six.

As soon as I found out that you could get free books out of the library, I was the happiest person ever. I could never imagine such a thing. I could never get my hands on enough books, and I didn't really grow up in a house where there were many books. My mother bought books if they matched the furniture or something.

The Fort Worth Public Library had this wonderful thing in the lobby. It was a big dinosaur with tusks, and next to it was a Chinese model of a rickshaw. It was frightening to me, and I would rush into the library and run past them. That was the only way to get upstairs.

The library would let you check out anything whether it was fitting for you to read or not. So I read things I didn't even understand. I read every book I could get my hands on. I would have somebody take me to the library, and I would spend the whole Saturday there. My brothers did not like for me to read; they'd rather tie me to a tree or shoot me with BB guns.

I lived in a sort of dream world. I remember one time I was being given a birthday party and I opened all these nice presents and then I opened a book of *The Wizard of Oz*. I left the party and started reading it. I was going to go read the whole book right then. My mother was furious with me. She had to come and take the book away from me. She wouldn't let me have it for three days or longer.

I also wrote things as a child. I was always writing something. I once made up a newspaper, and I took it to school and showed the teacher. I put out a newspaper for a little while until it got too hard to do it. I was doing it on a typewriter and setting it all myself. We passed the newspaper around; it was too hard to make copies. So everyone read the same one. I was in junior high school, I guess, at E. M. Daggett, where I'd started grade school.

I was a precocious child, in some respects. Poor at science and math. I remember at the same time as my newspaper, my main preoccupation was reading *Gone with the Wind*. That must have been about 1936.

My family was Southern Baptist. The only education I had until I got to the University of Texas really was between church and going to the Tivoli Theater every Saturday to the movies. Everything I knew I learned either at church or at the movies. I have a great classical, biblical education. I know lots of stuff from the Bible that has been a big help to me in a literary sense.

As soon as I found out that you could get free books out of the library, I was the happiest person ever.

I went to Robert Lee Paschal High School. I graduated in 1940. I went to more colleges than anybody in the world. I went to NTAC, the University of Texas at Arlington, and then to Hardin-Simmons in Abilene long before I got to UT-Austin. And to Abilene Christian College one summer to try to pass freshman algebra. Then I went to the University of Texas and graduated in 1950. I was divorced while back in college.

I studied journalism. I wanted to go on the stage, really, but I learned my lesson on that one. Actually, an interview I had done with Zachary

Scott while I was at the university helped me get my first real job as a journalist in New York. He had said if I ever needed a job in Hollywood to give him a call.

About four months after I went to New York, I saw in the paper he then lived in New York. So I phoned him, and he got me an interview with *Modern Screen* magazine. They hired me immediately, remarking on my "virile writing style." I didn't know what "virile" meant and had to look it up.

Liz Smith gained fame as a syndicated gossip columnist. *Photo by Nigel Parry, Liz Smith Papers, Briscoe Center for American History, University of Texas at Austin*

Liz Smith recalls reading the cartoon history in *Texas History Movies*. *1935 edition, Briscoe Center for American History, University of Texas at Austin*

Texas History, the Cartoon Version

I remember when I was a kid I used to go to Stripling's Department Store, to their bookstore. They had this marvelous cartoon book of Texas history. I went there every Saturday and read that thing. I just loved it. It was a very accurate history of Texas done in cartoons.

Texas was populated with real adventurers and outlaws and renegades and unusual people who were real survivors. They were the people who were told "Get out of Tennessee" or "Get out of Virginia or we're going to hang you" or "Go to hell or Texas."

And they went. And there was a lot of infusion of cultures—French, the Spanish, the Mexicans, and all of that Southern gentility. So because Texas really wasn't anything specifically, I think it developed a great deal of individuality all on its own. They were hardy and unusual. My great-grandmother went from Louisiana to Texas with her children in an oxcart when her husband died. She didn't speak any English; she was French. So these people were real pioneers and survivors.

Today I own this collector's item.

Ray Price grew up in Dallas with his mother but spent summers
on his father's farm in East Texas. *Photo courtesy Janie Price*

BIRTH NAME	**NOBLE RAY PRICE**
BORN	January 12, 1926, in Perryville to Walter Clifton Price and Clara Mae Bradley Price
DIED	December 16, 2013
INTERVIEW	Hotel, Houston, Texas, July 25, 1981

RAY PRICE

The Best of Two Worlds

R ay Price was often called the Frank Sinatra of country music for his rich baritone vocals and longevity in the industry. He crooned hit after hit from the 1950s through the 1970s, was inducted into the Country Music Hall of Fame in 1996, and shared a Grammy with Willie Nelson for Best Country Collaboration with Vocals for "Lost Highway" in 2008. After returning from World War II service with the US Marines in the South Pacific, Price dropped out of college to seek a singing career and soon landed on Big D Jamboree in Dallas. He moved to Nashville in the early 1950s, where he roomed with Hank Williams, was a regular on the Grand Ole Opry, and formed his own band, the Cherokee Cowboys, whose members at various times included hit makers Willie Nelson, Roger Miller, Darrell McCall, Johnny Paycheck, and Johnny Bush. Price was the first to snare success on the country charts with strings and backup singers to enhance his signature 4/4 shuffle beat.

When I was a little kid, I would sing just for my own amusement or to run the boogers off in the woods. I always liked to sing. I don't know why. When I was a kid, I dreamed of being a real famous singer, and then it drifted away. I forgot about it.

We sang songs that were popular at the time, like Jimmie Rodgers songs. That's probably where I learned to sing country. Of course, Jimmie Rodgers really wasn't country; he was a yodeler and a blues singer. They called him the Blue Yodeler. He learned to sing from the Blacks in New Orleans because he used to ride a train there all the time.

Of course, we sang gospel songs, too. Grandma had an organ, but nobody in the family played it that I remember. My mother played piano, but I didn't find that out until about twenty years ago. She had played piano in church.

I had a pretty good life because my dad was a farmer and my mother was the daughter of a farmer. But my parents moved to Dallas when I was little. Then they divorced when I was only four, and Dad moved back to the farm. He just couldn't make it in the city. And I can understand why: he loved it in the country.

He went back down to Perryville in East Texas, and I would spend the summers there and the winters with Mother in Dallas. When things were so tough in the Depression, I would spend the winters in East Texas, too, and farm. So I got the best of both worlds. I'm not going to say the divorce didn't affect me. I'd go every summer to see Dad, and I'd watch Mother drive off and then vice versa. That was kind of traumatic, but I didn't understand it because I was a kid.

Neither of my parents could take care of both my older brother, Weldon, and me. So they split us up. Because I was the baby, my mother kept me, which I think my brother has always resented. But it wasn't my fault, and he doesn't understand.

Ray is my middle name. They called me Noble up until I came out of the marine corps.

I look a lot like my dad. He was the one son out of about ten kids who stayed home with his dad to help farm and raise horses. I'm talking about 390 acres with horses. He was a hard worker, but he never owned a piece of land in his life. We sharecropped.

On the farm, we grew everything—peas, corn, cotton, and so on. It took a lot of work. We did everything. If it was too wet to plow, we'd cut wood for the winter. It was one of those "if you don't work, you'll starve" situations. And that really was a terrific incentive for work.

We lived with Grandma and Grandpa Price near Perryville. Perryville is two churches with a graveyard in between. The Baptist is up on the hill and the Methodist is down at the bottom of the hill. There were two grocery stores, both of them broke, and that was it.

There was a big family living at Grandma's, including my aunt and her three children. And then there were two younger aunts. That sure was a houseful for a three-bedroom house.

When my grandfather Price was thirteen years old, he got on a horse and rode from Corinth, Mississippi, to Hall County, Texas, by himself. He started work and was quite successful in life. He was a hardworking old man. He started before daylight and worked till after dark. You wouldn't believe how dark it was when the old man hollered, "Get up."

Grandpa Price was scary; he was pretty shrewd and stern. Of course, I understood him later. He was just trying to teach us the value of what a person had to do to make a living. And he did.

Religion was a big part of our lives. We never missed a Sunday, just like everybody else. The community was so poor it couldn't afford two full-time preachers, so preachers preached every other week. We'd go to the Baptist one week and go to the Methodist the next. And the only thing that I could see different was the Methodist sprinkle and the Baptist dunk. I was dunked.

Ray Price performs on the *Louisiana Hayride* broadcast on radio station KWKH in Shreveport, Louisiana, with Roger Miller on lead guitar. *Photo courtesy Janie Price*

At home, we learned to not lie and not steal; to work hard; to give a man value received for his money, not rip him off; to believe in God and Jesus; and to try to live a decent life. And that's it.

When I was a kid, if you worked for a man, you worked for him. You did everything you could. You didn't try to kill yourself, but you tried to make him a profit, because if you didn't, there was no reason for him to hire you in the first place.

My values haven't changed. I think things are a little faster; the pace has picked up. To me, if you don't have those values, you're not going to make it.

Dad believed in the part of the Bible about not building up treasures for yourself. That was his whole thing. The only vice he had, if it was a vice, was loving to go fox hunting and listen to the dogs run a fox. But he wouldn't kill the fox.

You ate what you killed or you didn't kill it. It wasn't sport; it wasn't fun; it was serious. I used to hunt a lot, but I don't like to anymore. I think a person gets older and sees his own time coming, so he doesn't want to deprive another living creature of its time.

Ray Price's smooth vocals drew fans to live performances for more than 50 years.
Photo by John Goodspeed

We had a lot of dogs on the farm. If it wasn't a hound dog, we weren't allowed to keep it, because a hound dog would make his own living. At the time, that was critical.

I grew up loving the outdoors. I love animals, birds, all kinds of things. I wanted to be a veterinarian.

My mother, Clara, was a Bradley. Her people went from Alabama to Arkansas and then to Texas.

I'm not sure if I got my talent from Mama, but I sure got a lot from her. She was the driving force. She was an artist; she did great hand-painted china. And, of course, she and my stepdad, known as Clare and Dominique, were two of the leading designers of women's wearing apparel for many, many years in Dallas. She used to do a lot of sportswear for Neiman Marcus.

When I was little, my mother used to rent a place in Dallas. She worked in a dress factory for about ten dollars a week, and it cost her ten dollars a week for room and board. To make her ten-cent or nickel carfare to ride the streetcar, she used to hand-knit brassieres and sell them for a dollar. She was pretty tough.

Of course, when I look back now, I realize we had a ball growing up. I really think the hard times are the best times. Times were different then. You didn't lock your doors. You didn't worry about people stealing anything. You didn't have anything to steal.

While I was going to college, I ran around with a bunch of kids who took me to a nightclub where people from the audience would sing. It was Roy's House Cafe on Singleton Boulevard in East Dallas. My friends got these people to get me to sing. I hadn't thought about making singing a career until I did that. I was about twenty or twenty-one.

I was more or less just trying to make it, trying to settle on something that I would want to do. I was taking veterinary medicine in college, so I think I would have been very happy doing that. But the music turned me around, and I quit college. Evidently, I found out what I wanted to do.

We got a little group together then, just playing around. And one of the guys who played the guitar, Dick Gregory, wrote country songs. He wanted to know if I could sing some country songs and I said, "Sure."

And he said, "Would you go down to the publisher and sing some songs for me?"

He was trying to get a song published, so I agreed. The first publisher we went to didn't have time for us, so he sent us to another place.

He really did us a favor. We got to the other place, and the guy was hungry. He was just starting in business, so he had time to listen. This company had just gotten through recording some radio shows for the Liberty Network. There was a group called the Frontiersmen, and Hi Pockets Busse was one of them. They heard me sing the songs and asked me if I would come back the next morning.

I said, "Well, I guess so. What do you need?"

They said, "We just need you to come back and sing them tomorrow."

So we came back the next day. When I got there, Bullet Records offered me a recording contract. That's what happened.

Lauro F. Cavazos, 1929. *Photo courtesy Lauro F. Cavazos*

BIRTH NAME	**LAURO FRED CAVAZOS**
BORN	January 4, 1927, on the King Ranch in South Texas to Lauro Faustino Cavazos and Tomasa Alvarez Quintanilla
INTERVIEW	His condo, Port Aransas, Texas, August 8, 2017

LAURO F. CAVAZOS
A Dutiful Son

L auro F. Cavazos took lessons learned in English and Spanish on the legendary King Ranch to the White House, where he promoted bilingual education as secretary of the Department of Education to Presidents Ronald Reagan and George H. W. Bush from 1988 to 1990. He was the first Hispanic cabinet official. After earning bachelor's and master's degrees in zoology from Texas Tech University and a doctorate in physiology from Iowa State University, he taught at the Medical College of Virginia for ten years and then moved to the School of Medicine at Tufts University in 1964, where he became dean in 1975. In 1980 he became the first Hispanic and alumnus of Texas Tech to helm the university. President Reagan honored him in 1984 with an award for Outstanding Leadership in the Field of Education, and the League of United Latin American Citizens gave him the National Hispanic Leadership Award. He wrote multiple books on medical science and medical education and received twenty-four honorary degrees. His memoir, A Kineño Remembers, was published in 2006.

The King Ranch was very large. At one time, it was about 1,250,000 acres. The ranch that I knew was about 850,000 acres, about the size of the state of Rhode Island. It was there that I learned all these lessons that were so deeply ingrained in me, that I learned from the men and the women and my parents on that ranch.

The original Spanish land grant that established the King Ranch was only 53,000 acres. This was the Santa Gertrudis de la Garza land grant. Captain King, Richard King, bought it in 1853.

Then in 1854, Captain King was in Mexico in the state of Tamaulipas in a little town out there called Cruillas buying cattle to stock his Santa Gertrudis Ranch. And these people in the little town had a small herd, 150 to 200 head of cattle. He bought them all.

The next morning, Captain King noticed the people were very unhappy, very sad.

"The cattle are gone. We have nothing to sustain us, just a few pigs and goats."

So Captain King said, "Help me drive these cattle back to my Santa Gertrudis Ranch. If you'll do that, I will build you your home, I will build you a school, I will provide for your family. We will be as a family on the ranch."

And, sure enough, they took him up on it. The little town practically evacuated. It was not an easy journey. Those men and women who drove the cattle from Mexico went to work for Captain King, and together they created the King Ranch.

Sure to his word, Captain King built a school and houses, and they went about creating a new home for themselves. They became known as *Los Kineños*, King's people, in Spanish. We were very proud of being King's people. I'm a fourth-generation *Kineño*. Their journey from Cruillas is what's called la entrada. My grandmother, Mama Grande Rita, was a Quintanilla. Her husband worked for the King Ranch, part of the original la entrada folks.

I was born on January 4, 1927, at home on the King Ranch. Mother wasn't sick. She was having a baby. My Mama Grande Rita and a couple of my aunts came over, as usual, to help the doctor, a little old country doctor. My aunts and grandmother lived in the barrio about three miles from the ranch.

I had one sister, Sarita, and my brothers were Richard, Robert, and Joseph, all born at home. Three of my siblings are named after the King Ranch Klebergs: Richard Kleberg, Robert Kleberg, Sarita Kleberg. Joseph was named after the country doctor who looked after us, and I was named after our dad.

I was nothing but a plain old little boy. Everything was of interest to me, I got into everything, and, obviously, my mother had to chase me all the time.

I don't remember a toy. I had a pocket knife.

I read a lot because Dad would go to the stock shows in Fort Worth, Houston, San Antonio, and up in Dallas and he would go to used bookstores and come back with boxes of books. Even encyclopedias. I read them all. I was the authority. I didn't have anything else to do, so I read, and I read, and I read.

Dad and Mother spoke Spanish to each other. They insisted that I speak English to him and Spanish to Mother. So that was my bilingual education. It was part of our tradition there.

As a youngster, I'd get all excited, talking in Spanish, and switch to English, and when I couldn't come up with the right word, I'd switch back to Spanish.

Dad would say, "Wait. Don't mix them. Each is a beautiful language. Speak one or the other."

The working language of the King Ranch was Spanish. It was tradition.

I'd watch Dad and Mr. Bob Kleberg Sr. and Jr. working cattle, and everything they said was in Spanish. All the Klebergs were good horsemen, spoke Spanish, and were committed to that ranch.

My life has been a life of education. The main thing Mother and Dad did was push us to learn.

Often he told me, "You're going to educate yourself, son."

All of their children got at least one college degree without exception. I didn't think I was bright enough to go to college. And secondly, I didn't think we could afford it. This was the depth of the Depression, and I think Dad earned thirty dollars a month.

Mother was illiterate. When she signed a check, she would draw her name. That's not to say she was not bright. That's how it was back in the twenties and thirties. We children used to read to her. Dad probably had a little bit of high school in Brownsville, maybe a couple of years. But he read a lot.

No other ranch in the United States has produced a four-star general and a US cabinet member, my brother Richard and myself. It's because of those parents saying, "Educate yourself, son. It's a treasure they can't take from you."

That's the life we led. It meant so much to me, the way they raised us.

I remember our house clearly still today. The boys slept on the sleeping porch, but my sister had her room next to Mother and Dad's bedroom. We never used our dining room as a dining room except if the priest visited or for special guests on holidays. The rest of the time we ate in a small area off the kitchen. It was the same way with our living room. We had a beautiful living room. Mother had decorated it. There was a wildcat skin on the table, snarling away. Every corner of our home had a happy memory.

There was no end to work on the ranch. If the house needed painting, I painted it. If there was wood to bring in, I brought it in. It was just constant, all kinds of chores. It bothered Mother if we sat down for too long. She struggled to beautify her front yard. It was more a fenced-in pasture. She had flowers and a fish pond.

In our house on the ranch, I made my first Holy Communion and I made my first confession. I'll never forget my first confession, as I was scared to death, not knowing what I was going to say. I barely knew what a sin was. I was only six years old. Somehow I made up a list of sins that I thought would be appropriate for this occasion.

They invited all the people on the ranch to come for the Mass and the first Holy Communion. They converted the dining room, moved things around, and made an altar. You had to fast in those days. Afterward, we had sweet bread and hot chocolate out back on the sleeping porch.

Dad was also the justice of the peace, and men and women would come from the ranch, and he would marry them there in our house. I remember Dick and I would peek into the converted living room to see what was going on. They would have skinned us alive if they had caught us.

We had a windmill right outside our home on this big pasture where we kept our horses and our horse trough. And it was a real high cistern. It's still there today. It's white. I remember when they built it. It had the Running W brand of the King Ranch around the dome. And it had a ladder. Now a ladder to a twelve-year-old is a challenge. I would climb all the way to the top. The windmill also had a ladder. When climbing it, you had to be careful that your head was not hit by the swinging tail.

We climbed up there because of the view. We could look out across the pasture there to Dr. [J. K.] Northway, our veterinarian, on one side, the dairy barns on the other part, the Big House, the garage. It was a kingdom to Dick and me. We treasured it.

I can still see it, the dust of the herd. You can't believe how much dust cattle can kick up, the hundreds and hundreds of heads of cattle.

We had a horse trough outside our house. It was tempting to two young guys; we'd jump in there and pretend to swim. We couldn't swim, but we'd wade, I guess. Mother would find out about it and raise Cain with us, and when Dad came home, he was really upset.

He said, "Cattle do not drink after there's human scent. Now I'm going to have to have that drained, scrubbed, and filled with water again."

So that stayed with me, "You don't swim in horse troughs."

You don't do a lot of things I did there on the ranch.

Maximiliano Garcia came to work at our place one day. I'll never forget it. We called him Vallejo because he came from an area of Mexico called Vallejo. Just like somebody from Texas is called Tex, he was called Vallejo. He came in our backyard and was being trailed by this dog behind him. I was nine years old.

I never spoke a word of English to Vallejo, although he could understand a little bit of English. He gave me some sound advice and told me some things that have stayed with me from earliest childhood to this day.

The first time I went riding with Vallejo, and at the same time Dick and Bobby, much younger, and Vallejo helped us saddle up the horses we kept in the pastures outside the house. Vallejo cinched it up for me, and I climbed up there and got on the horse.

Then he said to me, "*Bájate*, get off! *Bájate*."

"Sí, señor."

And I got off the horse.

He said, "Here on the ranch it is dangerous on horseback. You could be killed. Injured. Thrown at any moment. But before you get on that horse and seated, you say, 'Con el favor de Dios'"—with God's blessing.

I've remembered that always. So that carried on into my life.

I have flown thousands and thousands of miles, and every time I get on an airplane, walking up the ramp, I say, "Con el favor de Dios." It passes through my head. Every time I board an airplane, it is "with God's blessing."

I flew on Air Force One several times, but I always said, "Con el favor de Dios."

Vallejo taught me other things, too, such as how to take orders. Vallejo had given me a job to do, somewhere out in the chicken coops, and I halfway did it. I went in the house and was lying on the bed reading, probably a comic book.

Vallejo said, "Come here. I gave you a job to do. And you did not do it right. Now, Laurie, someday you are going to be a leader of men and women, but you cannot do that until you learn to take orders. Now get out there and finish up that work I gave you to do."

It's amazing that I remember that. I see him standing there. Vallejo was an incredible person. We had great affection for him.

Dick and I were constantly in trouble. He was really daring. Dad had taught us how to use a rifle since we were twelve years old, somewhere along in there. We fancied ourselves to be pretty good shots.

There was a lot of game out on the ranch, and every now and again Dad would say, "OK, boys, let's go hunting. Let's go pick up some dove or quail," or what have you.

We always got our limit. But he had one rule, "You kill it, you eat it."

And we'd come home with this sack full of birds, all these feathers, and, of course, it fell on Dick and me to pick these birds. We tried to con Vallejo into picking the birds.

"No, no, your father said you have to pick them, and if you don't pick them, you have to eat them with feathers."

Vallejo had this thing about armadillos. I had never eaten one until Vallejo came to work for us. Before long, I developed a taste for armadillo. Mother would not let Vallejo cook those awful things in her kitchen. He had to barbecue them outside, or when Mother went to town, Vallejo would come inside and cook them in the stove. It's a wonder we didn't all get leprosy, as they carry Hansen's disease.

Dad was a handsome man, tall and lean. Sat very straight and proud in his saddle. Bronzed by the sun, although he was very fair complexioned from the neck down. He had a way to walk, to dress.

He was a storyteller like you wouldn't believe. Oh, how I wish he had written down something or made some audiotapes, but he was always working so hard all his life.

He was a veteran of World War I, three battles in France. He took such pride in that and being an American. I remember Dad taking out this piece of paper and showing it to me, very fancy with colors. It was his honorable discharge from the army at the end of World War I.

He said, "It is the most precious piece of paper I have."

Our home was built on the highest hill on the ranch. It's pretty flat down there, Coastal Bend country, quite flat. But there is this one hill, and it's called Lauro's Hill, named after my father.

To everybody on the ranch, my father was Don Lauro, a term of respect. Tradition has it—oral history, I found nothing written—that Mrs. King ordered Dad's house built on the top of that hill in line of sight of her house, the main house, the Big House. Nothing obstructs the view from the Big House to ours.

Dad left the house around four or four thirty in the morning, seven days a week. No vacations. He got a full day on Christmas Day and he took off a half day on Thanksgiving. Everybody worked, and they worked hard.

I never saw my Dad in a pair of shoes. Never ever. He had these beautiful boots all handmade for him in Raymondville by a well-known boot maker there; he had Dad's mold. Like a man changes shirts, he changed his boots. He had boots for every day of the week and some left over.

The idea that my father could work cattle in a pair of unpolished boots was foreign to him. You know who gets to polish the boots. My brother Dick and I, the two oldest boys, we caught it all. It was just expected that we would polish his boots every day. Mother would line them up out there in the back for us. We had the saddle soap and the polish. He had fresh boots every day.

He was in the Texas State Guard in World War II, and I was, too, when I was sixteen in high school. It was kind of like the National Guard because the war was on and we'd be trained. Dad was a commissioned second lieutenant and we trained every other week, thinking we were going to be invaded and we could repel all these invaders.

Dad showed up in San Antonio because officers had to go for a week's training there. So they issued his uniforms and a pair of shoes.

They were just killing his feet. He went to his commander, told him his problem, and was told, "OK, you can wear boots with your army uniform."

After that they called him the "cowboy lieutenant."

When he died, we buried Dad in his finest pair of boots.

I t was greatly important to me that I saw so many things that were not good and learned from them. By that I mean, my Mama Grande Rita, my mother's side of the family, really insisted that her house was a very neat house. Her husband, Francisco Quintanilla, was what we called caporal. He was the leader of horsemen, a foreman, on the King Ranch, the part called Santa Cruz.

After he died, Grandmother moved into Kingsville and lived there in the barrio. It was here I saw some very, very sad things. We're talking about the 1930s. No paved roads, no gas, no electricity, everything required a lantern, no sidewalks. No sewer system; there were outhouses out there. The town provided nothing for the people of the barrio.

It was a town totally segregated. Even the restaurants were segregated. Even the schools were segregated, even in the cemetery. I remember going into the cemetery on El Día de Santos, All Saints' Day, and helping them clean up around my family's relatives' graves there and asking Dad, "Why aren't people cleaning up over there?"

He asked me, "Don't you see that road? We have to be buried over here, and they are buried over there on that side."

The Black people had their own cemetery, too. You talk about pointless. There's all these dead people, but you've got to sort them out.

I felt terrible that we couldn't do anything about that. It was just really bad, except on the ranch. There we were all a family. One family. It made all the difference in the world. Captain King meant it.

President Ronald Reagan welcomes his new secretary of education to the White House. *Photo courtesy Lauro F. Cavazos*

We started school at the Santa Gertrudis School. Total enrollment must have been about forty-five or fifty of us youngsters. It was a one-room schoolhouse with a sliding thing you pulled across and could make two rooms out of it. One row was for the first grade; the second row was the second grade. It was heated in the wintertime by a woodstove in the back. The big boys' job was to chop the mesquite wood and build the fires. My teacher was a woman named Ms. [Erna] Fisher. And my aunt Dell [Adele Cavazos], Uncle Steve's wife, was a part-time teacher.

We had no problem with discipline because everybody knew everybody on the ranch, and if you got out of line they'd talk to your parents, and you were done.

We all spoke Spanish on the playground, and, obviously, we spoke English in class. We were ready to learn when we got to school because our parents were raising us in both languages. But many of the kids who grew up on the ranch spoke only Spanish, so they had what we called in those days immersion in English.

The most important step in my education happened in 1935. That was when my parents transferred my sister and myself to one of those segregated schools, an Anglo school in Kingsville. Now, it was a real struggle.

The administrators told them, "No, you can't do that. You just can't do that."

Dad had bought a lot on the white side of town. The railroad track separated the town. You know the saying about the wrong side of the track? We lived that. I don't know how, but he managed to build a little house within walking distance of the elementary school, walking distance to the high school, and walking distance to a college. My father was thinking it through all the way. Now he had to get us transferred. It was 1930, and you just don't cross school lines.

Dad told them, "I'm a property owner. I am a taxpayer."

Dad had such a record in Kingsville and the whole area. He was a good man. He worked hard. He had a tremendous record of accomplishment there on the ranch. They respected him greatly.

So they said, "Oh, all right. You let that oldest girl come over here, but you have to bring her."

There were no school buses. The first day of school, she was just scared to death. Can you imagine, a little old girl about eight in the third grade?

I got beat up on my first day of school. You know, it didn't take much to hear, "I don't like Mescans."

Some big kid jumped on me, and I didn't know what the heck was going on.

Once Mother and Dad managed to pull this off, the idea kind of spread a little bit more in town. A few more children got transferred, and it blurred a little bit, and finally it just all went away, thank God. Looking back on it, I think of segregation, the way people were treated, and I'm amazed that we didn't have a rebellion, but we just passively accepted it. That was the way it was.

I remember on another occasion I was out front waiting for Vallejo or Mother to come pick us up, and this bully came along. He started in on me. I wasn't much of a fighter. I was more of a nice, quiet kid. He was beating me up and knocking me down, when this other kid on a bicycle comes speeding up, skids to a stop, jumps off, grabs this bully, beats him up a little bit, and the guy runs off.

He was an Anglo kid. His name was Dick Mosley, and his father was the town sheriff and had been for many years. Dick and I became friends.

I remember one night there on the ranch and I was in bed. I was perhaps nine or ten years old, and Dad came in that night. He woke me up and said, "Son, I have some bad news for you. Sheriff Mosley was shot and killed today. He was sitting in a café drinking coffee, and this guy came up, disgruntled, and shot him in the back of the head. And it killed him."

I remember that just as clear as a bell. I felt so bad for my friend Dick. It was a wild, tough part of the world.

Mother was going to drive us to Raymondville, a little town about seventy miles south of the ranch, to visit our cousins and aunts and uncles. I remember, we children were already in the car, and I was watching Dad as he checked the air in the tires, checked the water, the oil. And then he leaned over, and he handed Mother a pistol.

He said, "Be careful. It's loaded. I don't think you're going to need it, but it never hurts to have a little protection."

Mother was perfectly capable of using that pistol because Dad had taught her how to shoot. She tucked it under her car seat. We had enough discipline to know we did not touch that pistol. You could trust us not to do that. Everybody had them. I got shotguns and pistols, rifles for Christmas, because it was all part of it.

We lived near a highway and from time to time, during the Depression, people would stop by our house and ask for food. Mother sent them away with extra food for their journey.

I remember on one occasion, she saw this man come across the highway into our yard and up to our front door. She didn't recognize him. He looked awfully shabby. She told us to go to the bedroom.

"Don't you dare come out until I tell you."

She got one of Dad's pistols, put it behind her back, and went to the front door. She said this man looked at her, got a surprised look on his face, and took off. Well, obviously, he was up to some kind of mischief. Then she recognized that she was holding a pistol behind her back and that a big mirror hung behind her on the wall. He saw this woman with this pistol in the mirror. So he took off. That was the way it was.

Every Christmas the ranch had one heck of a big party. About four or five days before Christmas itself, they would dig big pits, fill them with firewood, light the fires, and they would start barbecuing huge sides of beef. People would paint the barbecue sauce on them with mops. Some people put together potato salad, all the things that you'd need for barbecue.

Then they would have a baile, a dance, in the school building not far from where the pits were dug. The bandleader was the maestro; his last name was Saenz. He had this little band, and so the people were dancing and having a good time. It was dancing for old folks. We kids didn't pay much attention.

But the best part about it to us was afterward in what we called the commissary, not far from the schoolhouse where the dance was. They had gifts for every child on the ranch. It was Dad's job to hand out our gifts. When I came through, I said, "Dad, I'd like a knife."

We had knives so sharp you could shave with them.

He said, "Oh, no, no favors. You get what I reach for."

I remember so clearly watching Dad get dressed on Christmas. He always wore his suit, beautifully made, and stickpin, finest boots. Then he put a .38-on-a-.45-frame pistol in his belt. Dad's job was to keep the peace, making sure there were no rowdies or somebody from Kingsville coming in crashing the party.

We were so trusting. It was a very open kind of a thing. Even though we were in economic trouble during the Depression, a truck would come by every now and then and drop off fifty-pound sacks of beans and rice and a big side of beef. Also, we had milk delivered every day from the dairy farm.

The ranch also had what we called health insurance. If you needed health care, you had to come talk to Dad. I remember being out in the yard, and this man came there and asked in Spanish if Dad was home.

"Yes, sir, he's home."

"Tell him I want an orden—an order—*para el doctor*—for the doctor."

And Dad would come out and write them a note. It was taken to the doctor, and there was no charge because it was taken care of by the ranch. If things got really bad, and you ended up in a hospital, the only bill you got was nothing. The ranch paid for it all.

When you retired or you got too old to work, you went to the barrio and received a certain amount of money to live on. You could see the townspeople were envious of us and other Hispanics who worked on the ranch and had all these things, and they didn't.

———

And the epitome of it, you died and the ranch buried you. That was back to the roots, to the story about Captain King.

"You are as a family, and we will look after each other."

Now many decades, years, after leaving the ranch, I recall my father's expectations of me. "Son, you will educate yourself, you will serve your country, and you will never disgrace the Cavazos name. Three things."

I remember where I was standing there at the ranch house when he told me that.

I think I met Dad's expectations of me. And I incorporated them into my life. I greatly value what I learned there. It was as fine an education as much as the degrees I earned from excellent universities.

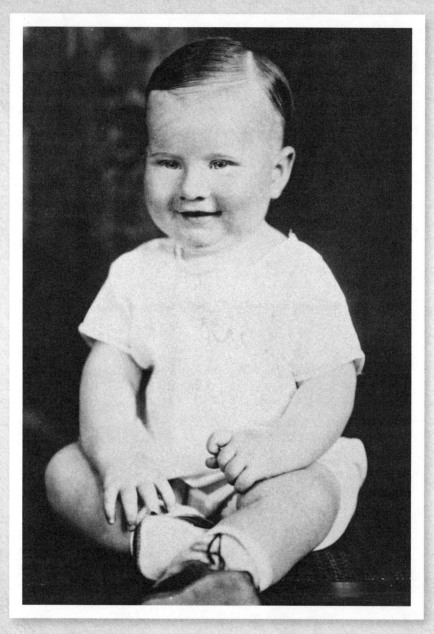

Billy Joe "Red" McCombs as a red-haired infant in his hometown of Spur. *Photo courtesy Red McCombs*

BIRTH NAME	**BILLY JOE McCOMBS**
BORN	October 19, 1927, in Spur to Willie Nathan "Slim" McCombs and Gladys Dempsey McCombs
INTERVIEW	McCombs Enterprises, San Antonio, Texas, December 1, 2017

12

RED McCOMBS
Money's Not the Goal

R ed McCombs is a San Antonio billionaire philanthropist and entrepreneur with ventures in auto dealerships, energy, real estate, communications, and sports franchises. Buying a radio station in 1972 with business partner Lowry Mays led to the foundation of Clear Channel Communications, now iHeartMedia. Since buying his first sports franchise at twenty-five, the Corpus Christi Clippers baseball team in the Big State League, McCombs has owned the Minnesota Vikings in the National Football League and the San Antonio Spurs and Denver Nuggets in the National Basketball Association. A lifetime of benevolence has resulted in donations of $30 million to the MD Anderson Cancer Center in Houston and $50 million to the University of Texas Business School named in his honor. His civic leadership in San Antonio brought HemisFair '68, the city's first major sports team, and recognition via television that the state's third-largest city was both multicultural and metropolitan.

My dad was born and raised in the Piney Woods. My mom was born and raised on a sharecrop farm close to Brownwood. They had good land, good soil, and such. They met at Spur, Texas, in West Texas, which is in the dry High Plains.

When I got to be a teenager and questioned his sanity, my dad told me, "Son, down outside Lufkin, I was the eldest of nine children, and we could only get forty acres to sixty acres to sharecrop. We heard of people going out west, and you could call for all the land you want. If you want two hundred, three hundred, four hundred acres, you think you can farm it, take it. But we didn't know it never rained. We didn't gain anything."

So, my dad came off the farm.

Spur is one of the few towns in Texas that's lost people. When I was growing up, it was 1,800 to 1,900 population, and now it's like about 1,200 or so. At any rate, it's lost population because it's not a county seat and they really don't have any jobs, and agriculture is just touch and go to begin with. It's really tough in that dry country.

The little town had nothing to offer, but we had great land around there. We were the little supply town for about six big ranches, Matador's, the Four Sixes, and the Swenson Ranch. The little railroad spur was run in there to where you could ship cattle. Then they didn't have to drive the cattle in the saddle into Kansas, where the railroad spurs were big up there.

All our family came from the East Coast. I thought I was told that I was Scots-Irish by blood. Finally, I got one of these fancy deals to where they really go back in the background and all. I'm 98 percent Scots. We were MacCombe, and the name got moved around. But the tribe name was MacCombe, pretty well known.

My mom's family was mostly Irish. Her father would get dead drunk and pass out and sleep out in the front yard if he had to if he could get ahold of some moonshine.

My mom's grandmother was almost six feet tall. You know, for an older person like that, it was almost unheard of. But even with that, my mom was only about five feet tall. But my dad was six foot three, and, fortunately, I caught those tall genes over from my dad. But you get it both ways.

They started calling me Red right away after I was born. In the little town, I was the only redheaded guy until my brother came along and he was red.

Both my grandparents on both sides had red hair. On one side, they were both redheaded. On the other side, one was redheaded. To get a red-head, you got to have both colors of red. We're very rare.

I tell my grandkids, "Marry a redhead. They're special, absolutely special."

They had a little old Ford dealership in that little old town. My dad was an auto mechanic there, but I couldn't even put a spark plug in. Although my dad had only a third-grade education, he really was a bright guy, a smart guy, and loved the power of the motorcar and what it did.

My dad worked all his working career virtually as an auto mechanic and a shop foreman, and many years as I was growing up, my dad made twenty-five bucks a week. And it never was any more, never was any less. He worked six days a week from daylight to dusk.

On Saturday, we'd gather around the kitchen table. I was the oldest of four children. My dad would open up his little envelope, and $24.75 would come out; twenty-five cents was deducted. My mother would take $2.50 of that and get a slip from the table behind her, put that in there. That went to the Baptist church. Even though we didn't have any money, we still paid that tithe every week.

I made the mistake one time of telling my mother, "You know, Mom, I hear you talking to Dad after we're in bed at night about how you wish we could get ahead and pay the doctors. It looks to me like that we're giving away 10 percent of that money each week."

Mom got mad at me and said, "You've been playing hooky and skip-ping Sunday school?"

"No, I've been going. Well, what do you mean?"

She said, "That's a tithe. We're not giving anything away. We owe that. The Bible teaches us that. You should know this."

If we got to the point where we had a lot of money, people asked, "When did you become a philanthropist?"

"When I got some cash."

I didn't have to worry about it for a while because I never had any cash.

I was working. I made more money than my father from the time I was about fourteen on. I always found a way to make money—mostly the typical things, cleaning up yards, cleaning up back alleys. I'd do this kind of stuff.

Then I got athletic scholarships to several schools, and I got six years of college and university. I never got five cents from home. Never expected five cents. I mean, nothing. I did well, very well, I might say. And I knew I was going to make a lot of money. So that was the way it worked.

Naturally, our kids going off to school didn't have the science subjects and all that they had in Lubbock. We didn't expect it. We all learned the basics real well.

I won a state essay contest when I was eleven years old with a crowd that was up to sixteen. They questioned whether I could do that perfect paper or not because you had to get it certified in your hometown and send it in to Austin. They'd call your school.

And they called and said, "This is not only the best paper we got this year, this is perfect. There's not even anything erased and written over. Every letter, every word is perfect."

Well, that's what we set out to do. We won.

I was pretty damn good at everything. I am good at arithmetic, very good at arithmetic. I was a kid who read. We didn't have a good library; we had a decent one, though. I'm sure I read nearly every book there.

My brother achieved the highest level of education of all of us. He got an earned PhD in classical languages. But he did that so he could study the Bible in almost any language.

One sister didn't really make it anywhere in school. The other sister didn't get a degree, but she was so good in the laboratory, where she just had a job being a gofer there, they moved her up. She got a lot of recognition for getting papers published that PhDs weren't even getting published, because she figured out a lot of stuff. She got married when she was seventeen, and that kind of stopped school.

There's no doubt about it, in our family, we got plenty of smart. I'm not saying we're smarter than any other family, but we don't have to back off from that. What our parents thought about was getting their kids educated. That was the big goal for them.

My mom was a great mom. She was a high school graduate. She was a little bit of a snob; that was a big deal for her, and she let us know it from time to time, too.

My sport was football. We were the Spur High School Bulldogs. I was

94

an end, and we played both ways. Offense and defense. So, I played the whole game.

They made me play a little basketball, but I didn't like basketball. I thought basketball was a sissy's game. I liked that knocking people around, busting them in the mouth. You know, we didn't have those guards in the front. We barely had helmets, just a strip of leather really.

Frankly, we didn't want for anything. We didn't have any money. But we had running water. We had a telephone. We had an ice plant in our little town. Nobody had air-conditioning, but you wet a rag and blew a fan on it. When I was growing up, I didn't see that anybody else had a lot more than what we did.

But for both sides of my mom and pop, you go out to the farm, and it was a different story. Those people had nothing. They had to sell some eggs or some butter along. They just didn't have any money. If you don't make a crop, you don't have any money to split, and you still have to pay the company store, and that's added to last year. You catch up finally when you get a good crop, but it depends on that weather.

Red McCombs, high school graduation, Corpus Christi, Texas, 1945. *Photo courtesy the McCombs family*

My grandparents lived out in the country on the farm. It took us about an hour and a half to get out there to the farm from town. They made it out there. At the company commissary, you could buy the basics, and they didn't have anything but the basics. You could buy the flour, the basic spices, and such, but you made your own milk, your own butter, your own meat. You could get by pretty good.

We had a few mesquite trees, and they were really guarded. We had some ground, some really rich ground. We didn't know about fertilizer and what it can do for you. That came around a little later. But very little

---

of the ground was farmed because they couldn't irrigate. They didn't have a water system.

We had a garden, but you carried water to it to water the plants. That was one of my jobs. Yep! But everybody jumped in. That was kind of a neat thing because you were going to get to eat some tomatoes off the vine, get to eat a little watermelon, cantaloupe, always cucumbers. It worked.

We probably had meat in about one meal a week and sometimes two. Even though we had access to stuff from the farm, they had to sell it.

I never felt like I was out of the play or didn't fit. But the first time I went into a hotel to eat, I was with a doctor's wife, and her son was my buddy. I'll never forget, the special on the blackboard was fried chicken, and I said I'd have the fried chicken. They'd ordered something different.

And when the fried chicken came, I thought, "You know, at home I pick it up with my fingers. Here we are in a hotel. What am I supposed to do?"

The precious lady there sensed that I was having to think about that. She said, "Billy, pick it up with your fingers just like you do at home. Don't even give it a second thought. We all do it. They do it that way in New York."

"OK. Fine."

When I was about four or five, I guess, I wanted a horse of my own. I'd go out to my friends' houses, and they all had horses. About half of them rode horses to school, rode bareback actually. They tied them up to a mesquite tree and watered them at noon. And then they rode them home. We didn't have buses to take you around anywhere.

At the time, there was a little toy horse about that long and about that high. It had fake hair on him, like real hair, and all, and it had runners under it, so it would rock.

My mom knew how bad I wanted a horse, but when I saw what kind I got, I just almost couldn't take it.

My dad noticed it first, and he said, "Come on, let's go outside."

And he said, "That wasn't the kind of horse you were expecting, were you?"

I said, "No, Dad, I'm so disappointed. I wanted to get my own horse."

And he said, "You'll get a horse someday, but not now. So, don't make your mother feel bad. Make her feel good. She's worked hard to get you and your brother and two sisters toys."

———

We had toys, and they were made out of snuff bottles that we tied together with string. Some were made, as you might imagine, out of stuff you could whittle out of wood and such.

I was in Cub Scouts and I was in Boy Scouts, and then I embarrassed my father, who was the scoutmaster and drove the bus and all. I created a riot at the Boy Scout camp because I didn't like the guys from Floydada. They sent me home, which killed my soul.

My dad felt so bad about it, but he said, "Sonny boy, this is just the price you pay."

And I said, "Oh, Dad, I'm just so sorry. I'm so sorry. But those guys just got on my nerves."

I had told my guys, "As soon as it gets good and dark and we're sure everybody's asleep, we're going to pull those ropes on the outside and knock that center pole down, and they're going to have a hell of a time getting out of that big tent."

And we did. And they screamed and hollered and cried, "Who did it? Who did it?"

"I did it."

So they sent me home.

I always liked the element of business, and I thought anyone who had a business was rich, whatever their business was. Didn't know any difference.

So there was an old lady, like I guess every town has one, never married, with a little bun on the back of her head. She had a café, and she lived up above it on Main Street. She had two shifts, and her second shift was from five to eight thirty, and that was the close-up shift. I was the dishwasher and helped the lady, who worked the counter, just the two of us, and I had a day job and I had this night job.

So this Sunday night I came sliding in from my night job, and my mom said, "Call this man. He's been by twice."

"Who is he?"

She said, "His name is Cecil Ayers. It's there on the paper, but it says

> **I thought anyone who had a business was rich, whatever their business was.**

he is a recent graduate of Texas Tech and that he wants to talk to you about your going up into high school in a couple of weeks."

So I knew what he wanted. I called the man up.

And he said, "I noticed that you're not registered for vocational agriculture."

I said, "No." I said, "I would never, never, never do that."

And he said, "Why?"

And I said, "You'll get most of the guys, probably 90 to 95 percent."

He said, "No, I checked all the grades. You've far and away got the best grades going into high school."

He said, "I need you. I am going to win all these judging contests, and I'm going to go all over the state."

He said, "I bet you'd like to travel."

I said, "Yes, sir, I get to go to Lubbock twice a year with the Boy Scouts. That's my traveling. That's where I've been and that's where I'm going. That's all I ever thought about."

He said, "I'm going to take you to lots of places, mostly Fort Worth and maybe Kansas City, blah blah blah."

Red McCombs addresses the ranchers at the annual Red McCombs Fiesta Texas Longhorn Sale at his Johnson City ranch, 2010. *Photo courtesy Red McCombs*

And he said, "You're going to win these judging contests, and I'm going to become known for that. And you're going to become my leader because you've got the brains to do it."

And we did it. We won everything in the state. He got hired on at Texas Tech. He was the first guy in their Agriculture Hall of Fame.

I got to go to Fort Worth, and we did win. We knocked everybody out. We judged cows and pigs and sheep, those three elements. We were winning, and I liked winning. I liked being the big shot. That felt pretty good. So I wasn't thinking about anything else.

My ag teacher, Cecil Ayers, pushed me. He asked to write in my annual. He wrote in my little book, "I want to tell you how much I enjoyed having you as a pupil. You are far and away the brightest student I've ever had.

You can do well. Go great places. But you've got to calm yourself down on your temper. You've had three incidents this year. And if you don't fix it, it's going to get in your way and it's going to be a big price to pay."

I never had a professor ask me before, "Can I write in your annual?"

This teacher did.

I'd get angry about a lot of things. I don't know the meaning or even if there is a meaning. I always pretty much thought I was right. Took me a long time to figure out you didn't always have to be right. I'm not saying I'd always be the most popular person in class, but I'd be close to it.

My dad gets this job in Corpus Christi, and he goes when school's out.

In the meantime, in my senior year in high school, I didn't know there was any place except work. I got the key job in town, which was to be the local soda jerk at the one drugstore. You get to eat ice cream all summer. Anyway, it was a neat place to have a job.

I don't know how she picked up on it, but my mom kind of sensed, I guess, that I never intended to leave Spur, Texas.

But sure enough, in late August, I looked up, and my mom surprised me. She walked in. My mom had driven all the way from Corpus Christi in our old worn-out car. She came in, and we embraced, and she said, "I'm going over to Miss Smith's house for supper and I'm going to spend the night with her. Can you come over there and have supper with us?"

"Oh, yes, ma'am. I'll be cleaning up here and be over there about eight thirty, eight forty-five."

So when I walked in the door, I didn't pay any attention, it was hot in the room, and I got one step inside and my mom popped up in front of me and said, "OK, now I don't want any trouble out of you."

She said, "I've been over at Leon's house and I got your stuff."

My stuff was packed in a paper sack about that big.

She said, "We're going to drive at night, so the old car won't overheat. And you're going with me."

And she said, "I just figured that you're not planning on coming back."

I said, "Well, you're right, Mom. I don't intend to ever go back to Corpus Christi."

I said, "Spur's my home. That's where I plan on staying. I'll still call

---

you once a week like I do now. I love you and all my family, but I'm not going down there."

She said very calmly, "That's about what I thought you would say."

She reached on this little table behind her where my tennis racket was, and she hit me across the head with the wood. Knocked me down. Knocked me out. When you get knocked out, you know what happened, but it takes a minute to get your feet under you.

She said, "I don't want to hit you again, but you're going to Corpus Christi."

So I sulked all the way down that long drive. We left at four the next morning and got in at almost dusk. My dad had a furnished walk-up with two rooms for us to stay in until we got into our house on the base. I saw some kids down on the beach and walked down there and got acquainted. Mom had to come and get me, because it was so interesting, and I got so excited about meeting all these new kids.

M oney has never been my goal. My goal is to be a leader. And if I were a leader in a little town like Spur, that would be fine with me. It doesn't have to be New York City. I want the people around to choose me as their leader. I'll fight to be your leader.

I don't know what caused that desire, that drive. No one in our family had ever been in any kind of business. Never owned anything. On both sides they were sharecroppers up until the time they died. They had no assets. Wonderful people. But that wasn't a part of who they were.

I always had heroes. Always, always. I felt like the guys who were my heroes were the wealthy people in town because they made all the decisions. There were three or four people in town who decided about the schools; they decided everything. That's what I wanted to do. I wanted to be like them.

Money had nothing to do with it, you know. But along the way, I always come early and always stay late. I'll do more than anybody else is going to do. You do that, and you get noticed.

Red McCombs with the mascot for the San Antonio Spurs basketball team, 1973.
Photo courtesy the McCombs family

Just a Coincidence

After that first time leaving, I never went back to Spur but one time. My brother was a Baptist minister, and he was holding a revival there. My mom was getting very old, and she wanted me to take her out there. So I had my little jet airplane then, and I took her to Spur and she spent the day. We got to go to the old Baptist church one more time.

And then when we named the San Antonio Spurs the Spurs, they went crazy. I got a call from the school superintendent.

He said, "The whole town's gone upside down. We know you named the team after the town, and we're so proud of you."

Well, that had nothing to do with it. But I didn't tell him that.

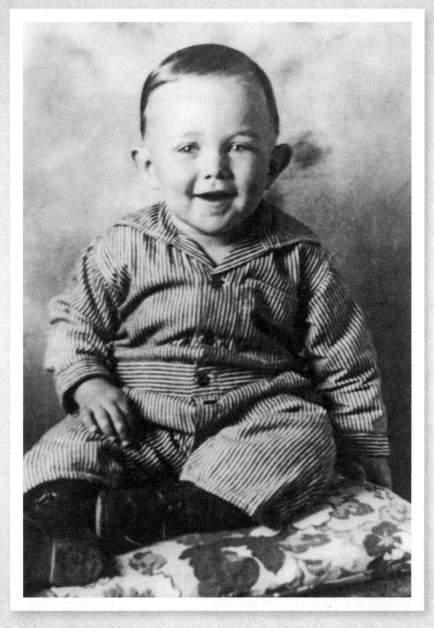

Jimmy Dean, eighteen months old. *Photo courtesy Jimmy Dean and Llano Estacado Museum*

BIRTH NAME	**JIMMY RAY DEAN**
BORN	August 10, 1928, in Olton to George Otto Dean and Ruth Taylor Dean
DIED	June 13, 2010
INTERVIEW	Jimmy Dean Sausage Company, Dallas, Texas, September 14, 1981

JIMMY DEAN
Propelled by Poverty

Jimmy Dean is an iconic country singer best known for the cross-over hit "Big Bad John" and a sausage empire capitalizing on his name. At twenty-five, he had his first hit, which launched a career in radio, television, and movies that mainstreamed country music. Before he reached thirty, he had turned a successful radio hour into The Jimmy Dean Show on CBS, where he introduced little-known country stars Patsy Cline and Roy Clark. He wrote "Big Bad John," the ballad of a heroic coal miner in a mining disaster, in an hour and a half on an airplane en route to a recording session. The song ensured his place among American legends when the single topped both the country and the pop charts and earned a Grammy Award for Best Country and Western Recording. With his signature twang and infectious grin, he was the first guest host for The Tonight Show Starring Johnny Carson in the early 1960s, had a role in the 1971 James Bond movie Diamonds Are Forever, and acted in Daniel Boone and other popular TV series. In 2010 he was inducted posthumously into the Country Music Hall of Fame.

Pop Taylor was my mama's daddy. I think I understood him better than anybody, even his own kids. It's a funny thing. A lot of people talk to me about wealth and success. I've always maintained that's a state of mind.

I tell them, "My Papa Taylor was probably the wealthiest and the most successful man I've ever known, and I doubt if he ever made $10,000 a year in his life. But he was the best farmer in Swisher County, and he knew that. His rows were straighter, his fences were in better shape, the end rows were cleaner, his barn was better, and his house was whiter."

He also had a marvelous relationship with the Man Upstairs. To hear him talk to the Lord was a very, very nice experience because it was just like talking.

He'd pray, "I need it, I wouldn't ask for it if I didn't need it, and I expect it."

And as a general rule, he got it.

I worked with him on the farm. He raised cotton, wheat, milo, and high gear [sorghum]. For some reason, when I was around him he had more humor than he did when he was around his own kids. We talked a lot and worked in the fields together.

He was about twenty miles from us. In West Texas we don't pick cotton, we pulled the bulb due to the drier climate. You could snap that stem off and pull bulbs and head mace and cut wheat.

My mama, Ruth, was a tough one. She's all wool and a yard wide. She had a lot to go through. I look like her. When she was a young lady, she was gorgeous. She did what must be done and got it done well. I think she raised me with a sense of loyalty, playing the game fair, that has sustained.

My mama cut hair. She started with an old pair of hand clippers shortly after my dad left, and she cut hair until she was seventy-five years old. This was in our house in Plainview. She didn't have a name for her business. People just knew that Ruth Dean cut hair in the evening, and you could go over and get your hair cut.

It was rough, but, hell, I wouldn't trade it for anything in the world. I wouldn't know how to act if all the good things had happened to me as a result of being born with a silver spoon. I now realize that poverty was the greatest motivating factor in my life.

We had a piano. Mama taught me how to play it. That was our entertainment on Sunday afternoons. The kids would come over and gather around and we would sing.

On Saturday night we used to go down to the old bank that had an entrance that was a little domed affair. It was so beautiful to sing in there because of the marvelous acoustical bounce coming back at you.

"Amazing Grace" was my favorite.

I was eleven when my daddy, G. O. Dean, ran off. I didn't really get to know him all that well. He was pretty much of a rounder, I guess. He tried a little bit of everything. He preached for a while. He preached in Presbyterian, Methodist, and Baptist churches. He was kind of an evangelist-type guy. I suppose if I have any talent, I probably got a chunk of it from him. He wrote a book. I've got a copy, but I've never read it.

When he left, I placed all the blame strictly upon him. Then I became increasingly aware as I got older that it is conceivable it was not all his fault. As I look back at the Taylor family, there were probably factors that would have prompted a fellow to stray a little bit.

When he left, I earned the family living. I was pulling bolls after school when I was seven years old. Any dirty job that anybody else didn't want, as a general rule, I got because I was big. I put up windmills and cleaned septic tanks and ran combines.

I knew I wasn't going to be a farmer. I used to be out in those damn boll patches or I was chopping cotton, and I used to say, "Boy, somewhere there's got to be something better than this."

We lived in a little community called Seth Ward. We looked up to folks on welfare. We were so damn poor that if you could go around the world for a quarter, I couldn't have gone across the street. I'd get a new pair of shoes and walk backward three days to look at the tracks.

My mama would buy those cloth sacks and bleach them and make our shirts. Then she'd dye them. That would make a pretty nice looking shirt. She was an excellent seamstress, and she had one of those old treadle sewing machines. We also wore bib overalls and brogan shoes, and you don't win too many popularity contests when you look like that.

I remember WPA [Works Progress Administration] was giving away trousers. They looked pretty good.

I said, "Mom, I think you ought to go down and get some of those clothes."

She said, "No, if we take clothes, that's charity, and that says we give up. We don't give up."

I've never forgotten that. Until this day I don't know what the word "defeat" means. Temporary setback, I'll buy, but you don't defeat me. No way.

They laughed at me at school, because kids are cruel. They didn't mean to be. But I used to think, "One of these days I'll show you that I can wear clothes as good as anybody."

Later I was back home after I'd done CBS and a few things. Things were going rather well, and I'd had some tailor-made suits. They called me from the new high school and wanted me to speak at assembly.

I said, "No. They didn't want me when I wore bib overalls and they don't want me now."

My mom said, "Why don't you do that?"

And I noticed a sense of urgency. She didn't say why. But when kids laughed at me for the clothes I wore, she was the only one I had to go to. Now that I'm a parent, I realize how much that must have hurt her.

The principal called back, and I said, "OK."

Jimmy Dean, right, around twelve years old, wearing a shirt his mother sewed from a sugar sack. *Photo courtesy Jimmy Dean and Llano Estacado Museum*

So we drove over there in my mom's little old car. She sat down in the front row in the high school auditorium. I found out they had called the assembly especially for me. The auditorium was full of these kids, and I was a hero. I walked out on stage. These kids started to stand up, and there was a standing ovation.

And I looked down at my mother and I saw the hurt repaid.

Fight, that's all I've ever known. That's all I think I can almost remember. I have the scars to prove it. They're not visible to you, but they're there.

Every time somebody pointed at me, laughed, and said, "That's G. O. Dean's kid and he'll never amount to a hill of beans," every time they laughed at my clothes or they laughed at the house I lived in or at my mother, it cut deep, very, very deep. And the scars are still there. They're all healed now and they don't hurt anymore, but they did then.

How very much I wish I could go back and find every one of those people and thank them from the bottom of my heart. I still don't like the haughty bastards, but those people made me what I am today.

Every finger that was pointed, every derogatory remark that was made, every smirking face built a fire in me, and there was only one way to put it out. That was to show every one of them that I was every bit as good and perhaps better than they were.

I spent those eighteen-hour days, and the fire in my gut kept saying, "I'll show you. I'll show 'em."

And, by golly, I did.

Most of my fond memories are always associated with food. The fondest memories are the really huge meals at my grandfather's house. Otherwise, we lived on pinto beans and cornbread. Somebody said we ate beans for breakfast and drank water for lunch and swelled up for supper. He used to tell me my legs were hollow.

"Nobody can get that much in their stomach," he used to say.

My grandmother, Ludie, and Papa Taylor were the funniest looking couple you ever saw. She was taller than he was. She had nine kids, and my mother delivered one of her sisters.

Ludie was a good cook, and I doubt if she ever weighed more than one hundred pounds in her life. She lived to be ninety-five or ninety-six.

Papa Taylor taught me how to make sausage. My grandparents raised hogs, and I first ate sausage at their house. I helped grind and I helped mix the sausage. And at hog-killing time every year, he bought a brand-new galvanized washtub, and that's what he mixed it in.

You knew it was hog-killing time when the stock tank had a little thin ring of ice around the edge for the first time. Then it was cold enough to kill a hog. To me, his sausage was the greatest stuff I had ever put in my mouth.

But your taste changes. When I was a kid, there was a certain kind of grape soda pop, Grapette or something. I thought that was the finest thing in the world. One time when I was grown and at home, I saw a bottle of it and I couldn't wait to try it. I couldn't drink it. It was the worst stuff I have ever tasted.

If I tried Papa's sausage now, I don't know that I'd like it. It wasn't the quality of our sausage today, because his was made out of the same thing that most sausage manufacturers make it out of—trimmings. What was left over went into the sausage.

He had a smokehouse. That was so nice. You'd just walk in there and get hungry. He'd take down one of those hams, and it would have mold all over it, which was nothing. Mama Ludie just trimmed it off, and that aroma coming out of the kitchen was so good.

At wheat harvest time, they took the whole grains of wheat and brought them in and washed them. Then they would put it in water and soak it overnight. You know, how you do beans. It would swell up, and then they boiled it in hot water the next morning. They drained the water off and put good, heavy country cream and some sugar over that whole-grained wheat. I still think I would like that a lot. That was a good, healthy breakfast.

As Papa used to say, "You better eat something that'll stick to your ribs. You got a long day coming."

At sixteen years old, I joined the maritime and celebrated my seventeenth birthday in Lima, Peru. I've always loved the water—still do. I just wanted to get out of those dust and boll patches and off those combines. My mama didn't encourage me to join the merchant marines, but she didn't discourage it either. She signed the papers to let me go.

I always sent the money I made back home, because when I worked after school and things like that, I never kept any money. There was no question about it, you just turned it over to Mom.

I remember still to this day the first whole dollar I ever had. I was probably thirteen. She gave it back to me. I'd worked practically all fall, and I guess she figured it was time I should have a dollar. I also remember what I did with it. I went to Bacardi's Store and bought six pounds of bologna. I went on down that dirt road and I ate all the bologna I wanted.

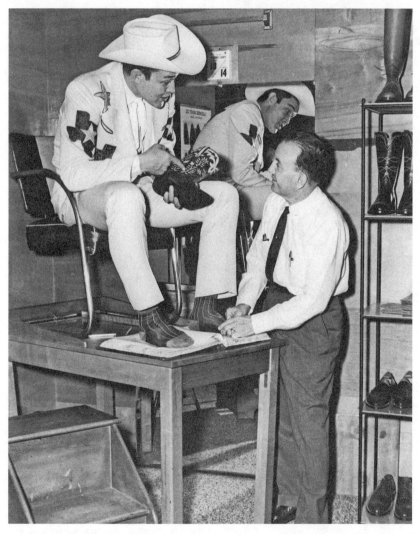

Jimmy Dean being fitted for a pair of Texas-made custom Lucchese boots, February 13, 1960. *Photo courtesy of Lucchese Bootmaker*

Humberto Reyes, the eighth of fourteen children, followed his older brothers to Texas A&M University. *Photo courtesy Humberto Reyes*

BIRTH NAME	**HUMBERTO VILLARREAL REYES**
BORN	December 15, 1928, in Berclair to Carlos Reyes B. and Maria Villarreal Reyes
DIED	February 13, 2018
INTERVIEW	St. Anthony Hotel, San Antonio, Texas, December 9, 2016

HUMBERTO REYES
A Cattle Future

H umberto "Bert" Reyes sold multimillions of dollars in livestock in more than forty years as a high-profile auctioneer on both sides of the Rio Grande. Noted for auctioneering in English and Spanish, he introduced Simmental cattle to the United States and sold Lyndon B. Johnson's herd at the request of Lady Bird Johnson after the former president died in 1973. For years he was recognized as the number one bilingual auctioneer in Texas and the Southwest. Headquartered in the historic San Antonio Union Stockyards, he auctioneered and managed cattle sales in twenty-eight US states, Mexico, Canada, and Venezuela. He graduated in 1950 from Texas A&M University with a bachelor's degree in beef cattle production, served with the infantry in Korea, and applied the G.I. Bill to a master's degree in cattle production and range management. Reyes dedicated his life to learning everything there was to know about Hereford, Angus, Beefmaster, Brahman, Brangus, and many other breeds. His archives reside at Texas A&M.

My father was from a very prominent family in Durango, Mexico. He was very highly educated in music, in his profession as a mining engineer, in religion, in everything. His family owned three silver mines. He had a perfect English accent because he learned his English from British miners in Durango.

Pancho Villa and my father were born and raised in the same little mining town in Mexico, San Lucas. My father saw him grow up and become a bad man. The rebels captured my dad, who was defending Durango, and all the boys in that community. They were lined up. The general started shooting them.

There was a colonel who said, "My general, the next one, please don't shoot him. He's my first cousin."

So the general said, "I will let him go, but you need to get him out of Mexico as fast as you can."

So my dad went to my grandmother's house, and she gave him enough money to come to the United States. He was a political refugee.

My father was about twenty-one when he got here. All he had was a backpack. He heard there was a rancher at the Bluebonnet Hotel in San Antonio who was looking for workers. My father, a college-trained engineer, needed a job of some kind. So he told this man, "I hear you're looking for cowboys."

This Englishman, Mr. Cyrus Lucas, owned a four-hundred-thousand-acre ranch, the Pryor Lucas Ranch. He turned my dad over to the foreman, and my dad became a cowboy. He hadn't been there very long when they made a big shipment of cattle, longhorns, to Kansas City. My father, being very well trained in mathematics, watched as they were loading up the train. When they paid the foreman, my father told him, "They didn't pay you enough for those cows."

The foreman said, "How do you know?"

And he said, "I counted them."

Mr. Lucas told him, "Well, I don't want you to get back out into the pastures. I want you to take care of my office and all the bookkeeping for the ranch, because they tell me you're not a very good cowboy."

My father and the owner of the ranch became inseparable. He trusted my father to the nth degree, and my dad trusted him.

My father came here with the hopes of going back to Mexico. But in that little town of Berclair in Goliad County, he met my mother.

My mother went to the fourth or the fifth grade. I often wondered how they got along all their lives, him being so highly educated, but my father said that my mother always had the last word.

In 1913 when my dad came over, the income tax bill was passed. All the ranchers were after my dad to fix their income taxes. In Mexico, if you are highly respected by everybody, they call you *don*. So in no time at all, he was Don Carlos Reyes B.

Dad leased a ranch between Beeville and Berclair. It was a very poor ranch. But we lived on that ranch for thirty-three years. Everybody in Berclair was a farmer or a rancher.

My mother's name was Maria Villarreal Reyes. She came from the most prominent Mexican family in that community of Berclair. My mother's family are the original Spaniards that landed in Goliad where La Bahía Mission is. They wound up having fourteen children. I was number eight. My oldest brother was named Lucas. Alvino; Antonio; Raquel; a girl, Otilia; Carlos Jr.; Cristina; and myself, Humberto; Florinda; Estella; Margarito; Martha; Pedro; and Ruben. We averaged two years between all of us. The most that were ever at home at the same time was six of us.

My father was gone from five in the morning until dark, so my mother had to supervise the farm. He was not a very good farmer. We planted cotton and corn and hay. We did that with mules and hand ploughs because there were no tractors then. We never had a piece of mechanical equipment.

We never had a penny in our house. But we never were hungry because my mother managed on the farm to provide meat, milk, cheese. We raised sweet potatoes, corn, watermelons. Nearly all the food we ate, we raised it on the farm. Every two weeks, my mother would go into our little town to get sugar and coffee, things we couldn't grow on the ranch.

At that time, the Hereford breed of cattle was not very popular for milk, but at the farm we had Hereford cattle, and that's what we used for milk. I was milking cows when I was six years old.

On the farm we learned how to be independent. I was a responsible, dependable kid from an early age. My oldest brother didn't have to go to war, because he had what you call a very important job for the war effort as a civilian, an essential agriculture job.

He supervised my life. Every morning, he'd say, "Now you go feed the cattle. You go feed the hogs."

And then he'd go off to work. So when I was eleven years old, I was taking care of hogs, cattle, and chickens. I didn't like my turkeys and hogs as much as I liked my calves.

On my first day of school, the teacher sat us in a long chair. I was at the end of the chair, not knowing one word of English. And the teacher said, "Stand up and tell me your name."

And I didn't move.

And she says, "Stand up and tell me your name."

She told me that three times. When I didn't, she hit me with a ruler on my shoulder. Then the older boys in the back told me in Spanish, "She says for you to stand up and tell her your name."

From that day on, I think that I picked up English just as fast as it could be picked up. I never spoke Spanish again in school. It didn't take long to learn English with a teacher who was mean as she could be.

It was a segregated school, a two-room Mexican school. We had a Mexican school, the Anglo school, and the colored school in that little town. We didn't go to school with the Anglos until I was a freshman in high school.

In about the third grade, my cattle interest started. I was sitting by the window, and I could hear the roundups from the big ranches coming in to be shipped by rail in Berclair. I could hear the cattle, all longhorns, because it was the end of the longhorn era. I could hear the men hollering and whooping. I slipped out the window without telling the teacher and headed for the shipping pens. I knew that my daddy would be there because he'd be counting the cattle. So I'd go up there and watch them load the longhorns in the railcars.

When I was in the fifth grade, the teacher came in and said, "Humberto, there's a man outside and he wants to talk to you."

There was this tall man in boots, a cowboy hat—looked like a Texas Ranger. And I thought, "What have I done wrong?"

He said, "Would you be interested in feeding the club calves from the county stock show?"

I said, "Yes, sir, but we don't have money to buy a calf."

And he said, "Well, I think I can arrange for that."

He talked to the ranch owner where my father was keeping books.

The owner, Mr. Lucas, said, "I'm going to let you have this calf, and if you win a blue ribbon, you don't have to pay me back. But if you don't, you're going to have to pay me fifty dollars."

I got to work, and sure enough, I got a blue ribbon and had the reserve champion. Immediately, I started another. I fed four calves during my high school grades.

I had the influence of that county agricultural agent, an older man from Texas A&M, who had heard about my older brothers there. That county agent's name was D. F. Berthower. He got me started, and he became my second father. He was very close to me.

I remember my favorite teacher. Her husband was in the cattle business, and she knew I was interested in cattle. They had a little ranch on the edge of town. Every day I would go out there and work for them an hour or two. He paid me twenty-five cents an hour. Mr. and Mrs. Robert Webb. My teacher's husband helped me show club calves in the stock shows. I started feeding club calves for the stock show when I was eleven years old. That never got out of my system.

When I was showing calves, I would be the only Latin kid. The A&M people who judged the stock shows kept seeing this Mexican kid at the 4-H club shows. And so the judges remembered me. I don't like to brag, but I was the most prominent 4-H club member in the area.

Humberto Reyes serves as auctioneer at the LBJ Ranch Hereford Dispersal in May 1973 after President Johnson's death earlier that year. Lady Bird Johnson and Luci Johnson watch the auction progress. Lynda Johnson and her husband, Charles Robb, also attend. *Photo courtesy Humberto Reyes*

I went to Goliad High School. My first two years of football were canceled because of the war. They canceled all the football programs in our area. For two years, I didn't have any athletics. When the war passed and everything was back to normal, I was a junior, and I started playing football. I was a quarterback.

Meanwhile, I joined the band and learned to play the trumpet. But that was during those first two years when there was no football, no basketball. The war was on.

On December 7, they bombed Pearl Harbor. I'll never forget it. I was at the pens taking care of my calf, and here comes one of my sisters. She was crying. I said, "What's the matter?"

Humberto Reyes during his interview at San Antonio's historic St. Anthony Hotel.
Photo by Marvin Hecker

She said, "Oh, they bombed Pearl Harbor, and they bombed the Philippines."

That's where we were when the bombing took place. The whole town was real sad.

The same time they bombed Pearl Harbor, where we had our navy, they bombed our air force at Clark Field in the Philippines. My brother, Colonel Alvino Reyes, flew B-24s and later B-17s. When the Japanese bombed Clark Field, they destroyed it completely, to the point the cook threw potatoes at the Japanese planes that kept striking.

My brother, all the other pilots, and a few crewmen got out of that island in boats. Luckily, my brother got to a little island called Java. He stayed there for a few days until they got organized and went to Australia.

In the meantime, we all thought he had been killed. Finally, after thirty days, we got a letter from my brother that he was alive.

My other brother, Major Antonio Reyes, went to Europe. He was with General Patton and became a major. They drafted my third brother, Lieutenant Carlos Reyes Jr., right out of high school.

These were tough times. We survived that. My mother suffered a whole lot.

There were very, very few Latin children who ever went to college at that time. My father and mother sacrificed a whole lot to send us, especially at that time. The Latins weren't supposed to go to college. As a matter of fact, most of them dropped out of school in the fourth or fifth grade so they could go to work.

My father always told us the only way we could make it was to get an education. He sent the oldest one to be educated in the university where he was educated in Mexico City. And then the next two were sent to Texas A&M. He visited the school and they loved it, so he said, "From here on, this is where my boys will go to school."

They sent all fourteen of us to college. Eight of us went to A&M, and the six girls went to different teachers' schools.

Being Latin kids in our part of the country, people wanted to know how in the world did they graduate from A&M. My brothers paved the way for me. By the time the first ones got out of college, they started helping the others, like myself. All my younger brothers and sisters, I helped them through college. Once we started going to college, there was a member of the family at Texas A&M in college for a long, long time. We are the largest family of Aggies.

My father did not want me or any one of the boys in the family to get into the farming or ranching business unless we had a profession to subsidize it. Sure enough, when all the brothers went off to A&M, they became engineers, petroleum engineers, and geologists. When it came time for me to go to college, my dad told me to take some kind of engineering.

When I was a senior in high school, I got a big, good scholarship called the Jesse Jones Scholarship. Jesse Jones was a very prominent man in Houston. It almost paid all my college.

When I got there, the first semester, I was taking engineering and I was barely making it. I was not interested. When I came home for Christmas, my mother said, "How are you getting along?"

I told her, "I'm fine, but I don't like what I'm doing. I cannot change unless I get a letter from my dad and take it to the dean at A&M. I know Dad will not give me that letter."

My mother said, "Go get the letter written, and I will sign it for you."

I got Dad's secretary to write the letter. I told her, "Don't you tell Dad."

Mother signed it. I went back to school and switched over to agricultural animal science. From that day on, I stayed with beef cattle production.

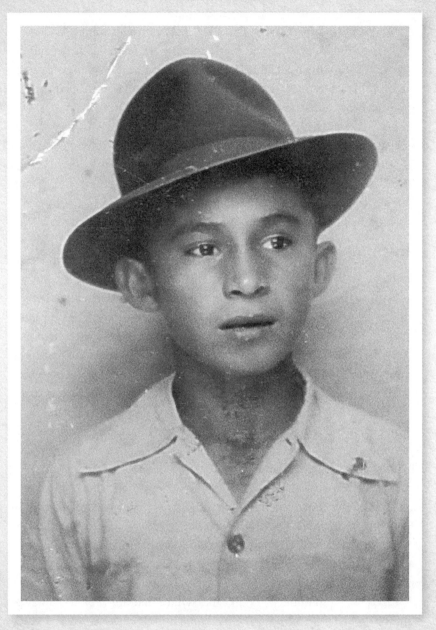

Patricio Flores, age eight. *Photo courtesy Archbishop Patrick Flores*

BIRTH NAME	**PATRICIO FERNANDEZ FLORES**
BORN	July 26, 1929, in Ganado to Patricio Flores and Trinidad Fernández de Flores
DIED	January 9, 2017
INTERVIEW	Archdiocese of San Antonio, San Antonio, Texas, March 1, 1984

15

ARCHBISHOP PATRICK FLORES

The Sting of Prejudice

rchbishop Patrick Flores was the first Mexican American elevated
to the hierarchy of the Catholic Church in the United States. He
entered the seminary in 1949, was ordained to the priesthood in
Galveston, and consecrated as bishop in 1970 as a symbol of Hispanic progress and the leading advocate for Spanish-speaking Catholics in the United States. In 1979 he became archbishop of the Roman
Catholic Archdiocese of San Antonio, the country's largest ecclesiasti-
cal province at the time. He founded America's first diocesan TV station
in 1981. He helped establish the Mexican American Cultural Center in
San Antonio and Padres Asociados para Derechos Religiosos, Educati-
vos y Sociales (Priests Associated for Religious, Education, and Social
Rights, or PADRES). In 1976 he co-founded the Teletón Navideño to
raise funds for charitable causes. On reaching the mandatory retirement age of seventy-five in 2004, he became archbishop emeritus. In
2007, A Migrant's Masterpiece, an hour-long PBS documentary,
examined his impact on the history of Latinos in Texas and the civil
rights movement in San Antonio.

I am from a farming family who were migrant workers at certain times during the year. We had our own farm and took care of our own things, but between crops we migrated, too.

I was born in Ganado, a little community ninety miles south of Houston and about forty miles north of Victoria. My mother and father married in Ganado and lived there twenty-five years.

My grandfather used to tell us three things that didn't make sense then but did later on.

"We did not come from Mexico. Mexico got away from us."

He used to repeat that over and over.

He used to say, "We didn't cross the border. The border crossed us."

The border was three blocks behind their house.

Then he used to say the Flores family was in Brownsville before Brownsville was ever Brownsville. It seems like we were Texans at least over 150 years back.

It seems like we were Texans at least over 150 years back.

We were nine brothers and sisters. I'm number six, and there are six men and three women. We also always had somebody else staying with us. For periods of years, we had other children with us. How we managed, only God knows, but we managed.

What I remember vividly is the fact that even though we were poor and moving, we were always together. There are powerful memories of family togetherness. We managed to do a lot of hard working but also to do a lot of entertaining.

My family was very musically inclined and very inclined to dancing. My father and mother could play several instruments. They wanted all of us to learn. I'm the only one who didn't learn anything. I could not play the guitar, even the harmonica. When I was quite young, I became the singer and dancer, while my brothers and sisters could play.

We would go to family parties on Friday, Saturday, and Sunday, but that did not stop us from getting up early the next morning and milking sixty cows before going to the field or to school. I never remember going to a social function alone, because the family went together.

We always took lunch and supper together at the table. The pots and pans went around and everybody got something. If we ever started an argument at the table, we couldn't finish our meal, and there would be nothing to eat until the next meal. But we could talk about anything. At the end of the meal, we would take turns leading the family Rosary.

My mother was very much with us in prayer. My father was much more with us in recreation. My father really liked to play baseball and other games. We had sort of our own baseball team. There were enough of us.

My mother and father were illiterate. My father never learned to write his name. My mother did learn to sign her name and read a little Spanish. Neither ever attended a school, yet they had a great interest in our going to school. However, we had to quit school early in the year, and we never started school on time. For several years, we only passed conditionally. We were told it wasn't because we were dumb but because we did not meet the requirement of being in school at least seven months out of nine.

I'm particularly grateful for the teachers in the public schools in Houston, where we moved when I was seven. Knowing that we were going to be leaving, they gave us books to take with us, and they would say, "Study them; read them."

Then when we returned from our journey, they stayed with us after school. Some of them took us to their homes on Saturday to help us catch up.

We were a Catholic Mexican family, and on both sides of us we had Catholic Czech families. We had religion in common but not language. My father learned Czech slang expressions, and our neighbors learned Mexican slang. My mother learned to make kolaches, the Czech pastries. And the neighbors used to say they were the only Czechs in the world who could make tamales.

The school policy was to use English. If we used Czech or Spanish, we got a *porrazo*, a whack. Several times I got hit on the hand because I knew the word in Czech or Spanish but not in English.

We learned English quickly. Since I was the number six child, the older ones going to school were using English at home. So I knew a lot of words even if I couldn't make sentences. I kept my identity by using the two languages. At home we spoke Spanish with my mother and daddy.

Food also gave me trouble in school. At home we always used flour tortillas for tacos. Somehow at school, we were not allowed or were made fun of if we took tortillas. My parents bought bread just to make sandwiches for us to take to school. I had never had a peanut butter sandwich, and all of a sudden, I was given two peanut butter sandwiches to eat at school. I almost choked trying to swallow them.

I was a school dropout for three years beginning in my tenth-grade year. My father was in an accident, and my older brothers and sisters were either married or in the service and could not help. I suggested to my mother that I quit school and go to work to help her pay the bills. She didn't want me to, but she had no alternative. So I immediately got jobs working in a filling station during the day and singing and dancing in a nightclub at night. We were able to pay off everything.

I became thoroughly convinced if I didn't finish high school that I was going nowhere. About that time, I began to think about the possibility of the priesthood. I fought with the idea, because that wasn't something I really wanted to do. I spoke to the bishop of the Diocese of Galveston and Houston.

Immediately, he said, "You've got to get back to high school, and I will pay for your tuition and transportation."

He supported me financially with the condition that every six weeks I would take him a report card. He would pay for me, but if I made too many Fs, he would drop me. He impressed on me that the seminaries demanded a high academic ability.

I entered an all-boys school run by religious Christian Brothers. They were fabulous teachers. They had a way of telling you things so you could immediately catch on. After classes and on Saturday mornings, they stayed in the classroom to help anyone needing additional assistance. The first year, I took advantage of that every day.

I decided to take Greek, Latin, Spanish, and English. I did not know the difference between a noun and a pronoun. But my language teachers were so good, I didn't have to take those languages in the seminary.

I made the honor roll the first six weeks. The bishop was very happy with me. I am eternally grateful to the brothers for the great support they gave me. I finished the seminary in seven rather than the usual eight years.

My father was an obstacle when I decided on the seminary. He had all kinds of dreams for me and was very apologetic that I had quit school because of him. His dream was that I be a doctor, a lawyer, or something, but not a priest.

He had had some problems with priests, especially in the area of discrimination. My father was a very light-complexioned man with red hair,

----

A young Patrick Flores, right, at a First Communion ceremony in 1944.
Photo courtesy Archbishop Patrick Flores

and he could pass as an Anglo anywhere. On the other hand, my mother was a brunette through and through. She could not deny she was a Mexican even if she had tried. In certain places, the whites sat in the front and the browns sat in the back of the church. Over that issue, my father had been turned off.

My mother continued going to church with us. My father would go only occasionally. His attitude was that priests were very unpopular because they were always bawling people out.

"Maybe that is their job," he would say, "but because of that, they don't have any friends."

That was his fear, that I wouldn't have any friends.

Our pastors were predominantly Spaniards and were very rough with us. He felt every priest had to be that way. For two years, he was so against it, he did not visit me at the seminary. He imagined it was similar to a penal institution.

When he did come to visit, of course, some of the students were singing, some were playing, and some were praying. He discovered we were acting as normal human beings. From then on, he was extremely supportive. Every visiting Sunday he was there.

My mother had tried to support me without my father knowing it. I admired the way they had always stood together. For two years, I would not accept anything from her. But after my father's conversion, I knew the gifts were from the two of them. And that was different.

We had a trailer to move around in. Some of the farms had little houses we moved into. Some farmers moved the cattle out of the barn so that we workers could move in. We had all kinds of living experiences.

For example, in our family we were brought up never to contradict or argue with an elder. In fact, we as kids would not enter a conversation when the older folks were talking. One time I did, and I was punished by my parents. I was ten or eleven.

We were in the Lubbock area picking cotton and living in a barn with a floor full of hay. We slept and ate there. At Christmas we went to a Catholic church. The priest gave a talk about Jesus being born in a stable. Jesus was poor, but Jesus never complained. The priest said we should not complain but be happy that we're alive.

When we went home to the barn, our neighbors, who were also cotton pickers, joined us. Mother had made chocolate and buñuelos, a Mexican dessert, to eat after the midnight service. The adults were commenting on what a good talk the priest had given and what he had said about Jesus being poor.

I entered the conversation uninvited and simply said that I did not like it, because Jesus was born in a stable but he didn't live in the stable all his life. As far as I could tell, Mary and Joseph then moved on.

My parents believed you should never contradict a priest. They did not believe in hitting us. One way they punished us was to make us stretch out our arms and kneel on the floor covered with cottonseeds. Talk about something painful. I had to kneel in a corner on seeds as a punishment for that.

Somewhere along the line, I was falling asleep, and they had compassion on me and let me go to bed. Years later I brought up the sermon again and that I thought they were wrong to punish me. We asked each other's forgiveness.

We never migrated out of Texas, and my parents were interested only in the cotton and corn crops. We generally were in the fields from the first of April until November. We were taken into the fields when we were quite young, five or six years of age. We were constantly challenged to be better at it.

We were paid by the pound. In the middle thirties, we earned thirty-five cents a hundred pounds cleaned. If you were a good cotton picker, you would pick three hundred pounds a day, so you worked for one dollar a day. A dollar then was a lot of money.

By the time we stopped picking cotton in the middle forties, it paid about one dollar a hundred pounds. We switched over to not have to pick it clean, so you could triple the amount you picked. The most I ever made a day picking cotton was four dollars. But way, way back, in a sense, that was a lot of money.

All the money the children made went to the family, but we were given back a little bit. We were told if we did well every day, on Saturday we would go to a movie or to a swimming pool. We also went to dances with other families in the backyards. We were always encouraged by looking forward to some function.

This was a seasonal job, and my parents were very conservative in their spending and their buying of clothing. I rarely got anything new; I knew I was going to get my older brothers' things the following year. My mother and sisters were good at sewing.

My parents believed if the girls were going to go to the fields, the boys also had to do the cooking, the washing, and the ironing. Everybody took turns cooking. And when it came time to do the washing, it didn't take us long because there would be six or seven scrubbing, rinsing, and hanging. Later, we had a little motor washing machine we carried with us. We took turns going to the machine from the fields to throw the dirty water out and put clean water in. The machine worked while we were working.

The same thing happened with ironing. We didn't have electric irons. We had the type that you have to warm on charcoal or on wood, warm up and clean and then do the ironing. When we improved our financial condition later on, we had two irons.

We had chickens and eggs, cows, and our own little vegetable garden with cabbages and radishes and whatever.

During the Depression days, when I was about six, the government was giving out baskets of food and goods. I remember one day this truck was coming toward our house, and my mother said, "Here they come. They're giving it away to everybody."

My father called my mother and said, "We do not want anything from them. We don't need it. The day that I take the government handouts, they will take away from me my last drop of dignity. As long as we can work, we're going to work for what we eat."

All of us heard that.

My father used to say, "It's not a punishment from God for us to have to work for what we eat. It is a way of letting us create our own lives."

And he used to say how boring life would be if everything was given to us. But we were very disappointed that my daddy would not accept the oranges and grapefruit they were giving away, because we didn't have that in our garden.

During those Depression days and my early childhood, we did not have a steak often or chicken every day. But we never skipped a meal, even though we were very poor. We had our own meat from our cows and calves and our own chickens and eggs. But we ate meat only on Sunday. The rest of the week it was rice, beans, tortillas, and eggs.

If we needed to buy aspirin, we would try to sell eggs or milk or home-made cheese or whatever we had available. We ground our own corn for cornmeal and used to exchange that, too, for something extra we needed.

Discrimination was a common practice in some places. Our family had a different phenomenon. We're a mixture because my father was very light and my mother was brunette. Some of my brothers and sisters are red-haired and freckled, and some are very light-complexioned with blondish hair. The other three of us are my color, and when we had hair, it was all very black. Three of us brothers were very good friends. But they were white, and I was brown.

When we were in places like Lubbock, Abernathy, and San Angelo, we'd go together to the movies. My brothers were told they could go sit downstairs, and I was told to sit upstairs. Sometimes my brothers would convince me not to say anything.

But sometimes I would ask, "Why?"

"Well, because Mexicans have to sit upstairs with the Blacks, and the whites sit downstairs."

And then I'd say, "We're all Mexicans. We're brothers."

Then all of us would have to sit upstairs.

In some swimming pools, if you were Black or Mexican, you couldn't get in at all. I think our biggest disappointment was after my mother and daddy had told us if we did well, we could go swimming on Saturday afternoon. When we got there, we were told we could not enter the pool. I could not stay quiet, although my brothers wanted me to.

I went ahead and said, "All of us are brothers, and we are Mexican Americans."

Discrimination also happened very often to us in restaurants. Some restaurants said, "We don't serve Mexicans," or "You have to go to the kitchen," or "We will sell it to you, but you can't eat it here. You can take it with you."

So we would eat outside or in the car.

When you are little, you don't question it. As you grow older, it gets you angry and you get into arguments.

I'd say, "I'm using American money. Isn't that what you take here? I take a bath; I don't stink. So why?"

Discrimination was especially hard to take when we were told, "You three can stay, but you two have to leave."

You don't want to betray your brothers, but yet you feel like you're betraying yourself if you accept that.

My father used to train and castrate farm animals and cut their horns. One time he was bounced into a fence by a bull and one of his lungs was crushed. He was flown from Lubbock to Galveston, where

---

he was in John Sealy Hospital for several months. My mother and half of the family went to be with him. Five of us stayed to finish the crop.

When we finished, we all got in the car around two o'clock in the morning to drive to Galveston. Finally, we stopped at a filling station and went into the restroom to wash ourselves. We had traveled all day and had the dog and cat with us.

We went into this little restaurant. My sister with the red hair was the oldest in the crowd and talked to the waitress.

The waitress pointed at me and said, "Honey, I'm sorry, but we don't serve Mexicans. So he can go to the kitchen and we can serve him there. But the rest of you can stay here."

Then my sister said, "We're brothers and sisters. We have the same mother and the same father. So we are just as Mexican as he is."

The waitress told her we'd all have to be served in the back. We decided to leave.

When we got into the car, my brothers started telling me, "It's your fault we didn't get to eat."

Archbishop Patrick Flores welcomes Pope John Paul II to San Antonio in 1987. *Photo courtesy Archbishop Patrick Flores*

I said, "It's not my fault. This is the way I am, and I can't change it."

They told me I should use some liquid to whiten myself. That was the first time I cried over it, because they were picking on me and we were hungry and tired.

We were in a Model A pulling a trailer and could only do twenty miles an hour. We got to Galveston at ten o'clock at night, and everything was closed. We couldn't see my father because it was after visiting hours. Finally, we found my mother, and she scrambled something for us to eat.

It wasn't until the end of World War II that my brothers, along with others who had come back, started legally fighting to eliminate discrimination.

Dan Jenkins swings a golf club for a photo in the Paschal High School yearbook.
Photo courtesy Dan Jenkins

BIRTH NAME	**DAN THOMAS JENKINS**
BORN	December 2, 1928, in Fort Worth to E. T. "Bud" Jenkins and Catherine O'Hern Jenkins
DIED	March 7, 2019
INTERVIEW	Juanita's, New York City, November 21, 1981

DAN JENKINS

An Old Typewriter from the Attic

S portswriter and author Dan Jenkins wrote more than five hundred articles for Sports Illustrated and contributed to Playboy, Golf Digest, and a host of other major publications. In the early 1970s, he produced the first of many popular novels, Semi-Tough, about professional football. In 1985 he began writing books full time. The 2014 His Ownself: A Semi-Memoir tells how Semi-Tough came to be written and published. For his six-decade career, he received both the PEN/ESPN Lifetime Achievement Award for Literary Sports Writing and the World Golf Hall of Fame's Lifetime Achievement Award in 2012. The next year, the Associated Press honored him with the Red Smith Award for his outstanding contribution to sports journalism. In 2017, he received the Ring Lardner Award for Excellence in Sports Journalism. Texas Christian University dedicated its football press box in Amon G. Carter Stadium to him, and the University of Texas at Austin created the Dan Jenkins Medal to be awarded annually to the country's outstanding sportswriter.

I was the only child of a mother and daddy who were divorced about thirty minutes after I was born, which is why my grandparents raised me. My grandparents were wonderful people who lived on the south side of Fort Worth, within sight of grain elevators and railroad tracks but near my aunt's drugstore and a golf course.

My grandmother lived to be ninety-six. She was born in Indian Territory, traveled in covered wagons. She was a very feminine lady, a nice lady that everybody loved. She was sweet to one and all, especially me. They don't make them like Mimmie anymore.

My mother lived on the same side of town. She had an antique business. I got all the money I needed from her, but I was too much of a problem for her to raise. She was working and agreed it was a good deal for my grandmother to raise me; and I did, too. I took advantage of it.

I could ride my bicycle from my grandparents' house to my mother's house in ten minutes. It was on the way to school even. I would occasionally spend weekends with my mother; I simply had two families.

My mother was eccentric and hilarious and had a good sense of humor. She enjoyed a joke. She was sick much of the time, but when she wasn't sick she was a good little spender. She liked nice things. She was the kind of person who would pick up the phone and say, "This is Catherine Jenkins. Send me a cab," and never tell the company her address. She expected the cab company to know it.

Catherine O'Hern Jenkins was widely traveled and had gone around the world when she was fourteen. She had a Packard convertible when everybody else had shoe soles. She was my Auntie Mame, I suppose. She had her antique shop and her bridge club and went to the theater and movies and went off to Chicago and New York to buy clothes and antiques. She made a lot of dough and managed to spend it all. She spent the last ten years inventing illnesses and going from doctor to doctor.

My dad was a bit of a rogue. He played golf every day and had about eight wives and drove with the top down. I think he married my mother because he thought she had money. I happened totally by accident, I think, and they dumped me at my "good" grandmother's doorstep and went separate ways, all of which was a good deal for me, actually.

My daddy had no influence on me at all. He was always a traveling salesman. He was the first to say that I was really lucky that he let his mother raise me, which is not to say he wasn't a good guy. He was.

I used to go to California in the summers when I was a little kid because my dad was out there working somewhere. My grandparents drove me to California for four straight summers. My aunt Sister worked in wardrobe at Paramount, so I was hanging around soundstages and watching movies being made when I was eight, nine, ten, eleven years old. I used to go over to a little diner just outside the Paramount gates and watch Jack Oakie and Gary Cooper eat a bowl of chili.

What made an impression on me in California was the palm trees, everybody's lawn being mowed, and double-dip ice cream cones. I had never seen double-dip ice cream cones in Texas. And very few platinum blondes.

I never worried about broken homes. My parents could have lived in a palace somewhere, and you couldn't have gotten me away from my grandmother's. There was never even a question that my grandparents loved me. It never came up.

I never said, "Where's Daddy? Where's Mommy?"

I kind of knew. From age five, my grandparents told me, "Your mother's busy and your daddy had to go to California, and here you are."

Looking back on it, I had the best of everything. I was practically born in my grandparents' house on Travis Avenue in South Fort Worth. It was a little white frame house with three bedrooms, which seemed huge at the time, in a nice neighborhood. My uncle Mack kept enlarging it.

During the Depression, relatives were in and out all the time. There were aunts and uncles and cousins sleeping over and staying over for weeks at a time.

Across the street lived my grandmother's sister, Inez, and my cousins Sid and Betty. Half a block up the street was another uncle and cousin. So it was a family compound. Aunt Inez owned a drugstore four blocks up the street, so I hung around the soda fountain, read comic books, talked sports with everybody.

Since I was the only little kid, I was terribly spoiled. This was the Depression, but it didn't seem bad at all to me. It was fun. We played football; we went to football and Texas League baseball games all the time.

Nobody was starving, and everybody had jobs. My granddaddy, Pap, was a barber, then a US deputy marshal.

They were all sports fans. There wasn't anything else to do except listen to soap operas on the radio, which I loved to do. I used to play sick and stay home and listen to *Vic and Sade* and *Pepper Young's Family*. And I went to movies—every movie that came along.

My dad was a golf nut, and my uncle played golf. So by the age of eight, I was out on the golf course, hanging around. When I was ten and wanted to play golf, my aunt gave me a set of lady's clubs. I'd get on my bicycle and pick up the golf clubs and ride a few blocks over to a nine-hole course that had sand greens. It was called Katy Lake. Ben Hogan learned to play golf there.

I was an ordinary student. Because I was such a sports fan, like all little kids, I kept scrapbooks. The newspaper would hit the front porch and I'd be up with a pair of scissors cutting out pictures of Southwest Conference football players before my grandparents could read the paper.

They did everything they could to stimulate my interest in whatever I was interested in. One day I found an old typewriter in the attic. It wouldn't work, but my aunt got it fixed for me. I wanted to be Clark Gable in those movies where he had a press card in his hatband. I started making up sports stories on the typewriter because I thought I could do it better than the newspapers.

My house was headquarters. All the kids were hanging out at my house because it was a friendly house. Everybody else had parents who were a pain in the ass. They didn't want kids hanging around, and their mothers always had headaches. But in my house, we always had food. I could bring the whole football team in the living room, and my grandmother would feed them. I realized later that the reason they encouraged me to hang around the house was because they wanted to know where I was.

Nobody in my family had gone to college—ever. And they said, "Well, you do what you want to. Be a newspaperman or be a golfer, but you will go to college. You're going to be the first one."

So I had no choice. I knew I was not going to let them down. I was going to get a college degree—for them if for no other reason.

I thought about becoming a professional golfer. When I was sixteen, seventeen, eighteen years old, I was going around winning little local tournaments. But then I found some guys who could really play, and I knew I was never going to be that good.

Since I was on the basketball team in high school, I got special treatment. Athletes always got special treatment. We had two lunch periods and the right study halls, and some of us had cars.

My first car was a 1936 Ford roadster. Convertible, rumble seat. My uncle gave it to me. I got that car in the ninth grade, and I was the only one who had a car then. It's still the best car I ever owned, although the girls didn't swoon over it, because it wasn't air-conditioned. When they started making new air-conditioned cars after the war in '46, I traded it in on a four-door Ford that was air-conditioned. It was the biggest mistake I ever made.

I can remember my grandmother trying to introduce me to religion. She took me downtown to a Baptist church. Here I was eight or nine years old, and it was hot. They didn't have air-conditioning. They had those old folding chairs, and they had huge crowds. Here would be this silly son of a bitch up there at the pulpit screaming to everybody, telling them they're going to hell.

I was sitting there thinking, "I'm only eight years old. Why am I going to hell? I didn't do anything. Why are these people buying that shit?"

That alone taught me he was an idiot, and my grandparents agreed. That's all I needed to know about religion. But they kind of wanted me to go to Sunday school and learn some history. So I did that some, and then that got boring. I would have kept going if they hadn't made it boring. My mother was Catholic. I tried that. But they didn't want to speak in English. What the hell did Latin mean in Fort Worth?

June and Dan Jenkins at New York City's 21 Club. *Photo courtesy Dan Jenkins*

Everybody had servants' quarters in the garage or apartment above you. We had a Black couple living in back of us. They had a lot to do with raising me. There was never any question about prejudice. I certainly knew they were Black, and I just thought this was unfortunate. They really got a bad deal is what I thought.

Warner and Florence were part of the family, and we all sat at the kitchen table together. They lived there just to have a place to live. Warner took care of the yard, and Florence did a lot of the cooking and cleaning. I was outraged the first time I ever heard anybody say anything derogatory about a Black, because those were my friends. It's hard to explain, but later I realized I was unique in that sense. Their church was the only church I ever went to that was fun. They used to take me to the Black church because they had blues singers.

There were other families on the same block who made the Blacks go to the back door. The mother of one of my best friends once told him that a "Negro" woman was not a lady. The first time he told me that, I was twelve years old, and I said, "Well, your mother is a fucking idiot."

We fought, and I'm sure he won.

In 1935, when I was seven years old and going to TCU football games, I saw Sam Baugh and people like that who were All-Americans. TCU was number one and won the national championship. In 1938, TCU won the national championship again with Davey O'Brien. TCU was only a few blocks from my house, and here we had the best football team in the world. Makes you arrogant is what it does. And then I started hearing about Ben Hogan and Byron Nelson being the greatest golfers in the world, and they're from Fort Worth.

I thought I was living in the sports capital of the universe, not just the US. It had a great effect on me.

I made my commitment to be a writer in junior high. I knew what I was going to do. I worked on the paper at Paschal High School, though I fancied myself as an athlete. My love for writing certainly didn't come from my family. It looked like a lot of fun, and maybe I'm a natural-born gossip or snoop.

I wrote a story in the high school paper, the *Pantherette*, making fun of all the local sportswriters. Blackie Sherrod read it and thought it was funny, and he hired me for the *Fort Worth Press*, the old Scripps Howard paper and the second paper in town. Blackie is my godfather.

Two weeks out of high school, I had my own byline in the local paper, where I thought I was really big stuff. So I was already a grizzled veteran in the newspaper business before I ever started college. At Texas Christian University, I semi-studied journalism. I mainly studied English and history and stuff like that, because I already had the newspaper job I wanted when I graduated from college. I was very lucky.

So I'd get up at five o'clock in the morning, go to the paper, and write eighteen thousand words. Then I'd go to TCU and go to class, maybe for half the day, and then I'd go to the Worth Hills Golf Course and play golf and hustle all afternoon. Then I'd go wherever I had to be that night, a game or a banquet or whatever. So I spent the next fifteen years sleeping about two hours a night and writing four million words, making $37.50 a week.

Nobody ever told me, "Don't try this," or "You can't do that." Certain things were just expected, and that was it. I didn't get whippings, except from coaches. I didn't need them. I knew what was right and what was wrong. I don't know why. I guess I lived by example.

My grandparents told me, "You're born, you're going to work hard at what you like, get educated, and have a happy life."

If you've ever been raised right and had the right influences in your life, you know about work. I had great coaches who really taught me discipline. I'm talking about kick-ass, whoop-ass discipline. My coach in high school, Charlie Turner, knew my background, knew I was a grandmother's boy, and he was going to whip me into shape. He did, and I learned from it.

And Blackie Sherrod was a real taskmaster. He'd say, "Write the column, then write the lead story, give me three shorts, give me four headlines, and then you can go to breakfast."

I learned to do all that in about an hour. I work well under deadline pressure. It's all I've ever done. I would never give up being a journalist. If I were F. Scott Fitzgerald, I'd still be writing about sports occasionally. On deadline.

Samuel W. Lewis Jr., just under two years old. *Photo courtesy Samuel W. Lewis Jr.*

BIRTH NAME	**SAMUEL WINFIELD LEWIS JR.**
BORN	October 1, 1930, in Houston to Samuel Winfield Lewis and Sue Roselle Hurley Lewis
DIED	March 10, 2014
INTERVIEW	American embassy, Tel Aviv, Israel, July 12, 1982

AMBASSADOR SAMUEL W. LEWIS JR.
An Early Wanderlust

T he diplomacy of Samuel W. Lewis Jr. laid the groundwork for Menachem Begin and Anwar Sadat to sign the Camp David Accords, receive the Nobel Peace Prize, and ink a historic treaty between Israel and Egypt in 1978. After graduating from Yale in 1952 and earning a master's degree from Johns Hopkins University School of Advanced International Studies in 1954, he joined the Foreign Service and began his career as a consular officer in Naples, Italy. He also served in Brazil and Afghanistan and held positions in Washington, DC, before becoming the assistant secretary of state for international organization affairs in 1975. From 1977 to 1985, he was the second longest serving ambassador to Israel. In 2011, the US Institute of Peace dedicated the Samuel W. Lewis Hall. He sat on the US Advisory Council of the Israel Policy Forum and was a board member of the American Academy of Diplomacy.

I was a city kid from Houston, but there was a big woods about a block from my house. I spent a lot of time in the woods, which now is the Texas Southern University campus. I used to climb and dig caves and fortifications and have wars with other gangs of boys. We did the things you do in the woods when you're a kid, but it was a very urban situation.

My first horse ride was on a Shetland pony at Hermann Park in Houston when I was about four. They had a pony ring there. I still have a picture of me on that horse, and I looked quite terrified.

I was born on Isabella Street in Houston about fifteen blocks east of Main Street. I went to Sutton Elementary School and to what was then Albert Sidney Johnston Junior High and then to San Jacinto High School. I transferred to Lamar High School and finished there.

I was a fat child and wasn't terribly good at athletics, and I wasn't a very good fighter. But since I was fat, I could kind of sit on people and keep them down. As a teenager, I got fairly skinny.

I was always a big reader. And I guess I was pretty bookish, but I also got along pretty well with the fellows on the block.

I never liked hunting. I've always had a soft spot for animals. I went dove hunting a few times as a teenager and deer hunting once or twice. I could never bring myself to shoot a deer. They're too nice alive.

But I did a lot of fishing. My grandmother on my mother's side had a little cottage at Red Bluff on Galveston Bay. One of the high points of my youth, particularly before World War II, was going down there a lot in the summer and sometimes on weekends through the year. Dad taught me to fish. And I learned to swim and became very fond of the water, something that has stayed with me ever since.

My mother's name was very unusual, Sue Roselle, which was a combined name of two of her ancestors, Ellen and Rosa. Her father was an insurance man in Houston. Her father had originally come from Baltimore and went to Houston via Galveston.

My father's name was Samuel, and I'm a junior. He was a Kentuckian. The Lewises trace our family way back to about the 1600s, when they left France. They first went to Wales, and then three brothers went to Virginia in the 1700s. One of the brothers ultimately ended up in Kentucky in the 1800s, and Dad was raised on a farm near Fort Knox. The farm was taken over by the army during World War I.

Dad could no longer be a farmer, so he went to Dallas to work. A few years later, he moved to Houston, where he met my mother. He was always a farmer at heart. He was really a country boy who had been transferred to the city. Dad was terrific any time we could get away with friends for a vacation to a ranch in West Texas. Sometimes we visited relatives on farms in Kentucky.

I was especially close with my father. For one thing, I was an only child, and he and mother poured a lot of their hopes into me. But besides that, I was born in 1930, and Dad's business collapsed about 1929 in the Great Depression. He never really got back on his feet financially. Dad tried many different businesses throughout the thirties and forties. Sometimes he would get on his feet for a while, but he never really found his niche in life. He kept his office at home most of the time, so he was home a lot and looked after me a great deal.

As a result, Dad did a lot of things with me that he wouldn't have been able to do if he'd been earning more money. For example, when I was in Cub Scouts, Dad was the den father. We had a much more interesting den as a result, because he was one of those people who could do anything with his hands—plumbing, heating, carpentry, repairs, machinery, anything of that sort. He was terrific at handling boys. All the boys in the neighborhood loved him.

In dealing with me, my mother was gentle, and she read to me a lot. She was a sweet person. But she could be firm, although they usually left punishment for Dad. He was the one to get the switch. I got switched a lot. We had some bushes right outside the screen porch that were very effective for switching.

Mother was one of the first women graduates of Rice Institute in the teens. She went to work for the Harris County Welfare Office in Houston and then switched to the Texas State Welfare Department, where she was the director. It had several hundred employees, and she was in charge of old-age assistance, aid to dependent children and the blind.

Her titles changed, and she was the state area supervisor for several counties. So she was one of the women executives during a period when there weren't all that many in Texas.

To me, Texas is a lot of things. Houston is flat, and I think of the flatness of the Gulf Coast. I think of pine trees and bayous. As a Boy

Earning the Eagle Scout rank is a proud moment for Samuel Lewis Jr.
and his father, right. *Photo courtesy Samuel W. Lewis Jr.*

Scout, I spent a lot of time fishing in dirty bayous for crawfish and going camping amid mosquitoes in East Texas. I also think of the sky because of my times in West Texas. One of my images of Texas is the cloud formations coming across vast stretches of landscape, horizons that have nothing but horizon.

Sometimes we used to visit a family who had a ranch near Blanco out in the Hill Country. A marvelous little creek ran down at the foot of the hill below the house. In the summer, Dad would buy these big watermelons and we'd put them in the cold water of the spring. They didn't have a refrigerator at the ranch. On a very hot day, it would be marvelous to sit down there and fish out the watermelons and eat them on the side of the spring. That's the kind of image I retained.

I had a very happy childhood. I liked Houston; I liked my friends. But I always had a wanderlust. I always wanted to see more of the world, and I wanted to get away from Texas and see some other cultures.

My wanderlust probably came from listening to stories about an ambassador in the diplomatic service. The stories came from the ambassador's friend, who was also a family friend of Dad's, a librarian at Rice University. She was a great traveler and would go on trips to Venezuela and Turkey and all around and visit her friend. Then she would come back, and we would sit around after dinner, and she would tell stories about what diplomatic life was like and about the countries she'd visited.

That's where I first got the thought of diplomatic service. But it was only after I was at Yale that I began to think about it seriously. From the time I was six or seven, I read history books almost as if they were novels. I think reading the history of other countries got me interested in seeing them someday.

We had some marvelous times at Galveston on the Gulf. Dad and Mother liked to camp, and we spent the night on the beach when I was a kid. We couldn't afford to do much. We had an old car, but we would drive on Saturday morning down to Galveston and way out West Beach, where it was really deserted, with nothing but sand dunes and sky. Nobody else was around.

We would spend the day and then put out some cots and sleep under the stars. We swam in the middle of the night, which was scary and quite exciting for a little kid. We had a little rowboat, and we used to go to the oyster reefs out in the bay. The big objective was to catch speckled trout. Dad was a wonderful fisherman. Sometimes we used to go out on the deep-sea fishing boats to the red snapper banks about fifty miles out in the Gulf.

One of the worst experiences of my life was the first time I went deep-sea fishing. I was about thirteen, and I'd never really been out in the Gulf very far before. We drove down to Galveston. The boat left at five o'clock in the morning, but we got there quite early. We brought along a big lunch and we were hungry, so we ate a lot of fried chicken and stuff.

About thirty miles out, we really got into some rough water, and I got seasick. It went on and on and it was only nine o'clock, and we weren't going to be back until six o'clock. I thought there was no way I was going to be able to live through that day. We got out to the banks, and I was lying on the deck throwing up every two minutes.

The fishermen threw out their lines, and somebody finally persuaded me to sit up long enough to hold a handline that was going quite deep.

I immediately caught a huge red snapper and somehow got it on deck. Just as I pulled it up over the rail, I threw up all over the fish. I really thought that was the worst day of my life.

My love of the ocean is one of the major things in my life. It started with those experiences on Galveston Beach. Since then, we've lived all over the world, and we've been to some spectacular beaches. For example, we lived in Rio de Janeiro on the ocean, one of the most beautiful beaches anywhere.

Later we went back to Galveston, and the sand was kind of brown and the water was kind of dirty, and it didn't look like I remembered. But nonetheless, in my memory, there was nothing like it.

I felt that somehow I had to be very Texan to stake out my own identity.

My professional role model was my mother's brother, Frank Hurley, who was a college professor at Rice University and later was a chemist at Case Western Reserve.

Frank was the one who really introduced me to books and art. He was a great art collector and used to insist on taking me to museums and concerts when I was a little kid. I thought I wanted to be a chemical engineer like him. Dad was just anxious for me to go to college because that was his great objective.

It was Frank who said, "Look, you want to go away to college. You don't want to go to Rice, although you've got straight As. Why don't you apply to some Ivy League schools, because they have a lot of money for scholarships."

So I applied to Harvard, Yale, Princeton, Columbia, and Cornell at his suggestion. In those days, there weren't too many Texans who wanted to go east to college, so the competition was probably easier than today. I got scholarships from several of them and blindly picked Yale. I didn't know what I was getting into.

When I went off to Yale, I was nervous and unsure. I didn't know what to expect from all these Ivy League characters and prep school products. I felt that somehow I had to be very Texan to stake out my own identity. So I took to college with me a skeleton of a steer head with horns that

I found out on a ranch. I had it up on the wall with a big Texas flag in my room. I was a professional Texan for my first year at Yale.

I also took cowboy boots with me, and my first Christmas there we had twenty inches of snow. Only once had I seen two inches of snow in Houston. So a bunch of us went out caroling and snowballing and romping around in the snow, and all I had were these cowboy boots. Most of the snow got inside my boots, and I almost lost both feet from frostbite.

That was an aberration in my history, but something about the Texan accent and manner is rather unique. Basically, I think Texans think they ought to behave like Texans.

When Lyndon Johnson was president in 1967, '68, I was assigned to the White House by the State Department. Johnson's staff in the White House—secretaries, messengers, officials—were practically all Texans.

When I'd been there about three days, I discovered when I called somebody in the White House to ask for an appointment or something, it worked a lot better if my Texas accent came back.

By the end of the Johnson administration, I was very Texan again just because it was functional.

Ambassador Samuel W. Lewis Jr. with President Jimmy Carter at the White House, May 1977. *Photo by Jack E. Kightlinger, Jimmy Carter's Presidential Photographs, White House Staff Photographers Collection, National Archives*

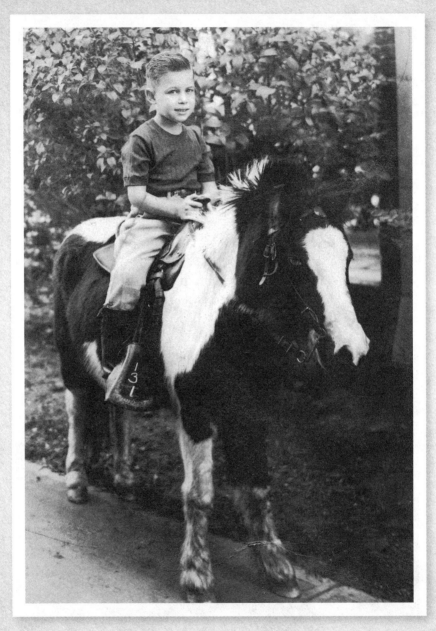

Les Wilk as a child. *Photo courtesy Les Wilk*

BIRTH NAME	**LES NORMAN WILK**
BORN	August 21, 1931, in Houston to Benjamin Wilk and Bess Caplan Wilk
DIED	November 21, 1995
INTERVIEW	Four Seasons Plaza Nacional Hotel, San Antonio, Texas, February 27, 1982

18

....

LES WILK
Educated in a Fine Ladies' Shop

L es Wilk set the pace for the state's fashion industry from 1969 to 1993. Wilk designed costumes for NBC's Comedy Hour *before working for several firms in Dallas and launching his own. Wilk was best known for attire worn by Miss Texas and Miss America contestants, and he designed wardrobes for the winners of the state pageant for fifteen years. In 1981, he became director of the Southwest Institute of Design at Texas Woman's University, and the university's Texas Woman's Collection houses more than one hundred examples of his creations. He and his students outfitted the state's popular female governor, Ann Richards, and Second Lady Jan Bullock for the 1991 inauguration using Texas textiles. He was the first Dallas designer to be the guest designer at the couture show at the Dallas Apparel Mart and was named one of America's Ten Great Designers by the apparel mart's "Decasalon" National Preview of Designer Collections.*

My parents had a little grocery store on Schwartz Street in Houston's Fifth Ward. I was the oldest child and a Depression baby born in 1931.

I came from a large Orthodox Jewish family, and most of them migrated out of the Fifth Ward into other areas of Houston, but my grandparents still lived there. Like many a family during the Depression, we had to move back with my grandparents. My father was the oldest child of three brothers and two young sisters, and we all lived in this big, old, wonderful house until I was five.

At the time, I was the only child, so I was the grandbaby and the nephew. My aunts were very young, as aunts go, and I was like a toy for them. We had a wonderful time playing.

It was very Orthodox, and they never cooked on the Sabbath. Grandfather Sam Wilk lived within the synagogue. As a child, I remember hard wooden pews in the little synagogue. It was so Orthodox the men did not sit with the women. My mother and grandmothers always kept a religious house.

All religious holidays were very boring and very dull for me as a child. You sat at the table and you listened to prayers and started worrying that you were going to fall asleep. The most vivid thing I remember is that my grandmother never sat at the table and ate. She was always too busy serving everybody else.

My grandfather had been a blacksmith when he came to this country from Russia. Later my grandmother Rachel and father came over with a younger son, who died on the way. They ended up dairy farmers.

I never could figure out what my grandfather really did. He was a blacksmith and had a dairy farm, but he owned lots of rent property, too. He signed his name with an X and never learned to read or write English. He communicated in half Yiddish and half English.

My grandparents never told me much about Russia and Poland. But I remember my grandmother saying she met my grandfather at the altar. It was an arranged marriage, of course, but they loved each other, because that was taken for granted.

My mother's maiden name was Caplan. Her father died when she was about seven. She had two sisters and one brother. She came from an Orthodox family, too. Her uncle on that side was a hazan, a cantor, in Dallas for many, many years. So there was quite a lot of Orthodoxy there.

———

The great-grandparents on my mother's side died within hours of each other. He was ill in the hospital and died, and she was home and died within hours after he died. It was like ESP, which was a beautiful way for two people who had spent all that many years together.

We used to go visit and play with cousins in the Third Ward. There was a lot of family closeness in my raising. When we moved out of the Fifth Ward, we moved to Isabella Street. We were surrounded by aunts and uncles and cousins. Then my grandparents moved about three blocks away from us.

Finally, when I was about six, I had a younger brother born, Edward. They taught us, "Don't get in trouble; be good always."

One of the most fun memories was going out to the end of Main Street to the pony ring and riding the ponies. It had Shetland ponies, which the adults walked around in this ring while the kids rode. I used to love to go out there and ride around that ring. One pony jumped the fence with me and drug me through a parking lot. I remember being in the hospital, being sewn up. For years they would never let me back on a horse for fear I'd fall off. I don't remember having cowboy boots. I rode in jodhpurs and knee boots.

My introduction into fashion was through my mother, Bess, because she was quite a fashion-conscious woman. She loved to go to town and shop, and she always used to dress me up and take me with her.

I'd wear short pants, berets, and white shoes, the whole thing. We have lots of pictures of me dressed up from the machines where you drop in a quarter and they give you three shots taken in a little booth. And we've also got some urchin-looking ones not taken on shopping trips. In those I am barefoot and wearing those short pinafore things.

We rode the streetcar downtown in Dallas. I remember I had X amount of money, and I brought back everybody a souvenir. For a nickel, I got salt and pepper shakers from Dallas for everybody. To this day, they've all got a thing for salt and pepper shakers.

My mother was a beautiful, beautiful lady and very active. She had dark, dark-brown eyes. She had long, deep-auburn hair, and for many years the pictures showed her hair to her waistline. She wore it in braids or pulled back in a bun. I remember her coming home after going to the beauty parlor and having her hair cut. The hairdresser had said to her, "You look like an old covered wagon."

My father, Benjamin, was extremely handsome, and he had blue, blue eyes. They were a beautiful couple. I remember happiness, their being well liked and having company over.

My mother became very ill. She had cancer as a very young woman. She got it in her early thirties and passed away in her middle forties. We were very, very close, and I was able to drive the car for her.

After surgery she had scars over her left shoulder and on her arm, so she couldn't wear a lot of things. Here was a clothes fanatic with this problem. So I used to go shopping with her. I used to drive her to Frost Bros. Some of the ladies there would stick you in the back room and say, "Well, how about this one or that one?"

We used to buy things, and we'd adapt them. For the swimsuits, we'd buy fabric and make one-shoulder cover-ups. We'd buy swim caps with rubber flowers all over, so she could have a swimsuit and a one-shoulder garland. So I became more involved in fashion the more I went through this misfortune. It gave me a big education in the back rooms of ladies' shops.

During the war, we moved to San Antonio when I was eleven. I was asthmatic, and Houston was terrible for me. Doctors told my parents to take me to either Phoenix or San Antonio.

We went on the train, and it was packed with soldiers. I'll never forget when we got to Flatonia between San Antonio and Houston. The train stopped, and they hollered, "Flatonia." I thought that was where we were moving.

We moved on Primera Drive in Alamo Heights and later to Mulberry Avenue. My father opened a scrapyard on the West Side.

I was still in knickers and so self-conscious because in Houston there were lots of knickers, but not in San Antonio. I remember saying, "I'm not wearing knickers anymore."

Houston schools must have been ahead of San Antonio, because I skipped a grade, which put me out of high school at seventeen.

As a kid, I was an artist. My mother could draw beautifully, and my aunt Rachel in Dallas was an artist and a fashion designer. She and my aunt Janet had very natural hands. Since I was asthmatic, I was forced to stay inside on rainy days and not do lots of things. I was kept busy by the force of my mother with a pencil and paper in my hand. It's lucky I liked drawing.

To be an artist, you have to be a little bit of a daydreamer. Not that you intend to, but you sometimes live in a world of your own. I was going to be a designer. When I was in junior high school, I wrote a theme on how I was going to be a fashion designer. I was already designing fashions.

I went to painting classes at the Witte Museum and took two buses to get there. They used to have little exhibits on the grounds and hung the pictures on clotheslines. I had a really steady art background.

I didn't learn to sew until I was in college, but I could sit down with a needle and thread and put something together if we had to make costumes for plays and puppet shows.

I remember in junior high having a teacher who was very inspiring and who encouraged me to do more with my art. Another teacher discouraged me from being in the art field because she felt it was a waste of time and certainly not a profession you go to college for.

But I did anyway.

Designer Les Wilk dressed Miss America contestants as well as Texas Governor Ann Richards. *Photo courtesy Les Wilk*

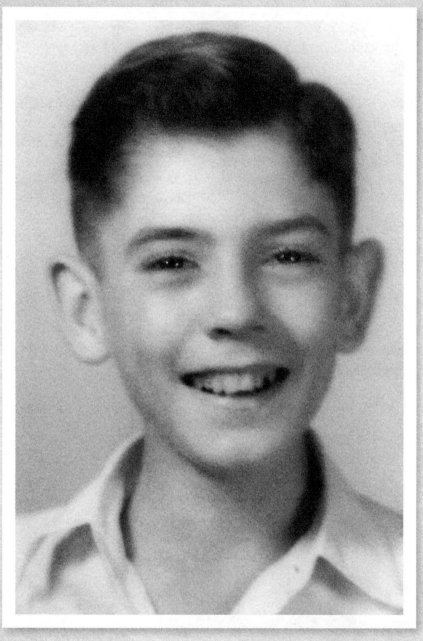

Dan Rather in elementary school, ca. late 1930s. *Dan Rather Collection, Howard Gotlieb Archival Research Center at Boston University*

BIRTH NAME	**DAN IRVIN RATHER**
BORN	October 31, 1931, in Wharton to Daniel Irvin Rather and Veda Byrl Page Rather
INTERVIEW	CBS News, New York City, May 3, 1982

....

19

DAN RATHER

Respect for the Land

Houston *broadcast journalist Dan Rather caught the attention of CBS News while covering Hurricane Carla in 1961. His reporting on the Kennedy assassination in 1963 led to the network assigning him to the White House. He went to China with President Nixon and covered Watergate and the president's resignation. He became a correspondent for the long-running* 60 Minutes *and a war correspondent in Vietnam. In 1981 he succeeded legendary newsman Walter Cronkite, the face of* CBS Evening News. *Inducted into the Television Hall of Fame in 2004, he also received numerous Emmy and Peabody Awards beginning in the 1970s for CBS News and ending in 2004 for* 60 Minutes II, *"Abuse at Abu Ghraib." After retiring as managing editor and anchor of* CBS Evening News *in 2005, he hosted* Dan Rather Reports *and* The Big Interview with Dan Rather *on AXS TV. In 2017 he created News and Guts, a news, media, and production company.*

From early memories, I can smell the beach at Galveston very strongly. I have vivid mental images of walking that beach with my mother and father and swimming with my father in the surf.

My father hunted some, ducks and quail, but he was much bigger on fishing. I can remember the flats at Port O'Connor and the salt air and the shrimp smells and those nice speckled trout and occasionally a redfish. I walked those flats with my father. He loved fishing.

We used to go to my grandmother's place in Bloomington, which is down near Victoria. I can smell that rich, black land as vividly as I can smell the sea, the salt air of Galveston.

Our grandfather Page was a blacksmith, among other things, and he would tell all the tales about the Pages—that's my mother's family—coming from Indiana to Texas well before the turn of the century. I couldn't have been more than seven or eight, but I remember very well saying, "Why did they come here?"

And he reached down to the land, the really deep, black soil that's down there. That rich land is why they came.

When I was fourteen, I worked as a brush cutter at Nacogdoches. That thick forest and the smell of the pine, I can smell to this day. I remember taking a deep breath of all those pine needles deep in the brush of Nacogdoches.

I worked one summer on a derrick out near Midland-Odessa. We stayed in Odessa. We had to work a lot of the time with wet kerchiefs over our noses. The smell of that dust is something I can smell from time to time. All these things are tied to land—pine trees, salt air, the wonderful, long beach at Galveston and the black loam in Bloomington. When you're from Texas, you share a respect for the land. No one can understand Texas and not understand how closely people are tied to the land. There's land everywhere.

I was blessed in having a steady family—a mother and father, first and only marriage. That's an asset and not everybody has that.

My father's name was Daniel Irvin. They named me Dan because he didn't want me to be a junior. Irvin is the name of a doctor who did something for our family before the turn of the century. Nobody knows what. My mother's name was Veda Byrl. She went by Byrl, and my father went by Irvin.

My father was five feet, eleven inches and about 165 pounds, with fairly dark black hair and features very much like my own. He had what would now be called good upper-body strength. He had a front tooth knocked out when he rode a horse under a chinaberry tree and didn't duck. Dentistry then was not what it is now. So he had a gold-colored tooth on one front side, which was not that noticeable.

I was as close to my father as I was to my mother. We were a close family, but I think every family thinks that they're close. Yet my father was not always home. He got up early and generally was at work certainly by six thirty or six forty-five in the morning. He very seldom got home until 7:30 or 8:00 p.m. Despite this, I was around him a lot.

I wouldn't see him before I went to school because he'd be gone. One night he came home just exhausted. His khakis were soaked through several times over, and you could see the white salt. That's one of my first memories of my father.

Dan Rather reporting for CBS News at the Democratic National Convention at Madison Square Garden, New York, August 1980. *Photo by Robert McNeely, Robert McNeely Photographic Archive, Briscoe Center for American History, University of Texas at Austin*

If you asked twenty people who knew my father, they would say, "Well, he was a hard worker and good talker." My mother was quieter. She was marvelously determined in a quiet way. She had absolute, fierce loyalty.

My first memory of my mother is her telling me that she loved me. I don't think I was even in school the first time I remember she said she loved me. And I know exactly where she said it—in the kitchen. I know exactly where I was going, which was next door, where there was a vacant lot and a swing. And before going out, she hugged me. My mother was big on hugging. She told me she loved me, and then I went out to the swing.

My mother felt strongly about being home when we got home from school. She had a lot of jobs over the years, particularly when I was very young. She worked hard, but I don't remember a time when she wasn't there when I left in the morning and when I got home from school. Whatever her work was, she managed that.

She did other things, too. She did waitressing and she worked for department stores. She worked for a while in a little office up on Shepherd Drive. My mother worked hard at home, too. Every morning my father went off in clean and freshly ironed khakis. That's a lot of work; you're talking about a hand-washing operation on a rub board. What a marvel it was when we got a washing machine, a Maytag, in 1939. The neighbors came from several blocks around to see this thing.

My father was an avid newspaper reader. I have a memory of sometimes getting up for a glass of milk maybe at two o'clock, and he'd be up reading. For somebody who worked as hard as he did and always got up early, that was extraordinary.

He read a lot of newspapers from front to back. He read the editorials, and he'd read columns. God help you, he knew everything in the classified ads. In a way, he had a good sense of prices. He knew what an old icebox was worth. My mother read quite a bit, too. She'd glance at the newspaper, but she was more of a book reader.

My being born in Wharton was an accident. My father was working in a pipe gang at the time. They started in Refugio and from there moved to Victoria, El Campo, or Edna and then to Wharton, Richmond, and Rosenberg. Then they moved into Houston. He and my mother had been married in Victoria.

There was always a pipeline running from some place to another. You'd build the pipeline toward the refineries up in Houston and the coast. Then they'd go out and build another pipeline. My mother and father were living in Wharton simply because that was the base out of which he was working, and I was born there.

They moved me from Wharton before I was a year old. We went directly to the Houston Heights. It's hard to get a vision of Houston in those times. The Heights Annex was a neighborhood in Houston, but it was out a bit. We were at the edge of the city limits. Today it would be called the suburbs. But I smile when I say that, and I laugh because it had no relationship either in look or atmosphere to what we call suburbs today. It was kind of half country, half town.

There were woods behind Buffalo Bayou right behind us. The woods were thick and deep within a quarter mile of our place. There was a big field between our place and the woods. We'd run and play in the thicket, and we rode on softshell turtles the size of number twelve washtubs. We'd track a turtle, wrestle it, and ride it and pretend we were slaying dragons. One big one took three other boys and me a whole day to catch. Then we took him home and Mom put him in a trough.

When Daddy came home at ten thirty that night, he first congratulated us on our triumph. Then he gingerly switched his tone to point out this was a living thing, and what should we do with it? We took it back to the bayou.

My mother was deathly afraid of me drowning in the bayou. Every year somebody drowned in the bayou. She forbade us to swim in it, but, of course, we did anyway. Buffalo Bayou is life and death to Houston. The water rises and falls so fast, it's transient. It came in our house once and often covered the field. The Johnny Cash song with the line "How high's the water, Mama?" means a lot to me. I can remember Daddy asking the same thing.

We lived in the house at 1432 Prince Street for all of my youth. Somebody opened a beer joint at the corner of our street down a block and a half. From that moment on, my mother felt that was not a good atmosphere for my sister. There are six and a half years difference between me and my brother, Don, and my sister, Patricia, is eight years younger. She eventually got the family moved to Garden Oaks.

I remember family discussions and my father saying, "Hell, we don't have any money to move anywhere. What are you talking about? This is where we live. Why do we want to move?"

This place in Garden Oaks was by far the biggest financial decision in the family's history. We bought this place, I believe, for $6,200. I don't remember details, but we had to get together something like $400 for the down payment. Everybody in the family struggled hard to get the down payment. We moved my second year of college.

A trip to Beaumont was a big trip for us. I don't think my mother or father had ever been out of the state until they took a trip to Mexico in about 1937, '38. I think they went to Monterrey. They brought me back one of those straw horses with a Mexican cowboy on it, which was a very dear possession of mine for a long time.

Then later, right after the war, they went to New Orleans. For us that was like going to Bombay or Nigeria. It was a long trip.

We were Baptist, hard-shell Baptist. My father didn't like church. He would go, but he was tough to get to church. He didn't especially like preaching. My father was a believer in prayer. He taught that, but not in a heavy-handed way. We had devotionals at home. One of the things I learned from him is to not confuse what you believe, what you honestly believe, with what people say you ought to believe. He taught me that faith is a very personal, individual matter.

I remember when the preachers would come to visit, usually from the West Fourteenth Avenue Baptist Church. We had a succession of pastors there. If my father knew the preacher was coming, he'd leave. But if he happened to be there when the preacher came, he would go out the back door. We had a little toolshed in the back, and he'd stay in there until the preacher left.

Mother was very good about getting us to church, and I went fairly regularly. This was your fundamental, total-immersion Baptist church. I was baptized there. Some of my Sunday school teachers were big influences on me. When I was a teenager, all the good-looking girls went to the large Baptist Temple up in the center of Heights. So I went there sometimes. I guess the Lord forgave me for that. For all I know, he led me there.

We didn't have any foot washing and there never was any snake chunking, but we had nearly everything else. From time to time, the tent preachers would come, which is a pretty big local event where people would come whether they were religious or not.

My grandmother Page lived out in the country. Grandma Page would say, "Is he going to chunk snakes? If there's going to be snake chunking, I'm not going."

They didn't do it regularly, but there had been a revival preacher come through from Tennessee, and he led the snake chunking, his technique for "testing faith." Nobody ever forgot it.

___

Before I was even in school, I went to work with my father. One time they had a leak in some pipeline. It was on a weekend. I sat on the back of the gang truck in what was called the "bear trap." All the men were stripped to the waist working in this ditch, which got progressively deeper and deeper, and they were soon in over their heads. They dug that whole day. They just kept going down deeper into the ground. It was frightening at that age to see my father going deeper into the ground.

They really worked hard and had what was called water discipline. You couldn't get a drink of water just anytime you wanted it. You'd drink once every two hours, and then maybe take a five-minute break and go back to the ditch.

My father also worked as a lineman. When the oil company put in its pipeline, it put in its own telephone line with its own poles and insulators. The lineman was a regular member of the pipe gang.

Dad worked for Houston Oil for twenty years, then he worked for Humble for almost twenty years—'Umble Oil. Nobody ever said Humble. You'd immediately be pegged as some easterner if you said Humble Oil. I remember a big family council and my mother crying over the big decision when he left Houston Oil.

When I was maybe eight or nine, he got a call about trouble on the line. His job was to find the trouble and fix it. We were down between Edna and Wharton, some no-blinker-light town. We drove at night in driving rain. The wind was blowing off the coast. The rain was coming sideways, and the windshield wipers were barely going back and forth. It seemed we drove forever, and we got there sometime well after midnight. It was dark and raining like hell.

We drove up to this telephone pole with one crossbar and an insulator on either side. The wire was down. My father put on climbing hooks that strap on and his waist safety belt.

He said, "Come on. You can grunt for me."

People who work on the ground for linemen are called grunts. He climbed this pole. He had a rope with a little bucket on it and a little pulley. He sent the bucket down and he said, "Get me a crescent wrench."

I put the wrench in the bucket and he took the bucket up. The rain got so bad that I went back to the car, a Ford coupe, a company car. I was in the car watching him. He slipped coming down off the pole. He had unbuckled the safety belt, his climbing hooks slipped on the slick pole, and he fell onto a barbed-wire fence. He had huge splinters in his hand from the slip on the pole, and he had a big rip on one side. There wasn't a lot of blood, but I was shaken by it, to say the least.

I remember that vividly. He came back to the car and checked his side and pulled some of the bigger splinters out of his hand and then went back and climbed the pole again. I'm not sure I would have gotten up and gone back up the pole.

With my mother there wasn't any doubt from day one that I was going to college. She was absolutely determined. I was the first child, and it was very important for me to go to college. If I went, then my mother felt my brother and sister would be much more likely to go. I wasn't particularly studious or precocious. I did well in elementary school in Houston mostly because I was there every day.

I can remember her saying things to me, maybe when I was thirteen or fourteen, about whether I would finish high school. My father did not finish high school; neither did his brother. That was not uncommon then.

My father wasn't opposed to education. As a matter of fact, he believed in education. But in his mind finishing high school was not the greatest thing in the world, and certainly going on to college was not something necessarily terrific. If I had quit school in the tenth grade, I probably would be working for Exxon. Humble Pipeline was a division of Humble Oil, and I probably would have gotten on there.

The last two summers I was in college, I worked in the pipe gang. That was clearly an option. I had made myself a good hand, as they said, and I could have gotten on there. I probably would have gone to Pierce Junction, which is where my father worked out of, and I probably would have gotten on full time working in the pipe gang.

To this day, I can smell the creosote. We put creosote on things like posts. We'd also do what's called dope pipe. We'd creosote the posts and tar and dope the pipe. Boy, in the Texas summer when it's over one hundred degrees, working around that dope pot and creosote was really something.

When I cut brush in Nacogdoches, I worked for a neighbor of ours. He was a civil engineer. With him I was learning "the instrument," which is on the civil engineering surveyor's tripod.

The progression was you cut brush, and you cut brush well, and you got to measure the tape. If you did the tape pretty well, then you'd be a rod man. The rod man holds up a red-and-white rod that the surveyor looks at. From rod man you could be trained to be an instrument man. Being a brush cutter didn't pay very well, and being a tape man didn't pay all that well. Being a rod man, you could make a living.

In other words, if you quit school and worked your way up, and if you became a rod man, you could probably make it. Certainly, if you were an instrument man, you could make it. Maybe I could have worked up to be an instrument man had I quit school. I cut brush and I was a fill-in rod man; that's as high as I got on that crew. It was a small, narrow world.

Dan Rather pays tribute to Texas in 1982 at a fundraiser at New York City's American Place Theatre. *Photo by Gaylon Finklea Hecker*

A Stronger Sense of Place

One grows up in Texas with a stronger sense of place than most people in most places do.

One of my early memories from first or second grade is learning all the words to "Texas, Our Texas," which is the state song. And learning Texas poetry, of which there was not that much. And, certainly, learning Texas history. That's part of giving you a strong sense of place. We had the American flag, and we had a Texas flag.

As you get older, it all fits into this good, strong sense of belonging. If you don't belong anywhere else, you belong in Texas.

Sixteen-year-old Frannie Reynolds, then Miss Burbank, poses with Emma Fischer Story, the widow of Burbank's first mayor, before a parade, May 12, 1948. *Photo by Paul Wolfe, Valley Times Collection, Los Angeles Public Library*

BIRTH NAME	**MARY FRANCES REYNOLDS**
BORN	April 1, 1932, in El Paso, to Raymond Francis Reynolds and Maxene N. Harmon Reynolds
DIED	December 28, 2016
INTERVIEW	La Mansión del Rio, San Antonio, Texas, January 20, 1982

DEBBIE REYNOLDS
Poor but Proud

A n actress, singer, and comedienne, Debbie Reynolds snagged her first leading role at nineteen in Singin' in the Rain *in 1952. By 1957, she had carved her niche in the cinema in* Tammy and the Bachelor *and on the music charts with "Tammy." Her star power stretched over the next six decades in television, Broadway, and Las Vegas with an Academy Award nomination for Best Actress, a Tony Award, and an Emmy. Among other films she made memorable are* How the West Was Won, Divorce American Style, The Singing Nun, *and* Mother. *She headlined her own television program from 1969 to 1970,* The Debbie Reynolds Show, *and for more than forty years starred in TV movies and made guest appearances in popular series. A 2016 HBO documentary,* Bright Lights: Starring Carrie Fisher and Debbie Reynolds, *traced the close relationship between two generations of entertainment royalty. The Screen Actors Guild honored Reynolds with a Life Achievement Award in 2015, and the Hollywood Walk of Fame immortalized her with a star in 1997.*

I was raised with my grandpa and grandma Harmon in El Paso. We lived with them because we couldn't afford a house. We didn't have our own house for years. For a while, we lived in the attic over the filling station where Daddy worked as a mechanic, and then Daddy couldn't even afford that. So we moved in with my grandparents.

During the Depression, you did anything you could. If you had a family, you just did anything. My daddy worked for the railroad, and it laid practically everybody off. Nobody was working; everybody was starving. We lived on jackrabbits, pinto beans, and enchiladas. My favorite food is still Mexican food.

I remember walking the railroad ties to school. I remember we had hobos, because in my innocence I'd bring them home. In the Depression, they had no food. We had no food, but Mother would give them a piece of bread. She was scared to death of them. But I'd pick them up along the railroad and take them home.

I would talk to them because I was curious. "Come meet my mama. She'd love to meet you. I love the way you look. Do you always go by yourself? What's in that bag?"

My mother was the disciplinarian. Daddy would whip my brother with a barber strap, but he never touched me. My mother could really deck me. She really could hit. We had the iron rule; there was no getting around that. I was a willful child and got stubborn and wouldn't do what she said, so she'd deck me. I'm sure I deserved it.

Mother hit me so hard one time I flew clear across the room and hit the wall. Knocked me out. Well, I never sassed her again. Maybe that's why I'm strong. I'm an Aries; my sign is strong. My mother also is an Aries. She held the family together.

My whole family are very proud, good, working people. My mother could never work at a job because my father would never allow it. He said, "Men work, and womenfolk stay home."

Everybody was poor. If you lived in Mexico, you were dirt poor. It was much worse. People were just starving. I remember they talked about the "ladies of the evening" across the border in Juárez. Over there it was very dirty. We bought huaraches, shoes, there for twenty-five cents. The cats were all starving. I don't remember anything pleasant about Juárez.

We were called "poor white trash." We were the only white family on the street. The rest were all Mexican and Black, called "colored" in

Actress Debbie Reynolds models costume accessories with designer Edith Head, February 27, 1960, before a charity benefit. *Herald Examiner Collection, Los Angeles Public Library*

those days. To us the rich people were the ones who lived on a street with sidewalks.

I played in the backyard. There weren't any playgrounds. I spoke very little English. All my friends were Mexican, so I spoke Spanish, Tex-Mex.

I remember tumbleweeds. As a child, I was short and little, and I remember the wind would come up and the tumbleweeds would scratch me to pieces.

But I never remember green. El Paso had no water. There was one big hill in El Paso; it was barren. Now that I can travel in a fancy manner, I see Texas is a very pretty state. I don't remember that as a child.

I think when you grow up rather poor and later become sort of successful, you never forget being poor. But you have to work very hard. It takes a strong spine and will.

I don't want to have to live in an attic. I don't want to have to be poor again. I can understand and appreciate people who are poor fighting to get out of it. I understand about welfare, but my family was never on welfare, and we were as poor as anybody could be. The pride was that you didn't go on welfare. You never would do that because it meant you weren't trying.

I was raised in tent meetings with sawdust on the floor, and I slept on the rows and rows of benches. When I was too young, I never understood the preacher. And then when I was old enough to understand, I was in church on Wednesday, Friday, Saturday, and Sunday. There were a lot of "hallelujahs" and "amens" and music, and I loved it.

My church was the Nazarene Church, and it had tent meetings like Holy Rollers. In El Paso you didn't have big, big churches. So when you had rallies or church conventions, you had tent meetings to hold all the people.

My grandpa, who was a lay preacher, was born on April Fools' Day. I remember very fondly on every April Fools' Day Sunday we would walk down the aisle together and put our pennies, one for each of his years, in the little birthday bank.

My mother was like a missionary. And I was, too, until I went into show business. The Nazarene Church was very, very strict. You couldn't even go to the movies. They considered that a sin.

I was born funny, a little crazy. Daddy had a very dry, English kind of humor, but my mother was just tired. She was always working. I have an uncle Owen who's totally nuts and an aunt Mary who is bizarre she's so funny. Aunt Mary ran a bar. She was a scream. Uncle Owen used to be a clown. He wore baggy, dumb clothes just for charity stuff. Rowdy. The rest were very quiet.

In my immediate family, there were six boys, and I was the only girl. I was the youngest. I had to fight my way like crazy because my older brother Bill would beat up on me all the time.

My parents stood beside me through thick and thin. Whenever I needed them, they were there. They've never asked for anything but love.

When I was five, I started to school in El Paso. I got to be the class cutup. I was a terror until I was about ten. I used to steal people's shoes and throw them out the window. I was always in the principal's office.

My teacher called Mama every day. "Mary Frances is out of line."

"What did she do?"

"Well, she was talking."

I was always talking. Then I'd take lemons to school. I used to suck on them. You know, it's very terrible to look at someone sucking a lemon. Then I'd throw them at the blackboard. Oh, I was very rowdy. I used to bring a jar of worms to school and throw them on the kids. I thought it was funny. That's when Mama said, "That's enough."

And it was enough.

Mother had thought she was going to have twins, and when she only had me, she said, "Thank God I didn't have two of you. You're enough. You are like two."

I had a lot of energy. You couldn't catch me. I was go, go, go. Later on in school, everybody liked me because of my personality. I was no competition to the other girls because I certainly wasn't sexy and I didn't neck with the boys.

> **My parents stood beside me through thick and thin. Whenever I needed them, they were there.**

Debbie Reynolds appears at a press conference at La Mansión del Rio in San Antonio, January 15, 1982, before a performance at the Majestic Theatre. *San Antonio Express-News Photography Collection, UTSA Special Collections*

Daddy should have been a ranger in the forest. He liked being alone. He's a very solitary man. Didn't need womenfolk, other than siring the babies and cleaning the house. He wouldn't cook. He wouldn't eat if you didn't cook. That was women's work. He would not do the dishes. That's women's work.

I helped around the house. I'm Miss Clean. When I'm upset, I clean. It's my release. Nobody cleans like I clean. Mother did the cooking; I did the cleaning.

My daddy moved us to California when I was seven. On the way there on the train, my mother cried all the time because she didn't want to move. We stayed in a motel that had bedbugs. We slept out on the sidewalk because Mother wouldn't put us in there.

We had no money. We went in a chair car. Daddy had a pass because he worked for the railroad. The railroad had rehired him after the Depression. We took lunches, but we couldn't afford to buy milk or anything like that.

We moved to California because Daddy wanted a better life. He thought the West was better because you could make a better salary there from the railroad. He saw California as the land of opportunity, the land of plenty. There were orange trees, and we could have a home. He just thought he could do better. And he was right.

He was a very courageous man to move his whole family to a different environment in California. From there I became a film personality. Who knows what I would have been had we stayed in Texas. Being so poor in El Paso, it would have been very hard to pull ourselves up. But I know we would have.

I got a lot of strength from my environment, which was Texas. As Catholics will tell you, if they keep you until you're seven, they've got you. So if Texas gets you till you're seven, you're Texan.

You can't be an adopted Texan. You have to be born here. Texans can like you, you can be a good old boy, but you ain't earth. Truly, there is a sense of earth.

I've had a wonderful life. If it went tomorrow, I've had an exciting, wonderful life. It all started in Texas, and the fact that we were poor was an asset. I've never stopped appreciating everything I have.

There's only one state and that's Texas. It's instilled in you from birth; at least, it was in our family. We were all supposed to be very proud of Texas. When I travel all over the world, I don't find that sense of national pride anywhere else. It's like we all should feel about America.

At sixteen, Rose Birenberg was a member of the National Honor Society and the Lasso dance team at Jefferson High School in San Antonio. *1949 Monticello, courtesy San Antonio Independent School District*

BIRTH NAME	**IDA ROSE BIRENBERG**
BORN	July 9, 1933, in San Antonio to Jakovo Birenberg and Sophie Weprinsky Birenberg
INTERVIEW	Her home, January 24, 2018, San Antonio, Texas

JUSTICE ROSE SPECTOR
Doing Good for Others

I n 1992 San Antonio jurist Rose Spector was the first woman elected to the Texas Supreme Court. She graduated from Barnard College of Columbia University in 1954 and was second in her class of seventy-five at St. Mary's School of Law in 1965. With experience as a municipal court judge in Olmos Park, she was elected to a Bexar County court at law in 1975 and the 131st judicial district of Texas in 1981. The election of Ann Richards as governor in 1990 inspired more women to run for office, and Spector, with more years as a trial judge than any of the Texas Supreme Court justices, entered that race in 1992. Despite a male opponent heavily favored by the editorial pages of influential newspapers, Spector carried San Antonio, Austin, and Dallas and garnered 52 percent of the vote. Among the appeals decided during her six-year term was Edgewood ISD v. Kirby, a landmark decision that overhauled the funding of education in the state.

Both my father and mother were born in small towns in Russia when the czar was in power and many Jews sought to leave Russia. My father supposedly came from a family that could afford to send him out of the country, and that's how he got to South America. He immigrated to Colombia, South America, sometime around 1910. He also lived in Argentina and Peru. Someone in my family did some genealogy and uncovered a marriage certificate for Jakovo Birenberg. Same age. Same origin: Russia. He was married to a young lady in Peru.

My father had gone from Russia to South America, but he had a partner who lived in New York, and the partner had a sister living in New York. My father was very handsome and personable and earned a living.

Well, he goes to New York, and the partner's sister is living with a Jewish woman. Instead of having a romance with his partner's sister, he falls in love with the Jewish woman and they married. The story is that he wanted to take her back to South America, where he was earning a living. My mother goes there after they were married and hates it because she misses her family still in New York.

By this time, my father is selling woolen goods and visits San Antonio on a selling trip. So the decision is made to come to San Antonio in 1922, where they speak Spanish. My father had learned Spanish in South America, and my mother also knew Spanish. Jack Birenberg had gone to South America from Russia and then to San Antonio.

All my mother's family originally went to New York and stayed there. *Fiddler on the Roof* was on the TV on Turner Classic Movies a few nights ago, and that's the way my mother described Russia. Farmlands. A shtetl. But my father's family must not have been farmers, because they had more money and sent him away, and he was a salesman and able to start a business.

When I was a child, my father had a store on Commerce Street where he sold woolens by the yard, and we've always laughed because San Antonio is the last place that anyone needs a wool suit. I don't know the years it was, but men wore wool suits. He had some customers who were tailors who made custom men's suits and would come and buy fabric. I believe they bought three and a half yards, which would make a man's suit. He also sold bindings, buttons, zippers, and things like that for the tailors. The tailor that used him the most was Black.

They made busywork for me while my father babysat me at the store.

I counted buttons. The buttons came in a container, a bucketful, and no one would buy that many. I could count by then, so I counted out 144 buttons.

And my father had a sign in the store window, "Se Habla Español," that brought him customers who only spoke Spanish. That's San Antonio and also Texas.

The store's name was Jack Birenberg, my maiden name, and later Jack Birenberg and Son. But the son never wanted to be in that business. My father had a secretary who was politically active. She did the accounting and probably wrote letters. She became the person who was prominent in running the store. She was Emma Tenayuca, who led the pecan shellers' strike in 1938 and organized labor unions. Friends called my father out for employing her, and he said she was just doing what she thought was right.

She told me to "do good," instead of becoming a fashion designer, as I had wanted to be.

During the Fiesta parades we used to sit in the display windows of his store and watch the floats and marchers go by. The store was on the parade route for the Battle of Flowers Parade. That was a big, fun time. We were not related to any debutantes or princesses or any of that Fiesta royalty, but we just loved the beautiful floats that would come by.

And at that time in San Antonio, most of the retail businesses had been started by Jews like my father. When I was young, downtown had Frost Bros., Carl's, The Vogue. I went to work at The Vogue as a teenager, and I guess they let you work in the summer and on Saturdays, the Jewish Sabbath, selling to young girls. There was also Joske's. The Kallisons had a mercantile, dry goods store. My husband's father [Jake Spector] used to have a small dry goods store, La Estrella, on West Commerce Street right next to Penner's, which was also owned by Jews. That was San Antonio back then.

My mother was very literate in Russian. She used to read letters for other Russian immigrants that were sent from their families. And she'd write letters back for them in Russian. She would translate for them, and she helped other ladies read and write letters back home.

We had bookshelves full of books. I guess my mother bought them. There was a time when she must have belonged to the Book of the Month Club.

But I don't remember her reading in English, except I do remember when she read *Gone with the Wind* in the late thirties. My father reminded her of Clark Gable. He was just handsome. He adored my mother. I had the original book. I stayed up two days and two nights reading it.

My mother had a beautiful singing voice, and having lived in New York, she loved opera. She knew classical music and opera. My mother had this beautiful voice, and she thought that I would be musical. At one point we had an upright piano, and she got a nun who taught music to come to the house to teach me. Then they bought me a grand piano. I didn't care for it. My mother would always be saying, "You're supposed to practice."

I never played well or wanted to play.

I remember going once to New York before my mother's father died. I remember he studied; that's all he did. I think maybe that's why they bought so many books later. He was very religious. And I remember him sitting at the breakfast table, with a yarmulke, reading or praying.

When her father died, we brought his widow, my grandmother, to live in SA, but she didn't like it. She wasn't meant to live in San Antonio.

My first home that I remember was on Aganier Street. In the evenings there was a streetlight at the corner of Agarita and Aganier, and we'd all go outside and play hide-and-seek or something. We had no air-conditioning. Children played outside, day and night, so we all knew each other and were friendly with each other. The parents knew each other, too.

I can remember different houses and who lived there. But they were all different religions. There were several houses with Jewish families, but then there were other families, too. It was not a Jewish neighborhood. On Aganier Street where we lived, even though we were Jews, we were accepted because all kinds of people lived there.

There was no TV until 1949. The reason we got television was my father liked to see the wrestling that was on television.

We belonged to Agudas Achim, which was a Conservative shul, and at one point I went to Temple Beth-El Sunday school. We considered ourselves Jewish. We were not really Orthodox. My mother lit Shabbos candles on Friday. We would celebrate Passover and most Jewish holidays. Women and men didn't sit together in shul. Girls did not become bat mitzvah back then, so I did not get bat mitzvah.

For some years, my mother kept kosher but became less so later on.

When she kept kosher, she bought chickens that were koshered from a shochet, a Jewish butcher, at his house. We used to go out, I remember, and pick up the chickens from his house. From one chicken she could make chicken soup, chopped liver, and fried chicken. Later, when she didn't keep strictly kosher, she still wouldn't have ham in the house.

Her special dish was a chicken stew, a mixture she called *zharkoye*, a Russian term. She made it on Friday for Shabbos. She made it regularly, and occasionally we have it now and laugh about it because it was mostly what my mother knew how to make. Everything was in it, like a stew with potatoes and carrots. You start it on Friday because you can't cook on Saturday. Now they call it cholent, with meat, for Shabbos, when you don't light a fire.

But when we didn't cook, we went out. Fried chicken at the Chicken Shack on Broadway was a big treat. You would pick it up and take it home. We also liked Mexican food. On Sunday we'd go to a place called Duran's or La Fonda on Main, which is where we'd eat Mexican food.

I have concluded that my parents cared about all their children, and their only hope was that the children were happy. I'm the baby of the family. There were two brothers, a sister, and myself. And it's my sister [Marcia Nasatir] who's the Hollywood mogul. The oldest brother was ten years older, and my sister about seven. The children were all close.

> My parents cared about all their children, and their only hope was that the children were happy.

My brothers kept track of baseball, and we did many things together.

I thought I was spoiled. And my brothers and sister thought I was spoiled, too. They actually called me Baby.

"Tell Baby to come in for supper."

My sister and I were very close. I always looked up to my sister, and I still do. She just worked her way up in the film industry when women were not expected to have any position except secretary. She became an editor, then became a movie executive, and has done lots of things. At Jefferson High School, she was the editor of the *Declaration*. Because she wanted to be a journalist, she wanted to go to Northwestern in Chicago, which had the famous journalism school. My parents just wanted her to marry a nice Jewish boy.

When we were young, we went to the movies together. That was probably my favorite thing to do during my childhood. They had movie theaters downtown. The Majestic, the Aztec, Woodlawn, Laurel. The shows changed on Thursdays. We also saw cowboy movies at the Uptown Theater on Fredericksburg Road. Every Saturday they had part of a serial and maybe two more movies, all for young people. It cost twelve cents to get in.

My mother was ill when I was a little girl. Because my mother was manic-depressive, what you'd call bipolar now, she had to have treatments at the State Hospital when I was a child. Mother was not able to do much. Mamie Chapa Guerra lived with us and acted as my mother forever. She lived by herself in a room next to the garage.

Mamie Chapa had a lot to do with my childhood. She took care of me. The other children were older, so often they went off to school, and I was the only one home.

Mamie would sew doll clothes for my dolls. I loved playing and dressing my dolls. My thought as a child was I'd be a fashion designer. Seeing the costumes in movies made me think of designing clothes.

My sister has a theory of why she became a movie executive and I became a lawyer and a judge. My mother never learned to drive, and my father let my sister and me learn to drive when we were about eleven and twelve years old so that we could drive my mother and ourselves. My sister thinks that driving a car at our young age gave us self-confidence.

My mother, who we loved, would get driving lessons by someone my father hired. She learned, but she was afraid. We weren't afraid. Many of our friends had cars. You could get your driver's license at fourteen back in those days, but my sister and I learned much earlier.

My father worked hard and was an example to us about hard work. The only time I remember that he was late for work was in 1948 when Harry Truman was running for president. The family stayed up all night listening to the returns on the radio, and he was late the next day.

I had light brown hair down to here. It fell in long curls. When I'd get up in the morning and go to school, my mother helped with my hair. We didn't have clips or anything; my hair was just curly. Somehow it looked like Shirley Temple or some movie star girl that had long curls.

I didn't like it. I didn't want to look like that. My mother thought it was very pretty.

M y first school was Agnes Cotton Elementary. Then I went to Horace Mann Junior High. After that, my parents moved close to Jefferson High School because we wanted to go to Jefferson and we could walk there. We lived on Mary Louise Drive near the high school, and Maury Maverick lived up the street. He became mayor of San Antonio, and we were supporters. We were Democrats, and he was very popular. Through the years, we didn't know anyone who wasn't a Democrat.

I was always a good student. I liked school. I was good in all the subjects. I was good at math. I took algebra and trigonometry. I can barely add now, and I don't know if I've had any problems that I've solved with trigonometry.

But I didn't do well in Spanish. My parents were immigrants from Russia and wanted their children to read and be educated in another language. My mother could speak any language. She knew not only Russian but Spanish and could pick up other languages, like Portuguese, easily. When I was in school, I took Spanish every year and never learned enough. I think knowing other languages is some ability that you must be born with.

We studied a lot of Texas history. When we were in school, history was all about democracy, the American way. We took field trips to the Alamo and the missions. I do not remember if we learned that many of our founding fathers had slaves.

In high school, my sister was a Lasso, and I was a Lasso. The Lasso outfit was a blue skirt, red shirt, and cowboy hat. It had a belt that was very wide where your rope hung that was for twirling. My parents allowed my sister and me to belong to the group even though we performed at football games on Friday night, which was the Sabbath. We marched in Fiesta parades and the Armistice Day parade. The Lassos were famous, and there was a Hollywood movie about them [*High School*, 1940].

My failure in life was I never could learn to twirl my lasso. At halftime at the football games, the Lassos would march in to music, twirling their ropes like cowboys herding cattle. Many Lassos knew how to march and twirl. Not me.

Teamwork was also an important life's lesson. I learned teamwork being a Lasso and performing at football games. It was like being on the football team. My husband was on the state championship Jefferson football team.

At Jefferson High School there was a Jewish group of students. We had an experience that was different. We were absent on Jewish religious holidays. Our parents wanted their daughters to remain religious. They didn't want us to marry non-Jewish boys. For instance, if someone would ask me to go to a high school dance, I either lied or didn't go. They were very strict about that.

We had friends of many religions. My best friend was Methodist. Her father was a Methodist pastor. All students of all religions were together for events like Christmas parties. This was San Antonio and Texas.

I met Ann Richards at Girls State in 1949. We were in high school and were both attending Girls State, run by the American Legion. We met in a camp somewhere in Austin for so many days and pretended we were part of an elected government. I nominated Ann for governor and she won, and I became lieutenant governor. She was from Waco. And Ann was Ann, very friendly. She was great to be with and always funny. Her name was Ann Willis before she got married, and we stayed friends.

Maryann Kallison was my age and a good friend, and her mother, Frances Kallison, encouraged me to go east to college. Frances went to one of those East Coast women's schools, like Smith and Wellesley or Barnard. She encouraged me to go east to a girls' school.

So I applied to Vassar and was refused even though I was at or near the top in my graduating class at Jefferson. But Ms. [Francis] Smith, our dean of girls, a tough lady, had a connection to Vassar and recommended me. That's how I went to Vassar. She had straight bangs and short hair, and she'd get after you if you didn't do what you were supposed to.

I wanted to become a fashion designer, probably from making doll clothes and going to movies with costumes, like *Gone with the Wind*. Ms. Smith wanted me to do more things that were beneficial for others. At the time, most high school senior girls stayed home after graduation. Ms. Smith wanted me to go on to college. Ms. Smith said to me that "you ought to do good for people."

Vassar is in Poughkeepsie, New York, and I was coming from sunny San Antonio. So my parents bought me a fur coat. I arrived at Vassar, and no one wears a fur coat. Everyone rides bicycles and you wore pedal pushers and maybe a sweater. My friends up there liked to call me Tex. At Vassar, everyone went to theater and museums in New York City. That was everyone's dream, to live in New York and go to the theater and read the *New York Times*.

And then my mother got sick, and I had to quit before graduating. I briefly attended Trinity University in San Antonio. Then I studied liberal arts and received a BA from Barnard. I lived with my sister in New York. I stayed in a room that was about the size of a table, with just a bed and chest of drawers.

Being Jewish is all about fairness and helping others. Judaism and the Jewish environment and morals and values I learned played a role in my becoming a judge and being considerate of other people.

Also, my teachers in public school influenced everything. Teachers in those years taught a

Justice Rose Spector was the first woman elected to the Texas Supreme Court.
Photo courtesy Rose Spector

lot of moral lessons. You shouldn't cheat on tests. You need to earn a good grade. You must study and do your best.

Even playing in school taught us to be fair. We played baseball and other sports and learned to be fair. We learned the rules of athletics. We learned to want to improve ourselves.

My parents were always very charitable. They raised funds for all kinds of charities that took care of people. From my parents, I learned we are all one family, and like family, we should share our resources and treat each other fairly.

Kathryn Grandstaff as a Bluebonnet Belle finalist. *1952 Cactus,*
Briscoe Center for American History, University of Texas at Austin

BIRTH NAME	**OLIVE KATHRYN GRANDSTAFF**
BORN	November 25, 1933, in West Columbia to Delbert Emery Grandstaff and Olive Catherine Stokely Grandstaff
INTERVIEW	*San Antonio Express-News*, San Antonio, Texas, May 12, 1983

KATHRYN CROSBY

The Virtues of a Small Town

Kathryn Crosby married widower Bing Crosby in 1957, trading a short but promising career as an actress for a twenty-year role as wife of one of the most beloved stars of the twentieth century. Under the name Kathryn Grant or Kathryn Grandstaff, she appeared in 1950s films, most notably Rear Window, My Sister Eileen, The Phenix City Story, Anatomy of a Murder, and The Big Circus. She may be best known for The 7th Voyage of Sinbad, a 1958 film with such advanced special effects it approached cult status. She earned a bachelor of fine arts degree from the University of Texas at Austin in 1955. After Bing Crosby's death in 1977, she occasionally returned to stage productions. She wrote three memoirs and in 2008 co-wrote Making the Most of the Best of Your Life: Enjoying the Challenges of Maturity, an inspirational guide for seniors. Her daughter, Mary Crosby, was the actress known around the world as the villainess who shot J. R. Ewing in the TV melodrama Dallas.

My hometown of West Columbia is on the Brazos River fifty-three miles out of Houston. I used to say it is two miles west of East Columbia, which is the original settlement. It was the first capital of the Republic of Texas. West Columbia is the new town. East Columbia was where the old settlers settled their plantations along, unfortunately, the wrong side of the Brazos River. When it flooded, the town fell off on that side and built up on the other side.

It was a very small town when I was growing up, fewer than five thousand. And it was lovely. It was filled with rice farmers and ranchers. It was almost like a dream, but I remember how ranchers used to drive cattle through the dirt streets of West Columbia. They had cattle guards around the schoolhouse, and there was a teacherage across the street where the young, unmarried ladies, the teachers, stayed. That's from the old, old times. There were lots of wonderful things about growing up in that town.

Daddy was Delbert Emery Grandstaff, and Mother was Olive Catherine. My mother taught for thirty-four years in the school system, first, second, and third grades. My dad was a teacher, too, and was also county commissioner for fourteen years. That was so important.

Everybody voted in the band hall. We'd stand on one block or the other and I'd say, "Vote for my daddy. He's the man for the job."

Sometimes we won and sometimes we lost, and that was all right, too.

Our schoolhouse had eleven grades, and I remember when it switched to twelve. I remember the home ec cottage because everybody took home economics except me. I skipped two grades and was having a hard time in the seventh grade. It was really tough; everybody was going through puberty except me. I kept wanting to climb trees, and the boys had other things in mind with the girls.

I remember my dad teaching me algebra. He taught me about πr^2. Suddenly, in the eighth grade, I was an honor student again.

I remember our yard. We had two acres in our yard and a big, old house that Daddy built. He bought an old hospital in Shreveport and brought all that good, seasoned lumber to West Columbia. He and some friends built our beautiful house. It's Cape Cod architecture, which I didn't realize until I played in Hyannis Port and saw other homes like it there. It has gables and is a story and a half, which was very tall for that area. There are a lot of pecan trees and elms in the yard.

In Texas there's room, there's time, and there's space. There's lots of dreaming time. We have such lovely trees. To lie under those trees in a hammock and look up through the leaves and see the moss and hear the sound of the june bugs, that's a nice time to dream.

I climbed a lot of trees, played Tarzan and Jane. I wanted to be a movie star as soon as I saw the movie. I had a big imagination. I thought that was just wonderful. I was happy as a child.

I spent much of my time up in the pecan trees or with a cow at the barn, an old pet. And we had Henny Penny, who climbed up the ladder into the tree where her nest was and laid her eggs up there. I had to go up and get them. Sometimes I made it down and sometimes I didn't.

Daddy was a hunter and once brought home a baby opossum that he'd found in the woods. He also brought home a baby bobcat one time, and his name was Chester W. Nimitz Please. Chester slept in the springs of the bed. I would wake up in the morning and he'd be sitting on my chest waiting for me to blink an eye, and then he'd slap my cheeks. He was a very cute baby, but as he grew older, of course, he had to be given to someone because he was wild.

Kathryn Grandstaff was a finalist for Sweetheart at the University of Texas. *1952 Cactus, Briscoe Center for American History, University of Texas at Austin*

I was the baby. I'm a junior named for my mother, but they spelled my "Kathryn" in the modern way. My brother, seven years older, is Emery Jr., although when he went to the service they changed it to Del because that was short for Delbert. My sister, Frances Ruth, was named after two aunts.

She's four years older than I, and she was the beautiful one. She was five foot eight inches and she became a model. She was tall and lovely and a tennis champion. She went to state competition in Texas, and she reminds me of Evonne Goolagong. She moved like a gazelle across the court; she had a hard serve like a man and then took the net and put it away.

I was slow and short and fat, and I played tennis, too. I was always slow and always too short to get to cover the court, but I really hated to lose. So I did all right, too.

I shared a room with my sister a lot. I'll never forget her coming home the night she was engaged to wake me up and tell me how wonderful it was. I must have been fifteen. I thought that was silly. Once again, I was out of step. I had just gotten so I could date a little bit, and here she was getting married. Then about the time I got old enough to go off to college, she had a baby and I was behind again.

I remember church a lot. I was a Southern Baptist, and I would go forward to rededicate my life about every three weeks. I was going to be a missionary to China or a Chinese missionary—I didn't know which, because I couldn't get it straight. The best first-grade teacher in West Columbia taught at the Methodist Sunday school, so I'd go over there, too. Mother taught at Vacation Bible School, and I went there and learned

Kathryn and Bing Crosby at the University of Texas when she was named a Distinguished Alumnus, 1969. *Prints and Photographs Collection, Briscoe Center for American History, University of Texas at Austin*

a lot of Bible verses. I was sent to the Baptist encampment at Palacios. I loved that.

When I was nine years old, during my second week at camp, my aunt and uncle, Mr. and Mrs. Leon Sullivan, came driving by with Mother. They were on their way to Mexico City. They took me with them.

I had never seen a foreign country, and I had never heard a foreign language. But soon I was speaking not only Spanish but French, because the telephone operator at the little hotel where we stayed was French, and she taught me how to sing "Frère Jacques." So I was bilingual.

I've had a love affair going with Mexico ever since. I love the country, I love the language, I love the people, and I love their love of poetry.

My daddy took me bass fishing on Eagle Nest Lake, and I caught a fish. Mother made him pull the boat while she collected lotus blossoms.

Dad made her stop teaching school once. He said, "My wife is going to stay home."

He got very macho.

And she said, "Of course, darling."

A week later, he looked up and there were two huge refrigerators, and the house was full of flowers. Mother had become a florist overnight. You talk about your women's lib. I mean, there's more than one way to skin a cat. We did all the funerals and weddings. I learned to wire chrysanthemums and carnations and roses, and I helped her make sprays. She was so creative.

She made my sister a beautiful corsage like a shoulder strap for her junior-senior banquet. She wore a strapless gown, and she had a whole shoulder strap of beautiful lavender hydrangeas that matched the lavender of the dress. It was so pretty.

At my sister's wedding, the crisis was, of course, the flowers, which had to come down from Houston. It was raining, and we were worried if the flowers would get there. I remember everyone wore peacock-blue satin and carried daffodils. Mother made all the flowers, and it was beautiful.

Celebrations were very important with Mother and Daddy. We had the biggest old house going, and everything was a celebration there. Everyone came to my big old house like they did when there was a hurricane.

At Christmas all the family got together, our aunts and uncles and cousins. The tree was in a certain corner by the front door. Aunt Frances and Uncle Leon came from the Valley bearing lots of wonderful gifts. Aunt Margaret made beautiful lemon chiffon pies and sand tarts. Mother played the piano and we all sang. There was excitement. Church, too, was very much a part of our Christmas.

Mother and Dad went to school in Humble, Texas, and they had a graduating class of six people. Daddy went to the First World War and told all his friends to leave Olive Stokely alone; he'd be back. They were going to the circus one night, and they got married instead. Then Daddy walked her home. That was it.

They were very much in love. They had fifty years of a very happy married life. There was never an argument that I heard. But I thought Daddy was going to divorce Mother once because she lost his fountain pen. That was so serious I thought it was all over. She often lost his pen, and he would say, "I'm really cross, Olive."

And that was it.

They were gentle people, and they were very much in love. Joy played a very big part in their lives. I know now that we didn't have any money, but I always thought we were very rich.

I remember as a lasting memory their big bed. We all had family discussions in the bed. We all learned the facts of life, all five of us sitting there talking. Everybody's questions were treated with respect even though I was seven years younger than my brother. My brother probably knew everything there was, and I had only found one book at the back of the library. I'd read that.

I remember my mother's left shoulder because I would come in and slip into bed with them. Daddy was on her right and she was in the middle and I was on her left shoulder. She would read to me, and I was very comfortable there, always.

Mother taught us to love beautiful things, not to covet them, but to enjoy and appreciate beautiful things of all kinds.

Daddy is very, very dogged. He is not a quick person. Mother had a quicksilver mind, very quick. It used to drive her crazy to wait for Daddy to come to the conclusion she had reached years before. But he got there, and Mother had great respect for Daddy and waited.

Once Daddy had a goal, he pursued it. Daddy thought it was quite logical for him to run for the United States Senate. He was teaching civics and government in school. How better for his students to learn what our government was like? It only cost him $150 to file for senator.

In 1960 we got on what we called the Grandstaff Bandwagon. Mother and Dad and I went all the way through Texas campaigning for the United States Senate. Daddy was in the top ten, and John Tower won. But we had a wonderful time, and Daddy learned to make a great speech.

Daddy was innocent. He didn't know anything about machine politics or working for parties, but he did know about working for government.

I went to Robstown High School and lived with my aunt Frances and uncle Leon. The schoolhouse had burned down in West Columbia.

Robstown was a great farming community. They had three crops a year and a big cotton gin. My uncle was a wonderful salesman of bags and produce baskets. He had a great shed that was down by the railroad tracks. We used to wave to the train conductor and ride on the carts that you hauled the bags out with. And we would jump off the baskets onto the piles of onion sacking.

High school was a great experience. I did well in school. I was reporter for the freshman class. I took Spanish my freshman and sophomore years, which was unusual. They usually didn't let you do that until you were a junior. I loved Spanish and used to get lots of help from all the Spanish students who were Mexican, because they had the best accents going. Then I was a cheerleader and editor of the annual as a senior. I fell in love several times, out of love several times. Robstown was a great place to grow up, and I loved it.

I spent a lot of time also taking ballet lessons and piano lessons in Corpus Christi. My aunt Frances drove me seventeen miles to Corpus Christi before school in the morning. She also got my teeth straightened at an orthodontist's there.

I was in two plays in high school, *Henry's Hired Aunt* and *Mama's Baby Boy*. You can imagine from the title the quality of that play. During the love scene in *Mama's Baby Boy*, the sofa broke down and the cushions and the leading man kept sinking out of sight.

I went to the University of Texas at sixteen and was in a play very shortly thereafter called *Dear Brutus*. B. Iden Payne directed it. He had directed it originally on Broadway with a young girl named Helen Hayes in the role that I performed, Margaret.

Then that spring, he did a Shakespearean play called *Much Ado about Nothing,* and the ingénue was the hero. I played one of the ladies-in-waiting until the day it was to open. The girl who played the hero got sick and I had to go on for her. I was wonderful. Iden Payne said I was a real trooper; it was the greatest compliment I ever had.

I got from Robstown High School to my acting career along the path that, thank God, is still open to girls in Texas. There were festivals everywhere. I was a Splash Day Princess in Corpus Christi at the age of three, and I returned there and was Miss Buccaneer Navy when I was fifteen. Because of that, I became Miss Fat Stock Show, or rodeo queen of the Houston Fat Stock Show. There I met Art Rush, who was Roy Rogers's agent and manager.

After going to the University of Texas for a couple of years, I was in the Miss Texas pageant and lost, which destroyed me. I was brokenhearted.

Dad said, "Do you want to visit Aunt Ruth in California?"

I said, "Yes, please."

So Mother and I flew out to California. I went to Paramount on Monday. I tested with Goldwyn on Wednesday. I signed a contract on Friday and celebrated at the Brown Derby in Hollywood under a picture of Bob Hope and Bing Crosby. I was eighteen.

In Hollywood no one called me Tex except Bing.

Kathryn Crosby autographs her book, *My Life with Bing*, during a book tour stop in San Antonio in 1983. *Photo by Harry Young*

A. J. Foyt's earliest racer was powered by a Briggs and Stratton lawnmower motor.
Photo courtesy A. J. Foyt

<table>
<tr><td>BIRTH NAME</td><td>**ANTHONY JOSEPH FOYT JR.**</td></tr>
<tr><td>BORN</td><td>January 16, 1935, in Houston to Anthony Joseph Foyt Sr. and Evelyn Monk Foyt</td></tr>
<tr><td>INTERVIEW</td><td>A. J. Foyt Racing, Waller, Texas, January 27, 2018</td></tr>
</table>

A. J. FOYT

Born to Win

A. J. Foyt, the first driver to ace four Indianapolis 500 races, is one of only two drivers to win both the Indy 500 and the Daytona 500, and the only one to also win the 24 Hours of Le Mans. In a driving career that spanned four decades and three continents, he won sixty-seven Indy car races and seven national Indy car championships, as well as fourteen national titles and 172 major races. He was victorious in seven NASCAR Winston Cup Series races and holds the records for the most 500-mile Indy car victories, nine, and the best percentage of Indy car wins in one season, 77 percent. Foyt ties with Al Unser Sr. for the most Indy car wins, ten, in one season. Accolades include the American Sportscasters Association Sports Legend Award in 1993, NASCAR's 50 Greatest Drivers and Driver of the Century in 2000, and induction into the Motorsports Hall of Fame of America in 1989 and the International Motorsports Hall of Fame in 2000. After taking his final lap around the Indianapolis Motor Speedway on Pole Day, May 15, 1993, Foyt retired and became solely a team owner.

I was born in Houston, St. Joe's Hospital off of Pierce Street, and I'll probably be buried in Houston. I was raised up in the Heights, 505 West Twenty-Fifth Street, which wasn't a good area.

My name is Super Tex because I brought all the championships back to Houston and to Texas. I probably brought more championships back here than anybody.

Everybody knew where I was from and where I was going to go back to. Houston is home.

I lived across the street from a pickle factory, and I went to Helms Elementary School. And the railroad ran across right there in front of my house. The Heights looked nothing like it looks like now. All of that's gone now, even my house. It's all big condos now.

Back then it was rock roads. I would drive my little car around the block on those rock roads. A lady used to come down there and jump on my daddy or she'd call the cops because I was throwing rocks in her yard.

I used to go to the Heights movie theater across the street from Harold's men's shop. I watched Roy Rogers and Gene Autry, mostly, at the movies. I only liked cowboy movies. And then my daddy had a shop there on Eighteenth and Ashland. That was the very early forties.

Years ago you slept with the windows open and the doors were unlocked. The Heights wasn't really safe, but we didn't lock our doors. Nobody did. We didn't have the thieves you have today. Back then they used to get punished quite a bit.

Walter Cronkite came here to the Heights to do a story, and he said, "You know, one thing about the Heights, the people who grew up here are either dead, in the penitentiary for life, or they made it."

There was no in-between.

I was probably a mean little shit. My mama used to come down Shepherd, and there was an orphans' home. She'd stop and say, "We'll take you up there."

I'd cry and plead, "Please don't take me up there."

I went to elementary school, and a lot of times when it was raining, I'd be playing and fall down in the mud and Mama would have to take me back home and change my clothes.

My daddy said, "Next time you do it . . ."

And he went and bought some girls' clothes. They made me go to school in girls' clothes. Once.

———

I went to Hamilton Middle School, and then my family moved over by West University, so I went to Pershing Middle School. After Pershing, I went to Lamar High School. That didn't last long. The first week I got in trouble for fighting. I'd fight about whatever you had to fight over.

I went from Lamar to San Jacinto High School, and from there I wound up at St. Thomas High School. It was a Catholic high school, and I'll never forget Father McGee and Father Ossa. Man, they gave you swats with a yardstick. If you jumped or moved, it was, "We said stand still and hold the locker. We're going to give you one more."

Damn, it hurt.

So that was a good school, St. Thomas, probably one of the best ones. The first day there, I skipped music class, left about thirty minutes in.

I said, "I didn't care about music class."

Damn. They threw me in the jug for two weeks.

A lot of stuff I just didn't enjoy in school. I liked science if it was something experimental. And I liked metal shop a lot. I liked math. I didn't care for English and all that crap.

I kind of liked football. I played football a little bit in junior high school. I played guard. About the time I was in junior high, I started messing with cars. Football was a secondary deal. Then I got tired of working out with them at football, and I just kind of dropped it. That's when I was at Pershing right off of Holcombe.

I dropped out of school my senior year. I had about half a year left. What happened was I started racing more and more and working in my daddy's shop. I was just trying to make more money and spend more time on my race cars. My parents didn't say too much. I was working every day.

Did I ever regret not sticking it out? To be truthful with you, no.

Education was important back then, but it's so much more important today than it was when I got out of school years ago. Back then you were just trying to survive.

I used to spend a lot of time with my [maternal] grandmother when my daddy was in World War II. Her side of the family owned Wilson Grocery Stores. They had a couple of grocery stores down on Shepherd, Twenty-Fifth or Twenty-Sixth. After school I always kind of hung out there. I used to eat Velveeta cheese and crackers that came in little boxes.

I'll never forget the man's name—Mr. DeLeon owned the hardware store, and my mama worked there during the war.

My grandpa Foyt was an auto mechanic, but I never knew him because he had died before I was born. I didn't have that much family. I never knew my great-grandparents. They had all passed. On my father's side, I think my great-grandmother was from Czechoslovakia. My great-grandfather was from Berlin, Germany.

I had a great childhood. The big things I remember most are my daddy's shop and going on picnics with my family and waiting for the weekend so we could go. Those were the highlights.

When Mama and Daddy had saved up enough money, we'd go on a picnic. We went down to Kemah or went somewhere in Galveston. We always picnicked in a park and picked up some wood and got it burning. The biggest thing I liked was roasting marshmallows. We also ate barbecue on our picnics.

My mother used to make divinity fudge for me and a devil's food cake. She also used to make a sweet brown rice. Mama was a good cook. She cooked fried chicken. I always liked fried food, I'm not going to lie. Mainly, I've eaten fried food all my life.

My sister, Marlene, used to teach dancing. A lot of times I'd pick her up in my car and take her to dance class. She'd want me to come in. And they'd have the dancers jump through my arms trying out routines. One little fat girl jumped, and, shit, I went down to the ground with her.

I said, "Man, I can't hold them."

I did that four or five times. Marlene was into professional dancing, and I was only interested in cars. I was always with my cars or motorcycles or bicycles. I wasn't interested in that dancing crap.

When I was about thirteen or fourteen, I had a little twelve-foot Marquis runabout, and my friends Bill Long and Bill Lure wanted to go out riding in my boat. We were in the bay. The only reason I'm here is that it was in January, and it was cold.

I said, "Give me a life jacket to put on."

You know, we were just out playing around. And all of a sudden, a little squall blew up. And I'm trying to turn the boat, and it fell between two waves and it turned over.

And I had on that life jacket when the boat turned over, and the only reason my good friend Bill Long survived was he had on a life jacket, too, because it was cold.

My good friend Bill Lure drowned, and they had to drag for him three or four days, I think, and he was a good swimmer.

And some way Bill Long helped me get to a buoy. Parker Brothers' boat was an oil boat on an oil rig. They dropped the crew off and came back to the buoy and said, "We just felt like there might be someone there."

You see them movies, where you're out there hollering in the water for help. We were hollering. We could see the boat, but they couldn't see us.

And as I woke up, they were slapping my face, and I was on a diesel motor. Later on the coast guard said I didn't have the life jackets on the boat, and I said, "No. The life jackets were on my boat. They were under the bow, you know, where the water pushed them under there."

I'm still scared of water. That was a hell of an experience.

I was in my daddy's shop all the time. When I was real little, they sat me on a shelf in the workshop, and I'd sit there watching everything they'd do. I liked to watch and learn from him. My daddy—he was a hard worker. He worked seven days a week. The shop was the size of a two-car garage back then.

I was about four or five years old when my daddy built my first race car. It was a little car with a rear engine in the back, a Briggs and Stratton

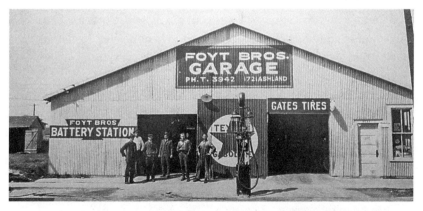

A. J. Foyt's family owned this garage at Ashland and Eighteenth Street in the Houston Heights neighborhood. *Photo courtesy A. J. Foyt*

A. J. Foyt after his second Indianapolis 500 victory in 1964. He is the
only driver to win the race four times. *Photo courtesy A. J. Foyt*

motor. It was kind of like go-carts you see today. I ran that on the sidewalks and the streets. Well, you didn't have a lot of cars then in the
Heights. You know, there wasn't much out there where we lived. I was
mainly on the streets.

My favorite race driver way back then when I was real young was
Doc Cossey. He was the guy who won all the races. He was my hero, even
though my daddy had cars. He was hard to beat here in Houston. They
said he just wanted to be the local hero that won everything at home. He
worked at Pollard Chevrolet downtown.

So my daddy painted my new car to look like Doc Cossey's car.
I remember driving around the racetrack with Doc Cossey in a match
race. He let me win, but I didn't really know that at the time. What I did
know was that I wanted to be a race driver when I grew up.

One time I was really scared. My daddy had midgets, and one night
they went racing in Dallas. So I got my friends to help me take his other
midget out of the garage. They pushed me to get the engine started. It was
a little V8-60 and I started it. I ran around the yard.

———

I hit the side of the house, but I didn't knock it off. I went around the big oak tree in the yard, and I knocked over the swing set and tore up the yard. Then the carburetor caught fire, so I had to stop and put it back in the garage. I didn't get hurt though.

Boy, I knew they were coming back from the race that night late, and I was laying there worrying because I knew Daddy was going to whip my ass. So I laid there in bed, and I heard him.

"That damn boy. I don't know what I'm going to do with him."

My mama said, "Oh, he's just a kid."

"Kid? My butt. He knows better."

My eyes were glued shut like I was sleeping, but I wasn't sleeping. He never did nothing to me about that.

There are certain things you don't tell your mama and daddy. You know, we'd have our cars and soup them up for drag races and all that. That was in the fifties. I had a Ford, a fifties model. I outrun the cops with it.

OST we called it, Old Spanish Trail, was across the street from Playland Park. OST back then was kind of an isolated street. It was straight and had no traffic or nothing. If I had somebody to drag race with, we'd block it off. We'd all meet at Stewart's Drive-In out there at South Main and OST. We'd always put up two dollars or three dollars, you know, maybe. No big thing.

I didn't always win. But I made sure I did the next time.

When I was still in junior high school I had a Ford, had it all souped up. Cops got after me and I outran them. So then I parked it at Bellaire School. There was a show there. I went into the show. I told the cops that I was in the show, which I wasn't.

And I lied to my daddy. Then the other two boys who were with me finally broke down and said, "No, we were all with A. J. We all jumped out and run."

Wasn't nothing that we did wrong, but they were going to get me for speeding. And they were West University cops.

I kept saying, "Naw, I wasn't speeding."

And they finally told me, "Look, all your friends that was with you out there, they said that y'all got out and went to the Bellaire show."

And finally they said, "We're not going to put you on probation. We're not going to do that. All we're going to do is turn you over to your daddy."

I said, "No, do not do that. I don't want you to do that."

They called my daddy, and he come from the shop. He drove a '49 Mercury convertible, a green one.

The cop told him, "Mr. Foyt, we think you've got a good boy. We're not going to file on him, but he told you and me a big lie." He said, "We're going to turn him over to you, but you can't lay a hand on him."

I'm thinking, "Oh, boy, yeah. He's going to beat the shit out of me and my friends."

But we're going back there to the shop and he said; "This is fine. Every day after school you better have your butt here at the shop. At three thirty. I'll take you home after work."

He said, "You don't go on dates. You do nothing."

OK, I'm still sitting there waiting for that hand to come and backhand me. My daddy was strong. He wasn't mean, but he could hold his own pretty damn good.

So I was punished for one year. Every day for a year I was in the shop working after school. He took me home. I saw my car parked there for a year.

On Christmas Eve, my grandmother and my mother said, "Aw, honey, let him go out."

He said, "I said one year."

I never forgot that. That was the day I quit lying.

When I was about fourteen or fifteen, working in my daddy's garage, they brought a car in. I was under it and water and ice was dripping on me. You didn't have all these hydraulic jacks to put it on stands back then. Everything was manual. So I decided it'd be better to be a race car driver than working on those damned things. I didn't like all that water dripping all over me.

My first stock car was a '38 standard Ford, and I bought it out of a junkyard in Austin and towed it home and built it in the yard to start with. I was probably sixteen. I think it fascinated me. It was just something interesting to try to learn to do and have a way to making a living. I liked engineering stuff.

I built my first race car myself. Knowing the mechanics behind it probably made me a better driver. I used to do all my own sprint car work, tow it to the races and work on it at the races—change the setup, mount my own tires, everything. It's so different nowadays.

What I like about the race cars is that you make your own decisions, and if you make a bad decision, you know it. And I guess that's one thing I really loved about racing even when I was young.

Me and my daddy, we were like brothers. When I was a young kid, my daddy had cars that won most of the races around here. Then a bunch of people started saying, "Your daddy's slipping. He can't build a winning car anymore."

Well, the guy who drove for him, Dale Burt, was not what you call a winning race driver. He was like a fourth- or fifth-place driver. Dale was good friends with my daddy, and they had a business together. They called it B & F Garage, Burt and Foyt. Super guy.

When you hear people bad-mouthing your daddy, you're out to prove them wrong. And that's what really started me wanting to be a race car driver. I wanted to win.

To be honest with you, I don't know if my daddy wanted me to grow up to be a race car driver. He built me race cars. He always let me race cars when I was a little bitty kid, but he never said nothing.

When my mama had to sign a release because I was too young to drive, she told my daddy and his friend Jimmy Greer, "Now if y'all hurt that boy, I'll kill both of y'all."

> **What I like about the race cars is that you make your own decisions, and if you make a bad decision, you know it.**

I remember my mama saying that. She started crying.

"Y'all better not hurt that boy of mine."

She worried about me. Guess I really was a mama's boy, kind of. My mother was a sweetheart of a girl. She didn't say much. I can't ever remember her coming to the shop. She probably did some, don't get me wrong, but she mostly stayed in the house.

The first midget I drove was for Red Fondren down at Playland Park, and because Daddy had a guy driving his car, he said, "I'd like to give you a ride in the midget."

I set a new track record—I mean I'm talking Johnny Parsons and Bill

Vukovich and all of them. I mean out-qualified all of them. And after that I started driving for my daddy.

I busted my butt to correct my mistakes. One time at Pan American Speedway in San Antone—I was about nineteen—my daddy got mad at me and fired me and put his midget on the trailer. He said I was going to get killed acting like an idiot on the racetrack, and I said the car wasn't running fast enough.

So I went to another owner, R. L. Furnace, and told him my daddy had fired me. He offered me his car, and I went out and won the feature with it. It was a long ride home with Daddy that night.

My daddy never told me I did a good job. He would probably kill you if you said anything bad about me. He was that type of person. Yeah, now if you started arguing with him about me, OK, that's a different ballgame. But he didn't want me to know it. He kept it all to himself.

I would have to say that nobody taught me—like a lot of people go to driving school, but I just taught myself. I have a natural ability to understand engines, I guess. I don't care what I got into, I was normally able to win. I still want to win.

When I started winning, I wanted more of that. And losing was terrible. You look at a lot of great quarterbacks. You look at great baseball players. I think that's something you're born with. I think that's something the Lord gives you. I don't think that's something that can be taught.

American drivers Dan Gurney, right, and teammate A. J. Foyt after winning the famed endurance race, the 24 Hours of Le Mans, Le Mans, France, 1967. *Photo by Flip Schulke, Flip Schulke Photographic Archive, Briscoe Center for American History, University of Texas at Austin*

Bob Schieffer as a child in Fort Worth. *Photo courtesy Bob Schieffer*

BIRTH NAME	**BOB LLOYD SCHIEFFER**
BORN	February 25, 1937, in Austin to John Emmitt Schieffer and Gladys Payne Schieffer
INTERVIEW	KENS-TV, San Antonio, Texas, December 4, 1981

BOB SCHIEFFER
No Excuses

L ongtime *CBS anchor Bob Schieffer garnered national attention at twenty-six as a reporter for the* Fort Worth Star-Telegram *when he snagged the first interview with the mother of the man arrested for assassinating President John F. Kennedy. His coverage of the Vietnam War for the newspaper attracted the attention of a Dallas-Fort Worth television station and in 1969 launched him into a fifty-year career in the competitive Washington press corps. As chief correspondent from 1982 to 2015, he reported on the White House, Pentagon, Department of State, and Congress. Schieffer anchored the Saturday edition of* CBS Evening News *from 1976 to 1996 and* Face the Nation *from 1991 until his retirement in 2015. He has interviewed every American president since Nixon and moderated three presidential debates. Schieffer was named a Library of Congress Living Legend in 2008 and was inducted into the National Television Academy of Arts and Sciences Hall of Fame in 2013. His alma mater, Texas Christian University, houses the Bob Schieffer College of Communication.*

I was born in Austin. We moved to Fort Worth when I was five years old. I grew up there and went to public school and to Texas Christian University there.

My father, John, was a building contractor in Fort Worth. He started out working in a lumberyard in Austin, and we moved to Fort Worth during World War II. He died at age fifty when I was a sophomore at TCU. My father was a very shy person, and I'm told I look like him. I guess because he was so quiet, he gave us all an opportunity to talk a lot. We're all nonstop talkers.

On my father's side, we're part of that group of Germans who came to Texas beginning in 1849. After landing in Galveston, they settled around New Braunfels and eventually Austin. The Germans had come from a Europe that was plagued by war, and when our Civil War came, many were war resisters to a war that was far away from Texas.

My mother, Gladys, was a very strong-willed, determined person who was the major influence on all of us. She didn't pay much attention to the adage "Spare the rod and spoil the child." She was the rule maker and the rule enforcer.

As a child, my mother's father walked beside a covered wagon from Tennessee to Texas. On that side of the family, some back in Tennessee fought with the Union, some with the Confederates.

We were a close family, more so after my father died. I was the oldest. My sister, Sharon, is five years younger, and my brother, Tom, is ten years younger. He was almost like a son to me because our father died when he was just ten years old. I am also close to my sister.

Our family values were very simple. There was no excuse for not doing your best—no excuse. I was reminded of that when I was sixteen and smarted off to my mother, and she whacked me across the shoulder with a broomstick.

When my brother was at the University of Texas, he got in an argument with her and told her, "You never had to come down to Austin and get me out of jail for smoking dope like some of my friends' parents had to do!"

She responded, "I didn't send you down there to go to jail."

You got no credit from her for doing what you were expected to do in the first place.

In Texas you grow up with the attitude that you are a little different because you're from Texas. I don't know how that reality manifests itself, but I do kind of have that feeling.

Most of my fondest memories about growing up involve baseball. I always played catcher, but in high school I got beat out and wound up second string. But I was a walk-on at TCU and made the starting lineup on the freshman team. Unfortunately, I got hurt at midseason when Dizzy Dean's nephew, Paul Dean Jr., who played for SMU, hit me in the eye. That ended my baseball dreams, and I turned my attention more and more to journalism.

We didn't have Little League when I was growing up. We had the recreation department's league in those days. When I was twelve years old, I hit a home run with the bases loaded. It won the game. It was like *Fantasy Island*. I was playing for a team called the River Oaks Kittens, and it was the first organized team I had ever been on. I can remember that day as well as if it were yesterday. I remember hitting that home run. Maybe because I never hit another one, but I remember where the ball went and watching the center fielder watch as it went over his head.

Later, in American Legion baseball, there was a game where I got

As a young journalist, Bob Schieffer interviewed Marguerite Oswald, Lee Harvey Oswald's mother, after the Kennedy assassination. *Photo courtesy Bob Schieffer*

three hits, and I can still remember every detail. I'd lie in bed and watch it again and again in my mind.

I have a funny memory in that way. When I used to do the CBS eleven o'clock news in New York on Sunday nights, I would get so enthusiastic that after it was over, I would go to the hotel and discover I had memorized the entire newscast, not only the words but the graphics as well.

Because of World War II, we moved a lot when I was in the first grade. We moved from Austin to Waco and then to Fort Worth and back, then to Houston for a brief period and then finally back to Fort Worth. We thought my father was going to be drafted. Then it turned out that he was too old, and they didn't take him.

After that, we lived in Fort Worth in a middle-class neighborhood in a housing project built by the company where he worked. When I was in about the eighth grade, we moved across town into a house he built in River Oaks.

My grandparents were old and lived in Austin, and we didn't see them much. It was very difficult with the war going on. Nobody had cars, and nobody had tires. I remember when we moved from Austin to Waco,

Bob Schieffer's first anchor job at CBS in the early 1970s was for the 11 p.m. Sunday broadcast. *Photo courtesy Bob Schieffer*

---

we borrowed the tires off my uncle's car and put them on our car because our tires weren't good enough to get to Forth Worth. My grandfather followed us in his car carrying our tires. He took my uncle's tires back to him.

I'll never forget that during the war our family had a '36 Ford, which was literally worn out. It had a canvas top, and there were so many holes in it that whenever it would rain, my mother would open an umbrella inside the car.

When the war was over, I remember the sense of relief. We lived near Carswell Air Force Base, where they made bombers. I don't think I really understood at that time what wars were, but I knew there was a war. It was something that was always there.

What I remember most was when Roosevelt died. I was with my mother and standing on the front of her shopping cart at the Loveless Grocery Store in River Oaks just outside Fort Worth. We got up to the checkout stand and someone was crying, and someone said that Roosevelt had died. I was frightened and remember thinking, "We can't go on."

My first-grade teacher, Doris Carroll, said she always knew Bobby was going to be a reporter because I used to make up little stories even in the first grade. I always wanted to be a reporter, but I always liked to draw, and sometimes it was in the back of my mind that maybe I wanted to be an artist.

I was a good student. I always liked English, reading and government. I was an all-A student except for a few Bs in high school. I went to North Side High School in Fort Worth, and I was the sports editor of the high school newspaper and editor of the high school annual. I had been on the junior high newspaper, too.

For some reason unbeknownst to anybody, I started out in premed at TCU. I guess it was because little boys used to think they were supposed to grow up to be doctors. It was a terrible choice. I was awful at it. After two years, I went to work at a radio station at night, and I switched over to journalism. I never looked back.

Whatever talent I have, I got it by making a lot of mistakes. Most of the things I've learned in life, I've managed to learn the hardest way possible.

While I always wanted to be a reporter, I didn't know about broadcast journalism because there was no television when I was a boy.

In the years after World War II, there were a lot of gamblers and gangsters in Fort Worth, which was a fairly wide-open city. When I was a sophomore at TCU, I worked nights at a small radio station that had panel trucks equipped with police radios. When the police radio reported a crime or traffic accident, we raced to the scene and did on-the-scene reports by two-way radio. That was a big thing back in the fifties. All the radio stations had these little mobile units, and we'd cover what we called the "three Rs": 'recks, rapes, and robberies. No car accident was too minor for us to report.

During that time, some gangsters set off a bomb at the Penguin Club, an underworld dive on the east side of Fort Worth. I went out to cover it. I walked up to the cop at the door and flashed my press card.

The cop said, "I'm sorry, I'll have to see your ID with your birthday on it."

I was the only reporter I've ever known that couldn't cover a bombing because the cop on the door carded me and said I was too young to go into a bar. It was a proud day at the station when I finally turned twenty-one and could not be turned away from a crime because of age—a victory of sorts for freedom of the press.

The first politician I knew about was Lyndon Johnson. In 1948, when I was eleven, he came to our neighborhood in the northwest side of Fort Worth. And it was big news because he came in a helicopter, and we had never seen one.

He had an electronic bullhorn, and as he was landing he started saying, "This is your candidate for the United States Senate, Lyndon B. Johnson."

It scared the devil out of us. We didn't know if it was God or what it was, but it was a great day, and I think that's where my fascination with politics really began.

CBS anchors Dan Rather and Walter Cronkite, like Bob Schieffer, claimed Texas as their home. Cronkite and Rather covered the Democratic National Convention in Atlanta, Georgia, in July 1988. *Photo by Dennis Brack, Dennis Brack Photographic Archive, Briscoe Center for American History, University of Texas at Austin*

Anchors Away from Texas

There was a time when all the anchors at CBS were from Texas. At one point I did the Sunday night news, and I was from Fort Worth. Dan Rather did the Saturday news, and he's from Wharton. Hughes Rudd did the morning news; he was from Waco. And Walter Cronkite did the evening news. He grew up in Austin and Houston, although he was born in Missouri. But Walter considered himself a Texan.

We all used to laugh when Nixon's vice president, Spiro Agnew, would rant about the "Eastern liberal press."

We were all from one place. He just didn't know what place.

Trini Lopez, age five. *Photo courtesy Trini Lopez*

BIRTH NAME	**TRINIDAD LOPEZ III**
BORN	May 15, 1937, in Dallas to Trinidad Lopez Jr. and Petra Gonzalez Lopez
DIED	August 11, 2020
INTERVIEW	La Mansión del Norte, San Antonio, Texas, October 30, 1981

TRINI LOPEZ

A Little Barrio Called the Alamo

Folk singer Trini Lopez was the original Latin pop superstar, whose 1963 rendition of Pete Seeger's "If I Had a Hammer" stayed in the Top 40 for forty-eight consecutive weeks and hit number one in thirty-eight countries. The single and his debut album, Trini Lopez at PJ's, sold five million copies. His version of the classic "La Bamba," later popularized by his friend Ritchie Valens, earned Lopez the nickname Mr. La Bamba. One of the leading guitar players and songwriters of the early 1960s, he also produced top chart singles such as "Lemon Tree" and "Sally Was a Good Old Girl." Hollywood gave him a cameo in Marriage on the Rocks in 1965 and a role in the ensemble cast of The Dirty Dozen in 1967. As a popular nightclub performer, he was inducted into the Las Vegas Walk of Stars. In 2015, PBS aired Trini Lopez and Friends: Live Again— A 50th Anniversary Salute.

I was born in 1937 and raised in a Negro and Mexican ghetto in Dallas. Our little barrio about a mile in radius was called the Alamo. The Mexicans were fighting the Blacks, and the Blacks were fighting the Mexicans, and there were no American white people around there. They didn't want to come close. Even the police hated to come into the neighborhood because they would get in trouble.

So there were a lot of killings. People were killed in my back alley. The Mexican and Black gangs would bash your head in just to steal a dollar or two from your pockets. I remember one killing in particular because it happened in back of my house. They found this wino with his whole head bashed in with part of a motor. They said he was killed for two dollars.

I was eight or nine years old then. I felt very insecure and very afraid to live there. All the kids I was growing up with were in gangs, and I was, too.

On a typical night with the gang, we'd hang out at a place called Pike Park. It's ironic. Because I hung around in this park, it now has a historical marker. But I hung around there for terrible reasons. The majority of the Latins in Dallas hung around this park.

I don't remember stealing. I remember running around late with the guys and having gang fights and breaking windows and stuff like that. Fighting was the big thing. A lot of my friends are dead because they got too carried away. You graduated from fistfights to knives and then to guns. Many of my friends ended up dead from gunshot wounds; they were killed in gang wars. A lot of them are in prison for life for murder.

My father and mother both always had been very strict. Even though they never went to school, they were very, very rich in spiritual guidance and caring for their children. My father noticed I was running around with the wrong kind of people.

He said to me three times, "When I come home from work, I want you to be home."

I didn't listen to him. The third time I wasn't home, he took his belt off and gave me a real good whipping. I cried all night long, not because I was physically hurt but because I was spiritually hurt.

To make up for hitting me, the next day he brought me a little old beat-up guitar.

He said, "Look, I went to the pawnshop on the way home and bought you this. I want you to learn something constructive, so I'm going to teach you all the songs I used to sing when I was a boy your age."

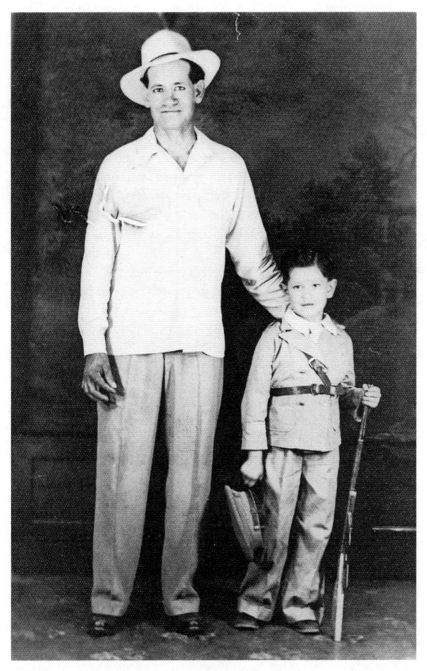

Trini Lopez with his father, c. 1942. *Photo courtesy Trini Lopez*

He started teaching me on this twelve-dollar guitar. He couldn't afford twelve dollars at the time. He started getting me interested in music. My father knew some singing and dancing when he was a young man in Mexico before he married my mother. He was an actor. The most famous song he taught me was "El Rancho Grande." He taught me songs like "Tú, Sólo Tú" and "Juan Charrasqueado," really old songs that were big in the thirties. Because of my father, I quit hanging out with the gangs. I thank him for giving me that incentive.

My friends didn't like me then because I was no longer part of the gang. I'd be studying in my room, and they'd say, "Come on, Trini, let's go play." When I would tell them that I had to stay home and study my guitar and my singing, they'd call me a sissy.

The minute my father gave me that guitar, I fell in love with music.

The minute my father gave me that guitar, I fell in love with music. Our family used to sing together. My mother had a beautiful voice. I started listening whenever I could to the beat-up, old radio at the house. I listened to rock 'n' roll and popular music.

One nice thing about being born in America is that you get into the American customs. I owe everything to this country and to my parents. President Franklin D. Roosevelt passed a bill that Mexican immigrants could stay in this country. Because of that, my parents did not have to be deported. Without that bill, I would be washing dishes in Mexico today.

My father and my mother were never educated. They came to Texas from Guanajuato, Mexico, in the 1920s. They came for survival. That's why all the Mexican people come here in the first place—to eat, to work, and to make a living.

My father first went to Chicago before he married. When he got a little money, he went back to Mexico and married my mother. When he brought her to the States, they came through Laredo.

My father worked in factories, and then he ended up in a place called Eunice, Texas. He worked there in the cotton crops and other things. A priest told him he should go to Dallas because he had a growing family and the children needed to go to school. In a little town, the poor people didn't go to school. So we moved to Dallas, and that's where most of us were born. There were six children in my family, four girls and two boys. I'm the fourth oldest.

My whole family spoke Spanish. In school we learned English, and at home we spoke Spanish. My parents never allowed English to be spoken at home. They were very proud. In school, we never were allowed to speak Spanish. I went to school without knowing English when I was nine years old. I cried like a baby my first day of school because I was so insecure.

In the old days, the families were very insecure because they were Mexican. In Texas Mexicans were treated as badly as the Blacks in the forties. Because of the insecurity, the folks kept their children at home as long as they could, thinking that as the children grew a little older, they would be more able to take care of themselves in school.

When I started kindergarten, it was basically Latin. My parents couldn't afford to send us to a parochial school, but they did. They made a big sacrifice. I don't remember what the tuition was, but it was expensive for us in those days, and we had to buy our books. I went to St. Ann's Elementary School and to Crozier Tech High School in downtown Dallas.

My father worked three jobs to support us. He was a maintenance man at Southern Methodist University. He worked at hotels as a houseman, and he used to cut the lawns of beautiful homes in Dallas, where we live now. My father worked hard so that we always had shoes to wear and clothes that were decent; he worked very hard all his life to support us. I had to quit school in the senior year to go to work full time. By that time, we were really bad off, so I had to help my father bring in a living. I had helped him do lawns until I was about fourteen.

Poverty is my most vivid memory. You can't erase that. As long as I live, I'll never forget that. We never had the right clothes, we never had the right food, we never had the right home, we never had the right anything.

We had one room and one kitchen. That was it for eight of us. We all slept in one room. We had little cots. When we went up north to work in the fields, it was worse because we slept on the floor and on the ground.

I was born at home. My mother had the babies all by herself, and then the doctor would come. My mother had nine children that way, and three died because of it. I'm close to all of my brothers and sisters.

My mother made our clothes from gunnysacks. When you bought

215

Trini Lopez, age ten, serenades girls in a play at St. Ann's Elementary School in Dallas. *Photo courtesy Trini Lopez*

flour in the old days, it came in cloth sacks. My mother used to wash clothes and iron for other people to help make a living.

Our whole family worked in the fields during the summer. Eight or ten families would go together in a big old truck with canvas on it. We worked in the rain, the sleet, the snow; it didn't matter what the weather was. By the time September came along, up north it was already getting very cold. Some years we would pick tomatoes and the vines were all ice. All this green stuff from the vines would be embedded in your skin for months afterward.

I started working at age eight. My sisters started when they were eight, nine, or ten years old. We did all kinds of things. I've been a busboy and a dishwasher. I used to wash pots and pans at big hotels. By the time I was nine or ten years old, I started getting into music. People liked my singing right away. I used to give all the money I made to my mother.

Then she would give me whatever she wanted to, and I would buy something I wanted, like a shirt.

My sisters weren't allowed to wear slacks. I wasn't allowed to wear blue jeans until I was twenty. I had to wear khaki pants. My mother pressed them, and they were starched like a soldier's. Poor as we were, my father never allowed blue jeans in the house. That's all that we really should have been able to afford. My sisters could not go out until they were twenty-one. Even though my parents were very poor, they were strict and so aware of manners.

My first singing for money was similar to mariachis in Mexican restaurants. We had a little rumba band and our outfits had ruffled shirts, Desi Arnaz stuff.

Music has always been very good to me. By the time I was thirteen or fourteen years old, I was making a lot of money singing. By age eighteen, I was making $200 or $300 a week, good money in the fifties. So when I would give the money to my mother, she would give me back more and more.

I used to see a pair of alligator loafers in a real pretty store in Dallas. I kept going by there and longing for these loafers. So one day, I came home with a pair of those $55 alligator loafers, and my mother nearly hit me. But she let me keep them.

My parents were very strict Catholics. I was an altar boy. My mother prayed all the time, and we had an altar in our home always. She put it anywhere she could find. In those days, we were lucky to have four walls. We always had a lot of candles burning.

She believed in saints and always prayed to them to keep us safe. She prayed to different saints for different reasons. She gave all of us saints' names. I'm Holy Trinity. My brother Jessie is Jesus. One sister is Lucy Grace. My mother's name is Petra and her last name was Gonzalez. My father's name is Trinidad. I'm the third Trinidad in our family.

On Christmas, we always went to Midnight Mass, and then we'd open up our presents. We didn't get any presents when we were young kids because we could not afford gifts. But as we got older and all started working, we bought presents.

The most important moral my parents taught me was to be an humble person. They stressed to always be a gentleman, to always treat everybody kindly, to never hurt anyone. Their virtues were great.

Frank Sinatra has always been my idol and my hero. I used to listen to the big band sounds of Woody Herman and Tommy Dorsey. I started listening to singers like Fats Domino and Chuck Berry. I used to sing all the hits from those days. I didn't stick to just Latin music; I did everything. I liked commercial music rather than the mariachi music I grew up with.

Buddy Holly was a friend of mine, and he heard me sing in Wichita Falls, Texas. He said to me, "How would you like to record one day? Why don't you meet this disc jockey in Clovis, New Mexico? Maybe I can help you."

So I packed my bags in my beat-up station wagon that had signs saying "Trini Lopez and His Combo" all over it. I had five guys in the group then and took them with me, as well as our uniforms and equipment. We went to Clovis, and it backfired.

The disc jockey said, "We can't have you sing and call it Trini Lopez. We're going to have to call it something else."

This was before people like Vikki Carr. I was the pioneer. I told him that wouldn't do because I'd been making good money for the last eight years and had been successful in Dallas and other places with my name and my group.

The guys in the group conspired against me. I'll never forget the next morning. They woke me up and said, "We've got some news for you. We're going to call this group the Big Bees and no longer are you going to be lead singer. From now on, we're all going to sing, and we're all going to make the same money you're making."

I told them that wasn't right, and I started crying like a baby. I was only eighteen. It was terrible. I started over again with another group. When it comes to success, life is destiny to me. If God wants you to do something, he's going to call for you. I believe in that.

That disc jockey had liked me. On New Year's Eve the following year, I got a call from him and he said, "I guess you know about Buddy Holly getting killed. His group, the Crickets, remembers you from Clovis. They would like you to be their lead singer and take over Buddy's place. I want you to come to Los Angeles and start rehearsing with them."

I couldn't believe it. I said, "Oh, my God."

I was working then in Lubbock, Buddy's hometown, in a beautiful place called the Millionaire's Club and making about $500 a week. The guy sent me cash to fly out to Los Angeles, but I kept it and drove out in my station wagon so I could save a little money.

I left my home when I was twenty, and I went to Los Angeles with just my guitar, my clothes, and $200 in my pocket. I wasn't coming back until I'd made it.

But it never worked out with the Crickets. The manager of the Crickets, who was a nice fellow but looked like a real Hollywood shyster, told me there was a place looking for an act to open a show at Ye Little Club.

At the audition, the man stopped me in the middle of the song and said, "You're great. You're hired. You open tonight for two weeks."

I stayed there a year. I got a big following in Beverly Hills, and I opened a show for Jack Jones and Gene McDaniels. Frank Sinatra, my idol, came to hear me, and he gave me an eight-year recording contract with Reprise Records, where I recorded "If I Had a Hammer" and "Kansas City."

I just wanted to see him in person one day, let alone work for him. That was the beginning of my career and my records.

Singer Trini Lopez grew up in Dallas. *Photo courtesy Trini Lopez*

Robert Crippen, age two. *Photo courtesy Robert Crippen*

BIRTH NAME	**ROBERT LAUREL CRIPPEN**
BORN	September 11, 1937, in Beaumont to Herbert Wesley Crippen and Ruth Cynthia Andress Crippen
INTERVIEW	Driskill Hotel, Austin, Texas, August 18, 2017

ROBERT CRIPPEN
Dreams of Flying

S huttle astronaut Robert Crippen piloted STS-1, the first orbital spaceflight of the space shuttle Columbia, America's first space-rated orbiter in NASA's space shuttle fleet. With a degree in aerospace engineering from the University of Texas at Austin in 1960 and a commission as a US Navy aviation officer, he served on the astronaut support crew for Skylab 2, 3, and 4 missions and the Apollo-Soyuz Test Project mission. He commanded three Challenger shuttle missions, including STS-7, in which female astronaut Sally Ride broke the US gender barrier in space. Crippen logged over 565 hours in space, orbited the earth 374 times, and traveled over 9.4 million miles. He served as deputy director of the space shuttle program at Kennedy Space Center in Florida from 1987 to 1989 and space shuttle director at NASA headquarters in Washington, DC, from 1990 to 1992. As director of Kennedy Space Center from 1992 to 1995, he oversaw twenty-two space shuttle missions. He accepted the nation's highest award for spaceflight accomplishments, the Congressional Space Medal of Honor, in 2006.

My dad, Herbert Crippen, was born on the wrong side of the Red River. He was from Oklahoma. My mother was Ruth Cynthia Andress, and she was born in Texas near Livingston. I think her dad's side came to Texas back in the 1600s or 1700s. They were here a long time.

My dad worked in the oil fields; he was a driller. I think he was working near Livingston, and that's how he and my mother got together. They traveled all over. I arrived when he was working in Beaumont, but we were only there probably about six months, and then we were off to California or someplace else. He worked mainly for small drilling companies that were subsidiaries that supported the big guys.

When I was very young, we traveled around quite a bit. When we were in Louisiana, he had an accident and lost two fingers of his right hand. He received a settlement from the insurance company and went through medical treatment in Houston. While we were living in Houston for a short period of time, he looked for another line of work. He ended up buying the location where I grew up, which was raising chickens on a small farm. I think we moved to the Porter area when I was about five.

Dad decided he wanted to open a restaurant and service station. He built the building and all of that, to the best of my recollection, all by himself. It was a beer joint—I'd call it a tavern—and a Gulf service station.

Dad and Mom were working there all the time, and my sister and I pretty much had the run of the house. The business was only fifty yards away from where our home was, so I ran back and forth. I worked pumping gas at their station and did those kinds of things growing up.

My sister is three years younger than I am. Her name is Betty Lou, and I named her. I was three or four, I think, when she was born. My sister and I kept care of the house. We cleaned the house, swept the floors, and even learned to cook at an early age.

Dad was a hard worker and good with his hands, much better than I ever was. I didn't feel all that close to him, but, you know, it was a terrible shock to me when I lost him later on in life. I admired the guy for the way he worked and provided for the family. Even though it was a kind of a poor area, we never really wanted for anything.

He only went through the third grade, because he had to go to work after that. My mom was a stay-at-home mom until they moved down to Porter. Mom was similar, a hardworking person, and she was pretty smart. She did graduate from high school, and if there was any writing or math to be done, she was the one who did that for the family.

My relationship with my mother was a mixed bag. There were times we got along and times we didn't get along. But in general, we had a pretty good relationship.

Mom was a good cook. She cooked country food—fried chicken, fried okra, barbecue, Texas food. One of my favorites was ham and scalloped potatoes. She knew how to make it better than anyone else. She made chicken and dumplings for Thanksgiving, as well as the turkey.

If we had guests, she would load the table up with food. There would be about five times the amount that was needed. I think that was common for people who grew up in the Depression where things were really tight.

I'm not a religious person. I don't know if my folks were religious. They worked all the time, but they took us to Sunday school. They'd take us and drop us off and come back and pick us up.

You name it, we did them all. We did Baptist, Methodist, Pentecostal, the whole thing. My sister and I went to Sunday school for quite a few years when we were growing up, probably six, seven, eight, nine, ten, something like that. My sister continued that, so it took on her.

It did not take on me.

I was just probably a normal kid growing up. Back where I grew up, Porter was just a little country town, and we didn't have that many neighbors close by. I was pretty much on my own most of the time. I played with my sister. I think I was probably adventurous, inquisitive, reasonably intelligent. Didn't get into too much trouble.

We had about twenty-five acres where we lived. My dad started out letting the highway department dig out a portion of it to make a pond. And then the highway people wanted more dirt and more dirt, and that progressed to about a twelve-acre small lake out there. I loved to fish. I grew up fishing on the lake and hunting frogs and doing that kind of thing.

I had a .22 rifle when I was eight years old. Got it for Christmas. I learned how to use it very safely. Hunting was pretty common way out in the country. The only thing I remember that I shot and killed was a bird, a big woodpecker or something, and I said, "Why did I do that?"

I walked around with my rifle and a shotgun and pretended I was hunting deer but never shot one.

I was in 4-H for a while. I had this little bull that I helped raise, but I don't know if I was raising him for that. But we had goats, rabbits. We ate rabbits, but one of the things we used to do when Easter time came around is get some bunnies, put them in a basket, and go over and sell them to customers.

I remember enjoying an Erector Set, and I think I remember building a Ferris wheel. I also remember having a chemistry set. One day I was making soap and trying to follow the formula. The room I was in had these varnished hardwood floors, and I spilled some on there and it took the varnish up. I got in trouble for that.

As I got older, I ended up getting a small motorbike. They didn't have so-called dirt bikes back then, but I used to ride it around the lake. I probably started tinkering with my motorbike. I knew how to take the carburetors apart and put them back together. I drove too fast as a teen, like a lot of kids. Almost killed myself a couple of times. Driving fast reflected the times and what everybody else was doing.

I think I was like any other kid growing up in Texas. I was proud to be a Texan and not shy about telling people about it.

I had horses. That's a very Texas thing. They bought my sister and me a Shetland pony when we were about six years old. Her name was Lady, and we'd ride her all over. And then I got a small horse named Sugar. She used to bite. Boy, I tell you, putting the bridle on her was some kind of a challenge.

And, certainly, I had cowboy boots but never got into them.

I started to school in New Caney. They didn't have kindergarten then. I think my folks lied about my age by a couple of weeks. I turned six on September 11, and I think school started about September 1. They didn't hold me back.

It was just a small school. It was all in one building, first through twelfth grades. My graduating class was about twenty, and quite a few of the people I started school with graduated with me. We went through all twelve years together.

I didn't particularly like English and don't know that we really studied much science. But math, science, and history, I guess, were probably three of my favorite subjects. My favorite teacher was Mrs. Henson. She was my eighth-grade teacher, and then she moved into high school when I went there, and she taught us history, in fact, as well as other things.

224

I didn't have to study hard to make good grades, and she would find ways to challenge me somehow.

When we lived in Houston and I was probably three or four years old, my dad would take me out to Hobby Airport. We would watch the planes come in, land, and take off over the fence. One day there was an airplane sitting there, and I'm pretty sure it was a DC-3. There was what we now call a flight attendant.

She saw us looking at it, and she said, "Do you want to see the airplane?"

You know, at that time you didn't have security, and we walked through the gate and we went on board. I ended up sitting in the pilot's seat. I was a kid and I was enthralled by it. After that I built model airplanes and flew them. I just knew I wanted to fly at a very young age.

I dreamed about flying. You know, at that time, when I was a kid, there was no such thing as an astronaut. I used to think, if I could just really fly myself, like Superman—go jump off barns and what have you. Flash Gordon was around, but none of us thought spaceflight would be a reality. Going into space was a thing unimaginable.

That fascination with flying started when I was four years old and went all the way until twenty-two, when I graduated college. Airplanes was something I wanted to do.

I had heroes like all kids growing up. My World War II heroes weren't the generals like Eisenhower because I was interested in the aviation part of it. I used to read about aviation a lot. There was a gentleman by the name of Chuck Yeager, first man who flew faster than the speed of sound. Jimmy Doolittle was a hero of mine. Doolittle was in World War II. If they flew and I could read about them, I was inspired.

I did read a lot, but don't ask me now what I read. We had a little library in the school, but there wasn't a library per se in Porter. It was just the school library. That's all we had. I liked adventure books, like Tom Sawyer and Huck Finn. The Hardy Boys—those kinds of books.

I grew up wanting to leave town. I was going to get out of there. Just not much there, you know, and I wanted to do bigger things, and it wasn't a place for me. I had an early wanderlust.

I thought the whole world was a steam bath until I went other places outside the Big Thicket. My folks never had an air conditioner. Mom used to think they made you sick. Going in and out of that cold air, you know, it's not good for you. They had big fans that blew hot air around.

We had mosquitoes and snakes. I can remember going out to collect the eggs and finding a snake wrapped around the eggs. I also remember once there was a copperhead in the barn area there, and I swore he was aggressive. He was coming at me.

I remember World War II. This was after we had moved to Porter already. Because of those two missing fingers, Dad was 4-F during World

War II. We were going to a movie in Humble. We were driving, and all of a sudden they were stopping all the cars and made us turn off the lights. We were having a blackout on the road. I think it was just a practice. That is my most vivid memory of World War II. Oh, it made you think that somebody was going to come and invade us.

I remember as a kid also throwing knives; sticking knives in stuff was a common practice. We'd draw pictures of Hitler and Mussolini and Tojo and throw our knives at them.

I was not a jock. We played six-man football because we had such a small school. I don't know if they

Robert Crippen played saxophone in his high school band. *Photo courtesy Robert Crippen*

still play that in Texas anymore, but it was prevalent at that time, and I wanted to play football. When I got to be a freshman in high school, I went out for football and was not bad.

But they were also starting a band. I had played piano as a kid, and I wanted to play the musical instruments in the band. I asked the school if I could do both, and they said, "Sure."

So my folks went out and bought a tenor saxophone for me. So here I was with a tenor sax, and about two weeks into the year the school said, "No, you can't do both. We got football practices scheduled at the same time as band practice. You have to choose one."

My folks had spent all this money on the tenor sax, and I didn't feel like I could give that up. So I elected to go do that. I thought I was pretty good, but I wasn't that good. But I enjoyed it.

Now looking back, I see all these kids with concussions from playing football, so I think that maybe playing sax instead was smart.

When I was in high school, I used to go stand out on the road and wave down the Trailways Bus and go into Houston and go to movies by myself when I was probably about fifteen years old.

My first job was in Houston. I was an office boy for Texas Company, which is Texaco Gas now. That was in downtown Houston. I just walked in and said, "Can you use me?"

I got my driver's license as soon as I turned sixteen, but I had been driving around in the country since I was fourteen or so. I wanted my driver's license as soon as I could get it. My first car was a '49 Ford sedan. It was a piece of junk.

I worked during the summers to earn money to help me go to college. Paying for college was a combination of my folks and me, but I paid a good deal of it.

One thing I did that I really enjoyed was working for the railroad for something called the Houston Belt and Terminal. They essentially had trains brought in by Union Pacific and everybody. They made up trains to send out and also delivered railcars to the various businesses around town. I was the switchman doing that. I got to run on top of the train and unhook the cars. It was a fun job, definitely, for a kid.

The way the union was set up then, I made as a starter as much money as the guy who had been working there for quite a few years. So it paid good. The first summer when I was finishing up and getting ready to go back to college, I told my mom I was going to give them my notice so I could start school again.

She said, "Bobby, you're going to quit that good-paying job to go back to college?"

I can't remember a time not believing that I was going to college. I think it was because Dad only got through the third grade. He was going to make sure that I somehow got a college education.

When I graduated high school, money was reasonably tight, so I elected my first year to go to the University of Houston because I had a friend who lived in Houston. He had come out to my house and lived with us, and we graduated high school together. He reciprocated, and I moved into his house in the Houston area.

It was tough. I mean, all of a sudden, I had to study, and I really didn't know how to study because I never had to do that before. I thought initially that I might study electrical engineering, but I knew from an early age that I wanted to fly planes. So I decided an aeronautical engineer was what I wanted to be.

I elected on my second year to go to Sam Houston in Huntsville. It was a smaller school, but I learned how to study and started making good grades again. I knew at that time my ultimate objective was to get into the University of Texas and study engineering. I had a cousin graduate from UT with a degree in engineering, and maybe that influenced me somewhat. I liked building things, tearing up things, and putting them back together, and that's what engineering is.

By the time I got to UT, I was used to studying. It was not as difficult as that freshman year at U of H. It was still a challenge though, and I ended up doing pretty good at UT. I figured that I needed to do something bigger than this big university to find a way to get on the right road. It was a matter of just finding the right road. No matter where you start out, if you've got the determination to do something, it's possible you can do it.

I think my parents seemed to have a great deal of confidence in me, and if I wanted to do something, I was usually able to do it. They never told me I couldn't do something, unless it was something that was going to get me in trouble. I'm sure all my youth combined together gave me some of that same self-confidence.

I was nineteen when Sputnik went up. I think I watched Sputnik flying over us in Porter. We went out in the yard to see it. There was lots of concern that not only could they see us, but they could put a bomb up there and drop it on us.

I don't recall having any hysteria around. It was a challenge that said, "Hey, if they can do that, then they are doing better than we are. So we need to find a way to overcome that."

Which is what Kennedy did when he gave us the goal of going to the moon. We hadn't even flown in space except for Al Shepard, who went up in the suborbital flight. We hadn't put John Glenn into orbit when he gave us that goal.

And then, not long after Sputnik flew, we selected the first seven Mercury astronauts. I quickly noted that all of them were military test pilots. Four of the seven were naval aviators.

And so I said, "I think I might try to do that."

In my senior year of college, I went home and told them I had decided I was going to join the navy. I think I wanted to be a part of helping us catch up and eventually get ahead. I don't remember any fear there. I guess if you want to do something bad enough, you just suppress all those kinds of things that say, "Hey, this could kill me."

Pilot Robert Crippen prior to his first space shuttle mission, STS-1, in the space suit he wore for launch and entry. *NASA photo, courtesy Robert Crippen*

Rex Reed has fond memories of his grandmother's farm in West Texas. *Photo courtesy Rex Reed*

BIRTH NAME	**REX ZACHARY REED**
BORN	October 2, 1938, in Fort Worth to James M. Reed and Jewell Smith Reed
INTERVIEW	By phone, New York City, April 26, 1982

27

REX REED

Memories Captured in Quilts

R ex Reed, acerbic film critic for the New York Observer, *is known for a fearless and freewheeling writing style that has been show-cased in* Vogue, GQ, Women's Wear Daily, *and the* New York Times. *He has issued often stinging critiques in regular reviews for the* Observer, *the* New York Daily News, *and the* New York Post. *Along with Tom Wolfe and Hunter S. Thompson, among other high-profile writers in the 1970s, Reed's no-holds-barred writing created the New Journalism movement that freed journalists to apply literary techniques to nonfiction. Reed authored eight books about the enter-tainment industry, including four celebrity biographies. He starred in the syndicated series* At the Movies *for five years. As an actor, Reed appeared in* Myra Breckinridge *in 1970,* Superman *in 1978, and* Inchon *in 1981. He appeared in the 2009 documentary* For the Love of Movies: The Story of American Film Criticism, *in which he recounted the influence of movie critics in the 1970s.*

I remember my childhood in quilts—beautiful patchwork quilts with cabins on them or in wedding band patterns. These quilts were made by hand; no sewing machine was ever used. I have most of them on display in my house on my farm in Connecticut.

When I look at those quilts, I relive my childhood. I see all my shirts and Mother's dresses in them. We'd send my grandma all our scraps. As a child, I could never understand why Mom would tear up shirts. But I never saw my grandma sewing. She didn't take time away from her grandchildren to quilt; she patched them together on long winter nights. Antique dealers have offered me a fortune, but I could never part with even one of them.

I was an only child. But both my mother and father were from families of ten children, so I had lots of cousins.

Daddy's name was Jimmy M. Reed. I was named Rex Zachary Reed for a relative, General Zachary Taylor.

I was born in Fort Worth and moved to Louisiana when I was six. But I came back to Texas a lot to visit my grandmother in a small town between Goldthwaite and Brownwood called Mullin. We moved to Lutcher, a tiny Louisiana town, because my father was an oil company supervisor for Humble, and this was a branch office for offshore drilling. My family finally settled in Baton Rouge.

I look like a combination of both parents. My mother stayed at home with me, so I was close to her. My father was away and didn't always come home at night. He worked rigs and quarter boats five or six days and then would come in for two.

My dad was the one who said "no." I grew up defensive about my father, but now we're good friends. As a grown man, I've been in analysis to deal with my childhood. In the last few years, I've come to grips with my feelings about my father. I was never close to him. I have no memories of my father teaching me anything.

Mom read Vacation Bible School stories and took me to church, shopping, and movies. She was young and beautiful. She was like my girlfriend. Years later I resolved the Oedipal complex in analysis, too.

My need for analysis would not have happened if we'd stayed in Texas. We wouldn't have had these problems if my father had stayed on the farm and we'd all been together. Family life was different in Texas when we had a farm. We loved animals and grew things. I was never into rigs and stuff; I didn't want to be an oilman.

Now this has come full circle. I have a farm in Connecticut. I spend weekends there up to my elbows in manure. I have peach trees like Grandmother had. I grow flowers. I'm a country squire with strong Texas roots. My father was never into that. He couldn't understand working in your spare time.

I spent summers, Thanksgivings, and Christmases at my grandmother's farm in West Texas. Ma Reed was striking when she was young. As a grandmother, she was the absolute epitome of Mammy Yokum. She wore a bonnet and apron and smoked a corncob pipe. She wasn't dressed without them.

Her house had what she called a "wind howl" in the north room through which the wind whistled. The wind off the plains did howl. I loved to sleep with her. Other grandchildren slept in other rooms. But hers had the feather bed and the wind howl. No bed ever felt better.

I remember her wood cookstove. At five or six in the morning, she would be up banging around, putting wood in the stove. She had real cream ready and gravy and biscuits cooked before the first light. She made elaborate meals.

She had an outhouse that was a horror. I'd beg not to go to the bathroom. Somebody had to go with me because I thought there were snakes in the hole. Years later she got indoor plumbing and running water. She hated it. She'd use the outhouse when nobody was looking. I remember drinking from a dipper by the door. It's a wonder we all didn't get trench mouth.

Farm life was like the movies; Westerns spoke of truth.

At my grandparents' farm, I did all the chores. I hand cranked the corn husker on a tree, which turned the dried corncobs by spinning them around. We fed the kernels to the chickens. But I didn't want to do this farmwork. I just wanted to get to Hollywood.

My only argument with my dad was when he would say, "What will this child do? He'll never get an honest job."

He was right.

My major memories of childhood are movies and food. My taste buds were cemented in Texas. More than anything else, foods make me nostalgic for Texas. Food from the South is so powerful. I have learned how to make all the foods I grew up eating—chicken-fried steak, cream gravy, biscuits. I can't live without Tabasco sauce.

We used to have figs in our yard, but it's impossible to get good figs in New York. I won't eat stuffing on Thanksgiving that's made with oysters and nuts. It has to be cornbread or it ain't real. I'm a purist on food.

To the rest of the world, anything cooked on a rotisserie or outdoor grill is barbecue. In Texas barbecue is cooked over mesquite or hickory with real tangy sauce and sopped on greasy Mrs. Baird's buns.

My mom took me to see *Gone with the Wind* at age two and I never recovered.

Early on I wanted to be a movie critic. I liked all the movies I saw. I had absolutely no taste. My mom took me to see *Gone with the Wind* at age two and I never recovered. I remember when it rained on-screen in *Tarzan's New York Adventure,* I told Mom she should go out and roll up the car windows.

The first movie stars I ever saw were on a summer trip to Grandmother's. They were Jimmy Wakely and his comical sidekick Fuzzy Knight. I couldn't believe here were two stars I'd seen on-screen in the little movie house in Goldthwaite. I loved Esther Williams. Over and over, I thought of Esther Williams. I couldn't stand it. In the water, she was so beautiful. She wasn't bad on dry land, either.

I liked movies because in them people ate beautiful things at dinner tables in Paris. I wanted movies to take me out of the humdrum of life. I drove my mom crazy wanting to eat exotic things.

In *Peggy*, Diana Lynn ate a chocolate éclair. So I wanted to taste an éclair. We ate homemade apple pie and cherry cobbler, but I wanted an éclair. No bakery in town ever heard of éclairs.

The theater in Goldthwaite was like *The Last Picture Show.* I visited Grandma and spent every afternoon at that theater. She sent me weekly flyers on what was playing the rest of the year because she knew I was interested. Like Larry McMurtry's book, the end of the theater meant the end of the town. It was the only entertainment, the only escape from a drab existence.

I remember family reunions. For one reunion, the Holiday Inn in Brownwood had a marquee that read, "Welcome, Reeds." We all stayed there and had a dance and barbecue. The first year I went as an adult, the family had a hard time adjusting to me. I was a Yankee. I didn't know anybody, and during the square dance, Tallulah Bankhead called me. Texans are not that impressed, really, unless something happens there first. I do think, however, they were shocked over the Tallulah Bankhead call.

I see Texas as sentimental, sweet, and country, but most of the world sees it like John Travolta in *Urban Cowboy* or the idiots on *Dallas*. There's no character in my memory or background like that. There were rope circlers, cow ropers, and people who'd starve to death but for quail and rabbit, but they were real people. Not paradoxes, not urban Texans dressing up to keep legends going and cash registers ringing.

As a Texas state representative, Senfronia Thompson serves her district in Northeast Houston, the same area where she grew up. *Photo by Marvin Hecker*

BIRTH NAME	**SENFRONIA PAIGE**
BORN	January 1, 1939, in Booth, to J. M. Proctor and Thelma Lee Waterhouse
INTERVIEW	Her office, Texas State Capitol, Austin, Texas, August 6, 2018

28

REPRESENTATIVE SENFRONIA THOMPSON

Looking Out for the Community

T he dean of women legislators in the Texas House of Representatives, Senfronia Thompson of the 141st District is the longest-
serving woman and African American in Texas history, with
almost fifty years in the legislature. She earned a bachelor's degree
in biology from Texas Southern University, a master's in education
from Prairie View A&M University, a master's in international law
from the University of Houston, and a law degree from TSU's Thur-
good Marshall School of Law. Affectionately known by her colleagues as
Ms. T, Thompson was inducted into the Texas Women's Hall of Fame in
2014. In June 2017, Texas Monthly named her one of the Top 10 Best
Legislators and described her as "a force of nature and a living argument against term limits." She is the last founding member of the Texas
Legislative Black Caucus still serving in the Texas Legislature and the
only recipient of the caucus's Rosa Parks Award.

I had a great-grandmother, Sadie Coleman Green, who was married to Sam Green. They were from Alabama. They were sharecroppers who moved from place to place. As they traveled from Alabama to Louisiana to Texas, they settled around Fulshear, Simonton, that area, Richmond, Booth, and Thompsons. They came to Texas long before I was born.

My great-grandmother had sixteen children. She later moved to Houston, and she owned her own business providing room and board on Heiner in the Fourth Ward area near downtown. She provided breakfast, a sack lunch, dinner, and a hot bath. Her customers could not find sufficient work in the small towns, so they sought work in large cities like Houston.

She was a good, successful businesswoman. She was illiterate but very smart. She packed a .44 pistol. She treated everybody with great respect and dignity, but she didn't let any rowdiness get into her business.

My great-grandmother was so sweet and kind. I enjoyed visiting with her and helping her with the work around the house even when I was just four, four and a half years old. She would place me on an apple box because I was too short to reach the washing tub to wash the handkerchiefs on a rubboard. Everybody had to work, and that included me, too.

My father was a white guy. My mother was an only child. She had married young, and that marriage ended with one child, my brother. My mother came home to her mother, who at that time was living around Simonton, Texas. During the time she was in Simonton, my grandmother had remarried, and so they moved to the tiny town of Booth in Fort Bend County.

My grandmother was the oldest of sixteen, and she was born in about 1900. Her name was Marcina. She's the one who reared me. My grandmother and her husband were sharecroppers. Mr. C. I. McFarlane was a resident of Houston and the owner of the farm in Booth. One foreman, a guy named Jefferson Mack Proctor, was over that farm, and he liked my mother, and they struck up a relationship, and out of that relationship I was born.

When my mom was pregnant with me, there was a Black guy, Mr. Lindsay Paige, who came and really knew how to farm. My mother was very dark and very beautiful. And this guy fell in love with her at first sight. He was kind enough when I was born to allow me to have his last name, but the people on the farm began to talk to him and tease him.

"You have this white man Mr. Proctor's child, and you have given her your name."

And they began to agitate him, and it became untenable for my mother to live there. Mr. Paige was always talking about killing us, and he got physical with my mother, and me, too.

So my mother had an aunt, the number sixteen child of my great-grandmother. And she never had children. My mother sent her a letter and told her how awful things had gotten for her. So my great-aunt hired a wagon and some horses in Houston and came down to Richmond. My mother packed our clothes, which would probably fit into a little grocery bag.

My grandmother begged her not to take my brother, because he was the first grandbaby. And she left my brother with her mother and stepfather. We got in the wagon and took off for Houston, and we landed at my great-grandmother's place of business.

Once we got to my great-grandmother's house, we were safe. It was just like being in heaven. We just believed no one could harm us at that time. My mother got to start all over, and my great-grandmother gave her a hand to help take care of me. My great-aunt somewhat adopted me, so my mother had a chance to get a job and do some things for herself.

I met my father one time when I was about twelve years old. I was bold. He was nice. He had a used car business on Washington Avenue in Houston. My grandparents thought he hung the moon. They loved him because he was very kind to them. My grandparents just kept talking about him.

And one day I got the nerve up, without telling anybody, to go see him. I could ride a bus from the time I was five years old. My great-aunt and great-grandmother taught me. I knew how to get around—and talk.

Well, when I first went into his office, there were some young teenagers with him. I surmised that those were his children. He had a hat on, khaki pants, and kind of like a plaid shirt with short sleeves. He didn't know who I was.

I said, "Sir, may I speak to you, please?"

He said, "Yes."

He walks outside, and he looks at me, and I tell him who I am. And the first thing he asked me was how were my grandparents. I told him how they were. He asked about my mother. I told him.

I said, "I'm your little girl."

He said, "Yep."

He said, "I'll tell you what. When I get off of work this evening, I'm going to come by and see you."

Oh, I ran to get to the bus to get home because I wanted to make sure that everything was in place and that I was there when he got there. And that day came and went, and the next day, and the weeks and the months and the years.

After school, kids would say, "Senfronia, come walk with us."

And I'd say, "No, I've got to get home."

I was in elementary school, and every day I would run home from school in case he came by. I didn't want to miss him. When you have a rejection, it's like nobody wants you. You see kids with their parents having a fun time and you wonder why you can't have your daddy. I told my mother that I had gone to see him, and she fussed with me a little bit. But she never talked about him from that moment on.

Later in life, I rationalized the times we were living in back then. I forgave him for not coming to visit me. He missed not knowing me and not knowing how God has blessed me to make some achievements in life. I missed the opportunity to have known him as well. The next time I saw my father was 2018 at his grave site. He passed away in 1965. I never realized that the cemetery he is buried in has been in my legislative district all these years.

My name's supposed to be Safronia. I was born on New Year's Day, and when the midwife recorded my birth, instead of recording Safronia, she recorded it as Senfronia. I've never met another person with that name.

I went to Chile some years ago. And we were in Santiago or somewhere, and a lady on the trip said, "What kind of name is Senfronia?"

A Chilean lady sitting on the bus said, "It's an old Spanish name."

I said, "I have to come all the way over here from America to Chile to find out what kind of name Senfronia is."

Finally, my grandmother and step-grandfather moved to Houston and brought my brother. They finally moved to an area where I still live in Northeast Houston. They bought a little piece of property, and the land is like 60-by-200 feet, enough room to put a house and plenty of room for a garden. We raised everything but flour, coffee, meal, and sugar. We even made our own soap.

When my mother was working, my grandmother says, "Listen, you're in the city. City life is not for children, and they need room to grow up. Why don't you let us keep them, so you won't have to worry about what's happening to them while you are at work and you need to rest yourself for the next day?"

We had well water as our source for cooking, washing, and drinking. And we had an outhouse out there. We were among the last people to get pavement on the street, because we had gravel for years and years and years. We still used gasoline lamps.

We were poorer than cushaw squash. We were broke, broke, broke. A lady asked my grandmother if she had change for five dollars. My grandmother responded by asking if she could see what a five-dollar bill looked like.

And my mother worked very hard, and my grandmother worked very hard, too. The only time we ever got a chance to see my grandmother was on Sundays. She'd leave at four thirty in the morning, and she'd get back at seven, eight o'clock at night. She cleaned and cooked and washed, and it was for low wages.

She was not able to comb my hair for school until Sunday night, but I had a teacher named Mrs. Nelson who would have me come thirty minutes before school started each morning and comb my hair. She would also see that my clothes were not so wrinkled, because I was only allowed to change dresses on Fridays. Later, when I got at the end of the third grade, I learned to comb my own hair and do a fairly decent job in ironing my clothes. God always puts someone in your path to help you, and he always equips you to help yourself as well.

I was my great-grandmother's favorite great-grandchild because I wouldn't cry. I was fearless and I could talk plainly. She would often send me to the corner grocery store, and I could recite what she was asking me to order for her.

The store owner was such a nice guy, and he always enjoyed seeing me come into the store. He knew where my great-grandmother lived. But he would pretend that he did not and said, "Where do you live?"

And I said, "I'll show you where I live."

And I just marched down the sidewalk made of bricks. I'd get there and crawl up on the steps. He would help me get up on the stairs, too, and then I'd open the door for him.

He'd bring the box of groceries inside. He'd wink at my great-grandmother and he'd say, "I didn't know how to get here, but your great-grandbaby showed me how, and I'm going to give her a nickel."

But I couldn't spend the nickel, though. My great-grandmother insisted on me saving my money. She had a sock, and if somebody gave me money, then she'd put those coins in there. My great-grandmother was very frugal. She was conscious of saving—just not taking something and spending it because you got it.

My uncle Sammy would always give me a nickel to make sure that I had milk. The real milk was sold in a bottle with a curly neck, and the milk would be at the bottom and the cream would be at the top. And my great-grandmother would always siphon the cream for the coffee or cake or whatever she was going to cook.

My grandmother was also very, very dark. In my family, they dogged me out. My step-grandfather loved me; he was just wonderful and good to me. But my grandmother always resented my complexion. She talked about my color as though I had something to do with it.

My step-grandfather would tell her, "Leave this child alone."

I wondered when I got grown, was it because she always had to explain me and not my sister and brother? You know, we had to ride the bus to town, and there she was with me. My brother was very, very dark colored.

She was always on me for the smallest infraction or smallest accident. She would punish me, whip me, for any little thing. After dinner, if I dropped something, I got a whipping. If I didn't say something and she thought I should have spoken up, I got a whipping. If I did speak up and say something, I got a whipping. If you smiled too much, she's fussing. If you didn't smile, she'd fuss.

She'd say, "You're never going to amount to nothing. You're nothing but poor trash. You're this. You're that."

Every night before we went to bed, we had to pray, and I'd say, "God, can't you take her on wherever you're going to take her, because I'm sick of her?"

But later in life, she had an opportunity to see me become a teacher, a politician, and a lawyer. I became her favorite grandchild. We lived down the street from each other. Most of all, I forgave her and appreciated all of the responsibility she took on.

My grandmother believed in religion, church, and all those things. We had to go to church sunrise Sunday to sunset. We had to sit on the front pew, and parents sat behind us to make sure we were behaving, not talking. My grandmother was Holiness, something like Assembly of God.

Once, a revival came to our community, and the minister asked for volunteers to take an envelope to raise money. I wanted my grandmother to be proud of me, and I took an envelope. When I got home, boy, did she fuss. I went through the neighborhood raising money for the minister, but I spent about twenty-five cents on myself, and I got whipped.

My step-grandfather was not religious but lived the Christian covenant. He just stayed home drinking some beer and listening to news over the radio.

"Listen, if you live by the Good Book, and you treat people right, you do what God wants you to do," he says. "I think I'm OK."

My grandmother and step-grandfather were illiterate. My brother was a genius. He would read the mail to my grandparents because they couldn't read at all. And he would help me with my homework.

When my grandmother was working for various families, one lady left her a note of what to fix because she was having a reception at her house. And it just so happened, this lady came home much earlier to get everything in place, and she noticed nothing had been prepared.

And she said, "Marcina, where's the food? Didn't you read? I left you a note."

She said, "I don't read."

She said, "I want you to make a cake. Here's the recipe."

And she said, "I can't read it."

And the lady looks at her and reads my grandmother the recipe.

The cake came out perfect. Flawless. She was just that good.

243

I remember when we got electricity. It was the early fifties.

My grandmother would leave to go to work at four thirty in the morning because she had to prepare the breakfast for the kids of the family she worked for. We had to do everything for ourselves.

My step-grandfather was always afraid to light the gas stove. One day I was getting ready for school, and my grandfather asked me to come light the oven so he could cook some cornbread or something. So I came and turned on the gas, but I couldn't find a match and forgot about it.

When I remembered, I got a match, and when I lit it, I got burned all on my face and on my arms. He heard me scream, and he ran and grabbed me.

"What's wrong?"

I told him I was burned.

We used to have this substance called bluing. It was like Clorox today. He put this bluing on me because he thought this bluing would help my face and my arms and my chest.

And he said he needs something from the store down the street from our house, so I go to the store. One of my neighbors, Mrs. Harris, saw me and said, "What's on you?"

She took some baking soda and Brer Rabbit Syrup and made a paste, and she put it all over my face and my arms and my chest.

She said, "Now, when five o'clock come in this evening, you rinse it off."

And I did exactly what she told me.

When I was in elementary school, we used to get outdated books. Pages were scratched up, torn up. We would have to wait until the white schools got through with the current books, and then that information would be outdated.

I went to school many days with holes in my shoes. I could step on a dime and know if it was on heads or tails because of the hole in my shoe. But you know what we did? We'd take a piece of cardboard and put it in that shoe to cover that hole and keep wearing that shoe because the other part of that shoe may be fine.

We didn't care if the neighborhood noticed. That was something common. We just didn't have money to go and buy another pair of shoes.

When I was in the second grade, there was a young lady who said, "You know what, you can hit Senfronia and she won't do anything to you. She won't fight back."

We were out on recess. And this little girl hit me, and I tell you, when I got through with her, nobody in the school ever hit me anymore. We had fights and all that stuff, but I had to defend myself.

And then the teacher was so upset with me, I got a whipping. That girl jumped on me. And the teacher spanked me because I scratched her during the course of my fighting. They called me "toughie." I was tougher.

Not that I wanted that reputation, but I just didn't want people picking on me.

Our dolls were white. There were no Black ones. But later during my childhood, they began to make Black dolls, and we didn't want them. What are we going to do with this Black doll? We wanted the white doll because that's what we'd been acclimated to.

We got a doll at Christmas. We got toys at Christmas, but that was it. We didn't buy Christmas trees, because we'd go cut a small, little pine tree down. We'd take construction paper and make the decoration for the Christmas tree. And one time we got a package of angel hair. It was wonderful. It was like fifteen cents.

We played ball. We'd take a sock, an old sock, and we'd stuff it with rags and things and make a ball and get a stick big enough to hit it and play ball. We couldn't afford a real ball.

The streets were sandy. My stepfather bought me a bicycle when I was about thirteen years old. I sailed down the streets, and I would come in looking like a different-colored person because sand would be all over me.

There was a lady who lived two doors down from me, and she wanted a bucket of water a day, delivered when she came home from work. We were not allowed to ask older adults for compensation for helping with things. We were not supposed to hang around like we wanted something, but if they gave us something, that was OK.

She was a maid and got in real late. She was exhausted, riding the buses long distances and working long hours. And I would always have a bucket of water waiting for her. She gave me a nickel a week.

Later in life, I bought her land from her daughter and built my house, where I still live.

From my great-grandmother, my grandmother, my mother, all the way down the line, my great-aunts, they were always saying to us: Be kind. Be helpful. That was always something that was instilled in us when we were children.

The church taught it. The whole community taught it. It was rare to see anybody in the community who was just terrible or doing anything bad. Everybody was trying to help each other.

You know, when you kill a hog, that was a big day. I get a chance to come to your house and bring you a bag of cracklings, a little piece of meat. All over the neighborhood, everybody was just having a good day.

And if somebody died, it was like somebody in our family died, too, because we were there to help you with your problems. Somebody got sick, it was like somebody got sick in our family. If something disastrous happened to you, it was like it happened to us. Everybody was trying to look out for not only the welfare of themselves but the welfare of their neighbors.

It was like a big community of family. Everybody loved everybody. They respected each other more.

Houston Sit-Ins Seek Justice

When I was in college during the civil rights movement, I said I was going to sit down at the lunch counter strikes. There was a Mading's Drug Store on Almeda Road and Southmore Boulevard, and I would go in there during my breaks in between my classes at TSU, and I would occupy those seats to integrate.

I just thought that it was so unfair that you couldn't go in and get a hamburger or a malt. At home, nobody talked about it, because I think people had conditioned themselves to accepting things a certain way. It was the younger people who said things should change.

One day, while I was sitting at the lunch counter during one of the sit-ins, a white man entered with a shotgun, shouting, calling us all kinds of names, and vowing to shoot all of us off the stools. No one moved. We stayed seated.

However, there were other white persons present who talked him out of taking that drastic action. He left the scene, and several Black citizens rushed to congratulate us for staying seated. I told one of the well-wishers that we were frozen in fear and could not move had we wanted to.

I continued going to the sit-ins. I was determined to keep fighting for equality and justice.

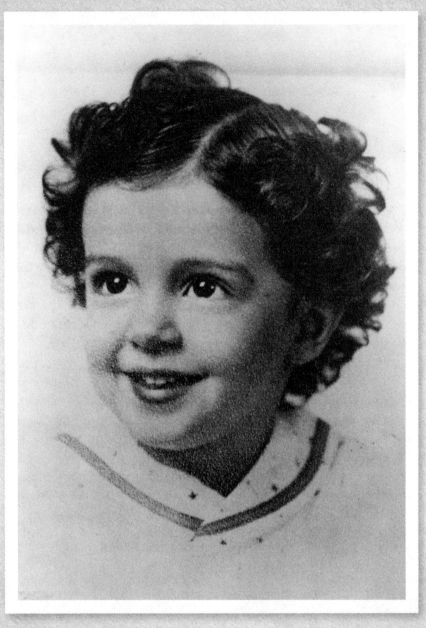

Tommy Tune was born in Wichita Falls but grew up in Houston. *Photo courtesy Tommy Tune*

BIRTH NAME	**THOMAS JAMES TUNE**
BORN	February 28, 1939, in Wichita Falls, to Jim Tune and Eva May Clark Tune
INTERVIEW	His apartment, New York City, October 26, 1982

TOMMY TUNE
Tapping through Adolescence

T he Tony Awards honored Tommy Tune with a Lifetime Achievement in the Theatre accolade in 2015. He added that tribute to
ten Tonys, eight Drama Desk Awards, three Astaire Awards, the
National Medal of Arts, the George Abbott Award for Outstanding
Achievement in the Arts, induction into the American Theater Hall of
Fame, and a star on Hollywood's Walk of Fame. In the early 1960s, he
danced in the Broadway musicals Baker Street, A Joyful Noise, and
How Now, Dow Jones. He scored his first Broadway directing and
choreography credits for the original production of The Best Little
Whorehouse in Texas in 1978. Off-stage, he also appeared in the films
Hello, Dolly! and The Boy Friend. After more than half a century of
choreographing and dancing in one hit after another, the tall tapper
took his talent around the country in a one-man show, Tommy Tune
Tonight!, billed as an "autobiographical stroll."

I was born in 1939 in Wichita Falls, but I grew up in Houston. We must have moved to Houston when I was two or three.

My father had his own business, but it changed a lot. Mostly, it grew out of the oil business. My mother was a mother, wife, and rearer of kids. My parents are Eva and Jim. I have an older sister, Nell, and a younger sister, Gracey. Each of us is ten years apart. We were all only children because of the ten-year span.

I was always tall. Both of my parents are tall, but not ridiculously tall. Dad was six foot two, and Mom was five foot seven. My little sister is about five foot ten, and I'm six foot six, which is ridiculous.

I look like both of my parents. I have my father's mouth, but my father was a very large man. I have my mother's bone structure, which is thin. They were both dark; there was Indian blood, I think, on both sides. So my coloring is the same. My younger sister and I look a great deal alike.

My family was very affectionate, a lot of hugging and kissing on the mouth. I'd go to other people's houses and they wouldn't kiss on the mouth. I didn't understand what a kiss was if you weren't kissing on the mouth.

In the early days, we lived on McClendon Street in what was called Windermere. We had a big acorn tree in the front yard and brick houses on the street. We lived in a duplex. The landlady and her daughters lived upstairs, and we had the downstairs. We lived there until I was in the sixth grade, and then we moved to Sunset Terrace, which now is out Buffalo Speedway, to our own big, kind of sprawling, ranch-style house.

Dancing school is my earliest memory. I was five when I started. We don't know if Mom wanted me to take dancing or I wanted me to take dancing. It was destiny.

This class was in Emmamae Horn's dance studio over the Piggly Wiggly on South Main in Houston. Mom hauled me to lessons. In the early days, we were not a two-car family, and she would ride me on the back of her bicycle over to the studio. She wore gabardine slacks and Nettleton loafers. One day we fell over in the street. Mom got skinned up, and I got embarrassed.

The dance studio was upstairs, and it was hot, really hot. This was before everything was air-conditioned. We just sweltered. We're talking Houston in the forties, and it was hot and wet, damp and muggy.

It was a class of all boys, which is unheard of, and we had thirty minutes of tumbling and thirty minutes of tap. I was so skinny that the tumbling was real hard for me because my bones kept bumping as we would do somersaults, and it hurt. But I was a whiz at tap.

I don't know how Mrs. Horn got all those little boys together. There were twenty at least. The first year we did our recital, we all performed, and we wore candy cane cocktail coats and white pants. Mom made all my costumes perfectly.

When I went back the next September to start up class again, I was in a class with all girls. It wasn't tumbling anymore, though. It was thirty minutes of ballet and thirty minutes of tap. That was all right with me because ballet didn't hurt as much as tumbling did.

The two dance teachers I remember are Emmamae Horn and Camille Hill, who came to teach at the studio shortly after my first or second year. They've both been tremendous influences on my career and on my life.

Actually, my emphasis went more toward tap after I got so tall and skinny. I kind of moved away from ballet because I didn't like appearing in class in tights. I was embarrassed.

I danced all the time. If I had to cross the floor, if I had to go from the kitchen to the bedroom, I danced instead of walking or running.

I wanted my little sister to dance so much because I wanted her to be my partner. I could tell she was going to be tall. It was very hard for me to find a tall partner who was skinny enough that I could twirl her around. So I tried too hard. You know how parents push their kids because they want them to be lumberjacks, and the kids rebel and go off to be lawyers? Well, I pushed my little sister so hard she just didn't want to dance at all, so she went off and rode horses.

Everybody would go out and play, and I would go to rehearsal. We put on musical shows in the garage in the summertime. And then it would get so hot in the garage that we would move outdoors. We called them the "patio revues," a very fancy spelling. I got all the kids together and bossed them around and put on shows.

I was naturally bossy. I must have been between nine and eleven. I think we charged a nickel to get in. We never made much money on the patio revues, but I learned to put on shows. This was the only game I knew. I've been doing it all my life.

My parents were both wonderful about my wanting to sing and dance and put on shows. My father was terrific about it, I think, because he was a wonderful ballroom dancer and had an appreciation for it. Mom and Dad met each other dancing. They were at a dance in Oklahoma, and he asked her to dance. They introduced themselves as they were dancing. So that's part of the predestination, I'm sure.

Dad trained Tennessee walking horses, and he would take me to Shelbyville, Tennessee, every summer to see the walking horse celebration. That was my early training for choreography. He would point out what made one horse better than the other. You would have to look very closely at them to get it; otherwise, it just looked like a bunch of horses. He would point out things, and I would see them. That enhanced my eye for dance.

At one point, Dad really wanted me to take over his business, L & H Machine Works, and I worked for him one summer. I think he realized that my head wasn't in it, because I would keep making up ballets in the machine shop. The sparks that came off of welding torches and the great brake drums rolling across the shop—I could see people jumping in and out. I created my machine works ballet there.

My dad really understood. He was quite wonderful about it, because that stigma about boys who take dancing being sissies never came up with him at all. He liked for me to entertain when he'd have people over to the house.

After the drinks were made, he'd say, "Come on, Bo, give 'em all arms and legs."

He actually called me Bo.

This was his favorite dance that I did, which was kind of a scarecrow routine like Ray Bolger did in *The Wizard of Oz*. I would do that, and everyone would laugh. I was made for entertainment, and I worked cheap.

I danced all through adolescence. I didn't learn a lot, but I learned how to make good grades. I got around the system some way, and then they loved me because I would put on the shows—the Christmas show and the Easter show and the May fete, all the shows. I was very big at that.

Because I choreographed, they needed me. I didn't know that I choreographed. We just made up dances, but that's what it really was. I had an early gift to choreograph.

I put on shows all through junior high and senior high school. I had a little more time in junior high school to be social with dances and all because the drama department was not as organized. I was popular and ran for things.

I remember in junior high school I always wanted to play Santa Claus in the Christmas pageant, but I wasn't the right type. So I played Jesus in the Easter pageant. They would sing, "I come to the garden alone, while the dew is still on the roses," and I would walk on and take the praying position at the rock.

When I got to Lamar High School, the drama department, headed by Ruth Denney, took up all my time. I remember the opening of the drama building. The drama building was a shack, one of those temporary army barracks. We painted it red, and we turned it into a theater-in-the-round.

For the opening of that, we did excerpts from three shows: *The Diary of Anne Frank*, *My Three Angels*, and *The Pajama Game*. I directed and choreographed the little thirty minutes of *The Pajama Game*, and it was a very big hit. That was the first musical comedy I directed and choreographed. We'd done revues and things, but this had a story.

Until my first year in high school, I didn't know what a musical comedy was. This girl I had the biggest crush on, Ann Lloyd, called me one day and said, "I'm going to see the dress rehearsal of *The King and I* at Theater Inc. Do you want to go?"

Well, I didn't know what *The King and I* was. I didn't know what Theater Inc. was, but I liked her a lot. So I said, "Yes, of course. Sure."

So she came by in her little Studebaker and picked me up. We walked in, and it had already started. It was this thing where the people sang and the people danced; they talked and it told a story; and it made you laugh and it made you cry.

And after seeing that—and I had no idea if it was good or not—I had a feeling it was sensational. My memory of it was that it was the most wonderful production of *The King and I* ever. That one little date changed my whole life. Prior to that, I just wanted to dance because that was all I knew. After that, I knew that musical comedy was what I needed to do, because that was a synthesis of it all. It was more universal than just dancing.

Nothing was the same after that. I went back to high school and talked Mrs. Denney into doing musical comedy. They'd never done one; they'd only done plays and variety shows.

For my graduation, when everybody was asking for a car and a watch and silver fountain pen and pencil sets, I asked my parents for a trip to New York, which they gave me. So at seventeen, I went to New York for ten days. I stayed at the Algonquin because I'd read about the Algonquin Round Table.

I came alone. Then after four days, Ruth Denney happened to be in New York, and we joined up and saw a lot of things. It was just unbelievable. I went to a play every night, sometimes two a day because you could get into a matinee.

The first night in New York City I had to see Ethel Merman. Ethel Merman, Ethel Merman—it was very important that I see Ethel Merman. She was in a dud called *Happy Hunting*, but I thought it was wonderful because I didn't know. I loved it all.

And I was standing out in front of the theater, waiting to go in, and our next-door neighbors, the Reeds, from Houston drove by in their Buick. I couldn't believe what I was seeing, that they would be driving by the theater district right before the show. They didn't even go to shows. I started running and yelling, "Mr. Reed, Mr. Reed, Mr. Reed!"

I bumped into a policeman on a horse because I was so excited.

I went to Lon Morris College in Jacksonville. After Lon Morris, I went to the University of Texas and got my BFA there. Then I went to the University of Houston and worked on my master's, but I never did complete it. It came time to go to New York; I had to make the big step.

The way it worked was my friend Phillip Osterman, who I've known forever down in Houston, finally said, "It's time for you to go to New York."

He threw me in a car and drove me up to New York. He knew I was procrastinating because I was nervous. I was so lucky. We arrived on Saint Patrick's Day. We were staying with a friend of his right off of Central Park.

Phillip said, "You've got to go out to the newsstand and get *Backstage* and *Show Business* and see what auditions there are today."

So I did. And there was an audition on Fifty-Sixth Street. So I said, "Well, I guess I just better go."

I had my song, "You Gotta Have Heart." I auditioned and I got a callback and I got the job. I danced and played a little part—twenty-two

254

weeks. We started in New Jersey, and we played on Long Island and toured all over, down to Florida and to Ohio.

I even put my tap shoes away. Tap dancing was not being done in any Broadway show. Tap dancing was corny. It was the Jazz Age. I didn't even admit that I knew how to tap dance because that meant you were from the sticks.

I remember kind of bragging about being from Texas, because they always talked about how tall I was, and I would always say, "Yeah, that's because I'm from Texas."

I was sort of like the epitome of a Texan—a tall Texan. I think it got me a lot of attention. I probably overused it and acted obnoxious. I was never really the overt, loudmouth kind of fellow. But the accent would get a bit thicker as they started talking to me and I'd say I was from Texas.

"Oh, are you really? Whereabouts?"

And it would get thicker.

Tommy Tune won Tony Awards for his performance and choreography of *My One and Only*, 1983. *Photo courtesy Tommy Tune*

Delbert McClinton, front, with his mother and older brothers.
Photo courtesy Delbert McClinton

BIRTH NAME	**DELBERT ROSS McCLINTON**
BORN	November 4, 1940, in Lubbock to Herman Louis McClinton and Vivian Fanny Dyer Bridwell McClinton
INTERVIEW	His condo, Austin, Texas, April 29, 2018

DELBERT McCLINTON

A Good Boy Unbound

S inger-songwriter Delbert McClinton made his stage debut at age sixteen at the Big V Jamboree at the Liberator Theatre in Fort Worth. Soon he and his band the Mellow Fellows, later the Straitjackets, were backing up the likes of Big Joe Turner and Bo Diddley in clubs on the outskirts of Fort Worth. His harmonica work on Bruce Channel's "Hey! Baby" led to a tour in the United Kingdom in 1962 with the Beatles as the opening act. After performing in Texas with his band the Rondels, he produced two albums in Los Angeles with fellow Texan Glen Clark before embarking on a solo career in the 1970s. That pattern of bands, pairings, and going it alone has continued for more than sixty years and touched just about every musical genre and movement, although McClinton is most closely identified with blues. He garnered four Grammys, a double-platinum songwriting credit for "B Movie Boxcar Blues," critical acclaim, and a loyal fan base as eclectic as he is.

I grew up in Lubbock when I was a little kid, but I moved away from there when I was eleven years old. Being in Lubbock is like being under a cake cover that you put over a cake to keep the flies off it. Clear. That's what it's like out there. You see the horizon in every direction. There's the sun and the sky and the horizon. I always thought that it gave me a sense of being boundless. I never understood "You can't see the forest for the trees," because I didn't know forests.

Nobody locked their doors at night. You might lock your screen door or you might not. Never entered your mind. The windows were always open for air circulation, and as far as I can remember, it never got too hot. But I was a kid. In fact, nobody had air-conditioning. In the winters we never had much snow, but we'd get sleet. And so that was fun, too.

My dad was a city bus driver. We used to have bus cards; we could go anywhere in town. But, of course, there wasn't anywhere to go much but to the swimming pool or movies.

I'll bet you, if you talk to anybody else from Lubbock, they'll also tell you they used to go out and run along the alleyway behind the DDT truck when they were spraying pesticides, in the fog, and just laugh and have the biggest time. If you had a bicycle, you'd ride it behind the truck. Nobody warned us not to do that.

We didn't have chiggers in Lubbock either. So how good is that? We'd play, rolling around in the grass all day long. Freaked me out when we moved to Fort Worth and I got chiggers all over me.

It wasn't that barren. It was just flat. Right behind my house was a persimmon tree. In front of the house next door was an apricot tree, loaded every year. It's interesting, you could water things and grow things. When you'd get outside town, there were cotton fields. That's what you do with fertile, flat land. And it's flat.

One of the other things that you've probably heard was if you stand real still and look as hard as you can, you can see the back of your head. Another Lubbock-ism.

I think I was born and grew up in the most interesting of times. You know, 1950, it's like a spring was sprung. I remember I was in the first grade in Lubbock and I saw the first two jet planes come over. Thunderjets. I've looked them up and found them. Jet airplanes. Oh, that was pretty amazing.

Everybody was poor, everybody was happy, everybody walked up and down the streets in the late afternoon and talked, and the kids would skate up and down. Never seemed to be a hurry about anything. I guess "quaint" is the best word I can put to it. That's the way we lived.

Oh, God, my parents, they raised me to be a good boy. I was taught to respect my elders; I was taught to be responsible; I was taught to be a nice guy. I had good manners and was respectable and respectful. I said, "Yes, sir," and "No, sir." I opened the door for women. I did all that.

I'll tell you, as a little boy, every time I would leave, my daddy would hug me and say, "You be a sweet boy."

He said that to me until he died.

The oddest attraction in Lubbock is Prairie Dog Town at Mackenzie State Park. It's named after [General Ranald S.] Mackenzie, who was the officer who led the last Indian battle right there. It's flat out there, but there are canyons, and it's really pretty—walls, cliffs, and grass.

All the family would go up there for picnics. You could spend all day at Mackenzie Park or you could drive twenty miles out of town to Buffalo Lakes, which was the big deal. It's a canyon that's a lake that Indians used to live in with caves. It's called Cañon del Rescate, Canyon of Rescue [Ransom Canyon]. It was a trading place for comancheros and Comanches. They traded people, rifles, whatever, something horrible.

If you went to Mackenzie Park, the topper was going to see the Prairie Dog Town. You had to see it. You drove out to the end of the park, where it got pretty bleak where they didn't tend it. There was this fenced-off part, and the ground is as dead as anything can be. It's a prairie dog community, and they are there in the thousands. You can sit up there and watch prairie dogs all day if you want to. For nothing. It's free. Still there.

On the other end of the park, there was an old man. He raised goats. I don't know if he milked them or what, but he was known as the "goat man." He lived right by a caliche pit. We would sneak up and try to get a look at the "goat man." But the rumor was if you did, he'd catch you and throw you in the caliche pit and that would be the end of you. No one would ever know what happened to you. These are the stories I heard as a kid.

S cots-Irish is what I've always heard the McClintons are. Mother was born in Little Rock, Arkansas, but left there soon and

Delbert McClinton in Fort Worth in 1985 with the 1960 Cadillac he
bought from his aunt Mildred. *Photo courtesy Delbert McClinton*

moved to Texas. She had five sisters. My daddy was born in Snyder,
Texas, one of five boys and two girls.

My mother was married when she was sixteen to a man named Jack
Bridwell. Well, he got some kind of terrible disease and died quick. He
and my dad were good friends and worked together at the Snyder Trans-
fer Trucking Company. So my dad already knew my mother from that,
and they ended up together.

When they got married, she already had a little one, two actually,
because she was pregnant when her husband died and when she got
remarried. So I have a brother six years older than me and one four years
older than me.

Lubbock is legally part of the Llano Estacado, as the Spanish called
it. Llano Estacado means "staked plains." It's so flat out there that the
conquistadors coming through there had to pile buffalo shit high as a
point of reference, or drive stakes with a rag on it, so they would know
where they'd already been. Lubbock's the Hub of the Plains—that's what

its credo is. It's the dead center of the flattest part of the world. There were rattlesnakes out there, copperheads. Where there's desert, there's rattlesnakes.

Going to Snyder, where my dad was from, was always a big deal, about a two-hour drive. We got to drive off the Caprock [Escarpment], see. When you get off the Caprock, that's when you get into Indian country. It's not flat anymore. You're off the plateau.

So we had family in Snyder and Sweetwater. That's where my mother's family was and my favorite cousin. That's about it. Some of my mother's family lived in Idalou, just on the outskirts of Lubbock. They later moved to Colorado City, Texas, which was not much more than a crossroads, and raised pigs.

I had family down there in East Texas—Hagansport. It's in East Texas black-dirt country, and it's a little old tiny town in the middle of nowhere. I went there to stay with my grandmother for a week. The Dyer family lived out there in some old house that had a breezeway. You know, the kitchen's over here and bedrooms were over there.

In the bedroom was a courting board. Sometimes when girls and boys had to share a bed, they shoved this courting board down the middle of it. It was about keeping people apart who didn't even know each other. It kept them from reaching over and grabbing the other one.

Until I got a bicycle, we played in the backyard. We had a rickety wooden fence around our yard so old that God must have put it there. And it leaned and wiggled and wobbled. We climbed on that fence and made it rock.

We raised chickens. In the chicken pen was this tree, and me and two or three friends built a house up on top of the chicken house for our club- house. So we hung out there and played up and down the alley.

The alley behind our house was just as dry as dust dirt, perfect, and we could run up and down that alley. If you were running away from the sun and looking at it, you could see John Wayne in the dust.

We played a lot of cowboys—"pla-lack." Pla-lack. "Let's pla-lack we're gonna do this."

"OK, but let's pla-lack I'm gonna be him."

I remember one time we found a baby buggy that was all gone practi- cally except the wheels. We went to the store and got a box and put it on there and built a stagecoach.

There wasn't any TV. I didn't see a TV until 1951. When I was eleven, that was the first time I ever saw a television.

Movies were a big deal. Old movies. Every one of the movies on Saturday had three or four serials before the movie—cliff-hangers. I loved all that stuff. Movies fire your imagination. And they were great, but you know, that's what you lived for, the movies and playing outside.

There was a theater called the Tower. The Tower and the Tech were down there across from Texas Tech. I'd have a quarter. Costs nine cents to get in. And then you go to the candy bar, and everything that's a nickel everywhere else is six cents there. That screws the hell out of a quarter. You know what I'm talking about? The impression that's left on me is magnificent. I guess it was the first time I ever realized the value of money and how somebody's always trying to take it from you.

I can remember waking up in the morning and rising up and the imprint of my head was surrounded by the finest dust. You could not keep it out of the house.

I remember coming back from Snyder to Lubbock one day when one of them dust storms blew in. The sand was so thick, you couldn't see. The cars on the highway—wasn't that many cars back then—had to sit on the road until the storm blew itself out before we could go on.

My time there was the last of those great storms. It's a very interesting thing to read about how the Dust Bowl happened.

I was the little guy in the family, and sometimes my older brothers were told, "Take him with you. He can go."

So, my older brother, Jack, and a friend of his were going to a drive-in movie and took me with them. For the old drive-in movies, you arrived just about dusk and you parked along the road and waited until the box office light comes on. So we're over here stopped, and I'm in the back of my brother's friend's faded red, almost rosy red, Dodge pickup truck. I was standing in the back, and my brother was inside.

And we saw those things [the Lubbock Lights]. And they were just there, and you couldn't judge how far away they were. But they were big, although I don't know how big they were, but in a V, and they were flying in formation. It was fascinating. Of course, the spinners start telling, "Oh, it was the reflection off that new roof of that old hamburger joint out there."

You know, some speculated goofy reasons, but I saw them. Everybody saw them that looked up. I was a little kid, and I saw them, and I watched them until they went away. It was not more than a minute probably, but it was longer than fifteen seconds. You know, I got a pretty good take on it.

I was eleven years old, so it didn't last long for me. I had playing to do. I wasn't concerned with spaceships. It wasn't a big deal for me for very long, but when it came up, you know what, I said, "I saw that."

What else can I say? "Two of 'em landed over here, and this old boy and I went over there and had a 'drank' with them."

See that building out there? They were just as plain as that.

My brothers were going to a Boy Scout meeting. Once again my mother said to my brothers, "Take him with you."

We'd have to go through a shortcut to the train tracks to that end of town. There was also a grain elevator there, which was pretty ominous—big, no lights. To get home we had to go through those tracks by the granary silo.

We were walking back home, and it was dark by that time. My older brother all of a sudden puts his arms out and stops me, and my other brother said, "Oh, no."

I'm like, "What?"

He said, "You see that?"

And I looked up and it was a full moon.

He said, "It's a full moon."

I said, "So?"

He said, "You know what happens when there's a full moon?"

I don't know what I said, but it must have been, "I don't have a clue."

He said, "The Ku Klux Klan comes out. We gotta run."

I didn't know the Ku Klux Klan from whipped cream. But it didn't sound good. They took off running, and I'm running, and I can't keep up with them. So, of course, I was starting to cry, and I was scared to death. They were running off and leaving me down on the tracks and the silo.

Then they stopped and said, "There's only one way they won't get us— if the littlest guy holds his arms up like this."

I said, "OK. OK."

So we're walking along, and I'm a little guy and I'm holding my arms up. Finally, I get so tired, I drop them down and I stop, and they run off. And I'm running, and snot is everywhere. I'm sobbing. So by the time we got home, it was obvious there's been a catastrophe. I told them that we were running away from the Ku Klux Klan.

My father was not their father, but he was the only father they knew growing up. He was always good to them. They didn't take his name, but that's all. Anyway, he had them stand at the dining room table like this, and they had their hands up, and every time they dropped down he'd take his belt and he'd—*bam!*—hit 'em with his belt.

My dad had worked for the railroad in the thirties as a young man, and he liked it. He had two brothers working for the railroad in Fort Worth, so we moved there in 1951, and he got a job on the railroad because he couldn't sit and drive a bus anymore because of back pain.

My daddy worked in Peach Street Rail Yard. It's called the Hump. They make up trains there. They've got ten or twelve trains down here, and they've got this one track. So they look at the information on the car, and it's supposed to go to the train on track nine. They set the switches to push it up over the Hump, and it rolls down there all by itself.

All night long you can hear *ka-bang*. It was what I went to sleep to, listening to them making them trains down there. It was really quite comforting because you knew just what it was. *Ka-bang*. You can imagine. Big old rolling box of steel hitting another one.

Fort Worth was considerably bigger than Lubbock, but it was still a cow town when I moved there. By that, I mean the stockyards were booming. I can remember my dad taking me down there, and they had all these big holding pens for cattle and walkways all around there so you could walk around and look. It was just amazing to see that many live animals, a shitload of them.

I can remember a night that Bob Wills was playing at the Cotton Club, a big old dance hall. And that's what they used to be, dance halls, because you did go there to dance. Day-ance.

Of course, the kids couldn't go in, you know. But the windows were open, and we could jump up and put our arms up on them and look in and watch them inside.

The Cotton Club was in the middle of a cotton field. We were more interested in going out and having clod fights, which was pretty stupid because some people got hurt playing clod fights. Throwing big clods of dirt in the night, God, that was stupid.

We were running wild through the parking lot listening to Bob Wills. He is still the king.

My uncle Earl was just not a pleasant guy. He had no time for kids. And he was alcoholic. He finally got over that, but I don't recall seeing him ever act nice either. I always visited them in the summer in Sweetwater, or they came up to Lubbock.

They had a bed that permanently stayed out in their backyard in the summer because kids slept out there most of the time. My cousin Walter and I were in that bed one night and a skunk came by in the yard and went under the bed. We didn't know what to do and finally it went way. It was too late to run when we saw him. He just walked right up there under the bed. Anyway, he didn't get us.

Walter and I were out in the backyard. I was singing some song, I think I was singing "Hey Joe." That's a Carl Smith song. The screen door swung open and hit the house. Uncle Earl came running out of the house.

"Who's doing that singing?"

I hesitated for a minute, but there was no way out.

"It was me."

He said, "Boy, that's good. Really good. Marie, come here."

He got my aunt out there, and I sang a little bit for her. From that point on, for those next two weeks, I was royalty. He treated everybody nice. He was just a whole different guy. And that made an impression on me because he was not a nice guy, ever.

In the morning, we'd get in the car with him and go down to the milk plant. We'd get his truck, and we'd load it with everything that was going out on our delivery to people's front doors, and we'd always go to the coffee shop and have a cup of coffee and a doughnut.

Well, of course, as soon as all that happened, Earl said, "I want y'all to hear something." He had me up on the counter right before sunup singing to all the milkmen. I liked it.

If you're a songwriter, you're a poet, period. I went to Arlington Heights High School in Fort Worth, and it was considered one of the hoity-toity schools.

The *Jacket Journal* was the monthly school newspaper. Yellowjackets were the football team. So somewhere shortly before Christmas everybody in every English class had to write a Christmas poem, and they were going to pick the best one and put it on the cover of the Christmas edition of the *Jacket Journal*. It's mine:

If you ever talk to a blind boy about Christmas on Christmas Eve
You'd find he has a more beautiful Christmas than we could hope to see . . .
The excited voices, the scent of the trees, are visions of a storybook
*   rhyme.*
His heart will be filled with Christmas cheer, and we'll be the ones who
*   are blind.*

I lacked a half credit in English for graduating high school, and I went to high school until I was twenty-one. My daddy told me once, "Son, if you don't get that high school education, you ain't gonna amount to a hill of beans."

He wasn't being mean. He meant it, because they were uneducated. They were the farmworkers; they didn't get a lot of schooling. My daddy always said, "Print big, boy."

He meant, "Write your name where they can see it."

He wanted me to show up.

My dad survived the Depression. He was a man of his time. My dad spent most of his time going around the house turning the lights out.

"Hot dang, all this is costing lots of money to run all these things."

Music has always been the driving force in whatever the hell I am—from the get-go. As a little kid, I can remember hearing the best music in the world on the radio. It was the most horrible time in our history, and the music was the most fun you could have. Still is.

My daddy should have been a professional tap dancer. He had the same rhythm in his tapping around that I do singing. Identical thing. I just loved to get him to do it.

I've got the same thing he had there. Rhythm. I don't know where I got my voice. I was at the perfect place at the perfect time to be influenced by Black musicians—not just meet them but play with a bunch of those guys. Plus, I love the music. We used to back up Howlin' Wolf, Jimmy Reed, Big Joe Turner, Bo Diddley, Chuck Berry. And I learned a lot. That's where I learned to play the harmonica.

We got to be in the Black clubs because we were the band. It was also at a time on the verge of rock 'n' roll. Who was doing it but the Blacks? And they gained an awful lot of respect from me. I'd always liked the rhythm of Black music.

Country music is white man's blues. So their blues I loved as much as I loved white man's blues. How can you not love the music? They came from the birth of rock 'n' roll.

There's a song going on in my head all the time. Always has been. If there weren't something going on musically in my head, I wouldn't know what to do, because I've never been without it. I can put horn parts to the hum of the city. Music is everywhere. That's powerful.

You are what you hear. The mix of music that I heard in Texas made me sound like I sound.

Delbert McClinton during a pre-taping for *Austin City Limits*, 1978. *Photo by Nuri Vallbona, UT Texas Student Publications Photographs, Briscoe Center for American History, University of Texas at Austin*

Kathryn Ann Bailey as a toddler. *Photo courtesy Kay Bailey Hutchison*

BIRTH NAME	**KATHRYN ANN BAILEY**
BORN	July 22, 1943, in Galveston to Allan Abner Bailey Jr. and Ella Kathryn Sharp Bailey
INTERVIEW	Her home, Dallas, Texas, June 16, 2018

AMBASSADOR KAY BAILEY HUTCHISON

A Pioneer Spirit

K ay Bailey Hutchison is the 22nd US permanent representative to the North Atlantic Treaty Organization and the second woman in the position. Upon graduation from the University of Texas law school in 1967, she became the first female reporter on television in Houston. Despite no political experience, she was elected to the Texas House of Representatives as a Republican in 1972, served as state treasurer, and won a special election in 1993 to become the first female US senator from Texas. After twenty years in the Senate, she returned to private practice in 2012. In 2017, President Donald J. Trump ramped up attention to NATO and appointed Hutchison to oversee US interests as ambassador at the organization's headquarters in Brussels. The Texas Women's Hall of Fame inducted her in 1997, and the Clare Boothe Luce Policy Institute gave her its Conservative Leadership Award in 1999. Hutchison has written three books on women in history, including Unflinching Courage: Pioneering Women Who Shaped Texas, *which draws from diaries and letters of her ancestors and other pioneers.*

My mother grew up in Nacogdoches, and that's where my great-great-grandfather [Charles S. Taylor] emigrated from England. In 1836 he was elected as a delegate to the Texas Independence Convention. He signed the Texas Declaration of Independence.

He was best friend and law partner with Thomas Rusk, the secretary of war for the Texians seeking independence from Mexico. Rusk was also one of the first two senators, with Sam Houston. My great-great-grandfather ended up being the alcalde of Nacogdoches, which was a big area of Mexico. And, of course, he went on the other side and became a rebel. After we won the war, he became the chief justice of Nacogdoches. I grew up hearing all that history.

Dad was from Beaumont. Mother and Dad didn't meet at the University of Texas. Mother was behind Dad, so Dad was already gone. They met in Nacogdoches and fell in love. They married and moved to Galveston, and that's where Dad started working in an insurance business and then decided to open his own insurance and real estate business on the mainland, which was La Marque. And so their first years were in Galveston.

La Marque is where I grew up. It was a very small town of fifteen thousand. And it was a great childhood. My growing up was just so happy and so American. We knew everyone. We had slumber parties and would be walking the streets at midnight, and the sheriff's deputy would come by in his car and say, "Now, you girls, which house are you in? You get in the car and I'm going to take you there."

He would drop us off and we'd sneak back in through the windows. And, of course, the parents wouldn't know we had ever left. Those are the kinds of things we did. And it was safe.

Our life was around the Episcopal church and the church socials and the church dances. So it was just a great childhood. It was easy.

I have two brothers. We were all five years apart. And so we were like five, ten, and fifteen, and the boys never didn't get along, but they were ten years apart.

When I was in high school, my younger brother, Frank, was in elementary and middle school, which was junior high then, and my older brother, Allan, had graduated when I went into the ninth grade. So we never played at home.

Toni dolls were the thing that girls had. Three of my girlfriends were the same age. We all got Toni dolls, so we played all the time with our

Toni dolls, and one of Mother's friends made precious clothes for the dolls. So we had ball dresses, bridal gowns, regular clothes, and we had nightgowns so they could go to bed.

I did have a Bonny Braids, but the one I really played with was my Toni doll.

I took ballet every day. That was sort of my outside thing. I learned ballet in first grade in La Marque with a teacher who was very good. And as I grew, we were the assistants with the little ones. And then she decided we could do the Houston Youth Symphony Ballet, so some of us tried out, and two of us got in. So I did ballet all the way through high school. I wasn't great. I loved it, though. That really was my life, every day, six days a week. It was a good thing. I could have a goal.

I remember one incident because I was riding my tricycle down the street, and my mother was running to get me because the explosion was very loud and the ground shook. Our house at the time was maybe two or three miles from Texas City [site of a series of deadly explosions on April 16, 1947].

I remember that terror in my mother's face, and I'd never had any trauma. It was something indelible in my memory, and Mother talked about it later. Just on my tricycle riding down the street. She was panicked because it was just too scary to have that explosion.

I can say I heard something like an explosion. I can't say I remember seeing it, but I remember the ground was shaking. I saw Mother coming toward me. It was 1947. I was born in '43, so I was four.

We did go to the beach a lot as groups, but my parents wouldn't let me go to Galveston at night because that was the big city. We had a bay in Galveston and we had a little Sunfish sailing boat, and so we did that.

We went crabbing. That was a big part of our childhood. We'd go crabbing with neighbors all afternoon. It was really fun. We'd bring all the crabs to one of the houses, put crab boil in a big pot, and cook the crabs. And we'd put newspapers on the tables, usually outside, and we'd pick crabs. That was a really fun outing.

We'd ride the ferry across to go see my grandmother in Beaumont. My grandparents lived on Broadway, right across the street from the hospital next to the Jewish synagogue. We would sit on the front porch and watch the ambulances come in. My grandfather's office was a block away, and he would walk to his office every day, and then he would visit his patients in the hospital across the street.

We had wonderful visits there with my aunt, my dad's twin sister, and my grandmother. We knew my grandfather, Allan Bailey, a little bit. He died when maybe I was seven or eight.

I had the best parents. My mother was a homemaker, and she always made sure that I was doing the right things. You know, it was always that I would go to college. She didn't push me on ballet, but she also saw to it that I played piano. And then she finally said I had to make a choice.

"Which one do you want to do?"

So I chose ballet. I wish I had chosen piano. But she made sure that I just did the right things. She was in a sorority at Texas, so she made sure I went through rush, and I joined the same sorority. I didn't know what she was doing until later.

She was just very smart, supportive. She was strict. She was the one who said, "You can't date a boy more than one year older than you. You can't go to Galveston."

I rebelled. I said, "Everybody can go to Galveston but me."

But now I know why and understand those kinds of things. She was always there.

Being a cheerleader in high school was so much a part of the school spirit. That was really, really fun. And we had good football teams. In our league, we were always in the running up to state, but we didn't win state until later, when we won several state championships. But when I was there, we went to quarterfinals. We were the La Marque Tigers.

Our uniforms were very traditional—"LM" in chenille letters and white sweater, maybe a turtleneck, and just a blue corduroy skirt with gold lining. Blue and gold were our colors.

At Texas, it was also really fun. The two years I was cheerleader, we went to the Cotton Bowl and the Orange Bowl. So you got to go on the

Kathryn Ann Bailey as a University of Texas cheerleader, c. 1964. *UT Texas Student Publications Photographs, Briscoe Center for American History, University of Texas at Austin*

trips and everything. At Texas we literally had one yell, "Give me a T, give me an E, an X . . . What's that spell? Texas."

It didn't take any talent. Now today, they are athletes. We were just cheerleaders.

We were elected by a panel of presidents of all the student organizations, probably about thirty people on the panel. It was in Gregory Gym. Everybody tried out, and then the panel voted, and they announced it right there. I was really so thrilled. That was really exciting.

I adored my dad. Everybody did. He was just the sweetest man. If you took a popular vote of the people in La Marque, Texas, at any time, he would be the most popular. I mean, he was sweet.

He always bought the book covers for all the kids in high school, the ones that we used to cut and fit on the books, the paper ones. Back then we reused the schoolbooks year to year. They would sponsor the Little League team and buy the ad in the annual—all those things, and always just doing something more.

And he said you have to give back, and I guess that's where I get that. Not that they demanded, "You have to give back."

But I learned by watching them.

Dad was very much a civic leader. He had this small business, and he was on the city charter commission. He would support the mayor. He actually sent money to both the Republican and the Democratic parties because he thought citizens should do that. It was good to have strong parties. So he did that. He sent twenty-five dollars to each party.

And they loved Eisenhower. I remember that, which was the first time I would think about politics at all. They liked Ike.

And so they were good citizens, but they weren't political at all. In fact, my only political experience was when Dad took me out of school

Senator Kay Bailey Hutchison chairs the Aviation Subcommittee in the Russell Senate Office Building on Capitol Hill, April 2001. *Photo by Melina Mara*

Ambassador Kay Bailey Hutchison escorts dignitaries, including Secretary of State Mike Pompeo and Defense Secretary Jim Mattis, during a 2018 NATO session in Brussels.
Photo courtesy United States Mission to NATO

to go see Bill Blakley when he was coming through La Marque and doing an event. He was a Democrat. That's when John Tower ran, and Tower won [the US Senate seat]. When LBJ became vice president, Blakley was appointed to replace him, and then Tower beat Blakley.

And Dad took me out to see him, and it was a civic thing, to say, "Here's a senator." And I thought that was really cool. Oh my gosh, he was in the bank lobby, *the* bank, and all the townspeople were there in the lobby.

And then when I was a freshman in college, I did work for my congressman as an intern, and he was a Democrat, Clark Thompson from Galveston. When I wrote him to tell him I was running for the legislature, I put in parentheses "as a Republican."

But he was so nice. He must have been congressman from Galveston for thirty years. He was just this grand old man, very sweet, good. And he wrote me a note back and said, "Even if you're a Republican, I think it's wonderful that you're running."

This is what was great about my parents. They never encouraged me to do anything. They never said, "Go run for student council. Or why don't you run for cheerleader?"

They never said that, but they were so supportive whenever I did something. When I said I wanted to go to law school, my dad was totally surprised. Never came into his mind that I would go to law school, but he was right there supporting me. And when I wanted to try to work and earn some of the money for law school, I worked in the legislature for my Democratic state representative from Galveston, Ed Harris. And I was working part time and I was really having a hard time having time to study, and Dad said, "Just quit. I'm going to pay for your law school. You study. That's what you need to do."

So I did. But that's what they always did.

I was definitely a reader. I loved Hardy Boys. I read every Hardy Boys book. In fact, in the sixth grade, I couldn't fulfill the requirement because I had already read every biography in the library. I loved them, and I think that's what gave me my ambition, honestly. It was George Washington and John Adams and Ben Franklin, and there was one about a woman, Betsy Ross. But I did see so much about great people, and I think it gave me a spark, even though I never gave it a thought of actually doing anything at the time.

My can-do spirit was from reading the history books. My most important trait would be perseverance, because I've been knocked down a lot. But I really think it's the people who get back up and keep on going who eventually succeed with whatever the goal is.

But I don't know why, other than reading the biographies in the school library—other than that, there was nothing remarkable about my childhood. It was wonderful, but nothing about it that you would think inspired me particularly. My life was pretty easy.

Kay Bailey Hutchison with Luci Johnson at a signing event in 2013 for Hutchison's book, *Unflinching Courage: Pioneering Women Who Shaped Texas. Briscoe Center photograph*

The Spirit of Texas

I am lucky because growing up I was always thinking about Texas history.

The women who did so much in early Texas created the spirit of Texas that you feel here today. The women were refined, they had pianos, they knew music, they knew languages, they were educated.

This is what Texans are. They [pioneers] are hardy, they are happy, they're not suffering, they are facing hardships, but they had balls and parties.

We've passed it down through the generations because we still have that love for Texas. And it's so important to continue to teach Texas history as a required course.

Joe Armstrong, 1954. *Photo courtesy Joe Armstrong*

BIRTH NAME	**JOSEPH CHARLES GRAVITT**
BORN	August 23, 1943, in Fort Worth to Emmett Charles Gravitt and Dorthadele Greathouse Gravitt; adopted in 1948 by Doyle Cameron Armstrong
INTERVIEW	His office, New York City, November 24, 1981

32

JOE ARMSTRONG
Joe's Party and Gift Shop

A s a young Texan in cowboy boots, Joe Armstrong made his mark on the New York City publishing world in the early 1970s by turning Rolling Stone, *an obscure underground magazine facing bankruptcy, into the chronicle for a generation. He convinced an older generation of advertising executives that the magazine was marketable with top-notch writers Hunter S. Thompson and Tom Wolfe and celebrity photographers Annie Leibovitz and Richard Avedon. From there, the list of magazines he published is equally impressive:* New York, New West, Saveur, Worth, *and* Civilization, *the magazine of the Library of Congress. He also advised publishers at* Time, Random House, Doubleday, American Express, Hearst, Gannett, USA Today, George *magazine, HBO, and ABC News. He applied his entrepreneurial skills to fund-raising and chaired the first of two mega-multi-million-dollar benefits for AIDS victims in the panic years of the 1980s and early 1990s.*

I've had a long association with print. I'd get the paper and study it, and I taught myself to read before the first grade. My mother was a very big reader of newspapers and magazines. I was ten or eleven when I got an old mimeograph machine and put out a family newspaper and a neighborhood newspaper. When I was in high school, I used to write for the newspaper in Abilene for ten cents an inch—travel stuff and high school news.

But I don't think I ever had one burning ambition. My mother would say, "Joe wants to find his ballpark."

I don't think money was ever very important to me. With the money I made as a kid, I took trips or went to camp or bought gifts for my baby sisters. I went to YMCA Camp Grady Spruce on Possum Kingdom Lake. Why would you ever name a lake Possum Kingdom? Anyway, I wanted money for adventures.

Joe Armstrong, editor-in-chief and publisher of *New York Magazine*, 1978.
Photo courtesy Joe Armstrong

But it has always been the sense of accomplishment that was important. I remember my mother telling me as a child how our family could never spend more than a quarter on anything in the grocery store. Now, I didn't feel deprived of very much, and we led a very simple life. My parents always taught me that being fulfilled is what it's all about.

I lived all over the place in Texas because Dad worked for a trucking company. I was born in Fort Worth and lived there until I was about five, and then we moved all over Dallas. We relocated to San Angelo for six months and finally Abilene. And we lived at several addresses in each city, so I went to thirteen schools.

And I never could take those stupid tests that said if a train is ten miles east of Tyler going twenty-two miles an hour and there's a train nineteen miles northwest of Throckmorton that's heading east, when are they going to meet? I'd say, "I don't know, and why is it important?"

So I did not get into the University of Texas. I talked my way into Trinity University in San Antonio. I entered on probation and ended up being president of the student government for two years. It was a great experience because it was the first time in my life that I started even with everybody else. Because I'd moved so many times, everyone else already had their cliques and friendships.

M y parents always encouraged me. I had a father who said anyone can do anything if he wants to bad enough. He also used to say, "It's just as easy to think big as it is to think little."

My dad started working when he was thirteen. He came from a very poor family and started working on the docks of a motor freight company. He worked his way up to become president of this little trucking company called Johnson Transport. Then many years later, it became not so little and merged with Merchants Fast Motor Lines. Merchants became the largest intrastate carrier in Texas. He was in charge of sales, and the company of just a few million went to more than $100 million in revenues in the 1970s.

My dad is the embodiment of the best values in somebody, allowing me to see that you can have those good values and do what you want to in life. My dad has always treated people like he wanted to be treated and was always a strong, decent, thoughtful, kind, completely honest man. And it worked.

My mother is a real optimist. She always gives a lot of credit to God and her Methodist faith. She has a real strong sense of goodness in people and seeks it out. She brought us up to look for the best in people.

My first father was killed in Europe in World War II, and my mother was a widow at nineteen with an eight-month-old kid to raise by herself. Five years later she remarried, and I was adopted by my father, Armstrong, who I consider my totally great dad. But my mother has always said she saw my natural father as my guardian angel, always pulling for me from above.

Raising three children was her full-time job. She was active in the church and volunteer work, but primarily her whole life was raising her children. My sister Mary was born in '50, and my sister Marilyn was born in '52. I helped raise them. I took the responsibility because I was seven when my first sister arrived. I rushed home every day to play with them.

I remember having a library where I'd arrange books so neighborhood kids could come and check them out. After getting old school desks out of an alley, I remember having a school for my sisters and their friends. One time I had a circus using piano crates in the garage. We had a stage, and my sisters were the performers. I was the director.

I'm really blessed by my sisters. We have always been very close. My best friends were always my family. Because we moved so much, I wasn't able to make a lot of long-lasting friends.

I was very, very fortunate that I had parents who allowed me a lot of space, a lot of freedom, and a lot of independence. They encouraged me to do my thing. My parents would either expose me to opportunities or allow me to find my own.

I tried, for instance, to go to a different place every summer. I worked in the Black slums in Milwaukee in the summer of '60 in a Peace Corps or VISTA kind of program before there was a Peace Corps or VISTA. I worked with a Quaker group and in the National Urban League. That's something my mother had found out for me.

I'd been rejected as a camp counselor by my camp as not being mature enough, and I was crushed. So my mother sought options for me. You had to earn your own money to go. You had to pay $150 for the food for the summer and to go to work in the Black slums and sleep on a cot in an old church. And you had to get your own way up there, and I went by train. I cut firewood and delivered groceries to get the money.

It was one of the most wonderful experiences I ever had in my life. We tried to get struggling people to clean up and fix up their places. We got paint for them wholesale, and we painted houses for the old and infirm. We tried to instill a community revival.

The summer of '64, I worked on the *Franklin Evening Star* in a little Indiana town of ten thousand people thirty miles below Indianapolis. It had two daily newspapers battling it out.

I worked in Washington, DC, once at the Peace Corps headquarters and another summer at the Veterans Administration. My parents made it possible for me to go on a bicycle tour of Europe in '61. We cycled 1,500 miles, stayed in youth hostels, and it was a wonderful trip. It was so long ago that jets had just started. My mother was afraid for me to ride on a jet, so we took a prop plane back to New York, and it took thirteen hours.

I loved those summer experiences growing up—going away and then coming back home. That was very important to me.

One of my first legitimate jobs and one of my proudest achievements—being a busboy at the Dixie Pig for two years. The name was so kooky that I thought it was cool. It is at Fourteenth at Butternut in Abilene on what's called the Friendly Mile and had a giant neon sign that was a hoot: "Eating Out Is Fun."

After being a regular busboy, I wanted more responsibility and asked if I also could be responsible for the frozen custard machine. I loved frozen custard. One time, I filled up the machine and the thing exploded. All these cowboys were sitting at the counter having chicken-fried steak and peach cobbler. This thing exploded, and I fell to the floor and all of it came on top of me like soap out of a washing machine. It covered me up.

The last thing I remember hearing was, "Look, that boy's done covered all up with frozen custard."

I think I blacked out after that.

I always wanted to work. There's just no substitute for hard work. My dad worked hard. He had the attitude that you've got to make things happen. In the freight business, they had a little store called Damaged Freight where they sold real cheap stuff that had been damaged. I remember going with my savings, starting when I was about five or six, and buying stuff and then taking it door-to-door and selling it for a profit.

I'd sell cosmetics or kitchen utensils that I'd bought at Damaged Freight. This was before I was even in the first grade. I remember shelling pecans and selling them door-to-door. I remember selling Christmas cards door-to-door, stationery and magazines door-to-door. I made pot holders, maybe a thousand pot holders on those little square looms, and sold them for a quarter.

In the third grade, I remember making doughnuts and selling them house-to-house. My mother and dad—this is how wonderful they are—ended up helping me make the doughnuts, which means they probably made them and sacked them. The neighbors would say, "Here's that Armstrong kid again. What's he got to sell now?"

When we moved to San Angelo, I was in the fourth grade and too young to have a paper route. So I got a bus downtown every afternoon after school. I went to the *San Angelo Standard-Times* and bought the papers for three cents. I sold them on the downtown corners and in stores for a nickel. Then I did that same job when we moved to Abilene.

I remember as a little kid looking through the help-wanted ads every day. I'd apply for jobs, and they'd say, "You're too young."

Back in San Angelo, I also remember saving up to have a huge wooden piano crate delivered to our house. I put it in the front yard and sold all kinds of penny candies and popcorn and snow cones and cold drinks in it.

My parents probably stayed in constant shock. We had this little two-bedroom house in San Angelo, and my dad came home to find this huge structure in the front yard. When we moved to Abilene, which was about the fifth grade, I got five piano crates and stacked them on top of each other and had a hotel for kids in the backyard. I had it wired with electricity, and all the kids in the neighborhood came to my hotel.

I remember having a restaurant in the sixth grade in Abilene, and I called it Little Mexico. It was three giant crates put together in the front yard. I served Cokes and fried pies and claimed it was Mexican food.

Then I had Joe's Party and Gift Shop, which had a huge sign in the front yard. I took over one room in our home and sold cheap little Japanese imports—the joy buzzer, little tricks and games, cheap party favors, and those stupid gorillas or monkeys that banged cymbals when you put a battery in them. That was not the kind of thing that would have been in the Neiman Marcus catalog. And I'd also truck this junk over to people's homes and I'd put on parties.

Friends of my mother would call and say, "I'm having a birthday party for little Nellie Lou. Can Joe come and give it?"

I also babysat and mowed lawns and washed cars for fifty cents an hour. And I used to play the piano at the Paramount Theater in Abilene between features on Saturday to get free passes. No one had done it there probably since the silent movies.

Then I worked at about three or four grocery stores. I remember working at a Safeway sacking groceries. I worked at drive-in groceries where you walk out to the car and take the order, go fill it, and bring it back to the customer. The lady would come up and say, "Give me a Bab-O and a Tide, and give me a jar of mayonnaise and some chili pie."

So I'd say, "Be right back."

And you'd go get it, take it to her, and she'd pay.

And I was a Santa Claus. I would go to Mrs Baird's Bakery and borrow their spare Santa Claus uniform on Saturdays. I went to the Metro Theater on Butternut and was the Santa Claus for the little kids. They'd all sit on my knee. I took them candy. Here I was thirteen or fourteen, and I was Santa Claus. Who said Santa Claus had to be somebody ninety years old?

There was a Creative Arts Club in Abilene. I would sit for artists who painted still lifes. Then in return, they let me use their facilities. I would rent a projector and get free films from the telephone company and have movies there. I'd get thirty to forty kids to come and watch movies on Saturdays.

How I got movies out of the phone company, I don't know. I knew they had educational films like "The Life of Alexander Graham Bell."

I used to sell Cokes and programs at the football games. Back then a lot of people thought you didn't want others to see you in public doing this or that. That kind of stuff never did bother me.

Texas is a way of life, an attitude, a state of mind, and a big menu. It's a way to act and a way to dress and a way to be that I feel so comfortable with it, it's almost like another mother. My parents gave me love and encouragement, and Texas gave me everything else.

Joe Armstrong with Phyllis George, 2006. *Photo courtesy Joe Armstrong*

Guich Koock with his aunt Martha Stansbury. *Photo courtesy Guich Koock*

BIRTH NAME	**WILLIAM FAULK GUICH KOOCK**
BORN	July 22, 1944, in Austin to Chester Lewis Koock and Mary Faulk Koock
INTERVIEW	Menger Hotel Bar, San Antonio, Texas, June 18, 1981

GUICH KOOCK
Talk and Tolerance

C haracter actor *Guich Koock played country good old boys in movies and on television. He and rancher-folklorist Hondo Crouch bought a ghost town, Luckenbach, in the Texas Hill Country for $30,000 in 1970 and created such attention-grabbing events as the Luckenbach World's Fair featuring the town's post office, general store, saloon, and dance hall. The town was memorialized in the song "Luckenbach, Texas," performed by Willie Nelson and Waylon Jennings. A casting director spotted Koock there and cast him in Steven Spielberg's first theatrical feature,* The Sugarland Express, *filming nearby. Luckenbach also served as the location for the sitcom* Lewis and Clark, *in which Koock co-starred. His most notable TV role was in the 1970s* Carter Country, *but he also appeared on* Laverne and Shirley, Alice, Harper Valley PTA, North Dallas Forty, The Love Boat, *and* Walker, Texas Ranger. *He is the nephew of folklorist John Henry Faulk, whose CBS radio career ended when he stood up against the Hollywood blacklist.*

I grew up in Austin, where I was born the middle of seven children. We lived at my grandmother's place, which is now Green Pastures Restaurant. At that time, it was way out in South Austin.

My grandmother Faulk was one of the finest ladies I ever knew. She looked like everybody's grandmother ought to look, kind of gray haired, kind of chunky, a wonderful laugh. She was a very tolerant, accepting, wise, womanly woman, which is similar to being a manly man.

I remember her killing chickens every Sunday. All the kids picked chickens every Sunday. She wrang their necks, but I never could do that. I used an ax.

Guich Koock at the bar in the Menger Hotel in San Antonio in 1981 during the first interview conducted for this book.
Photo by Harry Young

A great cross section of people was always there. The restaurant was the first integrated restaurant in the state of Texas when it opened in 1945. My mother, Mary Faulk Koock, opened it. She was a remarkable lady. The women's rights movement never did have much strength for me because I came from a line of strong women. They were born liberated.

Her father came from Alabama, one of thirteen orphaned sharecropper kids. He went to the University of Texas and became one of the first civil rights lawyers in Austin.

My daddy's family has been in Texas six generations. His family on his father's side, the Koocks, came over from Germany with the first ox cartload of people that came to Fredericksburg. My father's mother's side of the family, the Barksdales, was influential, and they were in Texas before the Texas Revolution, under Spain and Mexico. Barksdale, Texas, is named after my grandmother's grandfather for his service in the Texas Revolution.

My uncle Hamilton told me the name Guich was a first name on my mother's side of the family. The rumor of a pirate named Guich Faulk was not true.

My full name is William Faulk Guich Koock. My folks said they didn't have anything to give us but names. All my brothers and sisters have multiple names.

Uncle John Henry said that my daddy raised dogs and he gave them all the good names: David, John, Steve. I had a cousin named Spot. His daddy didn't raise dogs.

I was fortunate to grow up in a multiethnic neighborhood. I had Mexican friends and a lot of Black friends and white friends, plus Italians, Poles, and Germans. My father spoke German and made his own cheese and that sort of thing.

There were a lot of prejudices, but none of them related to religion or race. If we didn't like somebody, it was because he was a creep and we knew why and could document it.

When my parents first opened the restaurant, a Black soprano opera singer from Austin had a big dinner party at Green Pastures. Mama got a call from one of the prominent ladies in Austin, who said, "Mary, I understand that y'all had a Negra eating dinner out there the other night as your guest. Is that true?"

My mama said, "Oh, you mean Virgie DeWitte. You know, she has just gotten back from her tour of Italy. Next time she comes, I'll ask her to invite you. You'll really love hearing her. I'm so sorry you missed it."

In addition to her own children, Mama would take all the neighborhood kids out to Barton Springs, which was the big swimming hole at the time, with clear springs. She took Billy Morris, who was Black, and all the Tayo kids, who were brown. She was pretty well known in Austin, and the lifeguard came up and said, "Miz Koock, oh, Miz Koock, you know this is a segregated pool. Colored are not allowed in here."

She said, "What do you mean? These are all my children."

He didn't know what to say, and, sure, they went swimming.

The first role I played was Jesus Christ in the Christmas pageant. Every year we have a great Christmas pageant at home, and Mama invited all the neighbors. It was really quite a tradition. Billy Morris was the Ethiopian wise man; the Mexican kids were the shepherds and angels. It was always really nice, an integrated affair.

The first year you were born, you were Jesus. The next year you were a shepherd, then an angel, and finally the biggest thing was to be a wise man, where you had the only speaking part, which was, "Come, let us hasten unto Bethlehem."

We always had very lively discussions around the table. We always had a lot of actresses and actors visiting us. My uncle, John Henry Faulk, was involved in entertainment. His first wife, Hally Wood, was a very talented folk singer, and a lot of her people would come stay.

In the flood of 1935, a friend of my uncle Hamilton Faulk moved a trailer to our yard to get out of the flood and stayed there until he died ten years later. Hamilton took us hunting arrowheads all over Texas. He took us dove hunting, and he'd shoot the doves and we'd go bird-dog them. Mom could fix doves and smother them in gravy. She was one of the best cooks in the world.

A Colonel Talley and his wife came to dinner one Sunday and just stayed. He had been in the Civil War and was a captain in the Texas Rangers.

We had fourteen rooms in that house and one bathroom. We really developed a lot of patience. It was great growing up there.

My daddy, Chester Lewis Koock, had the most beautiful singing voice I ever heard. He was a great storyteller. There were so many storytellers in that part of Texas.

Big Bill Meislin lived down the street from me, and I used to stay with him and he'd tell me ghost stories. Big Bill gave me my first job when I was five, buying chickens.

Mother Finney's parents had been slaves. She lived right down the street from us in the same house the slave masters had given her parents.

There were a lot of rich experiences.

When I went to school at Texas A&M, I began to remember all those stories I collected as a kid. And I began collecting stories of children of slaves in the Brazos River bottom as a master's thesis at the University of Texas. The Brazos River was essentially the western boundary of the large slave movement in Texas. There were communities of people who lived on the same plantation where their parents had been slaves.

While I was in high school, I worked for J. Frank Dobie, a writer and professor at the University of Texas. I drove for him. He was the first agnostic I ever met.

———

Daddy's family was Catholic, Mama's family was Methodist, and I was raised in both churches. My family was very open, and that's rare in Texas.

One time, Dobie picked up some hand-ground flour from Sarah Penn Harris in Austin, and I drove him out to the ranch. I went fishing, and when I came back he had on his torn-off khaki pants, he was barefoot, and his legs looked like gnarled cedar stumps. A little, round, brown cloud of flour rose around those gnarled cedar stumps.

He said, "Guich, grease up that pan over there. We're going to have some biscuits."

I greased up the pan, and he sat down. When the biscuits came out, they were hard and flat and leathery like shoe soles.

"By George, I don't understand," he said. "I must not have put in enough baking powder. Grease up that pan again, and I'll make us another batch."

And another brown flour cloud rose around those old gnarled legs.

He sat down and said, "By George, this batch'll rise higher'n Jesus Christ, and, in my opinion, a good deal higher."

Our family was stone broke, but we never did realize it. Everybody was broke then. We raised everything; we always had plenty to eat. My daddy did all kinds of things. He worked for the railroad, was a salesman, and farmed some. We raised our own hogs and plowed with mules. We mainly raised Irish potatoes and corn.

Mama worked at home, and all the kids worked at home. At the restaurant, we all did everything. We waited tables. We'd all complain like kids do, you know.

Daddy was bad about making us work. I milked two cows from the time I was eight. He believed in working hard. He didn't mind work. He mowed about nine acres of our yard with a push mower. We painted the whole house when I was seven years old. We didn't think it was unusual or hard; that's just what people did.

Sarah Ragle participated in the McMurry College homecoming ceremonies as a child. *Photo courtesy Catherine Ragle*

BIRTH NAME	**SARAH RAGLE**
BORN	February 5, 1945, in Abilene to Reverend Herbert Doyle Ragle and Lena Catherine Morrison Ragle
INTERVIEW	Home of Jane Macon, San Antonio, Texas, September 18, 1981

SARAH WEDDINGTON
A Preacher's Kid

At twenty-six, Sarah Weddington became the youngest person ever to argue a successful case before the US Supreme Court. That 1973 decision, Roe v. Wade, *legalized abortion within the first trimester of a woman's pregnancy. Weddington served three terms in the Texas House of Representatives from 1973 to 1977. Ann Richards, who later would be a popular Texas governor, was her legislative aide. In 1977 Weddington was the first woman to be general counsel of the US Department of Agriculture, where she supervised more than two hundred lawyers, and she became the first female director of the Texas Office of State-Federal Relations. Among many honors, she received the Margaret Brent Award for professional excellence from the American Bar Association; the Margaret Sanger Award, the highest honor from the Planned Parenthood Federation of America; and, from the Texas Women's Chamber of Commerce, a sequined boot that noted, "For a woman who kicks ass." A popular speaker on the importance of women in leadership roles, she established the Weddington Center in Austin.*

M y family is a West Texas family, and I was born in Abilene. My father was a Methodist preacher, so we moved about every four years to places like Munday and Vernon. My parents, Reverend Doyle and Catherine Ragle, also lived in Lubbock. My grandparents lived in Olton and Odessa. One uncle was the postmaster in Pecos.

I think of West Texas as being a wide-open space. I can still remember going out one Sunday afternoon with some people who had a ranch outside of Amarillo and riding a horse. It was the most powerful feeling because you're by yourself on a horse way out and you can just see forever. It's a sense of being in control and of being at ease and at peace.

We lived through many dust storms in West Texas. The air fills up with sand and is a reddish color. You go outside and you're in a reddish world. After it's over, you look around and there's dust all over everything. It comes in the cracks of the house, onto the windowsills, and all over. It's just like a cloud of dust or sand moving in. Everybody complains about it, but it's sort of taken for granted.

I don't think I grew up with the resentment some seem to feel at being "the preacher's kid."

Daddy never said to me, "You can't do that because you're the preacher's kid."

However, there were certainly times he said, "You can't do that because it's wrong," or "You can't do that because that's not the way we live."

Obviously, there was a different standard for me. Other kids didn't invite me to do a lot of things; they invited other people. But, frankly, it's just as well. It would have put me in a conflict situation.

There were a lot of advantages to growing up a preacher's kid. One was in starting young to learn leadership skills. I was always working as an officer in church organizations or doing devotionals in front of the church or singing in the choir or singing solos or playing the piano. From a very early age, I was in front of people and used to more or less performing.

People would say, "Gosh, you're so good at that."

So I would think, "Oh, I'll do that again."

In a large way, the skills I have today and a lot of what I've been able to achieve came because I learned to give speeches and to be in front of people and to be very comfortable doing it.

Second, I had to learn to meet people and make friends quickly. The Methodist Conference tells the preachers where they are going to live. We moved often, and each time, I had to make new friends.

In politics, being from a lot of places is very helpful. When I went to Washington, the Abilene papers had a story essentially saying, "Abilene Girl Goes to Washington." Vernon had one saying, "Vernon High Grad . . ." and Canyon had "Canyon Junior High Grad . . ."

My father was not primarily an evangelist, but rather a preacher who stressed social concern; he believed that we have a Christian responsibility to help those less fortunate than ourselves. A lot of that rubbed off on me. Many of the things I have done since then have been motivated by my concern for people.

> **In politics, being from a lot of places is very helpful.**

I was basically a serious, precocious child. I read a lot. I was always curious and always had friends. But because I was the preacher's kid, I grew up feeling different from other children. Part of being a leader sometimes involves not being everybody's best friend but being willing to be a little bit set apart or a little bit different. That doesn't make me terribly uncomfortable, because that's the way I grew up.

I would have been the valedictorian of my class except we'd only lived in Vernon a year, and the rule of the school was that you had to be there two years. I was always an officer in various clubs and competed in debating. My memories of growing up basically revolve around accomplishing things and being recognized for the quality of my work.

Early activities included being president of the Methodist Youth Fellowship. Then I was the president of the Future Homemakers of America and in the debating club and in the extemporaneous speaking club and on the tennis team.

I don't remember wanting to enter any particular profession. When I went to college, my parents encouraged me to get a teacher's certificate because "I could always teach." I have my secondary English and speech teaching certificate.

I was sixteen when I finished high school, since I had skipped two grades. I wanted to go to graduate school. I knew if I got a doctorate in English I could teach, but I wasn't sure I wanted to do that. I hadn't taken enough chemistry to go to medical school. So I decided to go to law school. That was a fortunate accident, because I have truly enjoyed my legal career.

Once I said I wanted to go to law school, there was never a period when my parents said, "You don't really want to do that. That's not you."

Any time I decided I was going to do something, or even said I was thinking about doing something, they were very encouraging.

My mother was born a little bit across the New Mexico line, and my father was born in the Olton area. They influenced me in different ways.

My mother and I did all the traditional things. We did all the house-work-type chores, and I sewed my own clothes for a while. Mother was a good Texas-type cook and liked to cook cornbread, black-eyed peas, and ham. She taught me to cook those things, but I don't have time to cook now.

It was always assumed I could do anything I wanted to do. Mother encouraged me to read and to do all the extracurricular activities. If it meant scrimping to buy me a clarinet so I could play in the school band, or to get a uniform because I was a drum major for the junior high band, she did it. Mother saw to it that all three of her kids had all the extra opportunities.

From my mother, I probably got much more of my drive. In a lot of churches, it's considered inappropriate for the preacher's wife to work outside the home and church. But she is expected to give an awful lot. It's hard for a preacher's wife to carve out her own sphere, because as hard as she works in the church, the husband is always the preacher. He is the one in charge.

Looking back, there probably were many times when Mother would have been happier had she been able to work in a regular paid position. That didn't work out until later in her life, when she went back to school and got her master's degree in education and began teaching in business college.

Like many other young women, I was very close to my father. We did a

Sarah Weddington during the time she worked for the Jimmy Carter administration, May 16, 1979.
Bernard Rapoport Papers, Briscoe Center for American History, University of Texas at Austin

From left to right, Sarah Weddington, Liz Carpenter, Kay Bailey Hutchison, and Ann Richards, c. 1984. *Ann W. Richards Papers, Briscoe Center for American History, University of Texas at Austin*

variety of things together, like playing ping-pong. We also went camping as a family.

From my father, I gained a sense of self-acceptance because he accepted me so readily. When I went to college, Daddy took me.

On the way there, he said, "No matter what you do, we'll always love you. Obviously, we hope the best for you, and there are lots of things we hope you will accomplish. There's a kind of life we hope you'll lead. But whatever you do, we'll always love you."

We always lived in parsonages. In Munday it was right next to the church. It was a two-story, white house with a big porch. It encouraged lots of running up and down the stairs. In Canyon the parsonage was a few blocks away and a three-bedroom brick—more the spread-out kind of house very common there. Each place was a little bit different.

I remember poundings. In the rural churches, they still have them. Preachers in small churches are not paid too well, and every once in a while there's what is called a pounding. In the old days, everybody brought a pound of something for the preacher and his family. I remember congregation members setting up long tables in the church parking lot and everybody bringing a pound of coffee or cans of vegetables. A lot of it was purchased, but some was canned by the parishioners themselves.

One year they gave us our first TV. One year they gave Daddy a trip to the Holy Lands.

In our family meetings, what was really fun was for all the kids to gather around and hear Grandfather tell his stories about when he was growing up. Most of the stories have to do with being on his own.

In one story, he talked about going deer hunting on horseback. Everybody laughed at him and said he could never shoot a deer on a horse, because the horse would scare the deer. But he was determined to do it his way. He rode all day and finally found a deer. Even though it was a long shot, he got it. He took the deer back to camp and everybody was astonished.

That story illustrates that once you make up your mind, you're really going to do it. It's in my family. We work hard to see that we do what we say we are going to do. We tend to be much more inclined to do things instead of sitting around and talking about them.

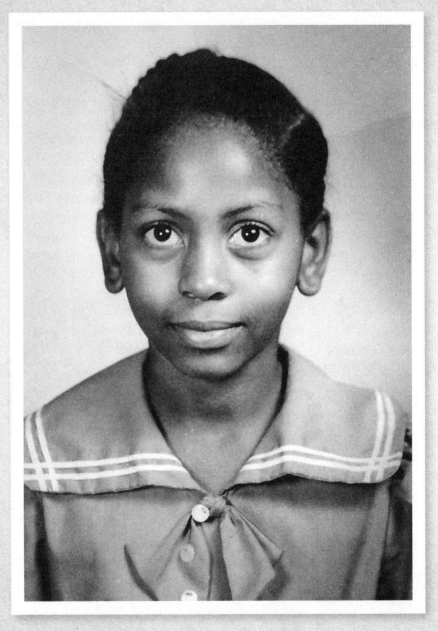

Ruth Stubblefield, age seven. *Photo courtesy Ruth Simmons*

BIRTH NAME	**RUTH JEAN STUBBLEFIELD**
BORN	July 3, 1945, in Grapeland to Isaac Stubblefield and Fannie Campbell Stubblefield
INTERVIEW	Prairie View A&M University, Prairie View, Texas, July 16, 2018

RUTH SIMMONS

A Sharecropper's Daughter

R uth Simmons was the first Black president of an Ivy League university. In half a century in higher education, she helmed Brown University from 2001 to 2012, headed Smith College from 1995 to 2001, and held other trailblazing roles at the University of Southern California, Princeton University, and Spelman College. Simmons was tapped by Prairie View A&M University in 2017 as its first female president. She earned master's and doctorate degrees in romance languages and literature at Harvard University and has received more than forty honorary degrees. Her honors include the 2001 President's Award from the United Negro College Fund, the 2002 Fulbright Lifetime Achievement Medal, the 2004 Eleanor Roosevelt Val-Kill Medal, the Foreign Policy Association Medal, the 2010 Ellis Island Medal of Honor, and Harvard's Centennial Medal. In 2013 she was named a Chevalier of the French Legion of Honour. DNA testing by the PBS series Finding Your Roots *traced her paternal roots to Gabon.*

Fundamentally, my family comes from the Grapeland and Oakwood area—my mother's side from Oakwood; my father's side from Grapeland. There were stories in the family all along that somehow we were related to a white family in town, but it was not proper to speak of it openly. Within the family, we certainly had heard stories, but nobody was bold enough to openly explore it so much, because that would have been quite a forbidden thing to do.

My great-grandmother was a daughter of a white family. Her name was Lucinda, a slave girl. My grandmother, Flossie, her daughter, was obviously the link to the white family, through the normal process of slaves on plantations basically traveling with the plantation and the racial mixing that took place. That's how my great-grandmother came to be in Grapeland.

In Texas there was no legal barrier to Blacks buying land. My mother's father and her brother saw that land was going to be critical to their being able to have a good future. So they probably worked for a while and then found the means to purchase this property, which I still own part of.

The original migration says something about what people thought about Texas: That is a place to have a future. Because in those days, right after slavery, it wasn't clear at all what people would do. I think they thought Texas offered the opportunity for a fertile start and also to be apart from the kind of the violence that enveloped other parts of the country. They purchased land where there wouldn't be enormous restrictions on what they could do.

My grandfather on my father's side also purchased property, but that property was lost somehow. Both sides of the family were aspiring. After slavery, there was one way that people could live: They could own land, farm, and they could raise animals. They could sell what they raised. They weren't going to get jobs.

In some instances, they were probably helped to purchase land by white relatives. I used to hear stories about a particular white person who visited us all the time, even stayed overnight, and was somehow related to us. If there were enough of a connection for them to visit, then there would be enough connection for them to help with the acquisition of land.

My grandmother, Emma Campbell, lived on the land that my grandfather had purchased in Grapeland, to raise her children after her husband died.

———

That's a very powerful story in my family, the fact that my grandmother was widowed and left with these small children and that she was able to make a way because of this act that my grandfather had taken to make sure the family had property and a place to live.

On my father's side, it's not so dissimilar, actually, because there, too, my father's father died young, leaving my grandmother, Flossie Stubblefield, with a large family to support. She subsequently remarried, but they had a very, very difficult time making a go of it. The boys, the Stubblefields, were somewhat isolated. These were the stories told in the family about the hardship my father had growing up. He was very close to his siblings.

The same was true on my mother's side. She was very close to her siblings, and so all of these uncles and aunts and their children formed a massively large family core for us to grow up with. And in a small town like Grapeland, this was very important. There were a lot of us.

We lived for a time on a plantation called the Murray Farm, a vast plantation of sharecroppers, both Black and white. Our family basically had a house on the Murray Farm, and most of us remember what it was like to be on this farm with all these families and having to pick cotton and harvest crops in that setting.

We were actually in Dailey [also known as Dalys or Daly's], far enough from the town of Grapeland that mostly my oldest siblings couldn't go to school enough to be able to graduate. If you were a sharecropping family, you worked in the fields. That was the most important thing. You only got to school when there was nothing for you to do on the farm.

The isolation in Dailey and the fact that we couldn't get away and go to school much of the time meant that we relied on each other. We have the happiest memories of growing up together with our father and mother because we were all hostage to this sharecropper system where you all had to be together. You all went to the field together; you all took every meal together; everything was together.

We were insular because we had so many people we could rely on. So there's something tribal, clannish about our behavior. Even to this day, people tell us often that we are not as friendly as some people might be, that we associate with each other too much.

We had a very modest home, obviously, with only the most essential things. I remember a place we called a kitchen and then a front room. This was an activity room, and anything that needed to be done was done in that room. Often my parents slept in that front room. Then there was a bedroom for boys and a bedroom for girls. So basically, it was three rooms with a small kitchen.

Most of the activity took place outside the home, so the porch was an extension of the house. Most of my memories of my mother are on the porch doing her chores, whether it was ironing or preparing things to get ready to cook.

Washing took place outside in a giant pot under which was a lit fire, and clothes were boiled. So most of the activity, all the chores, took place outside, and indoors was just a place for you to go into to sleep or if the weather was inclement.

We were fortunate to have pets, which augmented the satisfaction of that life, and some of us were fortunate enough to have horses.

Transportation in those days was very rudimentary. I remember as a child actually riding in wagons. My father was able to get a car at some point, but basically, there was very little room for any luxuries because you never earned enough on the farm to do anything substantial.

I was the last of twelve children. Five girls. Seven boys. They treated me like I was the baby all my life.

We all went to the fields because everybody else was there. I hear a lot of harrumphs from my older brothers and sisters, because they say, "All you did was ride on the cotton sacks."

Certainly, I do have memories of going to the fields with the rest of the family. It was an all-family enterprise. There were no babysitters. Everybody was working.

My next older siblings are two years older and are twins. In a family of twelve children, it would have been strange for me to have much attention from my mother. I would never have expected it, frankly, because there were lots of children around, and, furthermore, my oldest siblings were more like parents to me than siblings. My oldest sister thinks she raised me because she was old enough when I was born to do what a mother would do for a baby. She was consigned to doing that because my mother had a lot to do.

Elbert was first. I would say he was my mother's favorite because he was so like her in values and tone and personality and so forth. He was kind of a duplicate. Nobody had a quarrel with this. He was the oldest and carried a lot of authority and knew exactly what to do.

So there's Elbert. And Chester. Wilford, her second favorite. And then Atherine, like Catherine without the C or the K. And then Albert. Amazing, we had an Elbert and Albert. We just ran out of names. And then Arnold, then Nora, and then Ruben, Clarence, Azella, Ozella, and Ruth. That was all of them. Twelve.

My father was the dictator of the household—very stern, very much in control of everything in the house, except for me, because I was his favorite. He was not easy on everybody else.

So my father was very much conditioned by the difficulty of his childhood. He spoke of not having anything to eat. A very hard life. He was a very no-nonsense type of person, saw everything in black and white. There was no leeway, not for my mother or any of us. So we knew when he put down his orders, we had to do it. It was just that simple.

Ruth Stubblefield graduated from Houston's Wheatley High School in 1963.
Photo courtesy Ruth Simmons

He was more generous with the boys. He was very much a traditionalist, and he didn't believe in women's rights. So we couldn't wear pants, we couldn't go to dances, we couldn't do anything girls typically do when they grow up. It was very strict. We saw our brothers go out and do all sorts of different things when they were old enough, but never the girls. Understandably, this is the way these families protected the girls in those days.

I was very feisty as a child, and the last thing in the world you could do with my parents was to sass. I was constantly talking back, as they called it, and asserting my privileges, and so forth. I got into a lot of trouble with my sisters because I had more freedoms, and my father let me grow up absolutely wild.

My mother was less tolerant of it because she didn't like us being treated differently. She didn't like it so much that I got privileges that others didn't have access to. My mother was all about truth and decency and respect for people and fairness. She would sit on the porch, and while doing her chores, she would talk about life.

And she'd talk about things from the past—stories of people who had done something wrong and what had happened to them as a consequence. All of it was very instructive about how to live your life. That's how I learned. It was like Sunday school, but she was doing it on a daily basis. We just got this mantra over and over again.

"Never think that you are better than another person. Never speak unkindly about somebody. Never . . ."

For most of my life, that's the way I have functioned, just on those basic principles of decency. Such a gift and legacy for her to do that.

There were no social constructs really in this small town. And so going to church was where you saw people. It took all day, getting ready to go and getting there. Because travel wasn't easy, once you got there, you stayed all day. There was the service, then lunch on the grounds, and probably something in the afternoon.

We were Baptist. Absolutely. My father and his brothers had participated in the founding of a church in Grapeland, Greater New Hope Baptist Church. And so they felt a special obligation, because they had a position in founding the church, to support it. The gift that my father gave my mother when they married was a Bible, which I have.

My early recollection of going to church was that they taught us how to behave when we were in society. We had rules about how to act when you are in church.

And then, of course, the church was the anchor for a lot of people leaving that community. They would come back to the church on a big homecoming day to enjoy an elaborate lunch on the grounds. It was really the social center of the community.

You could raise many things sharecropping, but on the Murray Farm it was primarily cotton. The plantation also raised peanuts. Then around your own house, you had the ability to have a garden and your own animals. So we had chickens, pigs, and cows.

But the main thing was to get the crop in and transport the owner's crop into town for sale. You had to meet a quota and harvest a certain amount of cotton by a certain date and then transport that to the cotton mill or gin. That was your obligation to the owner of the plantation, and that was why it was so crucial that all the children work in the fields.

When not working, we played all the time, but there was no money for toys. That is the one recurring complaint from my sisters: they never had a doll.

Our parents were very diligent about doing things for us that were fun. For example, for Christmas we all got a shoebox with an apple, an orange, and some nuts in it. On some rare occasions, when it would snow, our father would collect snow and flavor it so we would have "ice cream."

We were desperately poor. Our clothes were mostly made by our mother, and they were made from discarded sacks in which you purchased flour or some large amount of grain. We were unaware that we were disadvantaged in any way, because everybody we knew was in the same circumstance.

The older children left as soon as they could move to the city. Fundamentally, the older children, when they married, went to Houston, found jobs, and as soon as they could secure enough resources and appropriate space, they encouraged my parents to move to Houston. I was seven.

When my father came to the city, my brothers had prepared the transition. They ended up getting jobs at Bama, the jam factory. They arranged for my father to have a job there as a janitor. They all lived in the same place. There were four or five houses clumped together where you knew everyone. It was very much a childhood filled with love and support and a sense of safety.

Children had a lot of freedom in Grapeland. You could just run around the fields, pick wild berries. You could hunt, if you were inclined to hunt. And you could jump in the creek.

City life was much more structured, and so you lost a lot of freedom as a consequence of the move to the city. When we landed on Lee Street, it was pretty clear there wasn't anything we could do outside of the sight of our parents, so after all of this freedom, it suddenly translated into, "Now you're in the city, and you can't do anything at all."

307

That was probably the right call, but I remember losing freedom. The second thing I remember is people making fun of us because we were country bumpkins. The kids made fun of the way we dressed, the way we looked. If I didn't have a complex before, I developed one when we moved to Houston.

When I started school, however, it was wonderful. I was an inveterate learner, so I kind of shut out everything else in the world.

My oldest sister thought that I was seriously maladjusted. She warned my mother that something was seriously wrong with me because all I wanted to do was have my face in a book. And I wasn't very social. I wasn't going out and playing with other children. I always had just a small number of friends. I was never a big joiner and never one to socialize a good deal. I was very much an introvert.

My mother died when I was fifteen.

It was a very, very challenging time for me. For us girls, my father didn't have the faintest idea what to do. My mother was gone, and we were at home. All he knew how to do was provide us a place to live and give us food. That was it. Probably he was in deep grief himself.

The worst thing that can happen in your young life was to lose a parent.

My first teacher, Miss Ida Mae Henderson, in Grapeland, was the first exemplar of education that I encountered. I thought she was the most wonderful thing in the world. Her enthusiasm was infectious. I just remember how exciting it was to be in her class.

When I got to Houston, I went to Atherton, and again I had teachers there who were resourceful. My excitement didn't end about learning. I never had a bad year in the classroom.

After my mother died, I got involved in stagecraft at Wheatley. Being in a drama program probably is a really good way to come out of yourself. I was salutatorian. We had a lot of smart kids in my class. I don't remember making a B, but I probably did here and there.

Nobody said I was the smartest of the twelve of us. My own assessment is that I had more advantages because of age. Any of them who had the advantages I had would probably have done as well as I have, frankly, because it was very much a factor of going to school. And they couldn't go to school.

In the fifties, college was not on the radar, period. I didn't know people who went to college. So I guess it was when I got to high school that one teacher in particular said, "Well, you need to go to college."

And when she said that, I said, "Um hum," politely, not thinking it was possible.

I remember once I came home before my mother died and said, "Mrs. Lillie said I could probably go to college." And what did she think of that? Could I actually go to college one day?

And I could tell from what she said that she didn't think it was possible. But not wanting to disappoint me, she said, "Well, maybe if the money could be found, it would be possible."

So in my senior year, Mrs. Lillie, my speech and drama teacher, contacted the university where she had gone to college to recommend me for a scholarship, and they gave me one. I also got a Worthing Scholarship from Houston, which was a godsend. Without a scholarship that would pay for absolutely everything, my father told me, there was absolutely no money for college.

Among the people that we know with large families, growing up in fundamentally the same way, I would say our family excelled in just a couple of ways.

First, we are closer than most. The advantages of that closeness are we had time together, that we lived together, that we had to work together, we had to go to church together. That bond that was cemented by that routine has just never been broken.

I can't think of anything any better for anybody than to have close friends and relatives, because it really helps enormously to face whatever you have to face in life.

When Ruth Simmons was installed as president of Brown University in 2001, she became the first Black person to head an Ivy League institution. *Photo courtesy Ruth Simmons*

Jaclyn Smith as a toddler growing up in Houston. *Photo courtesy Jaclyn Smith*

BIRTH NAME	**JACLYN ELLEN SMITH**
BORN	January 26, 1945, in Houston to Jack K. Smith and Margaret Ellen Hartsfield Smith
INTERVIEW	Her home, Beverly Hills, California, May 30, 2018

36

JACLYN SMITH
A Lucky Girl

W ith more than fifty films and television appearances over four decades and successful lines of apparel, wigs, skin care, fragrance, and home decor, Jaclyn Smith was one of the first TV celebrities to develop her own best-selling brands. She and fellow native Texan Farrah Fawcett starred in the iconic Charlie's Angels *TV series in the 1970s, and Smith was the only angel to remain for its five-year run and appear in two film adaptations. After* Charlie's Angels, *she became "Queen of the Miniseries," starring in a number of small-screen dramas and earning a Golden Globe nomination for her performance in* Jacqueline Bouvier Kennedy *in 1981. Hollywood's Walk of Fame added her star in 1989, and magazines such as* People, Us, *and* Harper's Bazaar *listed her among the world's most beautiful people.*

I refer to my childhood as the enchanted forest. Oddly enough, I grew up in a subdivision called Emerald Forest, 3510 Tartan Lane. There was a simplicity and goodness about it. My memories are ever present, so I am comfortable walking through the front door of my past.

I grew up in a neighborhood where everyone knew each other. I ran free. I rode my bike. I heard the ice cream man coming. I smelled fresh-cut grass. I am grateful for my childhood memories. I grew up in the fifties. It was a good time to be growing up. Lucky me.

I was born at St. Joseph's Hospital in Houston. I went to Mark Twain Elementary and from there Pershing Junior High and on to Lamar High School. At Lamar, we were known as the Tea Sippers. We got the name because at one end was the River Oaks Country Club and at the other end, our high school, which they referred to as a country club. I spent one year at Trinity University.

Daddy was born in Pittsburgh. No one was going to tell him that he wasn't a Texan. He thought Texas was the best place—a country unto itself. He never understood why I wanted to leave. It was really that he wanted me down the street near them.

Jaclyn Ellen Smith is my whole name, but as a little girl I didn't like Jackie. I do now, but I didn't then. So it was El or Ellen.

My dad's family was from Germany and came to the United States before World War I in 1901. They came through Ellis Island and settled in Pittsburgh. Daddy's family was Jewish. Their original family name was Kupferschmidt. Daddy's father later changed the family name to Smith. It was probably changed because of the prejudice that existed at that time.

My grandfather on my dad's side, Benjamin K. Smith, didn't speak English when he came to America. He took a dictionary and learned a new word each day. From this difficult beginning, he founded Big Three Industries, which eventually went on to trade on the New York Stock Exchange. Big Three Industries supplied the fuel for the first trip to the moon.

Daddy entered college at sixteen and graduated from Baylor and became a dentist. And in World War II, he served in the navy. My dad's appeal was that he was genuine and honest and pretention-free. He said exactly what was on his mind.

My mother's father was a Methodist minister. His name was Gaston

---

Hartsfield. He lived to be almost 102. He lived on a farm, picked cotton, and rode horseback and lived to see people land on the moon. And, oh, what stories he had to tell. He represented all that was good and right in this world to me. I loved him so much.

I called him PawPaw. He gave me my first base of understanding of what love truly is. Love is living beyond yourself, something he demonstrated all his life. He lost his wife when she was in her early fifties. My mom was only seventeen years old. Her grandmother, Maggie E. Moore, or Mamie to her, was there to help raise her and her brother.

He held his family together. His sensitivity and self-control perhaps concealed inner tensions about losing his wife, which resulted in a nervous breakdown. He recovered completely and went on to preach in churches across Texas for over fifty years. I am grateful for the depth and understanding of his faith.

My mother's grandfather left Mamie a two-hundred-acre farm in Luling, Texas.

He said, "If I leave you land, you will always be all right."

And, just like that, they struck oil.

The San Marcos River runs through it. I remember picnics with my mother and brother, Tommy, where we would put our drinks in the river to make them cold. I loved swimming in the rapids. It was a little scary, but I always had my brother watching over me.

My mom was born in San Antonio, Texas. Her childhood was idyllic. She lived in many small towns across Texas. She was a purveyor of surprise and sweet gestures. Our home was always filled with my favorite delicious treats. She learned how to make divinity, taffy, and fudge from her mother and grandmother. I was lucky to be raised by a devoted mother, one who put her family before herself. She had a talent for happiness.

She also had something money couldn't buy—style. My mother had wanted to be a fashion designer. She had this incredible sense of fashion, and so does my daughter. They're stubbornly original in their choices.

People would say my mom had a charisma about her that made everyone in her presence want to be her friend. I am starved for her energy, her choice of words, her smile. If I was worried about something, she would say, "Everything is going to be all right."

And I believed her, and it usually was.

313

I loved playing with dolls, and I played with them into my early teens, and because of that, I'd have to carry them in paper sacks to my friends' houses. I loved Madame Alexander dolls. One of my favorites was Cinderella.

I always loved redecorating my room, which my mother never held me back from doing. She supported that fact that I was creative. Mom was thrilled to see that I put all that early experience into my branding.

I was a goody two-shoes. My children still call me that. I was a very sensitive child, and I took things to heart.

I didn't talk back. I never had a spanking, but I was punished every now and then. I can remember one time my mother said, "It's raining out, so don't go out until I get back."

And I said, "OK, I won't."

The rain stopped, and I said to our housekeeper, Vera, who I loved very much, "I think I'm going to go and meet my friend down the street."

She said, "Oh, I wouldn't."

But I go out anyway, and I'm just singing in the street. I see my mother and brother, and I knew I was in trouble.

My brother goes, "Ha, ha, ha, ha."

My mother said, "I told you to wait until I get home."

Mom had popsicles for me, and my mom followed through and I didn't get them.

"Pretty is as pretty does." My mother always said that.

I grew up with very beautiful girls in my class, so I did not feel like a standout. They did not make a lot of it. It was more about the person, not about how you looked. I think the only time I heard my mother talk about it when I was younger was when she'd slick my hair back in a ponytail.

She would say, "I just want to see your face. It's so pretty. I just love your face."

My brother, Tommy, walked on the side of the good guys. He would do anything for me. He taught me to ride a two-wheeler. He could do magic. He was a builder of treehouses, and our Christmas tree fort, which was made of discarded trees after Christmas, was the biggest and best. I can still smell that scent today.

On our summer road trips we'd get up at 5:00 a.m., and I would sleep in the car. Tommy knew I loved Texas peaches. He would let me sleep. He would peel them, slice them, put them in a little bowl and wake me up in the car with them.

Mom, Tommy, and I would always pick bluebonnets on the way to our farm in Luling, and we would fill the house with that glorious Texas state flower.

I am stunned by all the places I still love in Houston. There's no better Mexican food than Sylvia's Enchilada Kitchen. It's better than the best. Mom and I were always sneaking off to Cliff's Hamburgers. Another favorite was Weldon's Cafeteria after church every Sunday. I can never forget the Bluebonnet Gardens. After my dance recitals, we sat on wooden picnic tables shaded by big, beautiful trees and were served sliced watermelon on big silver trays. Watermelon was my favorite food as a child.

Such memories—a treasure I wish I could reclaim.

Christmas was big and is still big, and I carried on my mother's traditions. The decorations on our tree are things we made, things from childhood, ornaments we made together out of

Jaclyn Smith, right, with Farrah Fawcett, two of the three original "Charlie's Angels" and both native Texans. *Photo courtesy Jaclyn Smith*

jewelry. They are still gorgeous. We had presents in the morning and a Christmas lunch with family and friends. I've never spent a Christmas away from my family.

My upbringing in Houston gave me this small-town feeling, but on the other side of the coin, there was this cultural side that filled my life with wonderful teachers who inspired me.

I loved ballet. From the time I was five, I was in love with tutus and ballet slippers. I thought that I would later teach and open a ballet school in Houston. I studied first with Florrie Olenbush and later with Patsy Swayze, Patrick Swayze's mother. With Florrie, it was classical training. Patsy introduced me to musical comedy, which would entail being a more well-rounded dancer. With her, I studied jazz and tap. Dance defined me in my high school years.

And then I met the amazing Ruth Denney, who was my drama teacher in high school. Ruth was ahead of her time. She knew how to talk to kids and knew how to give them confidence. She gave us every reason to be the best we could be. Many of her students went on to successful careers in the entertainment industry, such as Tommy Tune, Robert Foxworth, Paula Prentiss, and Tommy Sands, to name a few.

I will never under-estimate the power of family and of growing up in Houston.

When I went into Ruth Denney's Drama Shack, there was no turning back. We did *Bye Bye Birdie*, *Bells Are Ringing*, *Wish You Were Here*, and *West Side Story*, to name a few. We were lucky to have Tommy Tune choreograph some of those shows.

My dream was to go to New York. With my parents' support, off I went to study dance at nineteen. Even though it was my dream, I had a hard time leaving Houston and leaving my childhood behind. When it came time for them to leave me in New York, you know that feeling when you think you're going to choke and die on the spot? That's how I felt. When they pulled away, I sobbed.

I stayed two months and went home for Christmas. Some things just happen. I didn't really plan it. I just knew that I needed to go back, and I went back to New York City, and that's when my world took a different turn and my career began. Leaving Texas was when I realized that the world was larger and more complex than I ever imagined.

One of the most important things that my parents taught me was that my sense of worth did not depend on my career. Having their support made me unafraid of the newness of New York, of the oddness and vibrancy and contradictions I would encounter.

Going through the front door of my past is emotional for me. I will never underestimate the power of family and of growing up in Houston. It will always be one of life's true blessings. My childhood was really, really the best anybody could have. And, you know, the funny thing is, I knew I was a lucky girl. I knew it.

Even though I lived away from Texas more years then I lived there, I still consider myself a Texan. You don't find nicer people. Just hearing the dialect makes me feel safe and excited about what that life gave me.

Jaclyn Smith has had a successful career as an actress and businesswoman. *Photo courtesy Jaclyn Smith*

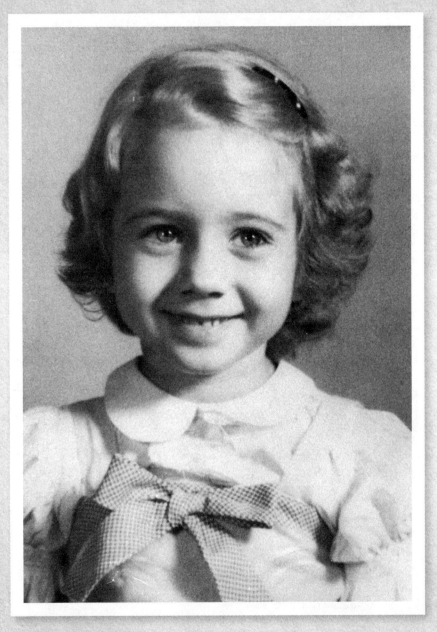

Sandy Duncan as a child. *Photo courtesy Sandy Duncan*

BIRTH NAME	**SANDRA KAY DUNCAN**
BORN	February 20, 1946, in Henderson to Mancil Ray Duncan and Sylvia Wynne Duncan
INTERVIEW	American Place Theatre, New York City, May 2, 1982

SANDY DUNCAN
Climbing Oil Derricks

T he second *Peter Pan from Texas, Sandy Duncan garnered atten-*
tion for her singing, dancing, and endearing stage persona in a
reprisal of the musical on Broadway in 1979. An earlier knock-
out performance in The Boy Friend *on Broadway in 1970 landed*
her a film debut in Disney's The Million Dollar Duck. *The elfish blonde*
with a pixie haircut and toothy smile starred in the CBS Saturday
night sitcom Funny Face *in 1971,* The Sandy Duncan Show *in 1972,*
and The Hogan Family *from 1987 to 1991. While filming her namesake*
TV series, she underwent surgery to remove a benign brain tumor and
lost vision in her left eye. In 1976, Duncan played the title role in Pinoc-
chio, *a made-for-TV musical, and appeared on the first season of* The
Muppet Show. *She was nominated for an Emmy for her role in the 1977*
epic miniseries Roots. *In addition to two other Emmy nods, she rated*
nominations for three Tonys and two Golden Globe Awards in more
than fifty years of entertaining.

The first primary influence in my life was my grandfather, Jeff Scott, because he was a big storyteller. He was like the Pied Piper. Kids would gather around, and Jeff would tell stories and he'd whittle. He had glasses; he looked the type.

I have forks and knives and spoon sets that he made. He'd make wood knickknacks for the kids and canes. He'd pass them out to people who needed canes. All over East Texas now, you see some of my granddad's canes.

He would sit and tell stories about the old days. My favorite story was that he was going to quit working and we were going to move to Arkansas along the Sabine River and get burros and live in a houseboat. That was my best fantasy. We never did it, but that didn't matter.

He was a pumper in the oil field. He'd be on graveyard duty all night, and he'd stay in those little doghouses down at the Humble Oil camp. He was a wonderful man. His yard was always like an oasis because he was a big gardener and he had flowers all over—crepe myrtle and chinaberry trees, gladiolas, you name it. He lived in the country around New London almost his whole life.

The important part of my life in Texas and the thing that was of value was the preschool time down in New London when I was wandering around in the woods by myself. I had an imaginary playmate, Ann Fuffenfooffer. She was my best friend because we didn't have a lot of kids around. And I would just play in the woods, and I'd say, "I want a drink of water," and I'd give one to Ann, or I'd give Ann a cookie, too.

Kids have a sort of animal instinct. They have no fear. An aura protects them. I would go down around the creek bottom. I remember climbing oil derricks instead of trees. They were all over the place in Kilgore and New London. My grandparents had one right there in their backyard. That was like my tree.

I never rode horses, except I sat on Hopalong Cassidy's horse when I was six years old. We went to the rodeo and they asked, "Are there any kids who want to sit on the horse?"

I sat on the tail.

Those were things that colored my whole feeling about Texas as being very special and beautiful. It had a mellowness and ease.

I'm a fifth generation Texan. I was born in Henderson and lived in Overton and New London. In fact, my mother had a brother killed in the

Sandy Duncan as Peter Pan. *Photo courtesy Sandy Duncan*

New London school explosion in 1937. Her younger brother, Sonny Boy, was killed in that. She would have been, too, except she had won a big county meet in typing and she was out of school for the afternoon. The bus drove up right after the explosion. But she has no memory of seeing any dead, and they were everywhere. She just blocked it out. She was about fourteen.

I started dance lessons in New London when I was five. Utah Ground came down from New York, and she started teaching kids from various little towns. We had classes at the American Legion Hall, where they used to play poker. We'd hold on to poker tables as our ballet barre in this dirty old American Legion Hall. We'd have our recital over at the New London school auditorium. We'd do pliés to the rhythm of the pumps.

I always had a single-minded kind of tunnel vision of what I wanted to do; I knew from five years on. In addition to ballet, I took acrobatics and jazz three afternoons a week and Saturdays. I used to go to Dallas for dance lessons every Saturday. I remember one specific afternoon after being at a slumber party the night before. Of course, we had stayed up all night. I had to get up at eight in the morning and drive to Dallas to make singing and ballet classes. My ass was dragging that day.

We'd do pliés to the rhythm of the pumps.

One big crossroads came when I ran for cheerleader at Hogg Junior High. My mother didn't really want me to get it, and my dance teacher said it would be bad for my muscles and it would take all my time. I remember really feeling torn that I didn't win. I came in seventh for six places, and I was devastated. It was the best thing in the world that could have happened, but I didn't know it then.

I also remember driving from Lon Morris College in Jacksonville to Dallas every Saturday to continue my lessons. Some days I would be so sleepy driving up in the morning by myself that I'd drive off into a ditch and wake myself up. But I'd get there, take the class, and drive home.

Early on, around sixteen, I moved away from ballet and got into musical comedies in Dallas. I'm sure if I had tried to pursue a ballet career, it would have been a little hard going. And I was always a little of a cutup—from observing my dad, I'm sure. I was also very studious. Nothing came that easy; I always had to work very hard. Even now I have to really work. That whole Puritan work ethic comes from my family. I come from a working class of people.

My daddy always had a service station. He loved the social life. He had a station in Overton before my parents moved to Tyler. They wanted to move to the big city. He went into the insurance business for about a year and was very successful, but he didn't like it because he was always away traveling. So that didn't last long.

One thing that made me different from the average little girl growing up in Texas was my well-read mother. She always had an awareness of an outside world. My parents had gone to San Diego when my dad was in the service. That's where they got pregnant with me. She had always been aware that there was something outside of East Texas.

I always felt set apart, and it bothered me quite a bit. I somehow knew in the back of my mind that what most people were involved in was temporary. But it was a hard time to get through. Everything was very cliquish.

My whole personality and the things I thought were important ran counter to a lot of what went on in Texas, like the picking and fiddling. I was very much a ballet person. So all that stuff that's typically Texan I fought as a kid. The accent was something I really wanted to conquer.

I found a lot of the values bigoted as I grew up in East Texas. I remember giving a paper in the seventh grade about a Black woman I'd seen with her child down at Woolworth's. I was amazed there were things that were for "coloreds" only.

One of the things that threw me for a loop was when I first came to New York at eighteen. The normal introductions back in Tyler had been, "Hi, my name is Sally. What church do you go to?"

I was thrilled to get into a town where the second sentence wasn't "What church do you go to?"

In Tyler we didn't go to church. My mother took us to the Unitarian church a couple of times. It wasn't even a church. It was in a house, and they read newspaper clippings. I told her frequently, "Mother, this is not a church that everybody else goes to."

As a kid, I can remember saying to Mom, "Can't we ever once be on the popular side?"

I used to be driven to school. Daddy would drive me in his truck, and the truck wouldn't slow down before I'd hit the pavement, so no one would see me getting out of it. When you're an insecure little teenager, everything is embarrassing to you.

I'm more like my dad, personality-wise. At least, that's the personality I adopted because it seemed to be more socially acceptable, easier to get through things. He sort of shined it on, whereas my mother read, was very quiet, and socially was uncomfortable for the most part. She was less and less so as she got older. She became more secure and just said, "To hell with it, this is what I believe."

Actress Sandy Duncan continues to work on stage and screen. *Photo by Marc Raboy, courtesy Sandy Duncan*

I remember when she took up oil painting. People who usually do that paint on velvet or something, and my mother got into very abstract paintings and collage. She got so tired of relatives and neighbors who would say, "Well, Sylvia, what is it?"

Finally, she said, "Well, goddamn it, it's an oil painting."

She got tired of explaining herself. John Connally bought one of her paintings.

I never felt pushed. I always felt exposed to a lot of things because of my mother. For that period of time and that area of the world, I never grew up feeling that I was any less good than a man. I was brought up to feel I was just as capable of achieving what I wanted to as anyone else. I never had the pressure of getting married, having children.

I was very quiet and independent at home. I was required to be well-behaved and to take orders. I wasn't asked to do a lot because I was always doing what I should be doing. I was never a problem or a rebellious kid, so they didn't impose a lot of arbitrary rules on me.

Because I grew up in East Texas, some foods always will be special to me. Like watermelon. I have one in my icebox right now. At the theater, I eat watermelon between acts.

When I was pregnant for the first time, I learned to make my grandmother's banana pudding. I dragged the recipe out, thinking I was going to make this banana pudding because it's something I remember as a kid. I used to go to Darlin's and she'd say, "There's something in the icebox for you."

And it would be banana pudding. She just sort of made it, and we were always asking, "Darlin', how do you make it?"

So she sat down and wrote this recipe for me called "Last Will and Testament of Banana Pudding." In her little, scribbly handwriting, she wrote things like, "You put in the butter and you beat the shit out of it."

It's a real colorful recipe.

Taste Buds Never Really Change

I have strong food associations from my childhood. I love fried green tomato rings and fried okra. Even as an adult, I still want Mama to make me macaroni and tomatoes. Other foods that remind me of childhood are all the greens and chicken-fried steak.

There were a lot of Texans in *Peter Pan* because we started the show there. When we had our parties after shows, we had Tex-Mex or barbecue or fried steak.

We would bring things back from Texas like Ro-Tel tomatoes and chili. When I was doing a show called *Canterbury Tales*, I used to bring Dr Pepper concentrate from home. You couldn't buy Dr Pepper in New York then, and I would mix it up in my dressing room.

Michael Levy as a young child. *Photo courtesy Michael Levy*

BIRTH NAME	**MICHAEL RICHARD LEVY**
BORN	May 17, 1946, in Dallas to Harry Aaron Levy and Florence Ruth Friedman Levy
INTERVIEW	His office, Austin, Texas, January 8, 2017

MICHAEL LEVY
Making a Difference

Michael Levy launched Texas Monthly *in 1973, when slick mag-azines were finding success defining locals and locales around the country. He helmed the popular state magazine for thirty-five years, eventually boasting a readership of 2.5 million and multiple national magazine awards.* Esquire *magazine included Levy in the 1984 Esquire Register of Outstanding Americans Under Age 40. He also was honored with the 1999 Henry Johnson Fisher Award, the industry's highest honor from the Magazine Publishers of America; the 2003 Missouri Honor Medal for Distinguished Service in Journal-ism from the University of Missouri School of Journalism; and the 2004 Lifetime Achievement Award from the City and Regional Magazine Association. He graduated from the Wharton School at the University of Pennsylvania and the University of Texas School of Law. He belongs to the World Presidents' Organization, a global organization of leaders of major business enterprises.*

My father was born in Poland. His father was a blacksmith who fought in the Polish army. I think they first moved to Detroit, then Colorado, back to Detroit, and then to Dallas because my grandfather had, I believe, brothers here. Dad immigrated through Ellis Island.

My dad's parents were definitely from the old country in terms of accent. They did know English and they spoke English. We had Passover services in their home. I remember going to High Holy Day services at Congregation Agudas Achim in South Dallas. It was very Orthodox. That's how Dad was raised. I was raised Reform.

Mother's parents emigrated from Hungary in and around either side of 1910. Today I am very cognizant of the fact that if they had not emigrated, they would have been in the ovens. There's no other way of saying that. Our family has been blessed from the early 1900s on.

Mother was born in Dallas. My mother's parents died before I was born. Mother was raised Reform. She was a member of Temple Emanu-El. When she grew up, she was confirmed there. And I was confirmed and became a bar mitzvah there, too.

I was born in Dallas. I grew up in Dallas. I remember Mom and Dad working very hard. That was a major influence on me, that if you wanted anything in life of significance, you've got to work hard.

I remember my father digging ditches. He had a plumbing repair company. He had four trucks, three or four other plumbers working with him. They wanted the best for my sister and me. They made it possible somehow for me to have the opportunity to go to St. Mark's School, one of the best preparatory schools in the country, and then on to college and law school.

In terms of life forces, obviously, my mom and dad were major life forces. My mom and dad, purely plain and simple, worked hard. They saved. They loved their family. Everything I've done is meant to honor their legacy. Period. But there was always fear of failure, of betraying my parents' confidence. It was not *Ozzie and Harriet* by any means.

There was never a doubt in my mind, never a thought, that my parents didn't love me and love my sister. They worked hard so we would have every opportunity possible.

Another of my life forces was a guy named Gordon McLendon, who invented Top 40 radio in Dallas with KLIF, along with KTSA in San Antonio and KILT in Houston. They were fifty-thousand-watt, clear-channel,

AM stations that did not exist back then for all intents and purposes. I never met McLendon. He basically invented Top 40 radio and in the process made me aware of rock 'n' roll music and media.

My third life force was at St. Mark's. I had an English teacher for four years named Ludlow North. Lud North was much like the Robin Williams character in *Dead Poets Society*. He had an enormous influence on me in the sense that he made me aware of reading and the written word and print.

The St. Mark's experience was very important to me. I remember few I went to school with at Wharton at the University of Pennsylvania or the University of Texas law school. Of sixty boys in my St. Mark's class, fifteen of us still gather in Dallas once a month for lunch and to talk. We are still close. It was another era.

My mother was a historical revisionist. She was always telling my daughters that I was a scholar athlete, neither of which was true. I was a goof-off and had a good time but with good teachers who were able to have an impression on me.

When I was in elementary school starting out at Preston Hollow Elementary, we were the first class, I guess in the fifth grade, to open up the new school, John J. Pershing on Meadow at the Cotton Belt Railroad tracks. And I remember Miss Bolger, third- or fourth-grade teacher, getting so angry because when a train went by my mind went immediately to counting the railcars. She was not happy about that.

My mother was very funny. And I am a clown. Make 'em laugh. Make 'em laugh. Make 'em laugh. I take what I do seriously. But I've never taken myself seriously.

I was confirmed and became a bar mitzvah at Temple Emanu-El in Dallas. It's the largest Reform congregation in the Southwest. It has always had a tradition of rabbis who were great preachers, which meant their sermons had a beginning, a middle, and an end and a meaning.

When I was being confirmed, we had to sit through compulsory Sabbath services, and the rabbi at the time was Rabbi Levi Olan, a legendary preacher, legendary rabbi. The tapes of his sermons are stored in archives and are still referred back to.

His core message that seeped through my teenage skull way back in the sixties was, "If you have an ability to make a difference and you choose not to, it's wrong. You can even call it a sin."

And that influenced me greatly down the road.

We didn't have much money, but we had a good time. Because we didn't have a lot of money, my mom and dad and sister would get into the car and drive down the old Highway 75 to Houston. We'd check into the Shamrock Hotel built by Glenn McCarthy. Dad would take us swimming in that huge swimming pool.

They would take us across the street to the Red Lion, which served great roast beef and Yorkshire pudding. When I go to London today, I insist that I have at least one dinner with Yorkshire pudding and roast beef, medium, with real horseradish.

Then we would go down to Galveston and we would check into the Galvez Hotel. During the day, we would take the ferry across to the jetties and we'd go crabbing. Dad would get some old bones from a butcher shop, tie them on cords, throw the cords across the jetties. Crabs would grab hold of them, and we'd bring them in. Dad, I think, gave them to cooks at restaurants. I don't remember if we had any.

We drove to Miami. We couldn't understand why everybody was passing us. We got back to Dallas and Dad figured out the speedometer was broken.

We drove to Los Angeles one summer. We stopped at a filling station, everybody got out of the car, went to the restroom, and so forth. Then we drove off. About thirty miles down the highway, my mother looked in the back, and my sister wasn't there. I hadn't said anything about that. It's one of those things.

Mother used to take us out of school every fall and take us to the State Fair of Texas because her parents did that.

Before everybody was distracted by television, the family—which included my mom's sister and her husband and my first cousin, my mother's brother, and his kids—used to go out to Flag Pole Hill at White Rock Lake, where there were picnic tables. Because Dallas wasn't huge and overgrown, there was never a huge demand for those picnic tables. We would have picnics during the summers with watermelon and fried chicken.

I remember in Dallas growing up eating at restaurants that no longer exist. Other people who grew up in that era remember Labella's for hamburgers on Northwest Highway in between Douglas and Preston Road. We remember Youngblood's fried chicken. We remember Salih's for barbecue. Looking back, I don't know if it was really just meat with some

Michael Levy. *Photo courtesy Michael Levy*

sauces on it. They put it on a roll and we had roast barbecue sandwiches. I remember Wyatt's Cafeteria also in Preston Center. I remember El Chico on Lovers Lane in between the old Cotton Belt Railroad tracks and Inwood Road near where the old Esquire Theater is.

I remember the motion picture theaters in Dallas. Many were owned by a man named Karl Hoblitzelle. As I recall, they were old vaudeville houses. The Palace and the Tower and the Majestic downtown. Either the Majestic or the Palace had an organ that in between different movies would rise up, and there would be an organ player who played lively music.

My dad used to take me downtown to see the Disney movies on the desert or the ocean, very realistic. They would have photographers out watching a long time—the flowers bloom, insects, snakes, wildcats, and so forth.

I used to come home every day and I would read the old *Dallas Times Herald*, which was the afternoon paper.

I remember as a kid bicycling up Preston Road to Preston Center, I think, on Thursdays, when the bookmobile was there from the Dallas Public Library. I would find biographies or the latest Hardy Boys book. That was in elementary school. That was a period when it was reasonably safe. Mom let me bike to the bookmobile.

I used to take the Preston Hollow East bus to the big library downtown to do research for book reports for elementary school and come back again. I also remember sneaking to the bookstore magazine stand on Elm Street and buying a copy of *Mad* magazine to sneak home.

Because under sixteen you couldn't get a job, I used to take the bus down early in the morning and get on these vans with other ne'er-do-wells, I guess, and they took us to various neighborhoods.

One summer I sold magazines door-to-door. Another summer I sold photography deals where we went from neighborhood to neighborhood selling photographs. A photographer would come and take a photograph of your family at night. I sold those.

Basically, I always worked. If I wanted spare change in my pocket, I knew I had to work. It was not said, "Go get a job." I was a kid and I hustled some extra money. I worked in my father's plumbing business one summer when I was in high school, making deliveries to his crews who needed parts and so forth.

Mother was always mad at me because for extra money I sold—what today would be worth a fortune—my Lionel train set for some extra change. What I spent it on, I don't remember.

I excelled enough. St. Mark's School in Texas is very hard to get in today. It's very competitive, and I could not have gotten in today. It is very hard to get into the University of Pennsylvania today. I was able to get in. At the University of Texas School of Law in 1969, basically all you had to do to get in was to be able to breathe on your own without having to be reminded. Obviously, things have changed. I went to law school not intending to practice law but to start a magazine.

———

Michael Levy's *Texas Monthly* magazine has been covering the state for decades. *Photo courtesy Michael Levy*

Just a Really Big City

What I saw about Texas is that it's this huge expanse of geography. But what it really was was a city, and its neighborhoods were Dallas and Houston and Marfa and Wichita Falls and Tyler and Longview. It really is like a small town. And everybody knew everybody else. We shared a common culture, lifestyle, and history.

The state was increasingly sophisticated, both because of the natives and the transplants, but the media hadn't caught up with it.

And I thought, "You know, if we put out a magazine of national quality with staff writers instead of freelancers, great photojournalism, we have a shot at success."

My dad helped me because he and mom believed in me.

Jerry LeVias's second-grade school picture. *Photo courtesy Jerry LeVias*

BIRTH NAME	**JERRY LeVIAS**
BORN	September 5, 1946, in Beaumont to Charles LeVias and Leura Wright LeVias
INTERVIEW	His home, Houston, Texas, January 21, 2017

JERRY LeVIAS
Only Big Enough to Run

Jerry LeVias broke the color barrier in the powerhouse Southwest Conference in 1965 as the first African American to receive an athletic scholarship. He led the Southern Methodist University Mustangs to their first football title in eighteen years and achieved both academic and athletic All-American honors, as well as the 1969 most valuable player title in the conference. He played wide receiver for the Houston Oilers and San Diego Chargers and has been an ambassador for the Houston Texans since 2008. The Football Writers Association of America voted him an All-American Alumni in 2004. The National Football Foundation and College Hall of Fame inducted him in 2003, the Texas Black Sports Hall of Fame in 1997, and the Texas Sports Hall of Fame in 1996. He also is a member of the halls of fame for Texas High Schools, Prairie View Interscholastic League, and Southern Methodist University.

Years ago my grandmother and my grandfather on my father's side started saying during slavery time our ancestors came over when Jean Lafitte came to Louisiana. My ancestors were sold to the French in Louisiana. As people bought slaves, they came to East Texas. Most of my family that I can trace back came to East Texas, in Biloxi, Jasper, Kirbyville, and Magnolia Springs. Logging country. Big Thicket. Real East Texas, right across the border with Louisiana.

LeVias is French. When they were sold to French slave owners, you took the name of the owner. It was spelled with a capital V, and it was pronounced Le-vee-yah.

The LeViases were more in Deweyville, Biloxi, in that part of the country. Dad just wanted to leave the farm they had in Biloxi, and he went out on his own. He worked in the sawmills.

On my mother's side, my grandparents, Fred Wright and Adelle Wright, lived in East Texas in a place called Magnolia Springs, right outside of Kirbyville. He had a couple of brothers, and they owned fifty or sixty acres apiece. My grandfather was light. He was part of a concubine family—the white guy had his family and then his Black family—and they were all light complected.

As a young boy I lived with my grandmother in Magnolia Springs while my two older sisters were in school with our parents in Beaumont. My grandfather would leave at the beginning of the week to go work at the lumber company in Kirbyville, Kirby Lumber. I was there with my grandmother. She had ten children, and by that time they all left.

We lived off the land, didn't think we were poor. We had to go to Kirbyville in a wagon, about twenty-five miles away. We had mules. No electricity. No lights. None of the modern conveniences. We were happy every month or so when a new Sears and Roebuck catalog came along. Made a little tissue paper.

My grandmother would get up every morning and get the wooden stove warmed up. She cooked the biscuits and cakes and bread. She milked the cows, and then we had buttermilk. So my job, when I was four or five years old, was to sit on the front porch and churn the butter.

There was one big heater. Some of those homes were not built well, with all the cracks. In each room, we had quilts that kept us warm. She and her friends saved all the scraps and got together on the front porch and made quilts. I still have her homemade quilts.

———

We had a well where you drew your water. If you were really fancy, you had a pump. When the well went dry, you'd have to go down to the creek, back up the mules to the creek with barrels.

We salted down the meat and hung it in the smokehouse. And you'd go out in the smokehouse and cut a piece of bacon or chops. You'd make sausage with a churn, and then you'd put it in casings. We had hog head cheese. They would eat cracklings. They made pickled pigs' feet in a jar. Nothing went to waste.

One of my duties on the farm was to pick the feathers when they'd kill the chickens. My grandmother would kill it and put hot water on it. She asked me to pick it, and then she'd singe it. I haven't eaten it since.

So we had fun with everybody in what you might call a colony of people. We'd go jump in the water at the creek and chase the dogs and the cats and the rabbits. After we got through with church in Kirbyville, all the kids would play baseball games, play some basketball, but no football. That was in the country, and nobody ever heard of football.

I would go with my grandmother to town. I would sit outside and hold the mules while she went shopping. This is Magnolia Springs. In Kirbyville, if you were Black, you better be out of town by five o'clock. Very few men would go to town, because women and children were treated better.

We had peaches, plums, pears. I didn't know what going to the store and buying jelly was. We had sugarcane and sugarcane syrup.

Grandma swept the yard with a switch broom. All there was was red sand. She'd sweep and burn the leaves. One day I almost set the woods on fire. That was the only time my grandmother whipped me.

We were sanctified. Church of God in Christ. Women wore dresses down to the middle of their calves. The girls in PE had to get special permission to wear long shorts. Couldn't listen to the radio, as that was devil's music. We didn't have but one Black station anyway, KJET. You were sanctified; you didn't do anything.

My grandmother LeVias's brothers, the nephews, were preachers. Our whole church must have been close to thirty people, and at least twenty of us were cousins. When Grandma said, "We leaving at nine o'clock," at five till nine you get in there. And she had on that big hat. You had your Sunday best going to church.

"You children are to be seen and not heard," Grandma said.

337

My grandmother played one of those little triangles. *Ting ting ting.* If we were talking in church, she'd get the Holy Ghost, swinging around, and just come by the children who were talking, go *ting ting ting.* The ladies would start jumping. And my grandmother would be skating all around. I wondered what struck them.

I'm glad I had that kind of bringing up, with church and the discipline that we had. Nobody was as good as the sanctified people.

Grandma, Ella LeVias, was the matriarch of the family. My grandmother on my mother's side was kinda quiet, but you didn't mess with the Wright women or the LeVias women.

She had seven girls and then three boys. My dad was the smallest one, the runt of the litter. Even the girls were bigger than he was, but he was the hardest working of them all.

If you were sick, Grandma Ella'd pray for you and get the home remedies. Everybody had Syrup of Black Draught, castor oil, and all that other kind of stuff they would make up. You wouldn't pull a tooth or do anything without talking to Grandma, because she did the almanac. If I had some kind of fever, she would wrap me up with greens and put that asafetida stuff on it.

In the fourth grade, I was kinda sickly—part of it was mental, and part of it was for real. It was difficult to walk. My legs weren't developing. Finally Dad took me to the hospital. And, of course, you had your Black part. One hospital in Beaumont was called Hotel Dieu. If you were Black and went to Hotel Dieu, you weren't coming out alive.

So they took me to the other hospital, and Grandma had wrapped me up in a mess of mustard greens. By the time the doctor got through examining me, they called it polio. I had a brace. When I was playing football, people teased me about my small little legs.

Daddy worked in that little place called Honey Island. They didn't want to pay him for a job he had done. He went home, packed up my mother, and went to Beaumont.

In Beaumont he started working in the shipyard. Then he went to work for Burrus Lumber Company, and he also worked with the soda company.

My mother was a housewife and laborer cleaning houses. A lady she worked for liked the work she had done and told her, "If your husband needs a job, my husband is the manager at Ideco."

He got a job there, kind of a maintenance guy cleaning up. At Ideco he was painting little bitty parts needed in the oil field, screws and bolts and nuts. My dad said, "There's got to be a better way to do this."

So he got two ten-gallon buckets and put a bunch of holes in the bottom of it and put one on top of the other one, and he put all the little screws and bolts in there and poured the paint out and let them drip dry. The foreman came by and said, "Charlie, you do a pretty good job. I'm gonna make you the foreman of the paint shop."

My dad didn't have much of an education, when you talk about the reading and the writing, but he had what you call mother wit. He knew how to do things. He came up with a lot of ideas to make things a lot better.

They cut out a section of Beaumont where the Blacks could live. We called it the Pear Orchard because it had a lot of pear trees. You better be back across the tracks before five o'clock on Washington Boulevard.

My dad saved up enough money to buy a lot for us and for my grandparents next door. He packed them up in Biloxi, because they sold the farm, and they tore down certain sections of their house that they could bring with them to build the house for my grandmother. I played under the house plenty of times because it was built on blocks.

There was a truck that used to come through the neighborhood and emptied the little container out of your outdoor toilets. They had all that white lime on the side of the truck. And we'd say, "Here comes the doo-doo man."

My dad did all there was to do to have commodes and running water in the house and neighborhood. A few blocks away, the city put the sewer pipes down. So my dad saved up his money and took off his hat and went and talked to the people at the city and said he had his mother there and she was elderly. He was very polite and humble.

And the man said, "Boy, you know how to talk to people."

My daddy gave him the money, and he said, "You'll have a spigot in your yard next week."

He knew how to go talk to white people and get things done, but when

Southern Methodist University supporters expected a blast of talent from
Jerry LeVias during the 1966 football season. Coach Hayden Fry is on the right.
Southern Methodist University Archives, DeGolyer Library, SMU

he got out of that, he stood straight up. He told me he never did want me
to have to do that. My dad broke a lot of barriers, too.

My mother was too nervous to drive, so she'd have to catch the bus.
But my dad would not catch the bus because you had to sit in the back.
They were downtown one time, and he was told to get in the back of the
bus, and he took my sister and got off.

When it was the county fair, they had Negro Day. We couldn't go to
the fair except that one day, and then they'd jack up the prices. White
people wouldn't go on that day to the fair.

Juneteenth was a big day. Everybody got together in that part of the
country and was just glad you were free. We had trailers full of food and
just had a great time. You'd be drinking that red soda pop.

People brought food, and my dad would say, "Stay away from the
potato salad," because it had the mayo in it, and it would be hot. After a
while, you see some people running back in the woods.

When you went shopping, Dad and Mom would say, "You drink your water here at home and use the restroom here," because there was colored fountains. My dad would not let us drink water from them. If you had to use the restroom, you better hold it until you got home. I don't think they had colored restrooms.

You couldn't try on clothes because if you put your foot in them, you bought them. That was just for Black people. You couldn't use the dressing room. They had a string that measured your length and your waist. They tell the story my uncle tried on some shoes one time, and they were a little bit too small for him. He had to cut them underneath to fit his feet.

Dad came home one evening from work, and all the people on our street on Glenwood came home early. All the Black men started putting furniture up against the doors. And everybody got their guns out. Somebody had talked to a white girl or spoke bad to a white man, and they were just going to come through the neighborhood and tear it up.

We slept on the floors. The men were outside. Everybody had their guns ready for race riots. But nothing happened. That's what you grew up with.

I had moved back with my parents in Beaumont when it was time for me to start school. It was like a country boy going to the city. I went to Blanchette Elementary School. Even though it was in the Black neighborhood, they had some stores, and some people had cars.

I found a way to get out of stuff. I was small, tiny, I guess. My nickname was Jelly Bean. I pretended to be sick a lot of times.

And mom said that was fine, "You can stay home with me."

Then she started giving me this castor oil, and I went to school.

The third grade especially was a little tough because they wanted you to stop printing and start cursive writing. I was still printing. I connected letters with a little line. I was left-handed, and they wanted you to write right-handed.

And they'd say, "You are a child of the devil, you left-handed, boy!"

I hated lunch because I knew we were going to have spelling after lunch. I could spell, but the teacher was going to make me get up in front of the class and write with my right hand.

And everybody called me stupid, afflicted. You kind of withdrew in yourself.

I played some flag football in sixth grade, and then they finally started an eighth- and ninth-grade football team. I was still too small, so I became a water boy. It was so hot. We couldn't drink water—two hours of practice and no water. We'd take salt tablets.

We had a football coach named Clifton Ozen. He was a big man. When it was cold, he'd have on short-sleeve shirts and short pants. He chewed tobacco. He had a two-by-four whittled down, and he carried it around all the time.

Our saying is, "Whatever Hebert [High School] does, it must be the best."

You had to be the best at whatever it was. If it was debating. If it was in the band. If it was in football, basketball, grade-wise. With our competition in Beaumont, then with Houston, Port Arthur, Orange, we won whatever it was.

When you made varsity, you got a chance to ride on that school bus on Thursdays. When it left the Pear Orchard, we had to go through town, through all the streets. You're talking twelve thousand to fifteen thousand people attended a high school game. Kids would start hitchhiking to the game after school to get to the stadium to get a seat.

That bus would pull up and everybody'd get on, and you could hear it through the neighborhoods, "Lift your head, and hold it high, Hebert Panthers passing by."

As a water boy, I couldn't get on the bus.

And I said, "I'm gonna ride this bus someday."

To be on the football team, you had to weigh, I think, 121 pounds. So the coach saw me over there playing with the other boys between practices, and he said, "Why don't you go out for the team?"

I had been sick all the time, and Daddy said, "I don't see nothing about that old football but a bunch of people smelling each other when you bend down. You going to fool around out there and get hurt."

So I didn't ask him. Before I went to weigh, my sister cooked, and I ate and ate, even though my sister's cooking wasn't that good. Drank a lot of water.

I got on the scale. One hundred fifteen pounds. I was heartbroken. I went outside, and I saw a brown paper bag and some rocks. So I put a bunch of rocks in the bag, and I put it in my pants.

I said, "That scale was not right. You had too many people weighing on it. I need to weigh again."

I got on the scale. One hundred seventeen pounds.

I said, "That is not right."

And I stomped my foot. Bag broke. Rocks everywhere. The coach looked at me, and I thought for sure I was gonna get it because I had lied.

There was this guy named Mr. Minix. He was a math teacher, a genius, and he was the junior high coach.

He said, "Coach, anybody who wants to play that bad, why, we're going to give him a chance."

Football was king in Beaumont. We had only two Black schools, and we played on Thursday nights because the whites had the stadium on Friday nights and Saturdays. We were in the South Park Independent School District, and the other Black school, Charlton-Pollard, was in the Beaumont ISD. We couldn't use the locker rooms in the stadium. You had to ride the bus dressed.

We were state champs. We had all those great guys, but you had to go to Black schools like Prairie View or Texas Southern, Southern, Grambling. Guys got scholarships. But when our first guy, Alvin LeBlanc, got one to Wichita State, to a white school, ah, man, that was big time. I used to polish his shoes to make a little money. He stiffed, me, too, for ten cents.

I wasn't big enough to play line. I wasn't big enough to do anything except run. So finally, Coach Minix, the junior high coach, told Coach Ozen, "There's nothing I can teach him over here."

And he put me on the B team with the tenth-grade B-team guys. I played quarterback. And all you did, just like sandlot, was take the ball and run. Then after I played four or five B-team games, they put me on the varsity. I was playing a B-team game, and then I'd play a varsity game on Thursday night. And the first time I touched a ball on varsity, I went sixty-five yards.

I was a big thing at school then. Man, I was ninth grade on varsity. I was big man on the campus, even though I had to tiptoe to try to talk to the girls. Everybody used to call me Shorty and Jelly, and they teased me all the time. But they didn't tease me about football.

When I got to be a sophomore, I played defensive back and a little running back, but the guys ahead of me were bigger than I was. They'd substitute me every once in a while.

As I got to be a junior, it was my time. I played quarterback, running back, and they couldn't believe some of my statistics on punt returns, everything else. We didn't do that much passing. It was all running.

There was the UIL, where the white kids played, and then there was the PVIL, Prairie View Interscholastic League, where the Black kids played. We had our own championship.

I was running track. When I was a sophomore, we were the state champs of the PVIL in Texas, and I got most valuable player for performance because I broad jumped, ran relays—100 yards, 220. I had more points than anybody in the whole meet, and I was a sophomore. I got to be the most valuable player in the state.

When I got to running track my sophomore year, I just broke through. Pshuuu! We ran about ten track meets that year. We won every meet we entered. We went to Houston, Jefferson Stadium, for a track meet. You couldn't stay in hotels. You had everybody staying in gymnasiums on cots. You couldn't take your team to some cafeteria and eat, so they'd stop at a market and buy us baloney, orange juice, and bread.

Most of the girls wanted football players for boyfriends, but I met this one girl who didn't care about football. She just wanted you to be smart. So I got smart. I was taking me some studies, too, along with football, baseball, basketball, and track. I got to be vice president, then president, of the student body, and I graduated third in my class. I got that smart girl. And after I did, she wasn't all that hot.

People had heard about me, and my cousin Mel Farr had gone to UCLA. So UCLA gave me a job in the summer when I was a junior, because that was the way they were recruiting. I got to be a senior, and I was more in demand because I played every position, quarterback, halfback, running back, defense, punt returns.

I'm taking off. My first ride on an airplane nobody wanted to sit by me, so they put me in first class. I had one hundred and some odd scholarship offers from everywhere. Utah. Washington State. Washington. University of Southern California, Wyoming, Syracuse. But not in Texas. I didn't even have a scholarship offer from the Black schools, because I was too small. The Black schools had their choice.

That was about the time that people wanted to start talking about equal rights. You didn't want Black guys who were "troublemakers," talking about equality, Black Panthers. I wasn't into getting beat up anyway, getting chased by dogs.

Every Sunday morning, people were knocking on the door, recruiters, and they'd say, "Is Jerry here?"

And my mother'd say, "Yes, he's here. He's about to go to church, and that's where you should be."

So I'm about to make up my mind and go out to UCLA with my cousin Mel.

Little did I know that Hayden Fry, a young coach at Arkansas, got his chance to have a head coaching job in the Southwest Conference. So he went in and he talked to them at SMU and says, "I will take the job on one condition: that you let me recruit a Black athlete."

And he left. They thought about it.

Willis Tate said, "OK, but he's got to be an outstanding young man. He's got to be a young man of character. He can't be in any trouble, so he can't set the program back. He's got to be smart."

The white guys had to have a 750 SAT score. I had to have 1100.

So then about April, Sparky Adams, the district superintendent, says, "We got some people who want to come to your house to see you."

Three carloads of white people pulled up in my neighborhood about five o'clock. Chuck Curtis, about six-three, six-four, had a big old Texas Ranger–looking hat. Hayden Fry was there. My coach. My principal.

And people stood in the neighborhood, "Oh, shit. Jerry's getting arrested."

So Hayden went over to my grandmother's house first, and the other coaches came into the house. Daddy's sitting there and Mama's in the kitchen. Coach Fry comes in and passes my dad, "How you doing?" and goes into the kitchen where my mom is cooking.

Coach Fry asked my mother, "What are you cooking?"

She said, "A little steak and pinto beans."

He said, "They give me gas. How do you do it?"

And she was in there telling him how to put soda in the beans and cook them.

Then he said to me, "We'd like to talk to you about coming to visit our school. We've got a lot of kids who graduate and do real good."

Every last one of the other recruiters had said, "This is where you gotta go."

But Coach Fry said, "You can come to school, and if you're lucky enough you can play. Life expectancy in football isn't long. What are you going to do with the rest of your life?"

He didn't talk about football, didn't talk about making me be the first Black athlete to be offered a scholarship. He talked about education.

And I said, "Where is it?"

He said, "It's in Dallas."

My daddy said, "That's where they shot the president, right?"

My grandmother said to him, "If my grandson goes to school there, I just want to make sure that you make me a promise. Before every game, you have him call me so I can pray for him."

Coach Fry did his homework and went to talk to my grandmother first. And I listened to my grandmother. I was smart enough to sign the letter of intent.

All crap broke loose. LeVias. First scholarship. "Negro Offered First Scholarship to Southwest Conference." All the publicity was unbelievable. You know, the Southwest Conference was better than the Big East. They had all the money, all the rich people and the oil, and it was right here in Texas.

So I got to SMU. I got to freshman football practice, and they couldn't show me any special favors. They put all the highly recruited defensive guys and offensive guys all on one team. They put the rest of us on the third team. When they scrimmaged, they put the first-team defense against the third-team offense.

By the time I got through with them, doing all that running, people said, "Uhhhhh, look at that Mexican run."

A couple times they caught up with me, I got spit on, kicked in the back; they wedged a vertebra in my back, cracked my ribs, because I was Black.

People on Mockingbird were stopping on the street to see us scrimmage, you know, to see the colored boy. Some of my teammates didn't like that. They hit me after the whistle had blown, and all this kind of stuff, but I was still running.

When we were going to play Arkansas, the first freshman game, Coach Fry and his staff came to Texarkana to make sure nothing happened to me. We were behind 7-3, and I'm sitting on the bench because I had broken ribs. I went up to Coach Morgan and said, "If you want to win this football game . . ."

At his grand-
mother's request,
Jerry LeVias wore
No. 23 for the
SMU Mustangs.
*Southern Method-
ist University
Archives, courtesy
Jerry LeVias*

He said, "You're hurt. You can't play."

But he looked back in the stands, and Coach Fry indicated it was OK.

He put me in in the last three minutes. I called the plays. I was the wide receiver and I told them what I wanted to do. The first pass I caught was a down and out, out of bounds, didn't get hit. We got ten yards.

I told them, "This time I'm going to go down and fake up."

Caught the winning touchdown pass and never did get hit.

I took such a beating the rest of the time, they would keep the medical center open. Out of five games, I only played probably two, because they beat me up so bad during practice. Sometimes I'd stay late after practice running because none of the other guys wanted to shower with me.

I got flatfeet, and they'd laugh at me and say, "All y'all got flatfeet?"

The head trainer, Eddie Lane, he would tape my feet; some of the student trainers never wanted to touch me.

I was ready to go. Didn't have a roommate. Didn't have a friend on the team. Only Tony Patron from New Jersey would talk to me. They all were white, and none of them basically had ever played with or against Black players. I told my sister I was about to leave.

And my sister said, "You know what Daddy said, 'You make your bed. You sleep in it.' You gave those people your word that you'd play there."

Every morning before I would leave out of my dorm room, I said the Serenity Prayer. "God, grant me the serenity to accept the things I cannot change, the courage to change those I can, and the wisdom to know the difference."

When I moved in, I saw these Black people in white coats and black pants going back and forth. They were maids and butlers moving these kids into the dormitory. I never made a bed in four years. We had maid service. I found out SMU stands for Southern Money University.

I played against Texas Tech in Lubbock. And I had a good game and newspaper reporters were asking the coach, "Coach King, LeVias had a pretty good game against you today. When you play them again, what kind of defense you gonna use, what you gonna do?"

He said, "I'm going to put a sign on the locker room door that says, 'For Whites Only.'"

> My grandmother wanted me to wear number 23 when I played football. "Be like David. The Lord is my shepherd."

My grandmother wanted me to wear number 23 when I played football. "Be like David. The Lord is my shepherd."

If you read the twenty-third psalm, it tells my story.

"Lead me in the path of righteousness for his name's sake. Yea, though I walk through the valley of the shadow of death, I will fear no evil."

Because of that, I was a brave man. Once I decided to stay, I was unshakable.

I met Dr. [Martin Luther] King. He was going to speak at the university.

Dr. King said, "A lot of things are going to happen to you, but whatever you do, keep your emotions in control."

I overdid it. I had no emotions. They spit on me. I had to develop a way of dealing with it. Coach Fry was instrumental in it.

He used to tell me, "Levi, the more touchdowns you make, the whiter you get."

When he liked me he called me Levi, and when I was in trouble, he called me Jerry.

He was a wise West Texas boy, and he said, "If you don't want them to get your goat, you don't tell 'em where it's hid."

Coach Fry never did break his promise to my grandmother. Long distance was expensive. When everybody on the team was down eating, he'd leave his door open to his room, and I'd go upstairs and talk to Grandma and charge it to his room.

One time I tried to call Grandma and the line was busy. We were going to play the University of Texas, and I was a sophomore.

He said, "You talked to Grandma?"

"No, sir. The line was busy."

The team was going out to play, time for the kickoff. And there Coach Fry and I were under the stands, talking in a telephone booth, calling Grandma. I think he got the money from a band student because he didn't have any change on him. The game started. We were under the stadium. He honored that vow he made.

Nolan Ryan, the youngest of six kids, grew up in Alvin. *Photo courtesy Nolan Ryan*

BIRTH NAME	**LYNN NOLAN RYAN JR.**
BORN	January 31, 1947, in Refugio to Lynn Nolan Ryan Sr. and Martha Lee Hancock Ryan
INTERVIEW	His office, Round Rock, Texas, January 9, 2018

NOLAN RYAN

Blessed with a Great Arm

Major League Baseball pitcher Nolan Ryan holds the record for strikeouts, with 5,714 in his four-decade career. Drafted by the New York Mets upon his high school graduation, the eight-time MLB All-Star also pitched for the Houston Astros, Texas Rangers, and California Angels during a twenty-seven-season career with seven no-hitters. He retired in 1993 at age forty-six. Ryan was inducted into the Texas Sports Hall of Fame in 1985 and the National Baseball Hall of Fame in 1999. Beloved by fans and sportswriters, he made the MLB All-Century Team in 1999, entered the Texas Rangers Hall of Fame in 2003, and was voted both the Rangers' and Astros' DHL Hometown Hero in 2006. He is the only player to have his uniform number retired by three teams. He served as president and CEO of the Texas Rangers, executive adviser of the Houston Astros, and major owner of the Round Rock Express, a minor league franchise he helped bring to Central Texas. An avid outdoorsman, he served on the Texas Parks and Wildlife Commission.

M y mother's family came out of Louisiana, and my father's family came out of Mississippi. And my mother's father died of pneumonia when his three girls were very young. Don't hold me to this, but the sisters were three, seven, and ten, and my mother was in the middle of them. And they moved to Kenedy, Texas, because of relatives living there, to try to help support those girls.

And my father's family came to that area as farmers. They were cotton farmers in those days, sometime in the 1800s. That probably makes me a third-generation Texan at least.

So both my parents ended up attending school in Kenedy.

The only reason I was born in Refugio was because we lived in Woodsboro, which is south of Refugio, and the only hospital in the county was in Refugio. And then my parents moved to Alvin. My dad worked for the old Standard Oil Company and was transferred up there to what they called the Hastings Field, an oil field north of Alvin. They were building a plant up there that made diesel and gasoline. He was a supervisor.

There was six of us kids, and my mom had a full-time job at home. I was the youngest. My oldest sister was eleven. So it went eleven, ten, seven, four, my youngest sister is a year older, and then me. I was disliked by all my sisters and my brother. I would say I was a brat, and they thought I got away with murder, and I probably did. Being the smallest, I probably pestered them a lot.

In those days your environment was your neighborhood and the kids in the neighborhood. Every spring we'd build us a baseball field and play baseball until school started again, and everybody started thinking about football then. So as a group in the neighborhood, we didn't play much basketball, because nobody in the neighborhood had paved driveways or anything. And we had no access to the gym. So it was football, a little basketball, and then it went to baseball.

And those houses weren't air-conditioned in those days, so you spent all summer outside. Our mom wanted us out of the house in the summertime. We wanted to be out of the house because in those days there wasn't anything on TV, and she didn't want you hanging around inside underfoot anyway.

You went outside, and you learned to let your imagination create games and stuff with other kids in the neighborhood, because everybody was in the same boat. Alvin was a small town during my childhood, about five thousand to seven thousand people.

There was a great sense of freedom. You never worried about anything. You got on your bicycle, and you might go up to the school and go over to somebody else's house. If you weren't playing ball, you were on your bicycle. You went to school, and all the activities were at school.

People would ride their horses up to the school. Nowadays you wouldn't see that, but kids had horses. Or you're on your bicycle or whatever. We lived in town, so we never had horses. I always got a hand-me-down bicycle; that's just the way it was. But that didn't really matter to you because you had a bicycle. You never got anything new.

My mom and dad both were very hardworking and dedicated to the family. Our lives revolved around the family. You know, when you have that many children, and you're washing clothes for all of them—she worked all day. Both of them worked all day. That's all they did was work.

He took a second job to put my sisters through college. And because he worked two jobs, we didn't go on vacations or do anything like that because he didn't have the time to do that. We had a lot of cousins, but they lived in different places. You didn't travel in those days. You know, you didn't get on the airplane. And you darn sure didn't drive to Oregon or California or wherever people lived. So you didn't see much of them.

In those days, you had two kids in each room, so you had at least a four-bedroom house. But one thing about it, you only had one bathroom. People couldn't survive today with only one bathroom for more than one person.

I shared a room with my brother. He was seven years older. The rest were all girls. We were a little long in girls. The first three children were more like aunts and uncles to me, because by the time I was ten, they were all out of the house, going to college. It was really my two youngest sisters and me at home by the time we became teenagers or a little earlier.

We always had a dog. The dog was mine because I got her on my sixth birthday. She went with me everywhere I went. They say it was a rat terrier, but I never believed it because I believe she probably was a fox terrier. Her name was Susie. If we went to play ball, she went and hung out there.

In those days when you grew up in Texas, you fished. Sometimes, maybe on Sunday afternoon, our dad might take us fishing in some of the rice canals around Alvin. That was all rice country in those days.

I was in Cub Scouts. I didn't go into Boy Scouts, and it really was because of sports and just not having time.

Church was a big part of our lives, and we all went as a family. We were Methodists. Growing up in a small town in that era, the only two activities were through the church or the school. We went to a lot of church camps, which was a big deal for us, and we went to camp in Palestine. You never as a kid got to go anywhere, but at camp we swam in a lake. Then MYF [Methodist Youth Fellowship] was a big deal with Methodist kids, so you spent a lot of time at church. And you went to Bible School in the summertime.

I had lots of chores. I had to paint the house every other year. It was an all-summer job, I'll tell you that. Mow the yard. Put out the garbage. Rake leaves. All that kind of stuff, depending on what time of the year it was. When I was, I don't know, ten or eleven or twelve, I'd go to my uncle's dairy and stay there two or three weeks in the summertime and help him on his dairy.

I learned most of my values from my parents, and we were held accountable at all times. That's another thing. You never got in trouble in school or anything, because not only were you going to be disciplined at school, you were going to have to pay the piper when you got home, because they were going to know about it before you got home. And in those days, you just didn't want to do that.

I got whippings from both my mom and my dad. I have no earthly idea why, except being mean to my sisters, probably. My daddy had the belt, and my mother used whatever she could put her hands on.

For a second job, my dad was the distributor of the *Houston Post* there in Alvin for twelve years. We threw somewhere between 1,000 and 1,500 papers a night. They would come in at one o'clock in the morning, and we would throw them.

And people say, "You built up your arm throwing papers."

Well, that's not true, because when you drive a car and you throw a newspaper, you throw it with your left hand.

I threw papers from the time I was in the first grade until I graduated.

And it's like a dairy; you do it every day. It's not four days a week; it's seven days a week. And so that's all we knew. That's what we did.

Now, when you get up at one in the morning and get back to bed about four thirty, you have to go to bed pretty early if you're going to get caught up on your sleep. Or you don't get caught up on it. You slept when you could. I'll tell you this, on Wednesday morning after Tuesday night basketball games, I'd miss the first couple of classes, but the teachers knew, so that wasn't a big issue.

He woke us up at one when the papers come in. You go down there, and I would roll while my brother and my dad were delivering the papers. And he'd come back and get me after I'm through rolling, and he'd take me back to the house, and he and my brother would finish throwing papers.

In Texas then you could have a driver's license at fourteen, so when I turned fourteen, I had the rural route, and my route was fifty miles a night. I drove fifty miles a night and threw papers in the country.

I knew everybody, because in those days, when you threw the papers, you had to go collect from people every month. They didn't mail in their payments. People used to go down to the gas company and pay their bills and go down to the electric

Nolan Ryan threw his first no-hitter while in Little League. *Photo courtesy Nolan Ryan*

company and pay them there. But we had to go by and collect from them.

I can remember in those days, and I was pretty young, I'd go collect $1.25 a month. Nowadays, you're thinking, "A dollar twenty-five? How can you even live on that?"

But that's what it was.

I want to tell you something, on that paper route I learned a lot about people, because I'd sit down there at that Sinclair station at ten years old by myself rolling papers at one thirty and two in the morning. And people would come by and want a paper. They'd come out of the beer joints, and I couldn't give them away. You know, that was pretty much an education.

And then going to collect from people—you're dealing with the public, and they didn't care if their dog got after you. And I can't tell you how many times I got bit. People didn't pay you sometimes. You had to go back two or three times, trying to get a payment. And as a kid you learn a lot of things that had never crossed your mind.

I had responsibilities and I was expected to do them. When I have something to do now, I get up and do it, because it's been instilled in me. I got in trouble one time with my dad because of his expectations.

Every morning before the papers came, we'd go down to that station and wait for that truck at one o'clock. One of my earliest jobs was to clean out the car and make sure there weren't any old newspapers left in the car so we didn't deliver somebody a day-old paper.

We rolled papers at a Sinclair station right on a corner in downtown Alvin, and I'd have to go around in the alley and throw the old papers in the garbage can. And as a kid, seven or eight years old, I hated that job because it was dark in the alley. You couldn't see, and you didn't know if there was somebody back there or not. So what I started doing was I'd walk around acting like I was going in the alley, and when I got out of sight of my dad, I'd throw them up on top of the service station.

I was a kid—out of sight, out of mind, right? So it's a flat-roof service station, and it rains a lot in Alvin. The rain washed those papers down in the gutters and stopped them up, and the roof caved in on the service station.

So I came home from school one day, and my dad said, "Nolan, we need to go down to the Sinclair station."

I wondered, "What's that about?"

We drove down there, and there was a big hole in the ceiling of the service station.

My dad said, "Nolan, you know anything about that?"

And I'm going, "I don't know what that is."

He said, "Let me show you what they got out of the gutters."

The rest of the summer I paid for that hole in the service station. I didn't make a penny one rolling papers, mowing yards, or whatever I did, because any money I got went to pay that bill. I learned a lesson, sure did, about shortcuts. You learn them the hard way a lot of times, but they stay with you.

Y ou were expected home for dinner at night, and you'd better be there. We prayed before we ate. My mother cooked dinner every night, and we sat down, and we ate as a family, and there wasn't coming and going and all that stuff like you have today with people with all their activities.

We never ate outside the house. One, you didn't have the income to go buy something. If we ever got an ice cream cone outside the house, that was something special, because there just wasn't any income for it. Alvin had restaurants, but they were these little independent Dairy Queens and stuff like that around.

Education was important to my parents, very much so. They worked themselves to death to give those girls opportunity. They were all really good students. So two of them went to Texas and two of them went to Sam Houston, and my brother went to both. I think he went to Texas and enjoyed his freshman year too much, so he ended up coming home.

I was the only one who didn't graduate from college, because I signed with the Mets after my high school graduation and went to play baseball. I would have liked to have had a college education; it just didn't work out that way. I'd come back in the off-season the first couple of years and I'd go to Alvin Community College, but, you know, things interfere with those schedules, and then you start having children. Going to college just gets pushed to the side.

I was one of the fortunate ones. I was able to make a career out of baseball.

I can't say that Nolan Ryan was the favorite of the teachers; however, the further removed I was from school and the longer I played baseball, the more popular I got with the teachers.

Being the baby of the family, most of the teachers had had some prior experiences with my siblings, and they were all very good students. School wasn't that important to me. Then when I got into junior high and high school, I went to school so I could play sports.

I am dyslexic. It's hard to learn, you know, when you reverse numbers, and spelling is hard for you, and so I struggled through school with that. But in those days, they didn't know what it was. You learn to deal with it.

I first learned I had it when my boys were diagnosed with it. I went through all my schooling never knowing. If you told me something, I'd remember it, but if I read it, I wouldn't. I reversed numbers. If I look at a number, I'll remember it. But if you told me, you know, your phone number, I'd get the numbers right, but they probably would not be in order.

I am an extremely slow reader. I enjoy reading, and I had a teacher in the fifth grade that would read to the class after lunch every day for forty-five minutes. And she'd read a book, and she'd stop, and the next day she'd read it out loud again to the class. She really spurred my interest in reading.

English was always hard. Math was all right as long as I didn't reverse

Nolan Ryan threw seven no-hitters during his long major league career.
Photo courtesy Nolan Ryan

numbers and stuff. I can't say there was one subject I looked forward to or one class I didn't want to go to. I was the last person picked for the spelling bees and the first person who got to sit down.

I went to our fiftieth class reunion, and there was a little girl there that was telling my wife, Ruth, how she just loved me, because when we played dodgeball, she was horrible—she couldn't walk and chew gum, right?—but I always would pick her as one of the first girls to be on my team. You had two captains, and you had to divide the kids up. I'd always pick her, and she was always so proud she wasn't the last one picked.

But I knew what it was like to be the last one picked. I didn't like being that person, and I wasn't going to do that to her.

I would say my earliest recollection of playing baseball would be around six years old, first grade or something, in an open field with the neighborhood kids. In those days, the first team sport and the only team sport was baseball. There wasn't any Little League football or Pop Warner or any of that stuff.

And so it was a big deal when you got to be the age that you could go out for an organized team. I think in those days you could only play Little League at twelve, ten, and eleven, and anything else below that was called Minor League.

It was the first time you were ever on a team and that you got a team cap. And that was a big deal because nobody wore caps in those days. Nobody had them. And so the only cap you ever had was the team you played for. That meant that you made the team. I probably got my first cap when I was seven or eight. The first kids' team I was on was the Rangers. Our cap was golden. I was a pitcher or a shortstop or played centerfielder. I don't remember if we were winners.

I played Little League and Babe Ruth League, and I wasn't any different than any of the other kids. You wouldn't walk out there and say, "Well, that kid there, that Ryan kid's going to be something special."

In Little League I pitched my first no-hitter. I was eleven, because the kid I pitched against was a year older than me in school, and he was twelve. To be honest, at eleven years old, I don't really remember it. But did they say it meant something? No.

Kids at that age don't put the ball in play a whole lot. Their hand-eye coordination isn't that good. It was a progression for me. It was a long process, learning your delivery and what you had to do. It wasn't something you did overnight.

Not until my sophomore year in high school did I start showing that I was blessed with a great arm. In those days, freshmen were still in junior high school. So when I went out for the baseball team as a sophomore, I had hit my last growth spurt. It was like I had a totally different arm. And that's when the velocity showed up. That meant I could throw harder than the other kids, but that didn't mean I was good, because I was a long way from being good. The catcher I had, by the end of the season, his hand was so swollen, so beat up. But he was a tough kid.

As a kid, I thought if I pursued any sport, I wanted to be a baseball player. As a kid you have no clue what it takes to play sports on any level but in the town that you're in. But once I got into high school, I wanted to go to college on a basketball scholarship. That was my passion, but thank goodness, my baseball ability overshadowed my basketball ability. I quit football after my freshman year because I wanted to focus on basketball. I was six-two and I weighed 150 pounds, so you know, I wasn't really a football player. I ran on the track team, so it wasn't like I was slow.

Having a strong arm was a gift. Nobody taught me to pitch. I was a visual learner, just watching. I watched TV. You know, once in a while, you got the Saturday Game of the Week.

When I was younger, I liked Mickey Mantle, and when I was older, in high school, I liked Sandy Koufax. They were my heroes.

When I signed with the New York Mets out of high school, I had no idea whether I could play professional baseball or not because we had nothing to judge it on. Being from a small community, all you ever saw was other kids from small communities.

I got to the Big Leagues at nineteen, and I was a fish out of water in New York City. I was about as prepared for that as I don't know what. I don't know how I adjusted. I think it goes back to how you were brought up.

I can remember walking into that clubhouse for the first time, a Major League dugout, and looking at those guys, and they were older and they were out of shape. They smoked, and I'm going, "That's not going to be me."

In those days, I think everybody smoked. I never smoked. My dad was a smoker, and it killed him. My mother was a smoker, and I never had any desire to ever smoke.

My wife, Ruth, grew up in the same town. Her sister was in my class, and Ruth was two years younger. I started dating her when she was fourteen. I was sixteen. I'm surprised her mother let her go out with me, but there wasn't a whole lot you could get in trouble in Alvin without somebody knowing about it. There was a movie theater and that was about it. And we'd go to the Dairyland.

I was riding down the street on the back of a moped with a friend of mine and we were going by the front of the high school. Ruth was a tennis player. That would have put her in the seventh grade. She was walking down the street, and he honked at her and waved. And I turned around and looked at her and said, "Who's that?"

And he said, "That's Lynn Holderoff's little sister."

And that was the first time I ever saw her that I remember.

We've been married fifty years. We raised our kids in Alvin, even when my career was in California and in New York. We wanted to try to give them the same opportunities we had.

I learned about being held accountable and not lying and being honest with people, even when it's not what you want to end up doing or what you want to tell somebody. I just think your overall values are instilled in you by your parents.

When I look back on my childhood, I think the thing that I was blessed about was the freedom that we had, the fun that we had as kids. And when I look back on that, I was very fortunate to grow up in that era, to have an opportunity to have a childhood like that.

Like many Texas schoolchildren, Nolan Ryan recalls field trips to the San Jacinto Monument. *Bob Bailey Studios, Bob Bailey Studios Photographic Archive, Briscoe Center for American History, University of Texas at Austin*

Texas History Makes an Impression

If you asked me what class I enjoyed most, it was probably Texas history in the seventh grade. Alvin was only twenty miles away from the San Jacinto battlegrounds. The only field trip I ever took in school was when they took us to the San Jacinto Monument. When you don't go anywhere in your life, that's pretty special.

After I took Texas history, we'd go down to Beeville to visit my grandmother and go through Goliad. I'd convince my mother and dad to stop and let us go to the old mission there or the Fannin battleground. And then going to the Alamo—it just really stimulated my interest in Texas history. It's been a lifelong pursuit of mine to read Texas history and to have kind of an understanding about how Texas developed.

Henry Cisneros and his sister, Pauline, at their grandfather's business,
Munguia's Print Shop, 1951. *Photo courtesy the Cisneros family*

BIRTH NAME	**HENRY GABRIEL CISNEROS**
BORN	June 11, 1947, in San Antonio to J. George Cisneros and Elvira Munguia Cisneros
INTERVIEW	His home, San Antonio, Texas, December 10, 2016

HENRY CISNEROS

A Cocoon of Family and Tradition

The first Hispanic mayor of San Antonio since 1842 and the tenth
secretary of the Department of Housing and Urban Development,
Henry Cisneros started his public life working for the National
League of Cities in Washington, DC. In 1975, at age twenty-seven,
he became the youngest person ever elected to San Antonio's city council. He bridged the divide between the entrenched Anglo and rising
Hispanic populations, and at thirty-three became the second Hispanic
mayor of a major US city. His legacy of economic growth, a locally
financed Alamodome, a visit by Pope John Paul II, and $500 million in
improvements to neglected neighborhoods explained his four terms and
Texas Monthly *naming him Mayor of the Century. From 1997 to 2000,
he served as president of Univision Communications, the nation's largest Spanish-language broadcaster. Cisneros returned to San Antonio to
build affordable homes and later joined an investment banking firm as
an equity partner.*

My grandfather and grandmother came with my two-year-old mother in 1926, during the height of the revolutionary turmoil in Mexico. My grandfather was an alternate to the constitutional convention in Querétaro, which created the Mexican constitution.

A young, up-and-coming political figure, he got crosswise in the political currents and received warnings that he was going to be executed. So he decided the wiser thing was to come to San Antonio. Since printing was his profession, he went to work at *La Prensa* for a man named Ignacio Lozano. He was the publisher of *La Prensa* who went on to create *La Opinión* in Los Angeles and a network of Spanish newspapers across the country. The editor was Leonidas González, the father of Henry B. González.

My grandfather and grandmother had seven children, four of whom were born in Mexico. They created this colorful, rambunctious family. They were very dedicated to the American idea, the American dream, and also had loyalty to their Mexican heritage. My grandfather sponsored professors from Mexico to teach at Trinity University under the auspices of a group called El Patriate. My grandmother created the first Spanish-language radio program in San Antonio, *La Hora de la Estrella, The Hour of the Star.*

He built a printshop that in its prime on Buena Vista Street employed forty-five people, one of the largest printshops in San Antonio. Grandfather was kind of a Charles de Gaulle figure. He wasn't from Mexico— he was Mexico. He was of Basque origin. People called him Don Rómulo. His name was Rómulo Munguia, and *don* is an honorific.

I used to go with him as a child to what is called El Grito, which is on September 16, Diez y Seis de Septiembre, and they played the Mexican national anthem. I was maybe ten years old. I was standing next to him and could feel him shaking. He had tears running down his cheeks.

I spent a lot of time in my grandparents' home, and we still live in it today. The dining room is where we gathered every Sunday. Every single Sunday. After church, all the brothers and sisters and their families came together.

We grew up with my cousins in this house. The living room is where we saw Elvis Presley for the first time on *The Ed Sullivan Show*. That's where we saw the Beatles for the first time. We would sit here on New Year's afternoon and watch the Rose Bowl.

They were all strong-willed, and, therefore, they didn't always agree. And more often than not, someone would leave those Sunday gatherings in tears because they had had an argument on some aspect of the business or family life. They'd make up during the week over the phone.

My fondest memories are of stepping out that door on Sunday night, at seven o'clock on Sunday evening, going down the porch, and the cars were parked at the curb. My grandmother would follow us out. She would make the sign of the cross over each car and say, "Nos vemos entre ocho días, si Dios quiere." We'll see you in a week, God willing.

My dad grew up one of twelve in New Mexico in a family of poor tenant farmers. During the Depression, the older kids stayed behind in New Mexico, and my grandfather took the younger group of kids in search of better farming country. He was the second from the youngest. He lost his mother in childbirth with the youngest. His father remarried and eventually built a farm in Brighton, Colorado, where they raised beets.

My dad, who was very smart and read multiple books at the same time, was the only one of the twelve who finished high school. He went

The Cisneros family in 1966. Henry, age nineteen, is in the center of the back row. *Photo courtesy the Cisneros family*

to business college in Denver and worked for the Indian Service in New Mexico, Colorado, and Utah, until he was drafted right before Pearl Harbor and spent most of the time in New Guinea. He contracted malaria in 1944, and they sent him to Randolph Field in San Antonio to recover. His roommate was one of the Munguia boys from the printshop family.

He was reading one Sunday afternoon. Ruben Munguia comes in and says, "Come on, Sarge, you've got to come meet my family. My sister's in the car. Come down and meet my family. They came out to see me."

They also came to see an airplane, the B-29, which was the type of plane that dropped the atomic bomb, and no one had seen it in San Antonio. It had just flown into Randolph.

That afternoon they went to have a malt, they saw a movie, they drove into San Antonio, and the next Sunday he was at their house. Six months later, he was asking permission to marry my mom.

And my grandfather said, "You can marry her, but you can't take her from San Antonio."

He wanted to go back to Denver, but they made their life here.

It was a kind of Norman Rockwell existence, but all our faces were brown.

I couldn't have had better parents. It was a kind of Norman Rockwell existence, but all our faces were brown.

I lived on a block where every single household was a World War II veteran raising their kids after the war. Some worked at Kelly Field. Some worked at Lackland. Some worked at Fort Sam Houston.

All my younger brother and I had to do was go out on the sidewalk and whistle, and sixteen boys between my age and his age were out there to play football, to play baseball. We were Boy Scouts. We were altar boys. My sisters were Brownies, in the Girl Scouts. We played baseball, football, boxing matches in the backyard.

Our fathers protected us from the worst of the discrimination visited upon people who might be less educated and who were severely underemployed as laborers, custodial workers, and household workers. We knew we were not any better than those folks.

Our church and parishes were good buffers against the disappointments of life, because the Catholic tradition teaches patience and humility and understanding. Our neighborhood church is Sacred Heart, but the school we went to was Little Flower at the Basilica of St. Thomas.

My brothers and sisters and neighborhood friends lived in a cocoon, which was the Mexican American community, and we really didn't know the degree of segregation or exclusiveness. We had no connection to the world of country clubs or golf courses or downtown businesses or banks. We were the other San Antonio.

So there was the Texas of ranches and oil wells, and the growth of Dallas and Houston. We didn't know a lot about the entrepreneurial or wildcat experience that characterizes Texas.

We were much more deliberate. You go to school. You get good grades. You'll probably be in some career where you are rewarded for your progress. We were on a different track.

There was also the pride in Mexican traditions. My sister and I danced in the city recreation programs wearing the traditional garb of Mexico. We danced on the stage of the Arneson River Theatre. We were taught the beautiful things about Mexican culture, from the cuisine—not just tamales and tortillas and tacos, but mole, for example, and good home cooking in the Mexican style. Mexican candy. Mexican desserts. Mexican drinks, like atole at Christmastime. The literature, the language, the poetry, the music, for sure, from mariachis to the great balladeers. The golden age of the Mexican cinema. About that time Spanish television came into existence, so we had access to Spanish TV.

They tell me I spoke Spanish before English. My grandfather was very proud of my Spanish. He would trot me out in front of the elders, his generation, to speak to them in Spanish.

But my dad said, "You'll never get anywhere in the United States if you don't speak English and speak it well, unaccented."

So we spoke English in the household because my dad was insistent that we were going to learn English and learn it well.

***

I was the oldest of my parents' five kids, and the first boy among the grandkids. I was shy. You know, when you grow up with an achieving father but a strict mother, you don't know how much latitude you have to be mischievous. So you aren't too troublesome.

Secretary of Housing and Urban Development Henry Cisneros, center, serves Thanksgiving dinner at a homeless shelter with President Bill Clinton and First Lady Hillary Clinton, November 22, 1995. *Photo by Dirck Halstead, Dirck Halstead Photographic Archive, Briscoe Center for American History, the University of Texas at Austin*

I was a pretty straight-arrow kid in part because they imbued in me a set of obligations related to being the oldest. They were pretty strict and pretty prudish about all the modern stuff. There was no girlfriends, no boyfriends. There were expectations. A lot of chores. Playtime was only after washing windows, sweeping the patio, cutting the yard. We painted the house.

They insisted on music lessons, so I played piano. Summertime was required reading every day, thirty books, and summer school most years.

I was skipped from the third to the fifth grade. So that meant that I was younger than everybody in my class. At twelve years old, I was going to high school. I graduated at sixteen. I went to school at Central Catholic, a boy's school, a good school, college prep. Never a doubt I wasn't going to college. My dad made sure of that.

Being younger than my peers was especially serious with respect to things related to girls and dating. I wasn't old enough to drive to my high school prom.

I met my wife when I was about fourteen and she was about twelve, one block from our present home. I was invited by my neighborhood friends to go to a talent show and style show at Sacred Heart Church. Mary Alice [Perez] was in it and walked across the stage wearing a green dress.

And I said, "Who is that?"

And they said, "Well, that is Mimi. That's Mary Alice. She's in our class."

She was beautiful, feminine, and graceful. I have known Mary Alice all my conscious life.

My earliest remembrances of politics were listening to the national party conventions. We listened to the 1956 convention, Stevenson against Eisenhower that year. I was about nine. I remember asking them, "Tell me the difference between Republicans and Democrats."

My father respected Eisenhower because Eisenhower was commander of the World War II forces, but he was for Stevenson because Stevenson was for the working guys.

My dad was the ultimate believer in the American way. He was a wonderful civil service worker, an army reservist who rose to the rank of colonel, conscientious, a play-by-the-rules kind of guy.

He would say, "You've got to study, because what you learn is the one thing that no one can take away from you. They can take away your home. They can take away your money. They cannot take away the knowledge you have in your head."

On Sundays my grandmother was the principal cook, although I think the daughters helped. It was always a full meal, like roast, sometimes brought in from Tai Shan, a Chinese restaurant on Broadway, or Youngblood's, the best fried chicken place on Broadway.

Sometimes it was food brought in from the picnics that the political organizations had, like the firefighters or police picnic of barbecue chicken. At Munguia Printers they did all the printing of programs for the police and fire unions. My uncle Ruben was running the printshop by then. My uncle would load all us older grandkids in the back of a pickup truck, which you could do in those days, and drive us all the way to Mission County Park or A. J. Plough Precinct 4 Park.

When I was ten years old, I was meeting the police union, the fire union, the letter carriers' union at their picnics because he was making the rounds.

He would say, "Hey, we're going to finish eating, get in the truck, and go do some politicking."

When I was growing up, I wanted to be an astronaut or a fighter pilot. I knew everything there was to know about airplanes—the name, the number, the capability, the performance. I competed to go to the Air Force Academy, but I was sixteen years old when I graduated from high school and weighed 135 pounds. I didn't get a nomination, but they offered me a chance to go to the Naval Academy. I'd never seen or been on a ship.

They told me I had to bulk up for a year before I tried the Air Force Academy again and suggested I go to a place with a military corps of cadets. This is why I went to Texas A&M. I got to A&M and studied aerospace engineering. What I really liked was courses where I could write, conceptualize, articulate, and persuade, so my majors became English and government. I was elected treasurer of my class and selected the best-drilled cadet.

This is 1965, '66, '67, and '68. The civil rights movement is happening. The antiwar movement is happening. The cities are burning. The urban crisis is being defined.

As a junior, I was active in a group called SCONA, Student Conference on National Affairs. Students run this massive conference with students from all over the country. I was treasurer and had to raise the money, a modest sum by today's standards. The director of the Memorial Student Center, Wayne Stark, said to me, "Here's a list of names of people in Houston who will give, but you have to ask in your uniform."

I called on executives from Gulf, Humble, Shell, all the oil companies in Houston. Here I am, eighteen years old, walking into corporate suites. They were predisposed to give because Aggies give for a good cause, and we raised the money.

Then Mr. Stark said, "I have selected you to represent A&M at a conference at West Point, the student conference on United States affairs. This is going to be a different group of students than you've been exposed to before. This isn't going to be Sam Houston State, it's not going to be West Texas State, it's going to be Harvard, Princeton, and Yale."

I don't think I opened my mouth for three days. In fact, I said to one guy sitting next to me, "How the heck do you know so much?"

He said, "I read the *New York Times* cover to cover every day."

I thought, "What's the *New York Times*?"

Wayne Stark, who was one of the most decisive people in my life, said, "What you did in Houston, I'm going to have you do in New York City."

I'd never been on an airplane. I'd never been to New York. And here I am walking the streets of New York, going to the major corporations, law firms, Wall Street, government agencies. The whole point wasn't really so much to raise money; it was to get me to understand who these people are, what their career patterns were.

On the flight up, I'm acting like a big shot, sitting on an airplane for the first time, looking out the window and reading *Time* magazine. And on the cover is an urbanologist talking about America's urban crisis. It was Daniel Patrick Moynihan.

We get to New York, and the stories there are about the newly elected mayor, John Lindsay, who's walking the streets, trying to keep the city from burning the way Cleveland and Los Angeles and Detroit did.

And synonymous with the cities were the great social movements: Dr. King, the civil rights speeches, the emerging young leaders, like Julian Bond and John Lewis in the Black community. All these new experiences stimulated my thinking. This is a life's work, trying to make things better for those who had been marginalized, and to get the cities to work.

I wanted to be in service to the country, defending the country in a military uniform or in the foreign service, but it very well could mean trying to make it better right here in the United States. So everything in my life changed to gear toward the cities. I selected different courses, looked at scholarships and internships that would get me on that course. That's what I've been doing the rest of my life.

I've never really articulated this, but when I was little, the things that I liked to do were concrete. The things that I played at were graphic and concrete when I was seven, eight, nine. For example, my first memory of ever thinking about cities or urban planning or anything like that was playing in the dirt driveway of our house, drawing out streets and blocks and putting buildings and trucks where they go—laying out cities.

It's my frame of reference. Building homes for people and changing the skyline is a concrete accomplishment. No one can deny you have advanced the world or helped somebody, because there it is. You can see it. You can put the pieces together.

Sandra Cox, ten months old. *Photo courtesy Sandra Brown*

BIRTH NAME	**SANDRA LYNN COX**
BORN	March 12, 1948, in Waco to Jimmie Ramon Cox and Martha Jean Norwood Cox
INTERVIEW	Her home, Arlington, Texas, June 14, 2018

SANDRA BROWN
Always Books

S andra Brown has written more than eighty books in the romance, mystery, and thriller genres. More than eighty million copies are still in print, and her books have been translated into thirty-four languages. Since 1990, every one of her novels has made the New York Times *Best Seller list. After she was laid off from a nationally syndicated* PM Magazine *show in Dallas, she began writing romance novels under the pseudonym Rachel Ryan and sold her first manuscript within a year in 1981. Beloved by readers, she has received the Romance Writers of America's Lifetime Achievement Award, the 2008 International Thriller Writers' ThrillerMaster honor, and the 2007 Texas Medal of Arts Award for literature. At book signings she hears from fans who still want her to write more about the Tylers, the fictional family in the Texas! Trilogy she created in 1990 to 1991. Now in its forty-fifth domestic printing, the three-book series brings to life a family trying to save their East Texas oil business.*

My mother's people came from Tennessee and Kentucky in covered wagons at the turn of the twentieth century. Both great-grandparents' last name was Denison. My great-grandfather spelled his Dennison with a double *n*, and my great-grandmother spelled hers Denison with a single. He was illiterate, but she could read and write. They settled somewhere around Frisco, which was then prairie, and she filed all their property documents and used the spelling "Denison." I don't know if my great-grandpa ever knew that. They lived in North Texas and raised cotton, picked cotton.

We lived through the 1953 tornado in Waco, and I remember it vividly because Mother was scared.

My grandmother was the youngest of the whole slew of children. That was a very close family, and I was very close to my mother's parents. My grandmother, Myrtle Denison, married Gene Norwood, and he had a rather tragic childhood. He was an orphan and the middle of three brothers. His mother died when she was twenty-nine. So his daddy had to work to support these three little boys, and he would temporarily put them in orphanages.

My grandpa Norwood didn't talk a lot about it. There were probably times when he went hungry, because in later life his thing was feeding everybody.

"You're going to come to my house and I'm going to feed you."

He and Grandma were dear people. He was also a part-time Southern Baptist minister, so that whole side of the family was very faith based.

I was born in Waco because Lorena didn't have a hospital. There was an ice storm, and my grandmother, my mother's mother, and my mother and daddy drove on icy roads from Lorena to the hospital in Waco.

My paternal grandfather, C. M. Cox, had a dairy farm outside Lorena. There was a shack on the farm half a mile down the road from my grandparents' house that Mother and Daddy lived in. But we moved to Waco when I must have been about three, and we lived in a garage apartment. Daddy worked for the *Waco Tribune-Herald*.

We lived through the 1953 tornado in Waco, and I remember it vividly because Mother was scared. I would have been four or five. I had a little sister, and she was barely walking at that point. We lived on Bagby in Waco. And our house sat catty-cornered on the corner of the street. And I remember Mother being panicked.

We could see this cloud. It was raining so hard that water was coming underneath the doorframe in the kitchen, and Mother was frantically mopping it up. Daddy was at the newspaper office, and they had all gone down into the basement. On the floor where he had been working, all the windows were blown out. So they would probably have been killed or injured had they been there.

I remember when the storm was over, we walked out in our neighborhood and there was debris. Devastation. The next day we drove around town looking at the destruction, and I just remember thinking, "What happened?"

If you are familiar with I-35, you've driven past the Elite Café and the Health Camp where the roundabout is. I remember driving past those, and the buildings just being demolished, and Mother saying, "Look at that Dr Pepper bottle."

In all of this destruction, there was a Dr Pepper bottle sitting upright with Dr Pepper still in it.

One of Sandra Cox's school photos.
Photo courtesy Sandra Brown

The buildings were just gone; sides of buildings were just gone. You could see inside of buildings and everybody's house. I don't remember our house being damaged. I remember water running in the street and a lot of tree limbs in the streets. I think it was worse downtown than in the neighborhood. It practically demolished the town.

I didn't know it was a funnel cloud. I just remember how Mother kept saying, "It's got to be a tornado because the sky's green."

But oddly, I don't really have a fear of storms, maybe because I lived through it. Soon after that, Daddy got a job at the *Fort Worth Star-Telegram*, and we moved to Fort Worth. That's where I grew up.

I never really knew I wanted to be a writer. But my mother was an avid reader and a romantic. She loved Lloyd C. Douglas, Thomas Costain, and all of those writers who told wonderful tales. And then Daddy went to work every day and had to produce an editorial, five hundred words about something. He had to express an educated opinion.

Mother was the fanciful one. She was the one who would say, "*Jane Eyre*'s so wonderful."

I have four little sisters. Mother used to read us fairy tales out loud before we could even read. And always books in the house. Always books.

Daddy was paid maybe fifteen bucks to do book reviews as a sideline. And so the publishers would send him books. Advance reading copies, and whether or not he reviewed them, they were just there in his office. And every two or three months, he would bring home boxes of books. To me, it was just like a treasure trove. And I would go through them— probably read a lot of things I shouldn't have at the age.

And then our big outing in the summertime was to the library, and we would check out as many books as they would allow, plow through them, and then we'd go back. Mother was an avid reader, too. It was just a part

Sandra Cox and two younger sisters practice cheerleading in their Fort Worth front yard. *Photo courtesy Sandra Brown*

of our family life. I credit both my parents with giving me a love of reading and books, storytelling.

My first school was Richland Elementary in North Richland Hills. I remember learning to read when I went to first grade. I'm sure I probably knew my alphabet. I don't remember being taught to read and write before I went to school. But then I read all the time.

Mother would get upset with me for not doing my chores because I had my head in a book. I read the Hardy Boys and Nancy Drew, the Bobbsey Twins, and all of those over and over and over. I bet I read every Nancy Drew book twenty times.

Writing was never hard for me, and I was a good student. First of all, it was expected. So I always made good grades. My parents were strict on me, I guess because I was the oldest. We were all four years apart. My youngest sister was born on the last day of my junior year in high school. I am seventeen years older than she is.

The first time I actually thought about writing was my first semester at TCU [Texas Christian University]. English composition was compulsory, and I remember the professor assigned an essay based on the John Donne quote "No man is an island." We could practice. We could plan out what we were going to say, but when we went into the classroom, we had one hour to write the essay without notes.

After they were graded, the teacher came into the classroom and said that most of them were pretty dismal. But he said there were two that were really good, and mine was one of the two.

Everybody was like, "This is the hardest thing I've ever done."

And I thought, "Not really."

The writing just wasn't that hard for me. Algebra was hard. Mathematics and sciences I never was interested in, except I did like physiology, the human body. But you give me history or English, I never had any trouble. I thought I'd probably be an English teacher.

My friends and I played all the things that kids can't play today—cowboys and Indians, cops and robbers. We had fake guns, all of that which is discouraged now. There were woods behind our house, with a little creek, and we'd go there and play Annie Oakley and the bad guy. Then my girlfriends and I would play movie star.

I never played with dolls much. Being a rockabye-baby mom was never my thing. And it was totally my mother's thing. When my youngest sister went to elementary school, Mother was forty-five. She enrolled in TWU [Texas Woman's University] and got her master's degree, got certification as a diagnostician and counselor and had a twenty-year career after raising five daughters.

Her name was Martha Jean, but everybody called her Mop. I think that was her name on her driver's license. Everybody loved her because she loved everybody. She enjoyed hearth and home.

That was her thing, never was mine. In a way deep down, I knew that my life was not going to be ordinary. I didn't know in what way it would be different. I just felt it would be.

My mother always said we grew up together, because she was only nineteen when she had me and I was born so adult. We were very good friends.

She knew I had this terrible paranoia about failure. To this day, each book is sheer torture. One day, I was just anguishing—this goes back early in my career, but after I had achieved a certain level of success—and she said, "You really worry me because you don't enjoy your success. You never let up on yourself."

And I said, "Do you remember when I had all straight As and I got a B-plus in algebra, and I was grounded for six weeks? I guess I'm still trying to get that A in algebra."

Obviously, my parents held me and my sisters accountable for our actions. We weren't punished harshly, but privileges were revoked. We got swatted on our behinds until we were too old to be. My parents instilled in us a moral code, which in our case was Christian. But even if you're not religious, there should be some basic morality. Decency should be taught.

There are two things I remember about the movies when I was a kid. There was a movie theater in Haltom City. This was when it was safe for parents to drop off their kids and leave them. We'd get a quarter. And for a quarter, we could pay our way in and get a Slo Poke and a Coke.

And you dipped your Slo Poke into your Coke. It would last the whole movie. We would see a double feature. It was a day's entertainment for a quarter.

I remember going to the drive-in a lot. All the little sisters would take a pillow, so they could go to sleep in the back seat. Sometimes my sister and I got to sit on the trunk or the hood of the car to be cooler. On the way, we'd stop at the A&W. Hamburgers were a quarter. Mother and Daddy would get a nickel mug of root beer, but the kids got a little tiny mug for free. Mother would have popped enough popcorn to fill a Buddies bag, from Buddies, a supermarket.

And nearly every time, when the movie was over, Daddy would drive off and the speaker would still be attached to the open car window.

We went to the grand opening of Six Flags Over Texas. Because Daddy was working at the newspaper, he got free tickets. That was a huge deal to us. Mother sewed all the sisters, three of us at the time, outfits alike to go to Six Flags. Shorts and tops. I think they were blue-and-white check.

Mother sewed a lot. She was working in the church office. She would come home from work, and I and or one of my sisters would need a new skirt or a new dress for a program at school the next day.

And she would say to me, "You cut out the pattern while I'm making dinner."

I would pin the pattern on the fabric, cut it out. After dinner she sewed it up for whoever needed it the next day.

When I was growing up, every summer at Vacation Bible School, you'd march in with the US flag, the Christian flag, and the Bible. I always wondered why girls only got to carry the Bible; we didn't ever get to carry the flags. I wanted to carry a flag. It was a total gender discrimination thing.

I resented never getting to carry a flag. I was way ahead of my time.

My sisters and I would fight over the last piece of fried chicken or the last pork chop. Journalists typically don't go into journalism to make a lot of money, and we were always extremely middle class and didn't have money for extras. But we always were well-fed.

Dinner always had a meat, a starch, a salad, a couple of vegetables. Mother cooked dinner every night. But that's why I don't know how to cook. She would do it, and I was doing chores, like tending to the little sisters or doing the laundry or folding it or whatever needed to be done.

I never learned how to cook like she knew how to cook, which was by ear. She just kept throwing things together, and it would taste good.

Another food memory—going to my grandma Cox's house. She was sixty-five when I was born, so I just remember her as being old. She had white hair, and she wore it in a bun. She had this blue ceramic cookie jar in her pantry. She made tea cakes, sugar cookies, and they were just heaven. Butter and flour that she'd cream up together, a little vanilla, roll the dough up into a log, put it in the refrigerator in wax paper, then slice it into disks. Dust on some sugar. They were just the best things in the whole world. We loved that blue ceramic cookie jar.

I also have food memories of my grandma Norwood. Grandpa worked on the railroad. He was a section boss. His crew rode those push cars along the tracks, looking for repairs that needed to be made along that stretch of the railroad. On lunch break, he would pick blackberries or dewberries off the side of the railroad and bring them home in a pail.

Grandma would make cobblers with them. I can remember her washing those dewberries and cooking them on the stove with a little sugar while she was rolling out the crust. She would pat that crust in the bottom of the Pyrex dish, put the berries in, and then cut strips of dough for the top. I can remember how her hands looked patting that dough down into the baking dish.

She would bake the leftover strips and sprinkle sugar on top, which is why to this day I still like the crust of the pie better than anything that's in it. Going to Grandma Cox's house always meant sugar cookies, and going to Grandma Norwood's meant cobblers.

Two other treats were homemade ice cream and watermelons. We bought watermelons out of big troughs of ice water. Daddy would drive around looking for the best price.

"Well, they are 2.5 cents a pound over here, but 1.5 cents a pound over there."

He'd pick up this huge, big, round watermelon. They tasted better than they do today. We'd take one to the park and put newspaper on the picnic table, slice the watermelon.

My sisters, cousins, and I used to fight over who got to sit on the ice cream freezer. When the crank started getting hard to turn, the grown-ups would pile quilts or towels on top of it, and then get one of us kids to sit on it to anchor it down.

We had a drill team at Richland. We were the Richland Rebels before the mascot was changed. I was a Dixie Belle the first year they organized the drill team. It was like the Kilgore Rangerettes. I had taken dancing, but in Dixie Belles I learned to dance enough to keep time to the music and not fall down.

In high school, I played the lead in *Bye Bye Birdie*. I was always in drama and speech. But in my junior year, they put on *Bye Bye Birdie*. This was the first time Richland High School had ever done a big musical production like that, and I was Rosie.

I guess I enjoyed high school well enough. I studied a lot, but I was also involved in student council, and I was a class officer. I had a lot of friends. My church [North Richland Hills Baptist] had a big youth choir. We toured every summer, performing concerts.

I remember John Glenn and Alan Shepard going into space. Both times I was in history class. My teacher wrote on the blackboard the importance of those days.

I also remember being in that American history class one day, and I looked out the window, and our pastor drove up. He entered the school, and I thought, "Wonder what he's doing here?"

In a little bit, somebody from the office came into the classroom and said, "You're wanted in the office."

I still didn't attach anything bad to it. So I went, and my pastor was there. He said, "Your aunt Ann has died."

One of my mother's younger sisters had had a bad heart ailment left over from rheumatic fever. In fact, she was one of Denton Cooley's first open-heart surgeries.

He was one of my heroes, and this was in the mid-fifties, later fifties. He had developed the heart-lung machine, where he could stop your heart and still pump blood through your lungs. It was very rudimentary technology at the time, and Ann was one of the first patients on which he tried it. And she lived for several more years. But she died about 1960. She was twenty-nine, very young.

And, of course, I have vivid recollections of the Kennedy assassination. I was in American history class again. Is that not bizarre? I had not ever thought about that. The first Americans in space and when John Kennedy was killed, I was in history classes both times.

Sandra Brown has more than 80 million books in print. *Photo by John Goodspeed*

I was in tenth grade when President Kennedy was shot. Daddy had seen him that morning in Fort Worth. Everybody was excited.

But at RHS we were excited also about the football game that night. It was Friday night, and we had held a pep rally. We had come back to class. My fourth period had a divided schedule. It was thirty minutes, then lunch, and then another thirty minutes. We were on the way to the lunchroom.

Somebody said, "The president's been shot. They've got it on the PA in the cafeteria."

And we were like, "What?"

In my imagination, it would be like in a movie. He was wounded but waving to the crowds. So the reality was unthinkable. We got into the lunchroom, and the PA was on, and all the teachers were crying, and everybody was in absolute shock.

We went back to our classroom, and my history teacher was sitting at her desk just sobbing, and then we heard Walter Cronkite say the words, "The president is dead."

Nobody could believe it.

I came home from school, and, of course, Mother was riveted to the TV, and even when she worked at the church, she came home for lunch to watch *As the World Turns*. She'd been watching her show when it was interrupted with the news.

We went to church that Sunday. Everybody was still reeling from shock. During the service, somebody came from the back of the church up to our pastor and whispered in his ear. He announced that Oswald had been shot.

Those memories are vivid for everybody in the nation. But for us right here in Dallas and Fort Worth, that day was particularly significant.

Mother told me that when I was growing up I had an imaginary friend I called Charlotte.

She said, "We didn't know a soul named Charlotte. I don't know where you got that name."

But Charlotte went everywhere with us. So even earlier than I can remember, I was making up people in my head.

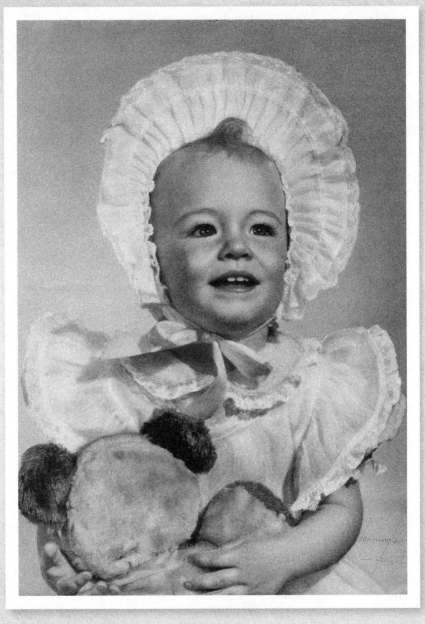

Phyllis George, fourteen months old. *Photo courtesy Phyllis George*

BIRTH NAME	**PHYLLIS ANN GEORGE**
BORN	June 25, 1949, in Denton to James Robert George and Diantha Louise Cogdell George
DIED	May 14, 2020
INTERVIEW	By phone, Lexington, Kentucky, June 15, 2018

43

PHYLLIS GEORGE
The Glass Half-Full

P hyllis George was the fiftieth Miss America and the second of three Miss Texas winners to wear the crown since the contest started in 1921. She was considered a breath of fresh air on CBS's The NFL Today *as the first woman host of a national pregame* show in 1975. She co-anchored three Super Bowls, became co-anchor of CBS Morning News, *hosted prime-time talk show specials, and appeared in the movie* Meet the Parents. As an entrepreneur, she developed successful companies Chicken By George and Phyllis George Beauty. As first lady of Kentucky from 1979 to 1983, she focused on her passion for creative work of the hand by founding the Kentucky Museum of Art and Craft in Louisville. She was a member of the James Madison Council at the Library of Congress and served almost fourteen years on the board of the Miss America Organization. She co-authored six books, including Never Say Never: Ten Lessons to Turn You Can't into Yes I Can.

I'm thinking how blessed I was to have had such an extraordinary life starting in Denton. Who knew that little girl growing up there would do all the different things that I've done? I do believe it had to do with my foundation and loving, supportive parents, who were always there for me and my brother, Robbie.

The Cogdells and the Georges lived in Denton or Denton County their whole lives. Several of them lived in Argyle. They're Texas people through and through. I regret not asking more about their lives.

My dad was a great dancer and charmer. He had a great smile with big dimples, which I inherited. Everybody loved to watch Mother and Daddy dance together. He met her when he was selling shoes in the Boston Store. He saw this beautiful woman standing there. She was very tall, very statuesque.

And he said, "I'm going to marry that woman."

After that, they were engaged. It was a lovely love affair of almost fifty years. He wrote her love letters all the time. Sometimes he put them on Post-its, and she would open the refrigerator and there would be little love notes from Daddy. Or by the coffee machine or in her purse.

I had the most normal, busy, what-can-I-do-now childhood that anybody has ever had. My brother once said our childhood was like the *Ozzie and Harriet* television show. My parents instilled that belief in me to think that I could be and do anything I put my mind to. That's the greatest gift I got from my parents. Win or lose, they were always there for me.

Denton, where I grew up, was like heaven. We had a square with all kinds of stores around it, and there's a beautiful, historic, old courthouse in the middle of town. When I was young, Denton was so safe we didn't lock our doors. The population was twenty-five thousand to thirty thousand, and then it swelled to seventy-five thousand when the two universities, the University of North Texas and Texas Woman's University, were in session.

I pretty much was an only child until I was seven, and then I told my parents I wanted to have a little brother. So I guess they got to work.

And then Robbie came, and I was very protective of him. But there was a big age difference, seven or eight years. So we were close and I adored him, but I was so far ahead of him in school that we were never at junior high or Denton High at the same time.

———

My brother's room was next to mine. I had the room facing the front of the house. Mom's and Dad's room was in the back. I didn't love doing housework so much, but I enjoyed vacuuming and dusting. I remember little things, like rearranging things and making my room look special. So I always had a knack for moving this here, putting that there, and moving this over here. I still do this today. We call it "tweaking by George."

I remember having a poster hanging over my desk in my room. It came from this store in Denton called Voertman's. I picked one of Portofino in Italy for my room. Every night, I would look at that poster and think, "I don't know how or when, but I'm going to go there one day."

And I did. How weird to have that dream for so many years. Then when we pulled in on a friend's huge yacht years later, it was exactly like it was in my childhood, exactly like I dreamed it would be.

The Power of Positive Thinking by Norman Vincent Peale had an influence on me. I was always the person with the glass half-full.

We were a middle-upper-class family. We were not rich in the financial way, but we were rich in love. I thought I had everything.

I played the piano every Friday at the weekly Lions Club meeting. I was the Lions Club sweetheart. I accompanied my mother on the March of Dimes Mothers March every year. I remember going door-to-door raising money.

I loved my Princess phone, and I loved to talk on it, a common pastime for small-town girls. I rode my bike and played the piano. I loved my animals. I had a life-size baby doll and the cutest clothes for her. My parents gave me a Madame Alexander doll every Christmas, so I had quite a collection.

I also went bowling, roller-skating, and horseback riding. I stayed up late at slumber parties. We created our own plays and performed songs from *Gypsy*. A group of friends and I started our rendition of the Beatles in the ninth grade. I was Ringo Starr and played the drums.

I started piano lessons when I was seven. Nobody knew that I would be good. I was told I was just a natural.

My mother wanted me to study with the internationally renowned Dr. Isabel Scionti. She settled in Denton because North Texas [University] has the famous Lab Band and a great music department. It was very expensive for my parents to send me to Dr. Scionti, because people would come from everywhere to study with her. She and her husband, Silvio

Scionti, were dual pianists, playing together with baby grands back to back. They played at Carnegie Hall and around the world.

I remember all the recitals and how Mother in those years would make my pretty little dresses. I remember being on a stage as a young girl at North Texas—back then it was North Texas State College—with Cindy Cole, playing "Dizzy Fingers." If you heard it, you understood why it was called that. It was up and down the keyboard and so fast.

When I was eleven, Dr. Scionti told Mother she wanted to start entering me in national recording contests. She would record me playing in her living room on top of the hill in Denton on a beautiful grand piano. At home, I learned to play and practiced on an upright. I didn't have a grand piano until the people of Denton raised money and gave me a beautiful Baldwin piano and presented it to me at my homecoming after winning Miss America.

And she would play the recordings back and say, "Let's do it again. Let's try it one more time. You can always do better."

That was a good lesson to learn early on in life.

I ended up winning all these recording contests and competing against twenty- and twenty-one-year-olds. I was a child prodigy at the piano. It just came naturally to me. I think they envisioned me playing at Carnegie Hall one day at Dr. Scionti's urging. When I got into cheerleading and being in school plays, it took away time from practicing the piano, much to Dr. Scionti's disappointment.

So, no band, no twirler, but I was a cheerleader. You did it through junior high and high school, and you had to try out before the student body. Once you win, they sort of know your name, and you keep winning. We didn't have pyramids back then. We didn't have guy cheerleaders. It was just us girls. Our outfits were purple and gold with insets.

Then we would go to SMU [Southern Methodist University] every summer for cheerleading school. We all had to do the Herkie jump. [Lawrence] Herkimer was a very famous guy in the cheerleading world back then.

The other cheerleaders would come over, and we'd go out in the street in front of my house. We'd just make up cheers. I learned practice, practice, practice at piano and cheerleading.

In Denton High School, we didn't win that much, but we would cheer our little hearts out.

———

"Two, four, six, eight, who do you appreciate?"

I could throw the ball farther than the guys. I think it's because of my older cousins who taught me how to play ball at a young age. I was a tomboy, although my mother loved to dress me in pretty little dresses and starched petticoats when I was a young girl.

Soccer wasn't a big deal back then. I played softball. I played some tennis, but that was because Schultz Park was behind my house. You didn't have to belong to a club. I was always very active. I used to go out on the golf course with my dad. We would practice putting and hitting long balls.

And football was a big part of my life growing up. Dad was a high school referee. I loved to watch football with him. Like most Texans, I was a big Dallas Cowboys fan and still am. Maybe that's why sports was a natural transition for me. My dad loved that I was working in sports.

Every Sunday we'd go to church, and after church we would go to different places to eat. Then every Sunday afternoon, we'd have Methodist Youth Fellowship. I was voted president, and I would go to the church camp. That was a big vacation for me to be away from home at such a young age. I was also a teacher during Vacation Bible School for the little ones.

Guess what our favorite meal was growing up? I'm a Texas girl—chicken-fried steak with white gravy, of course; fresh-cut french fries that my brother and I would fight over; black-eyed peas. Every Friday night, we'd grill T-bone steaks. And Mother would make the most delicious pies. The butterscotch and the chocolate pies—we would fight over them.

My mother was my best friend. I would sit on the bed when I'd been out on a date or with some girlfriends. Or I would go sit in my living room at night. Mom might be reading, and I would tell her everything. Just everything. I miss that so much.

Mother worked after I got old enough at a department store—the Boston Store. She did their bookkeeping for them. Later she worked for the dean of the North Texas art department and pretty much ran the show.

She graduated college at nineteen from Texas Woman's University right there in Denton. Mother was all about education. She was just

Phyllis George
as Miss America,
1971. *Photo by
W. Earle Hawkins,
courtesy Phyllis
George*

always ahead of her time. She was so smart, loved to play bridge—
probably could have been a master's bridge player.

She majored in home economics. She sewed all my clothes when I was
young on her Singer sewing machine. We'd go to a fabric shop and I'd say,
"Oh, I just love that dress, Mom, in the McCall's [pattern] book and the
Simplicity book."

And she'd say, "OK, good, honey, I'll make it for you. Let's go pick the
fabric and the buttons."

She dressed beautifully, with a hat, shoes, handbags, and jewelry. Her
jewelry was so much fun to play with.

Occasionally on Saturdays a few times a year, my mother would take
me to the downtown Neiman Marcus in Dallas to shop. We'd spend
the day trying on clothes and eat at the Zodiac Room, their restaurant

in the store. I would come home with two or three outfits. Those were memorable mother-daughter days.

And then my dad just did everything I wanted. He'd take me anywhere to do anything. I'd go off walking with him sometimes, and I loved being with him. It was just the two of us, and those times are the things I remember.

Daddy bought me a car. It was a yellow Ford Falcon with a stick shift that I smashed up the first day of high school. He didn't even get mad.

Daddy went to North Texas. He was an engineer and could fix anything. He was Mr. Home Improvement. He later went into the printing business with a friend, and then he was a Gulf Oil distributor in Denton. My mother worked for him there part-time, and my brother worked for him as well.

He volunteered at the Lutheran School for Abused and Abandoned Children and later worked there full-time. It was a labor of love for him. Those children didn't trust adults, but they loved Grandpa Bob because his space was safe. They never let anybody hug them, but they wanted to give him big hugs.

I was always eager to learn. I was very curious and asked a lot of questions as I was growing up. That's probably what made me a good interviewer and why I enjoyed it so much. I always made good grades. Mother expected it. I was an A student until ninth-grade algebra. Then I had to really work at it.

I was in algebra class when the principal came over the loudspeaker and told us President Kennedy had been shot. I remember exactly where I was and looking out the window. I couldn't believe it. I went home and cried my eyes out. It was especially hard because it happened right down the road in Dallas.

I never thought of myself as pretty. If anything, I was cute. I never relied on looks ever. I mean, I looked like Buster Brown. I had the bangs, a little Buster Brown hairdo.

My mother always said, "You know, Phyl, pretty is as pretty does."

Or how about, "Beauty comes from within"?

It doesn't matter how you look on the outside; it matters how you are on the inside. I was a people person. I was pretty popular. I had many, many girlfriends, but I didn't date a lot of guys; I usually had just one boyfriend.

I remember one year I was nominated for most beautiful, friendliest, and eleventh-grade favorite. I was already president of the junior class. And I preferred to be nominated for friendliest. I was homecoming nominee, Valentine's Sweetheart, and Miss Denton High School.

As a young girl, I watched the Miss America pageant every year with Mother. Back in the day, it was the biggest thing on television, and we would never miss it. Growing up as a little girl, I probably deep down had dreams that someday maybe I'd be Miss America.

And I would walk around with books on my head, so I have that perfect posture.

My dad always said, "Eat your carrots, Phyl. Your eyes will sparkle."

I hated carrots, but I ate my carrots. Although I must have dreamed of being Miss America, as I matured I started doing other things.

I modeled in Dallas and did some television commercials there for Kim Dawson [modeling agency], but I always thought I was the cute one. You've got these gorgeous, thin, tall models who walk in, and I'd go, "Whoa, what am I doing here?"

That's how I entered the Miss Dallas pageant. I entered the Miss Texas pageant the year before as Miss Denton and won second runner-up after winning all the preliminaries—talent, swimsuit, evening gown—and Miss Congeniality. I still had the bangs and long hair that flipped up like Marlo Thomas in *That Girl*.

I was disappointed. And my mother always said, "Your pride was hurt."

I remember telling the Miss Dallas pageant for four to six months that I wasn't interested in reentering pageant competition, that I was doing student teaching. I was a senior in college who was a Zeta Tau Alpha, and I had a boyfriend who was a Kappa Sig. I was the Kappa Sig sweetheart and also a *Yucca* [yearbook] beauty. I told them no many times. I've been there, done that, but they kept calling my parents. They were very persistent.

So Friday night before the Miss Dallas preliminary, after telling them no for months, the phone rang. My dad was asleep on the couch, my mother was playing bridge, the TV was on. I was bringing my dirty clothes home from college, and I had a big pile in my arms tied up in a sheet.

———

The *NFL Today* team of Phyllis George, Brent Musburger, and former
Philadelphia Eagle Irv Cross. *Photo courtesy Phyllis George*

The phone just kept ringing off the wall, and I ran, picked it up, and said, "Hello."

I was out of breath.

It was the official from the Miss Dallas pageant. He said, "I'm just going to give it one last shot. Why don't you come tomorrow? We really think you could go all the way."

And I said, "Are you kidding me?"

It was almost midnight.

"I have no idea where my swimsuit is or my evening gown that I wore. I mean, you've got to be kidding me."

He just flat talked me into it. I called my mother at bridge and said, "Mom, you've got to come home. We've got to dig out my swimsuit and my evening gown and those adorable pumps. I finally told the guy 'OK.'"

She said, "You what? You what, Phyl?"

I said, "I know . . ."

Winning Miss Texas was as hard as winning Miss America.

Well, I went back, and I won Miss Dallas, and then Miss Texas, swimsuit, evening gown, and talent. Winning Miss Texas was as hard as winning Miss America. These sixty Texas women I competed against were so talented and beautiful.

I didn't have the bangs the second time around. I pulled them back, and I pinned them up on the side of my long hair.

Miss America is the largest scholarship program for young women in the world, and the scholarship money was important for me and my family.

After I won Miss Texas, I thought, "You know what? I am going to work so hard, because if I go to the Miss America pageant, obviously you go to win."

That's where the Texas came out in me. I got very competitive. I played "Raindrops Keep Fallin' on My Head" and "Promises, Promises" in a medley but with a classical flair. All that classical training I had paid off.

It wasn't meant to be earlier, but sometimes you just have to lose to win. Sometimes you have to fail to be successful, and I took with me all the lessons that I learned from losing the year before and as the second runner-up.

I got to the fiftieth Miss America pageant, and I was the first one with the gold crown. Would you believe that it fell off of my head? It's a historic moment, and it would only happen to me. It hit the runway, and I had to pick it up and carry it to the end of the runway. And my banner came unpinned. My hair was sticking up from where the crown had tumbled off my head. I was holding this scepter and the flowers together in one hand and the crown in the other and crying.

I don't know if I was crying because I couldn't believe that just happened to me or if I was just so happy to win or it was just a surreal moment. There was so much going on.

I remember my brother saying, "Phyl, I'm going to miss you."

When I got back to my room, I called my mother and we talked for hours.

I said, "My life is going to change so much. I love you all and thank you for everything you did for me and for always being there for me. I just love you."

As hard as it was to leave the sheltered environment where I'd grown up in Texas, the Miss America pageant did change my life. You know, if we had had an answering machine back then, I wouldn't have answered the phone and given the Miss Dallas pageant people that last chance to talk me into entering. None of this would have happened.

People Ask, BQ or BBQ?

I remember when everybody said, "Do you think you can make it in New York?"

I mean, New York is so difficult, such different values, so challenging. But people are people everywhere. I never was afraid of meeting people. I was determined that I wanted to be known for more than just Miss America—a beauty queen. I called it a BQ.

And everybody said, "A barbecue?"

And I said, "No, silly, beauty queen."

"Well, we thought you meant 'barbecue' because you're from Texas."

Poncé Cruse in the early 1950s. *Photo courtesy Heloise*

BIRTH NAME	**KIAH MARCHELLE CRUSE**
BORN	April 15, 1951, in Waco to Marshall Cruse and Katherine Heloise Bowles Cruse
INTERVIEW	Her home, San Antonio, Texas, January 19, 1982

HELOISE

Inheriting a Household Name

Heloise is a popular authority on household hints, with a dozen hardcover books, syndicated columns running seven days a week in five hundred newspapers around the world, and appearances on television talk shows. The media-savvy Heloise exponentially expanded the business she inherited from her mother, the original Heloise, in 1977. As a military wife and homemaker in 1959, her flamboyant mother started a "Readers' Exchange" column in the Honolulu Advertiser on a bet to prove she could get a job. The column primarily attracted questions on household concerns and proved so popular that King Features Syndicate distributed it as "Hints from Heloise" to hundreds of newspapers. The second-generation Heloise and staff in her headquarters in San Antonio remain true to the model her mother pioneered—answering readers' questions with meticulously tested solutions. But while her compilations still sing the praises of nylon net scrubbers, she also relies on extensive research, regularly updates her advice, and has broadened topics and audiences. Today's loyal reader is anyone whose lifestyle demands saving time, money, and energy.

I was born on income tax day, April 15, 1951, in Waco, while Daddy was stationed at the air force base there.

My name is Poncé, with an accent on the *e*. Actually, that was a nickname. My father's mother's name was Florence McCullough Cruse, and her nickname was Floncé. The grandchildren couldn't say the *f* sound and they started calling her Poncé. When I was born, everybody said I looked like my grandmother. So they started calling me Little Poncé when I was two months old. And it stuck.

My birth certificate says Kiah Marchelle. Kiah is from the Bible, and Marchelle is a derivation of my father's name, which is Marshall.

I used to be called Little Hell once in a while. When I was eighteen, I had Poncé and Heloise legally added. My legal name now is Poncé Kiah Marchelle Heloise Cruse Evans.

My father is Marshall Cruse, and my mother was Katherine Heloise Bowles Cruse.

My mother was an identical twin. They were Louise and Eloise, later changed to Heloise. There were a lot of people who didn't know Mother was an identical twin. When Aunt Louise showed up at Mother's funeral, people were surprised. They said, "There's Heloise."

People had always said, "Heloise is going to show up at her own funeral."

Both my parents were born in Texas. My mother was born in Fort Worth, and my father was born in Rosebud. They were very Texan. My mother hadn't really been out of Texas until she lived around the world with my father, who was in the air force.

I am very proud to be and have always felt Texan. We moved to Virginia in 1952 and to Hawaii in 1958. Then we moved back to Virginia in '62 and moved to San Antonio in 1966.

There was a major tornado through Waco around the time I was born. My mother was a volunteer nurse. I can remember the stories of Mother taking action. Mother went to a department store and said, "Look, we need work gloves and this or that."

She really helped with the disaster.

I was born cross-eyed really badly. I have a picture where you can't even see the dark part of one eye.

Mother went through thirty-six hours of labor. Back in those days, the opinion was to save the baby; the mother comes second. They weren't really hip on caesarean. She had had four or five miscarriages or still-births before me. They think that much labor weakens muscles through the baby's soft skull. That's why my eyes were crossed. I had three operations to shorten the eye muscles, the last operation when I was seven.

I vaguely remember being in the hospital at Walter Reed in Washington, DC, and waking up and not being able to see anything because my eyes were patched. It's very strange when you're a child to not be able to see anything but to be able to hear and smell. You hear all the noises and smell the hospital smells, but you can't tell whether they're coming in to give you a shot or take your temperature.

We always knew home definitely was in Texas. Being in the military, we were always away. We spent only two Christmases that I can remember with the entire family. I remember going to my grandmother's in Fort Worth from DC and wearing shorts and going barefoot Christmas Day.

Mother was a Texan and dressed that way because that's the way she dressed in Fort Worth. Even though we may have been in Hawaii or Virginia, she still was the way she was raised. And it rubbed off on me.

Her father, Charles Bowles, grew up with Justin of Justin Boots, and they were friends. So when Mother had a custom-made cowboy outfit with a shirt and pants with zippers in the pockets and no place else, she would send a swatch to him and he would have a pair of boots made to match the outfit. I still have one pair left. He would sign the insides of her boots.

So I grew up with her wearing the pants, the shirts, and the belt buckles and the hats long before Texas became so popular. She always dressed me as a little lady, with patent leather shoes and Mary Janes and socks and crinolines out to here.

I started graying when I was twelve. We used to pull my gray hairs out when I was young. When Mother started her career, she was thirty-eight. She didn't think she looked old enough. She didn't have any gray hair. So she took that silver hair spray and sprayed the front of her hair gray so she would look more distinguished, more authoritative. So I always teased her that God was getting me back for her trying to fake it.

I got the blessing of the best of both my mother and father. My father is very systematic, does things correctly, keeps records, and knows how to organize. Mother was really a very creative, vibrant person, more the artist. I'm a little bit of both of them.

My mother was a cross between Lucille Ball and Auntie Mame. Yet she was a brilliant businesswoman. She was punk before punk was in. She used to spray her hair turquoise and purple to match her dresses when she would give speeches.

She had a sense of panache. I inherited some of her flamboyance. I've always worn hats; I must have fifty in my closet. I've been going to New York for God knows how many years, and sometimes I wear a cowboy hat and boots.

I remember when we moved back to San Antonio for good in 1966. When my dad retired from the air force, my parents did a systematic survey through chambers of commerce of the ten most desirable places to live in the United States. Three of them were in Texas. Even though we had relatives in Dallas and Fort Worth, they picked San Antonio.

I remember the first week of high school at Alamo Heights. When you're used to being military and bounced around, it doesn't make any difference whether it's the worst school or the best school. You make friends, and that's it.

The first week was Howdy Week, which I thought was real cute. Then after Howdy Week was over, the kids were still wearing their cowboy boots, belts, and hats. I thought that was strange then. But now it's wonderful and really makes me feel comfortable and Texan.

Mother never had an office. Her business literally started in the corner of the master bedroom with a typewriter on a card table. Then she bought a secondhand desk, which I'm still using.

When a hint would come in, she would try it out. And if a question came in that she couldn't answer, she'd write, "OK, girls, does anyone have the solution?"

If they did, she would try it in our home. I never thought it was bizarre, because I grew up like that. I'd come home and find Mother had put my sweater in the freezer because it was supposed to keep it from shedding.

At dinnertime, we'd say, "Uh, is this an experiment?"

She'd say, "I'm not going to tell you until you taste it."

You didn't want to taste it at all.

I didn't want to be Heloise, because I wanted a normal life. I wanted to be able to go to the grocery store and not have people stop me and that kind of thing. But the more I thought about it, I realized, since growing up with this and seeing Mother change from Miss Little Housewife to Heloise to internationally known celebrity, that I could handle it without letting it affect me.

I used to work in the office for my mother in the summertime. I'd come home and help sort letters and file and that kind of stuff. I really enjoyed reading and answering the mail and helping Mother run the office. I probably got treated worse than the employees because Mother wasn't going to show me favoritism. I worked on an hourly wage. If I checked in at 9:00 a.m. and checked out at 3:00 p.m., I only got paid for six hours of work.

In the parent-child relationships that I have run into, the parent is extremely proud of what you are doing. But it's very hard for the parent to say, "Hey, you're doing a good job."

Heloise inherited her mother's popular helpful hints column and the household name to go with it. *Photo courtesy Heloise*

I decided in 1974 to help Mother with the column full-time. She kept threatening to retire and turn it over to me, but, of course, I knew she never would retire. I graduated from Southwest Texas State University as a math teacher, and I already had signed my contract to teach in San Antonio. But I decided I'd probably spend two miserable years teaching seventh-grade math before I'd be back in the office anyway. So I decided to cut out two years of misery.

Young Ben Crenshaw works on his golf game. *Photo courtesy the Ben Crenshaw family*

BIRTH NAME	**BEN DANIEL CRENSHAW**
BORN	January 11, 1952, in Austin to Charles Edward Crenshaw IV and Pearl Vail Johnson Crenshaw
INTERVIEW	Lions Municipal Golf Course, Austin, Texas, May 16, 2018

BEN CRENSHAW
A Game of Conscience

O n a golf scholarship to the University of Texas in 1971, Ben Crenshaw snagged the individual title at the National Collegiate Athletic Association tournament and made the All-American collegiate golf team as a freshman. As a sophomore, he shared the individual title with teammate Tom Kite and won ten more. With NCAA title number three and other wins as a junior, he didn't wait to graduate to turn pro. He won the Texas Open in San Antonio in 1973, the second golfer in history to win his first PGA event; his first Masters in 1984; and his second Augusta victory in 1995. Outside the PGA, he racked up other wins, including titles in the World Cup of Golf in 1988. Crenshaw led the US Ryder Cup team to victory in 1999. He was inducted into the World Golf Hall of Fame in 2002. A golf historian with an expansive collection of books and memorabilia, he is a partner in Coore & Crenshaw, a firm that designs golf courses all over the world.

I am a first-generation Texan. I was born right here in Austin, but I have Alabama blood and Virginia blood in me. My father was from a small town, Andalusia, Alabama. He went to [the University of] Alabama his first year in college, and since they were raised Baptist, he and his brother, Allen, went to Baylor. My dad, through Baylor Law School, met Price Daniel, who became governor. And Dad worked in the attorney general's office. My middle name is Daniel. I am named after him.

My mom was from a real small town, Tazewell, Virginia, on the Kentucky border. When she met my dad, she was actually playing basketball at the University of Houston. She was from a big family. She was one of eleven. She taught sixth grade here at Bryker Woods Elementary School.

My brother is fifteen months older than I am—Charlie, who played baseball here at [the University of] Texas. We have a sister ten years older. She became a librarian. She got her master's in library science. We were much younger than she was, and she says, "I just merely tolerated the boys."

We tormented her, basically. But she was studious, and we were outdoorsy. Charlie was one grade ahead of me, and I was growing up with his friends, as well. Fifteen months is pretty close. We learned things together. Charlie's a good athlete, a good golfer. To this day, Charlie can make me laugh more than anybody in the world.

We played all sports. My father was a good athlete. I started golf when I was seven and my brother was eight. My dad became an early member of Austin Country Club when it was out on Riverside Drive. I met Harvey Penick [house pro and instructor for four decades] when I was seven and eight. We divided our time between the Austin Country Club and here. Our mother would drop us off here, and we'd play the whole day. She'd pick us up at dark.

I grew up right here, and it's very formative in my youth. There were a lot of junior golfers who enjoyed playing here who were really good, so I was watching good golf when I was very small. That helped in competition. Austin just seemed to have some real enthusiasts in golf, and Harvey, of course, helped that immensely.

Baseball was my second love. I enjoyed it. My brother was a pitcher, and I was a catcher. We played Little League Baseball in the neighborhood and in high school, and I quit baseball when I was sixteen to play golf.

Somehow I got a Sears Roebuck catalog when I was maybe six or seven, and I would get in my dad's lap and say, "Look at this catcher's mitt. This catcher's mitt has a little hole in it, and it will automatically catch the ball."

Dad said, "I don't know about that."

But I wanted that mitt for about a year and a half or two years.

And he said, "Now look, I will get you a catcher's mitt if you can go out there in the yard and catch your brother's fastest ball."

It took a while. We were always out in the yard playing with a lot of kids in the neighborhood. We had a little park, Enfield Park, where a lot of us would play. And, of course, I got beat up quite a bit, but I finally learned to catch it. And so then my dad got me that mitt.

There was a second story about how my dad liked to teach us to earn what we wanted. He wasn't hard on us, but he made us earn what we were thinking. There was a certain rod and reel that I wanted, too. My habit as a hitter when I was young was I'd step in the bucket; I would be fearful of the ball.

He said, "One day if you step toward that pitcher, I'll get you that rod and reel."

And I learned to do that, and I learned to hit better. He made us earn it that way.

My mother and Harvey Penick were the two sweetest people I ever met. Being a sixth-grade schoolteacher, invariably someone will come up to me and say, "I remember your mother being sweet and kind, and I just loved her."

She talked about how funny her students were, and I knew most of them, because I went to O. Henry Junior High, seventh, eighth, and ninth grades, but all the kids would say that their favorite teacher was my mother.

There's a story here that depicts her kindness. Nobody would play with me, so I was mad, and I was about nine years old. And I came over here by myself, and I played about four holes just by myself. And all of a sudden, I saw my mother come over the hill. And she said, "Bennie, I knew you were alone, and I wanted to be with you."

So sweet. We lost her very young. She was sixty-one when she died. My dad and mom were an incredible combination to bring me up.

Harvey Penick, in a subliminal way, was very much like my dad. I couldn't have had two better influences on me in my life. Harvey would want us to compete with all these kids. We learned to putt in little matches, play against each other in these matches, and he said, "In that way you're competing." And he encouraged us to play with the older juniors.

He said, "You'll get it in your mind's eye how well they play, and you'll pick up something."

So you were learning by osmosis that way.

I loved to putt as a kid on that little green right out there. Part of learning golf was to learn the little shots. You know, every youth wants to go and swing at it as hard as he can, and Harvey wanted us to do that, but golf is learned by these little, delicate strokes around here and getting the ball in the hole. He wanted all the youth, little kids, to learn to play a proper little chip shot.

So it's a game, but the little strokes are so vastly important.

It's so great to start out with your friends. If you are six, seven, eight years old, and if you go out with a buddy and learn together, it stimulates your interest in the game. And it's fun.

I just enjoyed being outdoors and being with my friends and playing something that we enjoyed. I think those rudimentary things have been a great part of my formation in loving the game.

It's an extremely healthy atmosphere. If you're starting as a youth, you can play the rest of your life regardless of your ability. You don't have to be a professional. The kids I hung out with played on junior high school teams and in high school here, and we are still in touch.

Dad was a good player, and his regular golf game had about four really good players. Actually, when I was so young, he wouldn't let me play with them, but I could tag along, and he'd let me hit one shot here and there, not to let me hold them up. But then I'd follow them and then play a few holes with my brother after that.

Again, I saw the way he treated people and stuck out his hand and was friendly, and he cultivated a lot of friends, so that was part of it, too. He basically taught us how to try to get along with people, and, importantly, how to talk to grown-ups. I think that atmosphere really helped me.

Ben Crenshaw and his mentor Harvey Penick at Lions Municipal
Golf Course in Austin. *Photo courtesy the Ben Crenshaw family*

I want people to get in golf and stay in it because it repays dividends
the rest of your life. It's kind of a way to live, and, more importantly,
there's something to be learned out there on that golf course every day.
It doesn't have to be about golf. It's about other things. It comes down to
human beings and getting along with one another.

There's certain rules—you don't have to be a stickler about it—but you
have to start trying to do the right thing, and not only for the game and
for the people that you play with. You are solely responsible not only for
how you play but how you interact with others and how you respect the
rules of golf. It is a game of conscience.

Mark Connally [son of Governor John Connally] and I were buddies
at Casis Elementary School. And I'll never forget that day in sixth
grade when the Texas state troopers came and got Mark and said, "Mark,
come with us."

His father had been shot with President Kennedy because Governor
Connally was riding with him. That was my friend, Mark.

It was like eleven o'clock in the morning, and he left school. Our school let the kids out. President Kennedy was coming here for a speech. But, no, that shook us. That shook us.

H arvey always repeated, "Play like Ben. Play like Ben." It's so simple, but it means "Trust your ability."

You have to learn to trust yourself, and I think that came from my childhood. I think it did, learning that there are different styles. There are a lot of graceful, beautiful form players. But everybody can't be like that.

Harvey didn't say it, but he imbibed in me, "That was good enough. Trust me. It was sound. Play like Ben."

When I was twelve or thirteen, I started playing better, winning a few more tournaments around here. My first kind of big foray was I played in the state junior golf tournament at Brackenridge Park in San Antonio. I was thirteen. At that time the age group was eighteen and under. So we were playing with guys older than you who could really play, and I started to do OK. There were six hundred entries in state play every year that played in the junior, and every junior in the state pointed to that. Some great players won that tournament, and I managed to win it when I was fifteen. But I qualified for the championship flight when I was thirteen.

When I was fourteen, fifteen, sixteen, I would get mad at myself and display a temper. And there was a TV show at that time that was called *Gentle Ben*, about this bear. Gentle Ben was a complete moniker given to me by a golf writer here for the *American Statesman* called Dick Collins.

And it was sort of a play on words because he knew I had a temper.

I was decent in school. Through my mother, I was pretty good at English and writing and things they don't teach now, like spelling and handwriting. I am part and parcel of that archaic age. I really enjoyed history as a student, and I love history. It's a huge part of my life.

When I went to Boston at sixteen, it was my first adventure up east. I played in the national juniors in Boston, and it was a big tournament.

I was fascinated, certainly, about Boston, and my dad took us on the Freedom Trail, and we saw where Paul Revere came, some historical things. We went to Fenway Park. I learned that the place we were playing, the Country Club at Brookline, meant a lot to the starting of the game in our country. That club was part of charter members of the United States Golf Association that formed in 1894. And I loved the golf course. That week started my interest in golf history and golf architecture. And my head has been in the book ever since.

Growing up around the people I did, I couldn't turn out too bad.

My mother taught David Royal, the coach's son. David and I were friends. My dad was good friends with Coach [Darrell] Royal. Dad was also a good friend of Governor Connally. He was handsome, and he had that grin that endeared himself to people. He would have made a great president.

There was a Christmas party each year for Coach Royal and all the Texas coaches, and I grew up with their kids. I probably went to some of my first UT football games at eight and ten years old and would sit in the knothole section in the north end zone. We were watching this program just blossom, and then the crescendo, winning national championships.

We followed the best and watched how it was done, and it helped me in golf. I was watching a winner in Coach Royal.

Being a Texan, I was expected to win. It was part of carrying on a tradition.

It was an incubation in this place.

We still go to Cisco's Bakery. It's in East Austin, a place that's been in existence for I don't know, at least fifty years, and it has the best Mexican breakfast. We used to go there with my parents, and my dad would entertain people coming up from Houston to watch the Texas football game, and they'd go to Cisco's for breakfast.

The Hoffbrau is still there. It was not air-conditioned back then. There was an old guy named Hamby who ran it, was the cook there. It's sort of an icon around here in downtown. It's anything but formal. I ate my steaks medium. I was never one with rare so much or well-done. They had these unbelievable salads, and it hasn't changed much. It's eclectic.

I really learned to have fun at Butler Pitch and Putt because all the holes are short. It's the one close to Peter Pan, the miniature golf course, and it's ideal for little bitty kids to learn the game because the holes are short. It doesn't take a long time to play. I played there some.

Muny [Lions Municipal Golf Course] was pretty much all we needed, but Butler Park was fun. We had little competitions over there. It's a pleasant little place. It's so crowded now; everything's engulfing Pitch and Putt now.

We swam in Barton Springs and Deep Eddy. Deep Eddy Pool was wonderful, right over here, not far away from here. Barton Springs is a revelation to any kid. The first time you go to Barton Springs, you just go, "Golly, this is completely different."

The water is ice cold, but then you start wondering, gosh, this is outdoors, this is natural. You can understand why people revere it and want to protect it. It's one of Austin's finest assets and has been forever. It wasn't far from our home on Bridle Path, where I grew up.

I couldn't have been luckier than to have grown up here—the schools, the people I've met here, the places, the freedom we had. I couldn't ask for any more. They're going to bury me here.

Ben Crenshaw reflects on his years playing golf. *Photo by Gaylon Finklea Hecker*

Rex Tillerson as a Cub Scout, ten years old. *Photo courtesy Rex Tillerson*

BIRTH NAME	**REX WAYNE TILLERSON**
BORN	March 23, 1952, in Wichita Falls to Bobby Joe Tillerson and Patty Sue Patton Tillerson
INTERVIEW	Cutter's Farm, Bartonville, Texas, June 16, 2018

REX TILLERSON

A Good Scout

R ex Tillerson's reputation as a global negotiator preceded him as the sixty-ninth US secretary of state for fourteen months in the Trump administration. He signed on after retiring as chairman and CEO of ExxonMobil after forty-two years with the largest oil company in the world. After graduating from the University of Texas at Austin in 1975, he joined Exxon Company, USA as a production engineer and worked his way up to CEO and chairman of the board from 2006 to 2017. In 2015 Forbes magazine listed him as the twenty-fifth most powerful person in the world. Tillerson sat on the boards of the Center for Strategic and International Studies and the American Petroleum Institute and was a member of the Business Roundtable and the National Academy of Engineering. He served as the national president of the Boy Scouts of America from 2010 to 2011, and the Eagle Scout Hall of Fame of the Greater New York Councils inducted him in 2009. The World Petroleum Council honored him with the Dewhurst Award in 2017.

I was named for Rex Allen and John Wayne. My parents were both big Western fans. Rex Allen was a famous singing cowboy in the movies. And then John Wayne, of course, the famous movie actor. They just loved John Wayne.

So I think I was six, and we had just moved to Vernon, Texas, and they had the big Santa Rosa Roundup. That's the Waggoner Ranch outside of Vernon, one of the largest ranches in Texas. They always brought in rodeo entertainment. And we went to the rodeo, and the entertainer was Rex Allen.

So he rode out and he sang from his horse and did all this stuff, and at the end of the show he was riding along the edge of the arena, shaking hands with people from his horse. And my dad grabs me up and my mom starts digging around in her purse, and all she's got is an envelope with the electric bill in it. She tore a piece of the envelope off and she had a pencil.

And my dad runs down there with me in his arms and leans over the rail and shoves this paper and pencil at him and says, "I named my son for you."

Rex Allen took that piece of paper and that pencil. It says, "Hi, Rex, Rex Allen."

I have it in my childhood scrapbook. I have a photo of Rex Allen on his horse that my wife found in an antique shop. It has sat on my dresser, where I tie my tie every morning, for the last thirty-five years just to remind me who I am.

I'm a fourth-generation Texan. My great-great-grandfather [Richard Henry Tillerson] came over from Ireland and then came to Texas right around 1846. My great-grandfather [John William Tillerson] was born in Collin County, the first one born in Texas. The maternal side of my family also dates back to my great-great-grandfather James Harvey Patton's arrival in Texas in the 1850s. So that's three generations on my mother's side and four generations on my father's side.

My grandfather was the third of eleven. He went through the eighth grade. The oil boom was on in the Burkburnett oil field, and he went to work in the oil field on a crew delivering casing with mule teams. And he worked at that until 1928. Then Conoco Oil Company built a refinery at Wichita Falls because they got tired of getting ripped off by John D. Rockefeller. He got hired by the refinery, I think in 1927 or '28. The Great

Depression hits in 1929, and he always had a job because the refinery never shut down.

I have an older sister, Jo Lyn, who is three and a half years older than I, and then my younger sister, Rae Ann, is only fourteen months younger than I am. My younger sister and I were kind of best buddies.

We grew up in a little part of town in Wichita Falls called Faith Village, and it had sprung up during post World War II. All little, frame, cracker-box houses. Everybody about the same age. This was the 1950s. I was born in 1952. The whole block, everybody, took care of each other's kids, so we had freedom to go everywhere we wanted to go and do what we wanted to do.

And so I kind of remember back there at four or five years old just doing whatever in the neighborhood the other boys and other girls were doing—playing baseball in the middle of the street, or we'd go down to the vacant lot and set red ants on fire.

We had a big sandbox in our backyard and it had kind of a little playhouse, and we used to jump off the roof of it into the sandbox just to see how daring we could be.

My first best friend was Bubba Whatley. I can remember going down to Bubba's house and listening to Elvis Presley sing on forty-five records on a little bitty record player. We'd listen to Elvis Presley records during the hot part of the summer because they had an air conditioner in their house. We didn't.

And I got my first bicycle there. I think we paid twelve dollars, and I learned how to ride when I was about five, six years old there. We'd ride two and three blocks away and go to the corner store and just do whatever we wanted to do.

In Vernon it was the same. We just wandered all over town with friends. We knew we'd be home in time for dinner. Somebody's mother was going to look out for you if you were on the other side of the neighborhood. And they knew when you were supposed to be home, and they'd send you home. I went everywhere on my bicycle. I mean, miles all the way across town.

Just tremendous freedom to roam, so that gave you a lot of self-confidence. A great sense of self-reliance. You had a wreck back then, you had to pick yourself up, get back on your bike, and keep going.

So that's how we grew up, self-confident, self-reliant, and not afraid.

We got hurt. We got injured—went to the doctor a lot, got stitched up, got your broken bones set. We just went on. It wasn't the end of the world. That's just life, you know. And so you kind of grew up with a real sense that bad things are going to happen to you and you're going to live. You're going to get through it; you're going to be just fine and go on.

My maternal grandfather, my mom's dad, Ray Patton, was one of the earliest Boy Scouts in Wichita County. He joined in 1912. Scouting came to the United States in 1910.

Rex Tillerson as a Boy Scout, wearing his Eagle Scout medal. *Photo courtesy Rex Tillerson*

My dad was an Eagle Scout. My dad's family was not involved in Scouting. But my dad got involved, and he and my uncle, my mom's brother, both were Eagle Scouts. And my maternal grandfather was a scoutmaster there in Wichita Falls, and he was very involved in the summer camp. And my dad and my uncle worked on the camp staff out at the Boy Scout camp for a summer job.

My dad was a Vigil member of the Order of the Arrow. He was big into Indian lore, and he led the Order of the Arrow dance team. My earliest memories of it were going out to Camp Perkins. Friday night was family night, when parents would visit their kids and have a picnic dinner and then have a big campfire, and the OA team would always put on a big Indian dance demonstration. I remember watching my dad do that.

He went off to the war in the Pacific when he was seventeen—and he had not finished his Eagle award. Under the rules, you have to finish by the time you're eighteen or you don't qualify anymore. Well, he came back, got married immediately, and went to work selling bread from a bread truck to grocery stores.

And he got back into Scouting and was a scoutmaster himself, and the Boy Scouts of America issued a temporary waiver for any young men who had gone to the war before their eighteenth birthday and were unable to finish. So my dad actually earned his Eagle Scout award after he returned from the war, and he was nineteen. And he received it with three boys who he had mentored in his troop.

Over time, he was always very involved, and so the professionals there in Wichita Falls approached him and said, "You seem to have a passion for this. Have you ever thought about doing it for a living?"

And so he gave up his job selling bread and went through the training up in New Jersey at that time, got commissioned, came back, and became a professional with the Boy Scouts, and that's when we moved to Vernon.

When I turned eight years old, I became a Cub Scout. That was the earliest you could join Scouting then. I've been a registered scout ever since. I couldn't wait. And I'd watched my dad and I'd gone to summer camps, and I said, "Man . . ."

So I was a very enthusiastic Cub Scout and a very enthusiastic Boy Scout, Explorer Scout. I just loved it. I loved the outdoors. I loved the challenge of earning all the merit badges, and you could learn so much.

All of my leadership skills came from the Boy Scouts. I've been through a lot of leadership training later, professionally. I didn't learn anything in any of that that I didn't already know. And I learned it all and practiced it all.

I always tested every decision against the Scout Oath and the Scout Law. Still today, that's what always guides me.

That's what the program does. It puts young people into leadership roles where they have to lead their peers. And you have to do it interacting with an adult who tries to make sure they're on the right track. And it's a great experience as a twelve-, thirteen-year-old kid, and then you apply it out of doors if you go on one of the High Adventures. I went to Canada, I went to the Boundary Waters, I went to Philmont for Trek, and you get out there in the wilderness, and things go wrong and you're the leader. So as a fifteen-, sixteen-year-old, you really learn a lot about yourself. But you're also learning a lot about how to motivate other people to accomplish the task.

I always tested every decision against the Scout Oath and the Scout Law. Still today, that's what always guides me.

The Scout Oath—the three pillars in the Scout Oath are duty to God and country, duty to others, and duty to yourself.

And the Scout Law is "Trustworthy, loyal, helpful, friendly, courteous, kind, obedient, cheerful, thrifty, brave, clean, and reverent."

And I always tell people, "The Scout Oath and Law are bookended by God. Duty to God and country. And a Scout is reverent. So the whole Scout program is bookended by God."

And it's God as you believe in him. That's why the Scouting movement recognizes all religions. Whether you're Hindu, Jewish, Muslim, Christian, doesn't matter, as long as you have a faith that there's a higher being at work in your life. That it's not about you.

My dad was gone a lot in his Boy Scout profession because his job was to train volunteers, recruit, put units together, charter partners, organize programs. But all that happened after everybody else got off of work because it's an all-volunteer organization. His work would start about five o'clock in the evening, and he'd get home after we'd gone to bed. And then on the weekend he was out running events for Scouting.

But my mom was the one who just gave us all this tremendous confidence. It was always, "You can do anything you want to do."

No matter what I wanted to try, she would say, "Well, sure. Go do that."

As a child you're always tempted to do things you shouldn't. Sometimes you don't realize you're not supposed to do them. So an innocent error is what I'd call it. You know, it's going to sound nuts, but every time something like that would come up, I was just such a Boy Scout, I just couldn't bring myself to do it. I had my share of silly stuff with friends, but nothing that came at anybody else's expense.

We were Presbyterian. My mother was. My dad was raised a Baptist. And when they married, though, they joined the Presbyterian church, and that was where he was a scoutmaster. So I was baptized a Christian in the church there in Wichita Falls. We were very active, growing up in the church. I've often said, my whole life as a child, all the way through my teen years, was built around the church and Scouting. My parents were Sunday school teachers.

I played football in high school, I played tennis, and I played a little basketball. And I was in the band. And all that stuff was important, but everything that shaped and molded me was church and Scouting.

I earned my God and Country award in Scouting before I earned my Eagle Scout award, and that's an eighteen-month program. To earn your God and Country, you meet with your minister every Sunday afternoon, and you do service to the church.

And so when I was working on my God and Country, I went to 8:00 a.m. church because I sang in the youth choir, then we went to Sunday school, and I went back for 11:00 a.m. because I served as an usher as part of my God and Country service, or I served helping with the service in some way.

Mom always had a big, traditional Sunday lunch. You know, pot roast, or chicken or ham or something. And then I'd get back on my bike and ride back to church at 3:30 for my hour and a half with my minister, and it was a whole bunch of studying the catechism and a lot of real deep study of doctrine. And then at five o'clock was youth fellowship, and my parents were youth fellowship advisers.

And so the whole Sunday I was at the church. But I loved my church. I loved Sunday school there. I loved everything.

I had a toy drum when I was five years old. My sisters and I used to hold parades in front of our house in Vernon. Jo Lyn was an AAU champion baton twirler. My mother started her in baton lessons when she was about seven years old. She did the fire batons. She did the hoops. Three batons.

We would do these parades, and my little sister and Jo Lyn would be out front doing the batons, and I had this little drum strung around my neck. We'd just get kids. Some would pull their little wagons.

"Come on your bicycle! Come on over here! We're going to do a parade."

We always had big disagreements about who was leading this parade. My mother and father actually have some old 8-mm film of me throwing quite an anger tantrum because I thought I was leading this parade, and my sister thought she was leading this parade. I turned around and tried to get everybody to follow me, and some were following her. And the whole thing just fell apart. I was mad. You can see it on the film. I was yelling at people. "Get back in line!"

We played a lot of army growing up. At Vernon, we had a huge backyard and this big hedgerow. And so I dug a foxhole back there in the hedgerow. At that time—this would be 1958 to 1960, '61—the big TV shows were *G.I. Joe,* and there was a program called *Combat!* And they were all World War II. These were weekly series, and, man, I watched every one of them.

And my uncle, who was career army and was in ROTC in college, gave me some of his old army helmets, his old backpacks and stuff. Man, we'd go out there and get in that foxhole. We killed Germans right and left. Every now and then we had to call the medic in because we'd get shot.

We'd go on until Mom says, "It's time for dinner."

I don't remember not having any jobs. In Scouting, they don't pay you a lot of money. My mom would try to give us a little allowance, but first I started collecting pop bottles as early as I can remember, on my bicycle in Wichita Falls. We'd look for pop bottles in the ditches. You get two cents for a pop bottle, a nickel for a quart. People just tossed them out of their car. We'd go along and pick them up and take them to the corner store. The guy would give us two cents for this bottle, a nickel if you had a big one. And we'd take that money and buy candy with it.

We moved back to Texas in November of 1968 at Thanksgiving. It was midyear of my junior year. I guess we'd been in Stillwater, Oklahoma, eight years, roughly. We moved up there when I was nine. My dad got transferred to the Sam Houston Area Council to be the district executive in Huntsville.

And that was the first year in Huntsville that the high school desegregated. They'd had two separate schools, grade school all the way through high school. Huntsville, deep East Texas—52 percent of the population was Black, 48 percent was white. I parachuted into this high school that they'd just integrated. And it was pretty tense.

And I'd come from a school that had always been integrated. In Stillwater, we didn't have separate schools. I just grew up always with Black kids in school and in the troop and in everything else. It just wasn't any biggie.

And this is when I got behind in math. I remember my math class was Algebra II that year, and we got to where I was when we moved down in November by the end of the year because they were trying to pace the program so everybody could keep up. Of course, everybody suffered as a result.

A lot of tension in the school. We had two class presidents. We had two homecoming kings. We had two homecoming queens. They were trying to figure out how to make this work because you had two football teams that all of a sudden had to be put together.

That's when I stopped playing sports. And I realized right away they're already struggling to put two football teams together and trying to make everybody happy. I'm not that great an athlete anyway. I was always kind of on B string.

But I stayed in the band, and I stayed in the choir. And then I played tennis because nobody else played tennis. Actually, I won my regional championship in tennis. So that's kind of the end of my high school years. My last year and a half was in a very strained situation.

I loved the band. That's where my closest friends in high school were, either in the band or in my math and science classes. I took physics. And I took chemistry. I took trigonometry. I took typing because I realized I needed to learn to type, and it was useful.

I'd got into the Explorer Post there. I did end up going to the National Jamboree in Idaho in 1969. The first time I ever got on an airplane was to go to that Jamboree with the Boy Scouts. Our Huntsville contingent went with the Sam Houston Council. So I was happy.

When I came to Huntsville, I was looking around for a rock 'n' roll band to put together or be part of. And my best friend in the drum section was already in a band, and it was with some college students at Sam Houston State. They needed a singer. And so I joined their band for the next fourteen months. Bobby and I were seniors in high school. So we played a lot of parties here and there.

We did a lot of blues. We did a lot of B. B. King. We did "The Thrill Is Gone." We did some Bachman-Turner Overdrive stuff, and then a lot of songs that didn't have vocals with them at all. These guys were really into blues and jazz. And so we had to have enough dance tunes so that people could dance. We had the full repertoire of what was playing on the radio, as well. Music has always been, still is today, part of what I really enjoy.

Throughout high school, I was a pretty good student. There were 212 of us, and I think I graduated tenth out of the class. I was an average student at UT. I was in the engineering program. But in my high school, the mathematics curriculum was not as strong as it needed to be, so I stayed behind in math. If you're behind in math in engineering, you're behind in everything.

Fortunately, I had a great professor, Dr. [James W.] Vick. He was my freshman calculus teacher. And I was struggling mightily because we didn't have precalculus in my high school. I took the preplacement exam, and I placed out of precal and went straight to calculus. Well, that was a big mistake. I just knew enough from my trigonometry that I was able to place out. I was so lost.

I went in to see Dr. Vick, and I said, "I don't know what to do."

He just spent time with me and got me through it, and it kind of saved me. And it didn't really start to click until about the time I got to differential equations. At the end of my freshman year, I started questioning if I should be an engineer at all. Maybe I wasn't smart enough for this. So I went to see counselors.

They said, "Here, take this test."

It was one of these aptitude tests. So I took this test, and they said to come back and see them in two weeks.

And I came back, and they said, "Well, the test says your three top occupations should be mechanical engineer, high school mathematics teacher, or civil engineer."

And I was majoring in chemical engineering. And organic chemistry was killing me, also. So I looked into mechanical engineering, and you had to take four semesters of thermodynamics. I looked at civil, and you only had to take two semesters of it. So I changed my major to civil engineering.

So my college academic career is kind of in two phases. My first couple of years I struggled mightily. But then after I got into civil engineering, I really loved it. And in my last half of my college career, I did very well, all As and Bs.

I guess that's what Exxon looked at when they hired me. They didn't pay any attention to that first part, because I never figured out how I got hired with that GPA.

I got accepted to UT and then went over and tried out for the band. Jo Lyn had always wanted to be in the Longhorn Band. And so she got into the band.

And Mr. D [band director Vincent R. DiNino] was great. He got me the paperwork necessary to apply for the Louis C. Wagner Scholarship. It was only available to engineering students who were in the Longhorn Band. I had that scholarship all four years. And Mr. DiNino just kind of took all of us under his wing, and when I was struggling academically, I would go talk to him about it.

"Don't give up," he said. "Everybody goes through this."

There have been eleven members of the family who have been members in the Longhorn Band. Mr. D said he's fairly certain we're the only family to have eleven members in Longhorn Band.

I tried out in percussion, and as a freshman I got put on the bass drum. I was down in the dumps over that, and Mr. D got me aside and gave me this lecture about how "you realize the bass drum is the most important instrument on the field."

He said, "When we get this band spread from one end of the field to the other, what do you think keeps everybody together?"

So I played bass drum for two years, and then in my junior year, to my shock, Mr. DiNino wanted me to be a section leader.

Rex Tillerson with his sister, Rae Ann, both members of the Longhorn Band at the University of Texas. *Photo courtesy Rex Tillerson*

And I said, "You want me to stay on bass drum?"

And he said, "No, you've got to move to snare drum."

I practiced like crazy because I didn't want to be the weakest guy in the line. We traveled everywhere, went to every game. I was fortunate to make the trip to Peru as a freshman.

There had been an earthquake down in Peru. And as a result of the earthquake, one side of a mountain had slid down into a valley and buried a city of thirty-five thousand people. The Indians that lived in the mountains fled to Lima, and there was a huge refugee camp with tens of thousands. It was just a horrible situation.

A group called Texas Partners for Peru organized a trip to Peru to raise money to draw attention to the calamity. The US State Department got involved, and so the Longhorn Band was asked to go down as part of this mission. They could only take one hundred of us—the first time I had ever been out of the country, first passport I ever got.

We left the day after the Cotton Bowl in Dallas. Mr. D would line us up, and we'd do these parades through downtown Lima. We would be in the buses, and he'd stop us and say, "Let's get out and play."

And so we were in the middle of Lima in Plaza de Armas, and we get on this plaza in the middle of this traffic circle with about five lanes of traffic coming. And he had had us learn the song "Perú Campeón," the Peruvian champions, because the Peruvian national soccer team had won their division at the World Cup that year and a Peruvian composer had written a song to celebrate it.

He fired up "Perú Campeón," and traffic stopped. People started getting out of their cars. People started pouring out of these office buildings, pouring into the streets. And then we did the Peruvian national anthem, and everybody was singing. We did "March Grandioso," and we did "Wabash Cannonball."

And we got back on the bus.

Rex Tillerson has traveled all over the world but feels at home in Texas. *Photo by John Goodspeed*

Texas Identity

I have a deep sense of pride in who I am as a Texan. Often, I loved to say to people in Washington, ". . . down in the Republic of Texas."

Native Texans have this deep sense of identity because we were a republic. We were multicultural in this part of the world long before anybody else was. We have a deep sense of pride in our ancestors. I think it's important for our children to understand it as well, so you don't lose track of who you are.

That's been the source of my success. I always know who I am.

Leon Coffee's yearbook photo, 1973. *Photo courtesy* The Texan,
David Crockett High School, Austin, Texas

BIRTH NAME	**LUKE LEON COFFEE**
BORN	October 11, 1954, in Blanco to Luke Coffee Jr. and Dora Ethel Upshaw Coffee
INTERVIEW	San Antonio Stock Show & Rodeo, San Antonio, Texas, February 11, 2018

LEON COFFEE
Littlest of the Herd

Leon Coffee achieved national acclaim as a barrel man and bull-fighter for the Professional Rodeo Cowboys Association and the National Finals Rodeo in Las Vegas. Not only did the US Army veteran win PRCA Clown of the Year in 1983, he was recognized for his antics in the arena as one of the top three candidates from 1984 to 2001. In his signature green cowboy hat, Wrangler baggies, and white face paint, he protected riders for more than forty years while entertaining crowds in major rodeo events in Texas and around the country. He was inducted into the Pro Rodeo Hall of Fame in 2018, the Texas Rodeo Cowboy Hall of Fame in 2004, and the National Cowboys of Color Hall of Fame in 2005. On the side, Coffee has appeared in documentaries, commercials, and movies, including 8 Seconds, My Heroes Have Always Been Cowboys, Jericho, and Blood Trail.

I live right now outside of Blanco in what we call Peyton Colony. It is an old slave community. I moved back up there and bought some of that old homeplace back. Peyton Roberts is the guy who started this community over there. We've got a cemetery that dates back to the 1800s.

With the abolishment of slavery and when they left South Carolina, some of them started out in Belton, and they settled in Blanco, Texas. My dad was born at my granddad's old house in Peyton Colony. That's where we kinda grew up.

In Blanco there's a town square. In the front of it was the courthouse, and in the back of it was a hospital. I was born in the courthouse.

People say, "What's your mama do, man? Why was she in jail?"

"She wasn't in jail; she was just in the courthouse."

Everybody who was ever born in that hospital is listed on that plaque there.

My dad had five kids. I was the second child. He had my brother and myself and one sister and then a set of twins, the babies. My dad married the last woman in Blanco County that he could marry without being kin to them. So everybody there, we were kin to, in some way or another. So he had to move us kids to Austin just so we could even have somebody to date.

My Coffee family has always had a pecking order. My granddad was Luke Coffee, my dad was Luke Coffee Jr., I'm Luke Leon, and my boy is Luke Anthony.

It's always been the second child that takes over as the head elder in the Coffee family. My granddad was the second child, my dad was the second child, boy. It could be the third, if there was a girl in there. I inherited that, and my son will, too.

If you were head elder you had to make sure that everybody in your tribe was doing what you're supposed to do. You take care of any problems. They had to approve all the marriages and to get them to the church to talk to the preachers before they did it. I've got books in my house of what they call tribes. And everybody had to make sure that their tribe was doing their tithing to the church. And so it was up there.

My mother was the baby of twelve kids. She was an Upshaw.

My dad shod and trained horses. You could drop a quarter through his ring. He was huge, but he was shorter than I am. I called him the baby gorilla. A bull hit a gate one time and lifted it off, and I have seen my dad literally catch that bull and take him over his head, a 1,300-pound bull.

My dad was shearing sheep and goats up there in the Hill Country, so I had to work before I ever went to school. At that age I was dragging sheep and goats to the pallets for them to shear. They couldn't afford babysitters so I had to go with them. They got like twelve cents a head to shear those sheep or goats, and I got a penny for every one I drug to them.

All us boys worked all summer long up there at the ranch. My granddad would cut cedar posts and have them mules drag them up out of the bottom of them canyons. My granddaddy broke mules for the highway department when they had mules for road teams and mule-drawn bulldozers.

My granddad was the vet for Blanco County for many years and had a third-grade education. A vet is the best doctor in the world because his patient cannot tell you what's wrong with him. You've got to figure out what's wrong with him, why it's doing it, and fix it. He was phenomenal with horses.

My granddad was head elder up there of all of it, and they wound up with 1,500 acres in the Hill Country. We raised a lot of Angora goats and Hereford cattle and a bunch of horses.

I was the littlest of the herd, so I had to ride all them colts. When you're breaking colts, you put the smallest guy on them because you don't want to put too much weight on horses at that age. So I learned to ride bucking horses at a very young age.

We trained a lot of horses. It was a way of life. It wasn't a choice; this is what we got to do. My whole family had been in the rodeo organization since day one. We always had an Easter Sunday morning roping. After church, we'd train all these horses.

I'm an adrenaline junky. I like to live on the edge.

When I was nine years old, my dad took us to a Little Britches Rodeo, my brother and me. Little Britches Rodeo is for kids, you know. I won the bareback riding, my brother won the bull riding, and I won second in the bull riding. That was my hook. I got hooked right there. We were riding little bulls.

So that was my introduction to what I was gonna do and how I was gonna do it. Convincing them of that was the chore. And that's what really set my tone there.

One time I got on one of them calves. I untied him and rode him down to the arena, and I said, "I'm gonna be a bull rider."

I'll never forget this day in my life.

And my mother said, "Nope, you're going to work behind a desk with a white shirt on and a tie."

I said, "No, Mama."

That's the first time I told my mother no. That was the first time I thought I was big enough to do that.

She said, "You're not gonna do that."

I said, "No, I'm gonna ride bulls."

My dad moved us to Austin when I was five. My dad worked two and three jobs to take care of us. He worked for the City of Austin maintenance and parks and recreation for thirty years. My mother worked at IBM, and so they didn't know exactly what all that I was doing. But I was slipping around.

When I was in high school there in Austin, I wanted to ride in the rodeos. You had to have entry blanks signed and a bunch of stuff, and I sneaked around and forged those things, their signature and stuff.

Oh, I was in trouble. I was supposed to have been running a service station over there, and I was supposed to close up that night and then go to the rodeo, but they didn't know I was going to the rodeo. The guy was running a little late, so I closed the station early.

Well, Mr. Schoen came by the service station and I wasn't there, and he went to calling my dad and said, "Where is he? Is something wrong?"

My dad said, "I don't know, but I'll find him."

Well, when he found me I was in Oak Hill, Texas, riding at a little high school rodeo. I had forged the entry forms and had saved up my money to pay the entry fees. I was gonna ride bulls, bareback horses, and roping every time if I got a chance to take over somebody else's horse. It was fun.

I rode a bareback horse, and I was really proud—I was big, I really done good, and I was supposed to be winning the bareback riding. I looked up at the gate and see my dad standing next to Mr. Hill, who was running the rodeo out there.

And I thought, "Oh, my Lord."

And I ran and I hid. Oh, I did. And I turned out my calf in the calf roping so he wouldn't see me again.

And then I said, "What am I gonna do? What am I gonna do?"

So I had my buddies put my butt up on my bull, and I was looking around and seeing if I could find my dad out there. I'm looking out and not knowing. I was not thinking about riding bulls at all. And this bull just whacks me to the ground.

When I get up, so help me God, my dad's standing there. That was scarier than riding the bull. He's got his belt off.

And he said, "Look at this. I'll tell you something, if you're gonna ride bulls you better not be thinking about me."

And he whipped me all the way out of that arena. All my friends saw that, and that was the most embarrassing thing that I ever had done to me in my life. I'm winning the bareback riding, and my dad's whooping me all over. Oh, man, I wanted to die.

My mother found out I was doing it and said, "You're not going to do that."

And I finally bowed up and said, "I'm gonna ride bulls. I'm gonna ride bulls. I'm gonna ride bucking horses."

You had to have grades up in school to be able to participate in any-thing. And I'm gonna rodeo.

I'm dyslexic. So I had a hard time reading things, and back then they didn't know what dyslexia was. They just said you were slow.

I started school in Blanco in the old one-room schoolhouse there. My birthday is in October, and you had to be seven by September 1 to start school. If you're not, you had to wait another year. So I was behind.

And then they said that I was not learning well, so they put me another grade behind. So I really had to hustle to try to work to learn things, because everything was jumbled up to me. Backwards. I could write backwards and read backwards.

I was actually left-handed when I first started to school. I always tried to do everything with my left hand, but they tried to teach me to use my right because nobody knew how to teach me to write with my left. That made it even harder.

Ms. Burgess—I'll never forget her name as long as I live—taped my left

Leon Coffee outwits bulls and protects riders by clowning around.
Photos courtesy San Antonio Stock Show & Rodeo

hand so I'd have to learn to use my right hand. That's what she did back then because she didn't know how to teach me to write left-handed.

She didn't know what was wrong with me. I didn't find out until I got in the army that I could look at something from the back side and I could read it.

432

Now, all dyslexic people are great with math. And math is my thing. Numbers don't lie. Numbers don't change. They don't switch around on you. But words do. Them letters get switched around and you can't deal with it.

When we had to read *Lord of the Flies,* I could read it, but to comprehend it and understand what I'm reading was difficult, because I was trying to change every word around. I was paying attention to do the reading, but I wasn't paying attention to what I was reading. And that's difficult.

Then Ms. Jackson, my English teacher at Crockett High School, finally took enough initiative to sit me down and talk to me. That was the one person that helped me overcome some things that were difficult and I didn't know why. I didn't know how to fix it. And I'm a fix-it kind of guy. She told me, when you picture that noun in your mind, then make a sentence around it, and you'll probably be able to read this.

Oh, man, it gave me headaches so bad. There were quite a few trying nights that I thought about, "I don't want to live like this no more."

Oh, I fought that so long that it was unreal, because I was never good enough.

Because of my defect of not being able to read, it was embarrassing to me, so I hid a lot of things with comedy. And I found out people like you if you're funny, and that was my defense of my defect. And otherwise, they just thought I was slow.

It started very early. Oh, I was seven or eight years old when I started telling jokes and trying to get people to laugh at me. I became the class clown. Kids are mean. They are honest. They don't know they are mean. They don't know how that feels. They've never experienced that.

I remember in junior high school, I was trying to read something, and I have to switch every word. "Was" is the worst one. That's "saw" to me. And I'd get to "was," "and they saw, and was," "No, Sam saw." "No, Sam was."

And the kids got to laughing at me about it. It was embarrassing. And challenging. I was bigger than they were, but they wouldn't stop.

When you're riding bulls, back then, there might be three hundred guys at this rodeo. They only pay eight of them. The winners. They pay the top eight. I was riding real good, but I'd be that ninth guy.

And I got into this really bad habit of eating, and I haven't yet found a methadone clinic to clean me up from it. So I had to figure out a way to feed me.

Clowning. I figured out that guy's getting paid every night.

I showed up at the rodeo one time. There were guys I went to high school with there.

One said, "Hey, man, the guy didn't show up to fight the bulls here. Do you mind stepping in and helping them out?"

Clowning. I figured out that guy's getting paid every night.

"Sure, man, but I don't know what to do."

He said, "Just run fast and act goofy."

"Excuse me? You're saying all I have to do is run fast and act goofy? They used to kick me out of school for that, and now you're telling me they're gonna pay me for that?"

There was one teacher, Mr. Howard King. He taught me a lot of things, but he'd always tell me, I was the class clown in high school, "Son, you can't make a living being the clown."

The first time I won Rodeo Clown of the Year, he was the first man I called. "Na, na, na, na, na."

He's the guy who taught me this: "I'm not going to teach you what I think, because if I do that I just create a clone of myself. If I teach you how to think, you become your own individual person."

I've never forgotten those things.

In the rodeo world, you are never judged on the color of your skin or how smart you are. You are judged on your ability. You are judged on how good you rode. How fast you roped. How fast your horse ran. That eliminated scrutiny of me; it only puts scrutiny on what I was doing.

I leveled the playing field.

Leon Coffee without his clown makeup. *Photo by John Goodspeed*

ACKNOWLEDGMENTS

For a project in our hearts for more than half our lives, the list of people, institutions, and organizations to whom we owe our deepest gratitude is, fittingly, Texas size.

Obviously, the forty-seven notable native Texans who shared their warmest recollections deserve the most appreciation. By allowing us to capture their childhood stories for the historic record, our lives are richer, our knowledge of Texas history greater, and our understanding of the human condition deeper.

We are forever grateful for forever-Texan Joe Armstrong, who dubbed us the Thelma and Louise of Texas Letters and provided foresight and frequent advice that made us laugh even when we wanted to cry. His inspiration and cheerleading when we needed it most boosted a forty-year project to the finish line.

Don Carleton and Alison Beck taught us that publishing goes far beyond print on pages or screens. They recognized the value of preserving the first-person stories of such impactful Texans beyond the covers of a book. Through their foresightedness, the archives of the Dolph Briscoe Center for American History at the University of Texas at Austin house our original interview tapes, photos, hand-edited transcripts, and correspondence ranging from handwritten notes to email streams. Holly Z. Taylor, the Briscoe Center's head of publications; Abby Webber, copy editor; and Derek George, designer, corralled decades of research into a digestible and publishable length and form. The Briscoe Center's collections provided additional photographs with considerable historical significance.

We are flattered and honored S. C. "Sam" Gwynne put aside his own considerable research and writing to craft a beautiful foreword that pinpoints just what made this book tick—the poignant, uniquely Texas tales of so many of the state's most accomplished people.

Early on, literary agents Charles and Mildred Stern, publishing-house-executive-in-the-making Ina Stern, and oral historian Esther McMillan validated our quest. James Michener endorsed the concept in 1983 and lit a fire under our ambitions. Later, author and friend John Williams provided advice and eagle-eyed copy editing. Other authors generously lent their expertise on everything from relationships with editors to protocols for book signings, and we're indebted to Suzanne O'Malley, John Pope, Bill Brett, Naomi Shihab Nye, and David Nelson Wren.

Capturing remembrances of the families of others made us even more grateful for our own. Our parents, Floyd H. and Dorthy Dennis Finklea and Lewis B. "Bert" and Laura Williams Odom, gave us the courage to believe we could do anything if we worked long and hard enough. Like many of our interviewees, we never outgrew wanting our parents to be proud of us.

We didn't say it often enough, but we couldn't have navigated such a circuitous course without the support of our spouses, Marvin Hecker and John Goodspeed. Among the countless tasks they undertook on our behalf, they shot and edited photos, captured sound, searched for wayward computer files, provided digital expertise, chauffeured us, and rarely wearied of being sounding boards.

A special thank you is in order for early ambassador Harry Young, who pitched in wherever needed and without whose contacts, photographic skills, and infectious enthusiasm this good idea would never have gotten off the ground. Several times Jennifer Hecker's expertise and library-archive connections guided us in the right direction. Other family members who share our Texas pride and listened, inspired, advised, cajoled, and encouraged us are Yael Young Akmal, Ari Akmal,

Patsy Reneau Ward, F. Ronald Callaway, David Young, Bridget Young, Kate Goodspeed, Zane Goodspeed, Mandy Goodspeed, Larry Odom, and Jere Hamm-Odom.

Interviewees Dan Jenkins, Dan Rather, Bob Schieffer, Liz Carpenter, Joe Armstrong, Phyllis George, Jerry LeVias, Kay Bailey Hutchison, Sarah Weddington, Red McCombs, and Jaclyn Smith graciously encouraged other Texas notables to participate, and we're indebted to them for their efforts.

We also appreciate family members of interviewees who facilitated the interviews, provided photos, answered questions, corresponded, fed us, and nudged the project along. Among them, Jean Rather, June Jenkins, Pat Schieffer, Don Correia, Marty Jenkins, Catherine M. Ragle, Mary Alice Cisneros, George Cisneros, Volma Overton Jr., Jo Lyn Tillerson Peters, Peggy Cavazos, Wendy Goldstein, Janice McKinney, Janie Price, and Dr. Morris Spector.

Others who supported this endeavor enough to reach out to potential sources or other key players are Mildred Whiteaker, Beverly Elam, Nancy Scott Jones, Tio Kleberg, Clyde Johnson IV, Sharon Rosenstein, Howard Rosenstein, Bob Furnad, Tranette Ledford, Bettye Ledford, Texas State Representative Elliott Naishtat, Jane McKnight Fender, Corky Hilliard, Ken Dabbs, Rabbi Aryeh Scheinberg, Mary Sue Neptune, Terry Milman, Jane Macon, Connie Nelson, Phyllis Fletcher, Russell Kaemmerling, and Judy Day.

Supporters who offered inspiration, connections, and expertise include Jane Chesnutt, Laurie Scott Mahaffey, Sharon Hanson, Jean Van Gee, Elaine Ayala, Francisca Aguilar Flores, Fred Bothwell, George "Punch" Shaw, and Madelon Rogers.

As successful people will tell you, they couldn't do what they do without a lot of help. We second that. None of this would have come to fruition without the attention to detail of assistants, agents, schedulers, publicists, and friends of our notable Texans. These behind-the-scenes fireballs include Lucretia Rodriguez, Dean Meadors, Joan Miller, Julia B. Sleeper, Jack Molthen, Kathy Cronkite, Betty Tilson, Judy Thomas, Pam Keller, Ronnie Spillman, Brig Berney, Sherry Clawson, Anne Fornoro, Charity L. Boyette, Sarah Majzoub, Darlene Mills, Amie Gray, Judith Dale, Milda Mora, Pam Watson, Suzy Thomas, Rena Jacobs, Jay Schwartz, Javier Delgado, Rose Hunter, Delphia Esters, Scott Sayers,

Judith Lampert, Michael Toland, Connie Coit Kitchens, OraLee Walker, Fredric Gershon, Todd Wurbia, and Mary Jo McDonough.

We owe a huge debt to museums, institutions, and professional associations that preserve slices of history. These include the McClendon House, Daye Collins; Jimmy Dean and Llano Estacado Museum, Elva Hipolito and Melissa González; Doss Heritage and Culture Center, Paige Baker; Fort Sam Houston Museum, Carlos Alvarado; University of the Incarnate Word, Paul G. Andersen; Daughters of the Republic of Texas, President General Karen Dannelly Thompson; Texas State Historical Association, Jessica Karlsruher; Archdiocese of San Antonio, Elvira Sanchez Kisser; Texas Country Music Hall of Fame; Sandra Day O'Connor Institute; and Army Nurse Corps Association.

Even in the digital age, brick-and-mortar libraries were instrumental in research and fact-checking. Tireless librarians and archivists located hard-to-find photos and yearbook images. Thank you to the Jimmy Carter Presidential Library, LaToya Devezin; LBJ Presidential Library, Claudia Anderson, retired; Los Angeles Public Library, Christine Rice; Howard Gotlieb Archival Research Center at Boston University, J. C. Johnson; Austin History Center, Madeline Moya; University of Texas at San Antonio Institute of Texan Cultures, Tom Shelton; Scobee Education Center at San Antonio College, Rick Varner; Austin Independent School District, Melissa Sabatino; Jefferson High School Library, San Antonio, Esperanza Garza-Danweber; National Personnel Records Center; San Antonio Public Library; Austin Public Library; and libraries at Brown University, Texas Woman's University, and Southern Methodist University.

Other venues and organizations deserve credit for hiring on-the-ball, public-relations-conscious employees who seized the opportunity to be involved, including San Antonio Stock Show & Rodeo, Lauren Sides; Houston Texans Ambassadors Program, Kandyace Mayberry; Gruene Hall, Krystal Kinman; Dallas National Golf Club, Britt Patton; and The St. Anthony Hotel, Debbie Gonzalez.

Other institutions that deserve praise for friendly and efficient staffs who furnished whatever we asked for are NASA, American Place Theatre, Texas Heart Institute, and the Majestic Theatre in San Antonio.

Legal assistance came from the insightful Richard H. Noll and Melynda Nuss. Our project was further spirited along by much-needed technical help. We are grateful for the audio magic of George Blood LP, Brandon Seaman and Jared Gibson; the website know-how of Vigasan Gunasegaran; the digital wizardry of FedEx West Lake, Luis Hernandez and A. J. Chappie; the lightning-fast transcribing of Monica Hasbrook; and the faithful copying of thousands of pages by San Antonio Copy Concierge.

Writers, broadcasters, bloggers and publishers who recognized the potential for this book-in-the-making warrant our appreciation. They are Kirk Bohls, *Austin American-Statesman*; Tonyia Cone, *The Jewish Outlook*; P.a. Geddie, *County Line Magazine*; Steven Dickey Arnold, *Texas Dabbler*; Natalie England and John Reetz, Friends of *The Daily Texan*; Rick Campbell, KPFT radio; Chris Heerlein, KLBJ radio; and Gordon Lothrop, *Lothropp Family Foundation Newsletter*.

And a special blanket thank you to everyone who, throughout the years, joined us in the parlor game of thinking of worthy native Texans, oohing and ahhing over well-known folks they hadn't realized were born in Texas, and sighing disappointment when seemingly big-name sure-things turned out to be only loyal transplants or simply wannabes.

ABOUT THE AUTHORS

Native Texans Gaylon Finklea Hecker and Marianne Odom have been collecting oral histories since 1981, and collaborated on *The Businesses That Built San Antonio*, a coffee table book of first-person accounts of business leaders, published to commemorate the Texas Sesquicentennial in 1986.

Finklea Hecker was a reporter for the *San Antonio Light* and *San Antonio Express-News*, associate editor of *SA: The Magazine of San Antonio*, editor of *Seniors San Antonio Style*, and contributor to *Newsweek*. She also served as editor of the *Jewish Journal* in San Antonio and *The Jewish Outlook* in Austin and worked in corporate communications. She is the author of four recent books concerning Texas history: *The Daughters: A Dozen Decades of DRT*, *Dusting Off a Legend: The St. Anthony Hotel*, *Enhancing Quality of Life for 75 Years: Bandera Electric Cooperative*, and *Bonjour, Y'all: A Squirrel's Nutty Tale of the Texas French Legation*, written especially for children. She is a journalism graduate of the University of Texas at Austin. An only child, she was raised in Hull-Daisetta, the Mayberry of southeast Texas, by her father, a lifelong ExxonMobil employee and drilling superintendent, and her stay-at-home mom. She fondly remembers wearing her fringed Annie Oakley outfit, Davy Crockett T-shirt, and cowboy boots to her aunt's small-town rodeo. She lives in Austin.

Odom covered fashion in New York, Paris, California, and around Texas for the *San Antonio Express-News* and won accolades for revealing profiles of designers and celebrities. She was a reporter for the *Tyler Courier-Times-Telegraph*, contributing editor for *Edible San Antonio*, and contributor to the *San Antonio Light, Seniors San Antonio Style*, and professional journals. The longtime educator taught journalism at Tyler Junior College and San Antonio College, where she directs the journalism-photography program and advises student publications. She has a master's degree from Texas A&M University-Commerce and a bachelor's from the University of North Texas. Born and reared in Tyler, otherwise known as the Rose Capital of the World, she was the younger child of the police chief and an elementary school teacher. She recalls the value of a cowboy hat, pointy boots, and flannel-lined jeans when taming the Wild West in her backyard, but she preferred the civility of the frilly dresses her mother sewed. She lives in San Antonio.

Gaylon Finklea Hecker and Marianne Odom outside the Briscoe Center for American History, 2018. *Photo courtesy Gaylon Finklea Hecker and Marianne Odom*